BARRIO
DREAMS

Camino del Sol

A Latina and Latino Literary Series

BARRIO DREAMS

Selected Plays

BY SILVIANA WOOD

Edited by Norma E. Cantú
and Rita E. Urquijo-Ruiz

THE UNIVERSITY OF
ARIZONA PRESS

TUCSON

The University of Arizona Press
www.uapress.arizona.edu

Printed in the United States of America
21   20   19   18   17   16   6   5   4   3   2   1

ISBN-13: 978-0-8165-3247-6 (paper)

Cover designed by Leigh McDonald

Publication of this book is made possible in part by funding from Trinity University and the University of Missouri, Kansas City, and by the proceeds of a permanent endowment created with the assistance of a Challenge
Grant from the National Endowment for the Humanities, a federal agency.

Library of Congress Cataloging-in-Publication Data
Names: Wood, Silviana, author. | Cantú, Norma E., 1947– editor. |
   Urquijo-Ruiz, Rita, editor.
Title: Barrio dreams : selected plays / Silviana Wood ; edited by Norma E.
   Cantú and Rita E. Urquijo-Ruiz.
Other titles: Camino del sol.
Description: Tucson : The University of Arizona Press, 2016. | Series: Camino
   del sol, a Latina and Latino literary series | Includes bibliographical
   references. | Plays are written in code-switching English and Spanish.
Identifiers: LCCN 2015032997 | ISBN 9780816532476 (pbk. : alk. paper)
Subjects: LCSH: Wood, Silviana—Criticism and interpretation. | Mexican
   American women—Drama. | LCGFT: Dialect drama.
Classification: LCC PS3623.O6427 A6 2016 | DDC 812/.6—dc23 LC record available at http://lccn.loc.
gov/2015032997

♾ This paper meets the requirements of ANSI/NISO Z39.48-1992 (Permanence of Paper).

With all my love to Tamara, Michael Pierre, and Adriana, all my grandchildren, and all my great-grandchildren.

—Silviana

A tod@s 1@s teatristas who bring us such joy with their art!

—Norma

Al teatro y la gente del desierto sonorense.

—Rita

CONTENTS

ACKNOWLEDGMENTS

I wish to sincerely acknowledge the love and support that I received from my children Tamara Valenzuela Cavazos, Michael Pierre Valenzuela, and Adriana Valenzuela Barrios when I wrote these plays. I now have a growing number of grandchildren and great-grandchildren in Arizona, California, and Colorado, and I wish to send all my love to them: to my grandchildren Michael Pierre Valenzuela Jr.; Francisco Javier Martinez; Pablo Andres, Dominic Alexander, and Cesar Santana Valenzuela; Dante Antonio Cavazos; and Javert and Cosette Barrios; and to my great-grandchildren Mikayla Elaine Verni and Alexander Lorencio Martinez; Mikey, Dominic Santana, Logan, Cayden, and Giovanna Valenzuela.

I wish to thank all of my other family members and friends who have always encouraged and nurtured my efforts even though they may not have completely understood the stress and pressure of the locura involved in the creative writing process. Here in my hometown of Tucson, Arizona, I especially wish to thank my brother William "Willie" Peter Wood, my sister-in-law Cecilia, my niece April Wood Figueroa, my nephew Carlos Wood, and their families for always including me in their holiday celebrations. I also wish to thank my niece Sondra Wood Gil and all of her family for inviting me to all their parties to eat the delicious fish that her husband, Robert Gil, caught and prepared! In Mira Loma, California, I wish to thank my niece Jenny Higuera and her husband Reggie Higuera and all of their family for their generous and warm hospitality. In Salinas, California, I wish to thank Angie and Paul Valenzuela (Pancho Villa is his hero!) for their invitations to visit them and for taking me all over Salinas so that I could recapture the memories of my youth in the town of my favorite author, John Steinbeck.

In San Antonio, Texas, I wish to thank my dearest friend Zulema Avila Pingenot (the sexy receptionist in my play *Amor de hija*), her husband Don, and all of her relatives and friends who have always treated me con amor y ternura as though I was truly a member of their family. Also in San Antonio, I wish to thank Jorge Piña for bringing my plays to the Guadalupe Cultural Arts Center without even reading them first, and for bringing in my comrade-collaborator-composer Raúl González Guzmán from Monterrey, Nuevo León, Mexico, who composed the original music for *Yo, Casimiro Flores*. And of course, I have to thank every director, actor, musician, and técnico who brought my characters to life, and my sincere gratitude goes to all the audience members who cried and laughed with them. ¡Ay, qué dramatic se pone la ruca!

I am very lucky to have so many loyal friends who are more than willing to yank me away from the computer and to share their good times with me. High on my list of grateful appreciation are the present members of Mujeres Que Escriben, our Latina writers' group, who have always provided me with their most positive encouragement and help: Valerina Quintana, Monique Soria, Estella González, Maria Elena Wakamatsu, and Mariel Masque. I especially wish to thank my best friends forever, Arturo and Barbara Martinez, for generously supplying me with copy paper, staples, ink cartridges, and Milk Duds, and for taking me to sushi dinners, movies, Tucson Meet Yourself, fiestas, and powwows. I also wish to thank my very dear friends: el Pancho "sin Rancho" Medina and Salomon Baldenegro Sr. for all the good conversations, rides, and support.

I wish to thank the staff at the University of Arizona Press, and I am very grateful for the help and guidance that I received from acquisitions editor Kristen Buckles and production editor Amanda Krause, two true wordsmiths with keen perception and vision and language acumen. Countless clerks, librarians, and strangers have tried to guide me through the mad labyrinth of computer technology, but I especially wish to thank my "computer expert" friend, Juan "el Güero" Villegas, who runs to help me navigate my way through the maze even though I will never learn how to use those chingadera flash drives that he and his wife Betty gave me and expect me to master.

This year I celebrated my seventy-fifth birthday, and I was surrounded by loving relatives and friends—too many to list here—but I wish to thank my three favorite excellent photographers whose talent made this occasion a truly memorable event: my niece Rebecca Higuera, and my dear friends Piper Weinberg and Brenda Limón. I also wish to thank my dearest friend, Helen Gutierrez, who did not hesitate one minute to help me with the Doña Chona skit and to demonstrate the dance steps to corridos, cumbias, and chotis with great rhythm. I would also like to thank Margo Cowan, Rocky Barilla, and William "Bill" Risner for their advice and encouragement. I especially wish to thank Luis and his brother Mario Gonzales, who not only provided me with the Yaqui dictionaries but who were also always willing to help me with the Yaqui language and culture. I wish to acknowledge my very dearest friend, Lupe Castillo, who gave me the best advice in the world when I told her that I didn't want to be a social worker and that I really wanted to write instead. She told me, "Silviana, we already have too many social workers and not enough writers." So the next day, I changed majors!

And finally, I wish to acknowledge two of my dearly departed friends: my beloved mentor, Mexican playwright and novelist Emilio Carballido, for all his help and advice that he gave me throughout these many years, and Franco Ontiveros, one of the most talented and dedicated San Antonio actors who breathed life and energy into my roles. I know that I've left out many other friends, but I will include them for sure in my next book, con el favor de Dios. ¡Mil gracias a todos! Y sigan soñando and keep telling me your dreams so I can write more plays!

—*Silviana Wood*

*   *   *

I wish to acknowledge the invaluable help and support of all who have traveled with us on the long road from the initial idea to the publication of this book, especially Elvia E. Niebla, who traveled with us to Tucson and who read the entire manuscript in its early stages, and my sister Elsa Cantú Ruiz, who also read the manuscript and offered her support, as always. ¡Gracias!

We acknowledge the support of our institutions, Trinity University, the University of Texas at San Antonio, and the University of Missouri, Kansas City. Their support secured the invaluable help of student assistants in transcribing and formatting the scripts; mil gracias to the institutions and to these diligent and dedicated students!

My sincere gratitude goes to my friend and colleague, Rita Urquijo-Ruiz, for her dedication and assistance as co-editor. Gracias mil, dear friend; I especially thank you for your research on Chicanas in early teatro y también for being my "partner in crime" as we traveled to Arizona, and for reading the many drafts of the plays and the manuscript con el ojo pelón, catching misplaced or missing accent marks. ¡Gracias!

Claro está, without Silviana Wood and her plays, this book would not have been possible. Gracias, Silviana, for your patience and for allowing us to publish your plays. Gracias también for your friendship, for the photographs, and, most of all, for your gift of storytelling ¡Gracias!

Finally, I thank the creator for all the gifts and challenges. ¡Gracias!

—*Norma E. Cantú*

* * *

Mis más sinceras gracias a nuestra querida autora, Silviana Wood. Thank you for your infinite patience and for entrusting us with your inimitable and necessary teatro creations. We are very honored to contribute our "granito de arena" to make this book possible.

Many thanks to the editors at the University of Arizona Press who believed in the importance of this project from the beginning, when it was merely an exciting idea.

At Trinity University, I sincerely thank my dear colleague, mentor, and friend, Dr. Arturo Madrid, whose personal and professional contributions to my work have been many. Gracias also to the Mexico, the Americas, and Spain (MAS) Program for its 2012 Summer Research Grant in support of this project. Thanks also to the Office of Academic Affairs for their generous support of Chicana/o scholarship.

Mil gracias to my sonorense querida Elvia E. Niebla, whose cariño y apoyo not only encouraged but sustained us during this project. A Norma E. Cantú, amiga, mentor, colega querida: your infinite support, exemplary Chicana scholarship y magia guide my path. ¡Gracias siempre!

Por su inmenso amor y por creer incansablemente en mí, le agradezco de todo corazón a mi querida familia sonorense: L@s Urquijo Ruiz. En especial a mi adorado hermano, Carlos Alberto "Charly" Barceló Ruiz, quien cada día hace sonreír a mi alma.

—*Rita E. Urquijo-Ruiz*

BARRIO
DREAMS

Introduction

CHICANA THEATER
AND THE PLAYS OF SILVIANA WOOD

Since the heyday of Chicano[1] teatro—that is, Movimiento activist theater—when dozens of other groups sprang up across the country in Chi-
can@ and Latin@ communities, teatristas have traveled a long and arduous path in pursuit of their art. We refer, of course, to the work of the
founders of such groups during the Chicano Movement as El Teatro Campesino, Teatro Aguacero, El Teatro de la Esperanza, Teatro del Pueblo,
Teatro Libertad, and Teatro del Sol, among many others. We are especially
cognizant of the teatristas who labored indefatigably to make teatro relevant and to produce plays that not only touched the hearts and minds of
audiences but moved them to action. Among the workers in this field, and
alongside Luis Valdez of El Teatro Campesino, we recognize Jorge Huerta,
Evelina Fernández, and José Luis Valenzuela in California, who, from their
early work alongside other teatristas, founded El Teatro de la Esperanza,
therefore shaping the nature of activist theater. It is the desire to recognize
and remember those whose work fed the spirits of the Movimiento that
led us to this project: an anthology of the plays of Silviana Wood from
Tucson, Arizona, who, over the course of her enduring career, has worked
diligently and consistently with her community to produce insightful and
relevant theater. Wood's teatro has elicited tears and laughter from young
and elderly audiences in barrios, in cities, and in academic settings alike.
At the Teatro Nacional de Aztlán (TENAZ)[2] festivals, as well as on Tucson television and in local theater groups in her home community, Wood
forged a reputation and established a name as a playwright, actor, director,
and activist. Now, it is time for her to take center stage and to make her
work available to newer audiences—hence this book, the first to collect the
plays of a Chican@ playwright from Arizona.

We begin with a historical overview of theater in that region from
the early days of the twentieth century, when Carmen Soto de Vásquez
had the vision of establishing a Spanish-language theater in Tucson, to
the present. We joined efforts to offer an overview of this Chican@ and
Latin@ theater history and to present here the invaluable writings of
one of the most prolific contemporary Tucsonenses, Silviana Wood. Her

work encompasses numerous genres and spaces, including comedy, tragedy, skits, public arenas, short fiction, poetry, and a novel that remains yet unpublished. Her dramatic works in particular address issues of social justice, linguistic marginalization, oppressions, gender and sexuality, and class, all within the larger schema of race and ethnic studies. It is within her oeuvre that we find a key to unlocking the many layers of Arizona's literary treasures.

Through this introduction, we present the playwright and her work within the context of the wider world of Chican@ and Latin@ theater production of the last fifty years, with a special focus on Arizona. We offer brief synopses of the selected plays included in this collection, along with a few words of analysis. As this is a joint effort, we each wrote different sections, but collaboratively edited these as we co-authored others. When necessary, we refer to ourselves in the third person, as Cantú or Urquijo-Ruiz, to indicate individual perspectives.

Origins: How This Book Came to Be

Back in the 1980s, Cantú participated in a program on pastorelas, the traditional Christmas shepherds' plays, at the state historical museum in Tucson, Arizona. Her work led her to a desire to connect the pastorelas to the Chicano plays of the 1970s, as they, too, were rooted in the traditions of the community.[3] When Cantú was considering a series of publications that would bring together the plays that had been produced at the Guadalupe Cultural Arts Center in San Antonio over the last forty years, she came across scripts by Silviana Wood, whom she had met at a TENAZ gathering in the early 1980s in San Antonio, where Wood had traveled from Tucson with her theater group. Cantú had memories of attending these productions, of meeting Wood at TENAZ festivals, and of her brilliant linguistic wordplay. After renewing their friendship while at the Border Book Festival in Las Cruces, New Mexico, Cantú went back to the Guadalupe texts and reread Wood's scripts with a renewed interest in Wood's work. Cantú then invited as co-editor Chicana/Mexicana scholar Rita E. Urquijo-Ruiz, whose work focuses on theater traditions and whose knowledge of the Sonora, northwestern Mexico, and southern Arizona region would enhance the project.

They subsequently scheduled a trip to meet with Wood, and it was during that trip to Tucson, while walking in Wood's childhood spaces—the streets of Barrio Anita—that the co-editors realized what an invaluable collection this would be. As they visited the elementary school Wood had attended and sat with her in her living room reminiscing, they realized that the plays she penned—and often produced and directed—were only a part of the whole picture, for hers is a transnational story that begins with her grandmother, María Concepción Durazo Romero Gonzales, also known as Doña Concha or Doña Conchita. Like many tranfronterizo stories, it is full of familial turns, often careening wildly into emotional precipices. It is a story of displacement: her grandmother moved from Sonora to Arizona as, for all practical purposes, a single mother with three children in tow; her grandfather had another family, and the older daughter, Wood's aunt Amparo, returned to Santa Ana, Sonora, to be raised by her father and stepmother. Wood has written a yet unpublished novel that details this story and more of her family's border life.

Figure 1. Silviana Wood with her mother, also known as Conchita Gonzales, circa 1942.

As a member of a borderlands family, Wood experienced the reality of that transfrontera community. The gifted child became a Chicana activist, a single mom, an older student, and a playwright who traveled a rocky and unsteady path; her story constitutes a testimonio of a Chicana's life, especially one seeped in art and politics during the Chicano Movement. The artist grows and flourishes with a purpose born of the lived experiences of a child growing up with an immigrant grandmother, whose own story proved resiliency as the key to survival; in Cantú's view, it is the writing that offers an anchor to the playwright's life.

No less formidable is the impact of her mother, who came to the United States as a child and in Tucson became a woman who relished life

Figure 2. Silviana Wood as a child, circa 1946.

and loved to dance and sing. Wood, armed with education and a passion for telling stories, does more than survive—she inspires with her words, her plays. She finds an outlet, a voice that proclaims loud and clear: "Aquí estamos y no nos vamos. We are here and we are not leaving." This book, then, is not just a representation of Wood's work; it is a chronicle of the linguistic and historical period in which the plays were written and first performed. To fully understand the great triumph that this collection signifies, we must go back to the history of teatro in Arizona and in the Southwest.

Chican@ Theater: Early History

From the outset, teatro worked its magic with audiences in Tucson, Nogales, and other border towns through the Carpas,[4] those early sites of entertainment and political satire for el pueblo. Our literary roots as Chican@s and Latin@s go back centuries and blend both Spanish and preconquest spectacle traditions where ritual and dramatic performances become one. The folk plays found in the Catholic practice—pastorelas and other dramatic works bound to the liturgical celebrations of the Church—as well as the loas and other Siglo de Oro productions, while rooted in European tradition, are still performed by groups of believers in communities such as San Antonio, Texas, and Tucson. Pastorelas, also known as "los pastores," are still performed every Christmas season, either under the auspices of the Church or, more commonly, in homes and neighborhoods outside of Church sponsorship.[5] El Teatro Campesino's ongoing productions of *La Pastorela* and *La Virgen del Tepeyac* are two professional adaptations that survive as remnants of these early plays beyond the folk plays found in the community, such as Tucson's Borderlands Theater's production of *A Tucson Pastorela*. Aside from the folk plays, Chican@ teatro has a lively and robust repertoire of authored plays, some of which have been published.

While the publication of the plays of Cherríe Moraga, Carlos Morton, Josefina López, or Luis Valdez attests to the very active theater scene in California during and after the Movimiento, this is the first collection of plays by a Chicana from a different region: a playwright equally immersed in the Chican@ civil rights movement, a regular participant at the TENAZ festivals, and a committed and devoted political activist. These plays clearly show Wood's penchant for wordplay and for an insistence on telling it like it is in the language of the region.

When in conversation that summer day in Tucson, Wood told us that her favorite book as a child was *A Tree Grows in Brooklyn*, and Cantú felt an even stronger kinship with her than when they had first met at the TENAZ festival more than thirty years before. They both had other favorites, though, and Wood spoke of her love of Steinbeck and how living in Salinas, California, she had come to know and appreciate his work, especially *The Grapes of Wrath*. Cantú saw in Wood a life paralleling her own; the child whose "facultad," as Gloria Anzaldúa (1987) would call it, is keen and sharp, functioning to assist her to transcend the conditions of her life. This facultad allowed Wood to enter into a literary arena that she was not born to—an arena in which she treaded lightly. Her decision to write didn't come easily, and it happened almost by accident. While working on a degree in social work, Wood became frustrated with the classes, for her real love was writing. So, encouraged to pursue her passion, Wood changed her major. As an older student and a single mother, this was a risky but fortuitous thing to do. She began writing short stories, at least one of which—"The Dragonslayer"—was later developed into a one-act play. It is included here as the third acto of *Una vez, en un barrio de sueños . . .*[6] Writing drama, though, differs from writing fiction or poetry in that a play remains a collection of words and a dream until it is produced—and Wood worked to have her plays produced. The very first collective she worked with—Teatro del Pueblo—included her brother and other local teatristas, and it was in working with this group that her dream became reality.

Figure 3. Silvana Wood, circa 2010. Photograph by Rebecca Higuera.

Wood explained that early productions were created in makeshift spaces, in collaboration with barrio folks who served as actors. And when she was finally granted a residency at the Guadalupe Cultural Arts Center in San Antonio, with a budget to pay the actors and to produce the play *Anhelos por Oaxaca*, Wood felt she had achieved success after the many challenges and obstacles she recalls facing along her path as a teatrista. In our estimation, the value of her artist's testimonio is that it chronicles and attests both to her resilience and to the power of her art, for even now, in the twenty-first century—decades after they were written and first produced—these plays remain relevant and speak to our recent past and our present.

An Overview of Chicanas and Latinas in Theater

One can say that the story of Chicano and Latino theater in the Southwest begins in the 1500s, with Juan de Oñate's production of an auto sacramental as the Spanish conquistadores stopped in what is now El Paso, Texas, on their way north into New Mexico. As long as the Southwest region remained under Spanish colonial domination, the religious drama that began in the sixteenth century lived on.[7] But it is not until the twentieth century that we can claim popular theater in what is now the United States flourished. As they made their way into small towns in Texas like Laredo and larger ones like San Antonio, and elsewhere in the Southwest, such as in Tucson and Los Angeles, professional touring companies developed audiences for their Spanish-language productions with a repertoire of plays drawn from both classical and contemporary playwrights. Thus, the itinerant and resident companies laid the foundation for an emergent tradition of political and activist theater.

It is no accident, then, that Chican@ and Latin@ theater would emerge decades later as a powerful political and social practice in the U.S. Southwest. Groups like Teatro Libertad in Arizona, and Teatro Aguacero in Albuquerque, along with the Guadalupe Cultural Arts ensembles, existed outside of the more recognized teatro groups in California like El Teatro Campesino and El Teatro de la Esperanza. The Guadalupe Cultural Arts Center, located in the west side of San Antonio in what had been a theater and movie house, became a premier venue for theater arts as playwrights were commissioned to produce plays. The Guadalupe was also the site where visiting groups from Mexico, Cuba, and Latin America performed. Similar locations existed elsewhere in Texas, California, and Arizona. Tucson in particular had a theater space devoted to Spanish-language productions; Teatro Carmen operated from 1914 to 1922, hosting innumerable touring companies and providing entertainment for Tucson's Spanish-speaking audiences. Built by the famous architect and contractor Manuel Flores and equipped with a state-of-the-art stage, the venue was managed by its founder, Carmen Soto de Vásquez, who realized her dream of having a cultural oasis in Tucson where the elite could enjoy various types of cultural productions. She produced a number of events, including music concerts, operas, melodramas, and serious theatrical works.

In subsequent years, Teatro Carmen, like the Guadalupe and other theaters, became a movie house and even hosted boxing matches. These early precursors to contemporary Chican@ and Latin@ theater remain as vestiges of an era when Spanish-language drama brought cultural affirmation to these Spanish-speaking communities. But with the advent of the Chicano Movement, theater artists and activists sought to fill the gap and, with a much more radical and political intent, sprang up all over the Southwest in the 1960s and 1970s. The founding of the TENAZ in 1971 brought together an international group of teatristas whose work revolved around social justice issues.

Historically—especially in the last three decades—Chican@ and Latin@ playwrights in general, and women writers in particular, have had few venues in which they can produce their work. Often relegated to obscure and inaccessible spaces, their work remains silenced and ignored by the mainstream U.S. theater world of Broadway and even local community theater companies. As scholars have shown, Latin@ productions in the United States are, in general, overshadowed by plays written by white males.[8] Such invisibility and the concomitant absence of ethnic communities, especially those of Chicanas and Latinas, on stage produce a misconception that the Latin@ theater scene remains marginal—that we have no playwrights. Therefore, issues of self-representation and empowerment are often themes incorporated in the work of Latin@ playwrights; their productions attempt to contest the stereotypical and racist depictions of the Latin@ community that were historically created. Chicana and Latina dramatic artists have chosen to voice their own concerns regarding issues of identity formation as subjects who constantly inhabit a liminal cultural space where multiple aspects of their cultures (mainstream and marginal) overlap. Furthermore, their contestation also addresses issues of gender and sexual discrimination from within their own ethnic groups, especially starting in the late 1970s when the first wave of third-world feminism produced empowering literary works that were later transformed and transferred to the stage.[9] In confronting the issues mentioned above, Chicana and Latina playwrights insist on making their voices heard; the preeminent scholar of Chicana and Latina theater and performance studies, Alicia Arrizón, states:

> [The Latina] subject is the one who replaces whispers with shouts and obedience with determination. In challenging her assigned position, she begins to transform and transcend it. . . . She is the . . . taboo breaker. She is the transgressive, the lusty and comical performer, the queerest among us. . . . Latinas today bring a rebellious sensibility to the task of dismantling the structures that have defined, silenced, and marginalized them.[10]

Several Chicana feminist writers have theorized the idea of rupturing the silence and defying the patriarchal roles assigned to Chicanas and Latinas. In their book, *Teatro Chicana*, Laura E. García, Sandra M. Gutiérrez, and Felicitas Núñez chronicle the difficulty they faced as Chicanas producing teatro at the height of the Movimiento in the 1970s. Yolanda Broyles-González describes Chicana performance artist, writer, and activist María Elena Gaitán from Los Angeles, California, as

> a crosswise woman (*atravesada*) . . . [who] crosses conventions, borders, and hierarchies with wisdom. When the *atravesada* is grotesquely comical, then she is a *traviesa*, a trickster. Laughter is the ingredient [that] magically changes everything, which turns the *atravesada* into a *traviesa*, the trickster who shocks us out of the complacency of seriousness. . . . She is an extravagant *traviesa atravesada pelada*. . . . *Entremeter* . . . carries the connotation of "voicing" and breaking decorum, breaking the established ongoing rules of his-story, interrupting and inserting new elements, and breaking onto the scene.[11]

In many ways, these definitions describe Silviana Wood, who, as an atravesada, a traviesa, creates work that challenges, questions, and incites women to consider their lot in life. Out of the many characters that Wood has created, perhaps it is Doña Chona, the iconic woman "que no tiene pelos en la lengua"—who tells it like it is—that most resembles this character who challenges and teaches at once.[12] She exists alongside theatrical representations like the ones performed and created by her predecessors as detailed below. These traviesas and atravesadas join in the tradition of entertaining, bawdy, and scatological representations of Chican@ and Latin@ social types, while also making strong political statements that challenge the status quo.

In their (re)codification of previously oppressive terms, Chicana and Latina writers and academics contribute theories of empowerment for women whose voices often have not been heard. Whether we apply the theoretical terminology created by Anzaldúa ("new mestiza consciousness") or by Chela Sandoval ("oppositional consciousness"),[13] we must situate the Chicana and Latina subjects in a "third space," or in between the cultures from which they are empowered to enact their own (re)presentation(s).

Historical and Cultural Differences: Initial Staging(s)

From its beginnings to the 1940s, U.S. Chicana and Latina theater and performance can be divided into three types: the professional, the popular, and the folk. The first kind was presented exclusively inside theater houses such as Teatro Carmen or Teatro Guadalupe, and it was created for the upper classes that preferred to attend these productions, primarily in monolingual Spanish, where the works of established Latin American and Spanish playwrights were highlighted.[14] The second type was a poor person's itinerant Teatro de Carpa—artists performed in Spanish (and sometimes incorporated English words) in tents set up in small towns or wherever working-class people gathered.[15] Many of these companies (both professional and popular) entertained audiences throughout the United States, Puerto Rico, Cuba, and Mexico. The third type comprised the liturgical folk dramas, such as pastorelas, which were mainly performed by common folks themselves, largely amateur performers who could memorize the long parlamentos and often performed them as a sort of prayer, a manda. In some ways, such theater served a didactic function as the Catholic Church encouraged the performances, especially around Christmas and

Holy Week, where the liturgical stories of the birth and passion of Jesus were dramatized. But alongside of these, we can find folk traditions of mojigangas and pastorelas that were often not sanctioned by the Church.

Professional theater is perhaps the most known, and women were critical in the development of both it and also popular theater. Among the women who were instrumental in the popularity of the formal companies is Virginia Fábregas, who was born and raised in Mexico and later relocated to California. As an entrepreneur, playwright, and actor, Fábregas offered professional theater to middle- and upper-class Spanish-speaking audiences in the U.S. Southwest.

Likewise, the previously mentioned Carmen Soto de Vásquez was not only the founder of Teatro Carmen in Tucson but also participated in Teatro de Carpa in 1915, performing for all types of audiences.[16] Around the same time, Lydia Mendoza and her mother, Leonor Zamarripa Mendoza, traveled throughout the Texas Valley, entertaining migrant agricultural field workers with their variedades, a kind of vaudeville show that included original skits, music, and stand-up comedy. Zamarripa Mendoza wrote and directed the comic sketches, taught her children how to play various musical instruments, and created costumes for the family; indeed, she was the one that held it all together with the support of her husband, Francisco Mendoza.[17]

There were two other women in Texas who left their indelible mark in the world of professional and popular theater: Josefina Niggli (1910–1983) and Beatriz Escalona (1903–1979). Niggli's Italian American father and Mexican mother were living in Monterrey, Mexico, when she was born, but the family fled to San Antonio during the Mexican Revolution. She was one of the first Latinas to study theater and performance in the United States, and she earned a bachelor of arts degree from Incarnate Word College in San Antonio in 1931 and a master's degree from the University of North Carolina at Chapel Hill (UNC) in 1937. Two years later, she published her collection *Mexican Folk Plays* with UNC Press.[18] As Urquijo-Ruiz writes, "Niggli was a pioneer in Latina letters in general, given that she also published works of poetry and narrative, when few Latinas/os had access to U.S. publication venues."[19] Niggli's contribution to popular theater in the 1930s is small but important, as her plays appear to be geared for an English-speaking audience. Her addition of folk themes and her desire to translate Mexican culture to a mainstream U.S. audience may not garner her inclusion in the world inhabited by Carmen

Soto de Vásquez and Beatriz Escalona, but in her own way, she, too, is a foremother to the Chicana and Latina playwrights who thirty years later struggled to publish and produce their work.

Unlike Niggli, Beatriz Escalona's work was rooted in the everyday and the common people. Their audiences were quite different, too, no doubt due to their respective social class positionality. Escalona was attracted to the stage from an early age and began working as an usher, gaining an education, albeit informally, in all things related to the theater. The rich artistic and performance scene in her hometown of San Antonio provided ample room for Escalona's resolute endeavours. She founded her own company, Atracciones Noloesca, and traveled throughout the United States and internationally. Escalona created a character, whom she called "La Chata Noloesca," that was to become the epitome of a peladita—a destitute, downtrodden Mexican social type.[20] In her use of what Tomás Ybarra-Frausto would identify as a "rasquachi"[21] aesthetic, we can see the origins of some street theater subgenres that relied on scatological humor to get their point across. Writing about Noloesca's performance, Ybarra-Frausto states, "The crude and ribald content of many such comic sketches centered around what Mikhail Bakhtin calls 'the lower stratum,' humor related to body functions: copulation, birth, growth, eating and defecation."[22] Escalona serves as a good example of a traviesa or atravesada, discussed earlier, a woman who is not afraid to speak her mind and challenge patriarchal power.

These women's contributions to the development of theater in the early part of the twentieth century cannot be denied. Teatro de Carpa constituted the root of popular entertainment that was to become Movimiento teatro, and often it was the women who wrote and performed their own work in these spaces. Unaware of this theater history in her own community, Silviana Wood emerged as a figure who continued this tradition by writing and performing her own work and often using humor to indict a society hostile to Chican@ and Latin@ experiences.

Silviana Wood and Chicano Movement Theater

Just like contemporary Chicana and Latina theater owes much to the theatrical productions of the civil rights movements in the 1960s, Wood's writing has benefited from the work of teatristas and ensembles like El Teatro Campesino that sought to make theater accessible to the masses.

Later, El Teatro Campesino offered writing and acting workshops, producing some of the most famous Chican@ and Latin@ actors and playwrights.[23] However, as Broyles-González has well documented, El Teatro Campesino, led by Luis Valdez, did not acknowledge the contributions of the women in the ensemble, such as those of Socorro Valdez, Diane Rodriguez, and Olivia Chumacero.[24] These three women developed solo careers as writers, directors, and producers after leaving the ensemble.

When TENAZ sought to establish a coalition of various groups with similar agendas to confront and deal with social justice issues affecting Chican@ and Latin@ communities at the time, many of us cheered, as we saw it as a move toward a national presence. And while TENAZ had a nationalist agenda that privileged male power, many of the groups were striving to include women, and a few were even led by women. El Teatro de la Esperanza, originally from Santa Barbara, California, and a TENAZ member ensemble, dealt with women's issues in their plays; for instance, one of their most famous productions, *La víctima*, has a female protagonist who was deported as part of the mass deportations that happened in that historical period; she is a heroine and a symbol of motherhood. Although the title may indicate that she is the victim, it is really her son who becomes a border patrol agent who fits the victim role better. But this ensemble was an exception within the umbrella organization; therefore, it was not long after the founding of TENAZ that the women who were members of separate ensembles formed their own organizations, such as Women in Teatro (WIT). Other spaces that welcomed all-women groups in California were Teatro Raíces and Teatro Chicana[25] in San Diego, and Las Cucarachas in San Francisco, which was led by Dorinda Moreno. In 1974, Moreno's group wrote and performed the play *Chicana*, which traced the lives of Chicana historical ancestors such as Sor Juana Inés de la Cruz and Adelita.[26] These activist mujeres that were members of both WIT and TENAZ advocated for women's inclusion and saw "[t]he need for women playwrights, producers, and directors; the need for strong women's roles in the messages through which we educate our public; the need of the individual woman, such as child care; and the need for support of all Raza for the development of women in teatro."[27] By the late 1980s, the most powerful positions within TENAZ were held by women: Lily Delgadillo was the chair and Evelina Fernández the artistic coordinator.[28]

The women ensembles within TENAZ also created *Teatropoesía*, a theatrical performance that incorporated theater, poetry, and music.

Chicana theater critic Yvonne Yarbro-Bejarano states that this subgenre "exploits the beauty and power of words, a dimension often neglected in Chicano theater, combining the compact directness and lyrical emotion of the poetic text with the physical immediacy of the three-dimensional work of theater."[29] Many of the women in this new hybrid genre were neither playwrights nor actors, but they utilized their artistic abilities to create theater that had a strong political and often feminist agenda. These women worked in solidarity against the struggles in Central America, especially for the people from El Salvador and Nicaragua.[30] One particular *Teatropoesía* performance piece titled *Tongues of Fire* took as its base feminist writings like the ones later published in *This Bridge Called My Back*, edited by lesbian Chicana feminists Cherríe Moraga and Gloria Anzaldúa. Throughout the 1970s and the 1980s—just as Wood was coming into her own working with the local theater collective Teatro del Pueblo, and later Teatro Libertad—Chicanas and Latinas were engaged in creating an impressive body of theatrical performance work, whether as part of ensembles or on their own. It was to the teatristas involved in this milieu that Wood's work in the 1980s and 1990s would speak, and it was these same teatristas in whom she would find an audience.

Contemporary Chicana and Latina Performance

The beginnings of contemporary Chicana and Latina professional theater followed this strong surge in theatrical production; Cherríe Moraga's first play, *Giving Up the Ghost* (1986), ushered in a new era. Although Moraga was not the first to write a play about Chicana/Mexicana lesbian desire, she was the first to treat the subject positively.[31] Originally from California and of both Anglo and Mexican ethnic heritage, Moraga occupies a special place of privilege among Chicana and Latina teatristas. Multifaceted, she has published dramatic scripts, poetry, essays, short stories, and memoirs. Other Chicana playwrights such as Edith Villarreal (*My Visits with MGM*) and Denise Chávez (*Novena Narrativas*) have written works specifically dealing with women's issues of identity formation and generational conflicts. Playwrights have come a long way, and some of the major themes have also changed: Josefina López's *Real Women Have Curves* and Milcha Sanchez-Scott's *Roosters* concentrate on themes about identity, self-image, immigrant labor exploitation, and life in the barrios.[32] A recent play, *Water by the Spoonful* by Quiara Alegría Hudes, is a case in point, as the themes are contemporary issues of generational dissonance—similar to those which we find in *Amor de hija*, but as a contemporary story set in New York and in a Puerto Rican family with other issues that differ markedly. Similarly, Virginia Grise's *blu* and *The Panza Monologues*, which she co-authored with Irma Mayorga, treat contemporary feminist issues surrounding sexuality and identity, as well as violence.

Contemporary performance art, a type of theatrical cultural production in which Chicanas and Latinas have participated since the 1970s but especially in the last two decades, may find one of its precursors in the work of Silviana Wood, given her mastery as a mime. Wood created a blend of performance that falls between strict dramatic theater and *Teatropoesía*. Many performance artists present their solo or one-woman shows in community and university spaces as Wood did. These shows often incorporate slides, music (recorded or live), visual art, photographs, and the artists' own bodies. Despite the economic production cost of their work, Chicana and Latina writers have had a recent proliferation of their productions in their communities and yet continue to occupy minimal space and time within the mainstream artistic world.

In her definition of Latina performance, Arrizón emphasizes the issues of resistance and agency when she states that,

> Performance art, with its focus on identity formation, enhances the cultural and political specificity of categories such as ethnicity, race, class, and sexuality. . . . This definition moves identity formation into the realm of indefinite processes unfolding in the bodily "acts" of the performer, the agency of production, and the spectator. . . . Chicana [and Latina] performativity must be located in the realm of negotiations which transforms silence into sound, invisibility into presence, and objecthood into subjecthood.[33]

Chicana and Latina performance artists often create and produce their own works just as their precursors did in the Teatro de Carpa. Additionally, they rupture stereotypes and raise awareness of social issues via humor and with an emphasis on the use of their physical bodies onstage. Through their performance and talent, Chicana and Latina actors, performers, and playwrights have created safer spaces for the marginalized—including the teatristas themselves. Wood belongs to this community of teatristas, playwrights, actors, and performance artists who take control of their own work, bodies, and lives in order to continue to assert their identities individually and communally. The hope and ultimate goal is always that the struggles will continue to lessen as more and more Chicanas and Latinas achieve their status as artists whose work is produced and published nationally and internationally. It is our wish that this collection of Silviana Wood's plays contributes to the achievement of such goals.

The Plays of Silviana Wood

In choosing to focus on Wood's plays—not her fiction—and in selecting the scripts to include in this book, we aim to both highlight her work and draw attention to the wider world of Chicana and Latina dramatic traditions. In preparation, we discussed various strategies: Which plays should we include? And once the plays are selected, should we do a thematic ordering? Should we present them chronologically as they were written? We arrived at a plan: compiling the writing that Wood felt best represented her oeuvre and following her guidance, we selected those that spoke to us and established an order that would work for readers who chose to read the book from cover to cover. Thus, the book-end plays—*Una vez, en un barrio de sueños . . .* and *Anhelos por Oaxaca*—provide what we sought to do: introduce Wood's work and entertain the reader. Choosing to focus on the plays, however, meant that we could not include an excerpt from her unpublished novel or a sample of her short fiction. It was not an altogether surprising choice; after all, it is for her dramatic work that Wood is most known. We hope that the short fiction and the novel will be published subsequently, and thus scholars and audiences at large can have access to the complete works of this remarkable writer. Because we feel that to understand Wood's overall trajectory one must focus on her key themes and look at her use of language, in the following section, we present some thoughts on language, as well as summaries and brief analyses of the plays included in this book.

Wood's use of language is specific to her geographical region of the U.S. Southwest. Her characters speak in a Chicano argot that is unique to Arizona and, in many instances, to Tucson specifically. The plays are a code-switching and punning tour de force in which almost every exchange among and between characters is laden with nuanced and deep-structured communications. For example, the very names that Wood assigns her characters constitute a well-thought-out and intentional statement; in *Amor de hija*, the mother Cuquita (from Refugio) and her daughter Consuelo (a.k.a. Connie) bring to mind safety and security. They represent a place—or a person—that offers succor and invites trust, as their names connote. The dialogue is often spirited, and even when there is a character offering a soliloquy, we are always aware that there is a message communicated to the audience. In *Anhelos por Oaxaca*, the language of Don Felipe and fifteen-year-old Rudy marks their difference in age, as well as the difference in their political views and cultural spaces.

In all of Wood's plays, the dialogue is in English, Spanish (formal and colloquial[34]), and Spanglish, representing the unique linguistic traits of a familia Latina living in the United States, especially in Arizona. In almost all plays, the language use is stratified according to generations. For instance, in *Amor de hija*, except for a very few words in English, such as "cake" and "ride," Tata Arcenio and Nana Cuquita (the grandparents) do not speak English, but they understand it perfectly, and while they speak only Spanish, everyone in the family understands them. Consuelo and Rogelio are fluent in both English and Spanish and code-switch with ease; in other words, they are true bilingual speakers who liberally use a Spanglish that is very much situated in the Tucson area. Their son Junior speaks both English and Spanish, but Kathy and Danny speak only English; however, all understand Spanish well. Heather, Kathy's daughter, similarly only speaks English but is determined to learn Spanish and exemplifies the quandary of many Chican@s who are raised speaking mostly English and who yearn to reclaim the language of their ancestors.

Now we turn to the plays themselves in order to analyze and contextualize them within Wood's oeuvre. We especially highlight the elements that make these plays representative of cultural practices and, in many cases, of a Chicana and Latina feminist sensibility.

Una vez, en un barrio de sueños . . . (Once Upon a Time, in a Barrio of Dreams . . .)
A very brief introduction opens *Una vez, en un barrio de sueños . . .*, a play composed of that introduction and three short sketches, or actos, offering glimpses into that familiar terrain—the barrio and its dwellers. The various characters are in fact identified as residents and each brings a unique

sensibility, thus setting the tone and mood for what follows. The play presents a site of struggle and joy, a space that Wood populates with typical stock characters. She uses the barrio as a palimpsest for her social commentary and as an indictment of a system that creates these often brutal and harsh spaces. She inscribes such characters from the "hood" in all her plays to illustrate both the pathos and the joys of living—or barely surviving—in the periphery, the outside of the mainstream. Part of her genius is the way she portrays life in what Anzaldúa called "el mundo zurdo"—that space inhabited by people of color, the poor, the female, the outsiders, a place for the atravesados, the odd, the different, those who do not fit the mainstream among us. The introduction and three actos center on the idea of dreams that go unfulfilled, that exist to offer surcease from the misery of life. The brief dramatic introduction to *Una vez, en un barrio de sueños . . .* sets the stage for the three actos that follow. The title harkens back to Pedro Calderón de la Barca's *La vida es sueño* and connects the three sketches into a coherent whole. In "El Militante y la Señora Martínez (The Militant and Mrs. Martínez)," we meet two disparate and seemingly opposite characters who find common ground. Both are as lonely as Samuel Beckett's characters in *Waiting for Godot*; they suffer from an inability to see reality for what it is. El Militante, a poet, is a dreamer who eventually gains Mrs. Martínez's trust and helps her to not only deal with her fear of the outside world but to learn to defend herself against racial discrimination. The two of them become fast friends in spite of the generational differences; el Militante supplants Mrs. Martínez's children, and she offers him familial affection as well. The generational conflict and the resolution is a surprising confluence that brings together some of Wood's favorite themes: intergenerational relationships and women's agency. Populated by barrio residents, el Militante's friend, and a chorus-like group of gossips, the short play is full of wordplay; for instance, in an exchange with Mrs. Martínez, el Militante explains that the chrysanthemums he is presenting to her are "clavelitos" (little carnations) because "me las clavé" ("I [el Militante] stole them"); "clavel" means "carnation," and "clavé" means "stole" in Caló, the barrio vernacular Wood uses so masterfully.

The second acto, "¿Y qué tiene que ver un turkey con Veracruz anyway? (So What Does a Turkey Have to Do with Veracruz Anyway?)" presents a husband and wife who see the world in completely different ways. She is the practical, frugal, down-to-earth matriarch, while he is a janitor obsessed with a dream to travel to Veracruz. The way in which Wood weaves in the classic Mexican film *Macario* (which makes references to both Veracruz and poverty) is evidence of her mastery of designing plots that, while not always possessing verisimilitude, are nevertheless believable. The film tells the story of a man similar to Wood's protagonist, but it elicits a different desire than what the filmmaker probably anticipated. The way Wood's plot unfolds makes the audience face a poignant and unexpected ending. The third acto brings together two unlikely characters engaged in an outrageous enterprise: "El Dragonslayer" makes reference to the barrio's neglected child and the neighborhood grouch. Wood describes it in the synopsis as "a Chicano 'Jack and the Beanstalk' tale," and the message is loud and clear: in unity there is strength, and we must take our allies as they come if we are to succeed. It is a powerful lesson, and one that a Latin@ barrio greatly needs.

Amor de hija (A Daughter's Love)

The play *Amor de hija* centers on a working-class family in Arizona. It hinges on and is held together by the interplay between the women, particularly the mother-daughter relationship. The four generations that populate the world Wood has imagined are Tata Arcenio and Nana Cuquita; their daughter Consuelo and her husband Rogelio; their grandchildren Junior, Kathy, and Danny; and their great-grandchildren Heather and a newborn baby. The protagonist, Consuelo, occupies what has been called the sandwich generation; she is the caretaker of her children, her grandchildren, and her parents. Now in her mid-forties, Consuelo, who has raised her children while working as the bookkeeper and receptionist for her husband's construction company, is at a loss as she begins to experience the proverbial empty-nest syndrome. Her children are grown and on their own, except for the oldest who is a college student still at home. Her husband's construction company is doing well, so Consuelo no longer has to work full time, and she feels unwanted and unwelcome there, especially when her husband hires an attractive younger woman as a receptionist. The plot's twists and turns bring strife and opportunities to Consuelo, who is affected deeply by difficult events: her life changes when her father, Tata Arcenio, dies suddenly as the family is celebrating her mother Nana Cuquita's sixty-fifth birthday. In act 1, the scenes of celebration and then of mourning are juxtaposed brilliantly as the festive tone and language shift to one of prayer and darkness, setting the tone for the rest of the play.

Tata Arcenio's death affects Nana Cuquita profoundly, and she begins to deteriorate physically, mentally, and emotionally. With *Amor de Hija*, Wood sets a thematic precedent, as it is one of the first plays by a Chican@ to deal with Alzheimer's disease; here we find elements that will surface much later in plays such as Lisa Suarez's *I'll Remember for You*. As the eldest daughter, Consuelo becomes the caretaker for her mother, and as the illness worsens, Nana Cuquita comes to live with her daughter's family, and the mother-daughter roles are reversed. This role reversal causes even more conflict when Rogelio, deeply resentful of Consuelo's new obligations, finds solace in a sexual fling with the younger woman (the script says mid-thirties, but a much younger actress was cast in one of the performances) who works as the new receptionist in his business.

Throughout the play, the author includes what she labels as IMAGEN (or the plural, IMÁGENES), which function to set the mood, to highlight a significant event, or to reflect the action. One such IMAGEN occurs in the surreal opening scene—before act 1, scene 1—which skillfully foreshadows these events with miming and the women's actions. The first act also sets the tone for the action on at least three levels: emotional, physical, and mental. At the emotional level, Consuelo (whose name means succor, consolation, or solace) pivots continuously from elation to despair. At each turn, she is whirled into emotional turmoil. At the physical level, we see her aging body mirrored in her mother's own aged body (Consuelo's future) and in her daughter's youthful body (Consuelo's past). The embodied knowledge that Consuelo exemplifies places her exactly in the middle—in nepantla, as Anzaldúa would say—between worlds or in a third space, firmly situated between young and old as a middle-aged Chicana. In terms of her mental state, she is also drawn into being of two minds: Had she not quit her job, her husband might not have strayed. Had she maintained her allegiance to her mother at bay, perhaps her children would not have left. Had she been a better daughter, perhaps her mother would not be suffering from her illness and loneliness. These kinds of mental imaginings allow us to locate her existence in the midst of various vortices.

Forced to choose between her allegiance to her mother or to her husband and family, Consuelo becomes the emotional, physical, and mental axis upon which her family (and the play) revolves. It is the strong familial bond that had been forged by Nana Cuquita before her illness, nourished and perpetuated by Consuelo, and reinforced by Nana Cuquita's grandchildren that allows the family to survive, but not without scarring and deep wounds. Junior, Danny, Kathy, and Norma all bring their own lives' worries to Consuelo, whether it is to take care of her grandchildren, Heather and the baby, or to support each of them in their career choices. Ultimately, the family would fall apart without Consuelo. Additionally, Consuelo is Norma's and Kathy's ally, and she strives to make things easy for them, knowing the stress and demands on their lives. She acquiesces and, in some ways, allows them to take advantage of her insofar as she is the one they always come to for assistance. But she is only doing what Nana Cuquita did for her. Norma, her daughter-in-law, is also a recipient of her and Nana Cuquita's cultural sabiduría, as we see below in the example of medicinal herbs being used for the baby's ailment.

A note on language and naming: Wood decided that Consuelo's children would all have Anglicized names: Kathy, Danny, Junior, and even Heather (Consuelo's granddaughter), whose name is mispronounced by Nana Cuquita. Consuelo also goes by the Anglicized Connie, but Nana Cuquita, who is of an older generation, has a name specifically connected to Chican@ culture. Her name is Refugio; Cuca—or the diminutive Cuquita—is a nickname used specifically for this name, which has no equivalent in English, although Cookie is sometimes also used as a nickname for Refugio. Honoring her name, she has been the family's refuge, but now she needs her daughter's protection and care.

Aside from such onomastic cultural knowledge, a closer look at Wood's use of traditional sabiduría is warranted. In act 1, as the baby cries and the discussion turns to empacho, it is Nana Cuquita who knows it is *not* empacho but colic, and she asks for chamomile tea for the baby. This scene also shows the ways in which neighbors share and work together. Norma is sent next door to ask for "un puñito de manzanilla" to make some chamomile tea for the baby. The older women, Nana Cuquita and Consuelo, instruct the young mother on caring for the baby. But it is done with warmth and compassion. As she waits for the manzanilla, Nana Cuquita cares for the baby and chastises youth and their modern ways:

NANA CUQUITA [*talking to herself as she tends to the baby*]:
Esta juventud de hoy día no saben nada. Ni se cuidan en la dieta. Salen del hospital en la mañana y ya pa' la tarde andan de compras en el Kmart, o peor, bailando cumbias en el casino. ¿Adónde dejé mi bolsa? [*Looking around and calling out*] ¿Arcenio, bajaste mi bolsa

del carro? [*Finding her purse*] Ah, aquí está. [*Taking a bottle of olive oil out of her purse and pouring a bit into her palm as she talks*] Un tantito de aceite de olivo, aceite de comer, pa' todo sirve. [*Rubbing palms together to warm up oil*] Calientito pa' no asustarlo. [*Rubbing it on baby's stomach*] Pobrecito, tiene el estomaguito bien duro. [*Checking baby's feet*] Y los piecitos bien helados. Le va a entrar frío al inocente. [*Bundling up baby*] Así, bien envuelto como un tamalito de frijol.

Indeed, the play is full of such asides and lessons from traditional culture. The generational divide is mediated by Consuelo, who inhabits both worlds—the old, as represented by Doña Cuquita, and the young, as represented by her children, grandchild, and daughter-in-law. All in all, *Amor de hija* is very much a 1980s play, but it remains fresh insofar as it deals with issues still relevant thirty years later: the sandwich generation's predicaments, Alzheimer's disease, young people's desire to learn Spanish, infidelity, and mother-daughter conflict.

A Drunkard's Tale of Melted Wings and Memories

This play can be considered a tragedy, as several of the characters live in despair and die. As in other plays by Wood, the linguistic word games are rampant and so are the allusions to cultural practices. Watusi and Artemisa, Helen, and Catungas remain in the audience's mind long after one reads the play—a testament to Wood's ability to enflesh her characters with real human traits and frailties, which, while reminiscent of almost stereotypical characters of the barrio on whom Wood embellishes and zooms in, magnify their weaknesses. In one exchange between Helen and Catungas, we get a discussion of nicknames:

CATUNGAS: La Molacha. My sister that's missing her front teeth—remember her?
HELEN: Yes, you mean Amalia. I can't figure out how you all start out with such wonderful Christian names and end up with those outrageous nicknames. What are your two brothers called? Andrés and Fernando?
CATUNGAS: El Huango y el Chueco.

HELEN: El Huango y el Chueco. I'm not even gonna ask how they got these nicknames.

CATUNGAS: But I'm gonna tell you anyway. El Huango loses all his strength in his neck, arms, and legs sometimes, so he walks like this. [*Showing her*] Y el Chueco has a crooked back, so he walks like this—

HELEN [*sarcastically*]: Well, that should make it easy to remember who's who.

Of course the nicknames in this case are all physical attributes—toothless, unsteady, crooked back. But the way that Helen points out that they all begin with perfectly nice Christian names and end up with nicknames that she seems to insinuate are offensive allows us to dig deeper even while laughing at Catungas's antics on stage.

A veteran of World War II, Watusi is also damaged and wounded. But the tragicomedy has a somewhat happy ending as the establishment of a cultural center promises to bring joy and healing. No doubt this is taken from Wood's own experiences with the cultural centers and activism in Tucson, which provided much-needed health care and basic assistance with educational issues. The play offers a panoply of characters who confront an equal number of situations that reveal the ways Raza lives in Tucson. Moreover, lighthearted and whimsical treatment of serious topics permits the playwright to introduce difficult themes in a way that an audience will not soon forget.

Yo, Casimiro Flores (I, Casimiro Flores)

The trilingual (Spanish, English, and Yaqui) tragicomedy *Yo, Casimiro Flores* is set at three times represented concurrently: the present, the past (through flashbacks), and the afterlife. The first part is set in a hospital in a town in the Southwest, and the second half takes place in the mythical Mictlán, the Aztec place of the dead. Casimiro is a Yaqui-Mexican hospital janitor who dwells in the basement, where his only companion is Geraldine, a discarded anatomy class skeleton standing in a corner. There is an intersection of mythical characters from Aztec cosmology, such as Mictlantecuhtli, alongside contemporary Raza characters from the barrio. In presenting the four dead characters whom Casimiro must prepare for their entry into Mictlán, Wood ventures into surreal and mythic representations of Chican@ social types. The four are: Rocky Road, a suicide case; Mad Dog Sánchez, a wannabe gang member; Xóchil, an innocent fourteen-year-old; and Don Prisciliano, an old man. Each represents an aspect of life that Casimiro must contend with, and each also allows Wood to introduce issues—such as suicide, gang violence, and aging—found in the barrio. The pun on the title character's name is worthy of mention as well; Casimiro Flores can be translated as "I almost see flowers"—no doubt an allusion to the Aztec belief that flowers are the hearts of the dead. In the closing scene, Mictlantecuhtli says, "Already we sit down to the flower, para recibir la flor, we sit down to the flower," as Casimiro is dancing La Danza del Venado, the Yaqui sacred dance of death.

The poignant, acrimonious way that Casimiro deals with his own demons and how he navigates his encounter with his past and with the underworld deity illustrate Wood's mastery of interlocking knowledges and cultural worlds. Casimiro sets up an altar for his dead friends and then brings all the action into focus at the end, highlighting the play's deeper meaning—for the play is ultimately a meditation on life and death that asks us to ponder our own mortality while instructing us on indigenous knowledges.

Anhelos por Oaxaca (Yearnings for Oaxaca)

The characters in this play are also time shifters, as we see them travel back in time through flashbacks. Don Felipe, his daughter Amelia, and his grandson Rudy live in Tucson, Arizona. The fun begins when young Rudy, who speaks only English, becomes a reluctant chaperone to his grandfather as they travel to Oaxaca, his homeland in southern Mexico, to visit Don Felipe's brother Antonio. The conflict is among the two estranged brothers, and they must now make peace as death is near. Wood uses flashbacks to fill in the backstory, and we see Don Felipe's fight with his brother and his girlfriend Juanita's refusal to go with him to the United States. As in the other plays, cultural markers abound. The baseball game that Rudy joins in Oaxaca and the foodways that become staples of his meals are now rooted in the new Rudy. At the train station, he delivers a lesson on mole, the traditional red chili and chocolate sauce:

> RUDY [showing TOURIST a page from dictionary]: My tata
> insists that mole was invented in Oaxaca, and you

can't argue with him. But really mole was discovered in Puebla. You see, the verb "moler" means "to grind." So anyway, these nuns lived in a very poor convent, and they barely had enough to eat. And one morning the mother superior announces that a very important archbishop is coming to visit the convent; they have to prepare something impressive for him to eat. The cupboards are bare, so they run around and gather herbs and spices and put one of the younger nuns who just arrived from the country, la provincia, to grind— moler. So she's grinding all the herbs and spices on the molcajete—isn't that a great word? Molcajete. Can you say it?

TOURIST [*pronouncing it slowly*]: Mol-ca-je-te. Yes, it's a great word. Like cacahuate, no?

RUDY: Right. So the archbishop strolls by the kitchen, sees her, and asks her what she's doing. And the nun replies, "Aquí nomás, mole, mole." And that's how mole came to be named mole. Got that?

As Rudy becomes more comfortable with his Mexican ethnicity, speaking some Spanish and spending time with new family members, he does not want to return to the United States. They must do so, however, and Don Felipe becomes ill and collapses at the train station, dying suddenly. Nevertheless, the play does not end on a somber note, as Don Felipe dances with a woman dressed in black who can represent both death and his old girlfriend Juanita. Everyone joins in the merrymaking and dances to "Llévame oaxaqueña," until all freeze and Juanita and Don Felipe embrace. As the out-of-body experience ends, Rudy cradles Don Felipe, and a new song—"La danza de la pluma"— comes on, allowing the reader or spectator to infer how critical music is to the plot, conveying messages of nostalgia, love, and family unity to the audience.

Conclusion

As we can see, the people who inhabit Wood's plays are common folk— janitors, mothers, grandmothers, and teenagers—hardworking people who, in one way or another, have made their way in life and who embody the cultural characteristics of life in the barrio. These are barrio characters at their best. In terms of setting, the plays weave in and out of present time, and they often present, via flashbacks, a nostalgic past. The locations are varied, although, for the most part, the plays are set in the Southwest, particularly in Tucson, Arizona. The language and settings of the plays serve an integral role as a vehicle for the political commentary, satire, and complex messages the plays entail. Additionally, the linguistic play often serves as comic relief.

The path of a playwright is not always smooth. Wood has had to travel a bumpy road, but she has forged her work from all of these challenging experiences. Using her early memories of growing up in Tucson and her later experiences as a young mother and an activist, a militant for social justice, she has consistently remained true to her calling—her writing. Although her autobiographical novel remains unpublished, she will no doubt continue to hone and polish the manuscript until it is. No se raja— she does not give up. And that is perhaps one of the most important compliments anyone can pay a Chicana working in the arts, given the obstacles and hurdles that she must overcome to remain true to her art.

As we conclude this introduction, we wish to invite our readers to go beyond the texts and to dream about seeing productions of the plays, to enter into Wood's imagined world, and to enjoy the journey. The mark of a successful script for a play lies in its ability to move audiences to both laughter and tears. Some plays are written to be read—George Bernard Shaw's *Back to Methuselah* comes to mind—but that is not the case with Wood's plays. They are alive and demand to be on the stage. It is our hope that her work presented here continues to be read, studied, and produced. With this in mind, we enthusiastically offer this collection to you, our readers.

Norma E. Cantú and
Rita E. Urquijo-Ruiz
January 2015

Notes

1. We would like to begin with a note on our use of certain terms. The terms Chicana/Chicano or Chican@ refer specifically to people of Mexican descent, and Latina/Latino or Latin@ to people with cultural or ethnic ties to Latin American countries (which sometimes may include Mexico). We use "Chicano" when referencing certain usage—that is, when it clearly means males—such as here, and we use the more inclusive "Chican@" when referring to both "Chicana" and "Chicano." We do the same with the words "Latina," "Latino," and "Latin@." However, in the many instances in which we are referring specifically to women, we use "Chicana" and "Latina." We also do not italicize Spanish words so as not to privilege one language over another.

2. TENAZ was founded in 1971, and while sometimes the acronym appears to signal the plural, Teatros Nacionales de Aztlán, we are following Jorge Huerta's use of the acronym's origin in the singular—Teatro Nacional de Aztlán—in his article "Concerning Teatro Chicano," *Latin American Theatre Review* (Spring 1973): 13–20.

3. Cantú was impressed with the trilingual—Spanish, English, and Yaqui—performance in Tucson, where such pastorelas are performed to this day at the Borderlands Theater downtown. See http://www.borderlandstheater.org/productions/2013-2014/pastorela/ for the latest information on this continuing folk tradition.

4. Teatro de Carpa (or the Carpas) refers to early twentieth-century itinerant theater groups that resembled vaudeville performances, with music and dramatic sketches created primarily for working-class audiences.

5. See Norma E. Cantú, "The Offering and the Offerers: The Generic Illocation of a Laredo Pastorela in the Tradition of the Shepherds' Play" (PhD diss., University of Nebraska–Lincoln, 1982), and Richard R. Flores, *Los Pastores: History and Performance in the Mexican Shepherd's Play of South Texas* (Washington, DC: Smithsonian Institution Press, 1995).

6. An excerpt of *Una vez, en un barrio de sueños* . . . was published in *The Chicano/Latino Literary Prize: An Anthology of Prize-Winning Fiction, Poetry, and Drama*, edited by Stephanie Fetta (Arte Público Press, 2008).

7. Nicolás Kanellos finds evidence of theatrical productions in Spanish in the eighteenth century as well. See *A History of Hispanic Theatre in the*

United States: Origins to 1940 (Austin: University of Texas Press, 1990), for a fuller discussion of the early plays.

8. We refer readers to the work of María Teresa Marrero, who, in studying the 1998–99 season, finds these statistics: "82 percent of all plays produced were of male authorship. That leaves 12 percent of female authorship, regardless of ethnicity. A paltry, appallingly miniscule 1.8 percent were written by playwrights with Hispanic surnames. . . ." ("Out of the Fringe? Out of the Closet: Latina/o Theatre and Performance in the 1990s," *TDR: The Drama Review* 44, no. 3 [2000]: 149).

9. In *"Teatropoesía* by Chicanas in the Bay Area" (1989), Yvonne Yarbro-Bejarano asserts that the writings of Lucha Corpi, Lorna Dee Cervantes, Sandra Cisneros, Alma Luz Villanueva, Gloria Anzaldúa, Cherríe Moraga, María Moreno, and Ana Castillo, among others, were responsible for opening up Latina feminist spaces on- and offstage in the Bay Area.

10. Alicia Arrizón, *Latina Performance: Traversing the Stage*, Unnatural Acts: Theorizing the Performative (Bloomington: Indiana University Press, 1999), xvi.

11. Yolanda Broyles-González, "Performance Artist María Elena Gaitán: Mapping a Continent Without Borders (Epics of Gente Atravesada, Traviesa, y Entremetida)," *Frontiers: A Journal of Women Studies* 24, nos. 2–3 (2003): 92, 94.

12. Wood created the character of Doña Chona for the Arizona Public Media station, KUAT, series *Reflexiones*. The character was at times described as a female Cantinflas because she played with language in much the same way as did the famous Mexican comic. According to Wood, she improvised and created the segments without written scripts. Teresa Jones, a former Teatro Libertad member, directed the filming of *Reflexiones*, which aired locally from 1982 to 1996. Doña Chona cemented Wood's identity as a local performer, and many Tucsonenses still remember the character with love.

13. Gloria E. Anzaldúa, *Borderlands/La Frontera: The New Mestiza*, 4th ed. (San Francisco: Aunt Lute, 2012), 79; Chela Sandoval, "U.S. Third World Feminism: The Theory and Method of Oppositional Consciousness in the Postmodern World," *Genders* 10 (Spring 1991): 11.

14. See Kanellos, *A History of Hispanic Theatre.*

15. See Yolanda Broyles-González, *El Teatro Campesino: Theater in the Chicano Movement* (Austin: University of Texas Press, 1994); and Tomás Ybarra-Frausto, "I Can Still Hear the Applause. La Farándula Chicana: Carpas y Tandas de Variedad," in *Hispanic Theater in the United States* (Houston: Arte Público Press, 1984), 45–61.

16. See Kanellos, *A History of Hispanic Theatre*. For examples of other women of Mexican and Latin American ancestry who participated in earlier theater and performances, see Elizabeth C. Ramírez, *Chicanas/Latinas in American Theatre: A History of Performance* (Bloomington: Indiana University Press, 2000), especially the first two chapters that offer the sociohistorical context before 1950.

17. It was Lydia's father, Francisco Mendoza, who drove the family from show to show and who came up with the idea of advertising with signs proclaiming "Familia Mendoza. Variedades. Lydia Mendoza" or "Lydia Mendoza, la Guitarrista, y el Grupo de Variedades de Sketches Cómicos." See Yolanda Broyles-González, *Lydia Mendoza's Life in Music/La Historia de Lydia Mendoza: Norteño Tejano Legacies*, American Musicspheres (Oxford: Oxford University Press, 2001), especially chapter 1.

18. Alicia Arrizón, *Latina Performance: Traversing the Stage*, Unnatural Acts: Theorizing the Performative (Bloomington: Indiana University Press, 1999), provides an in-depth analysis of Niggli's play *Soldadera* (published in *Mexican Folk Plays*), focusing on the Adelita character; in her discussion of this play about the Mexican Revolution, Arrizón writes,

> Contradictions abound: Anglo women play Mexican *soldaderas*; they wear clean and colorful skirts and shawls; they are surrounded [*sic*] by basketry and cacti meant to evoke folk art and a warm, exotic country side. . . . Despite her childlike qualities, Adelita is revealed in the end as an aggressive, valiant hero. Beyond the folklore and subjective historical interpretation of *Soldadera*, Niggli's depiction of Adelita and the other female soldiers centers the courage and bravery of these women. (60)

19. Rita E. Urquijo-Ruiz, "Staging the Self, Staging Empowerment: An Overview of Latina Theater and Performance," in *Inside the Latin@ Experience: A Latin@ Studies Reader*, ed. Norma E. Cantú and María E. Fránquiz (New York: Palgrave MacMillan, 2010), 155. See also Elizabeth Coonrod

Martínez, *Josefina Niggli, Mexican American Writer: A Critical Biography* (Albuquerque: University of New Mexico Press, 2007), which, according to the publisher, recovers Niggli's works and situates her amongst the lineage of influential Latina writers.

20. Rita E. Urquijo-Ruiz, *Wild Tongues: Transnational Mexican Popular Culture*, Chicana Matters Series (Austin: University of Texas Press, 2012), 39.

21. Although Ybarra-Frausto published the first article on rasquachismo in 1990, Broyles-González presented in 1994 a pertinent definition working from his contribution:

> The *rasquachi* aesthetic is the inventiveness driven by necessity: not only economic necessity, but also by the need to resist, to speak out, and to address the burning issues of the day. *Rasquachismo* makes the most out of very limited performance resources and, thus, is not ensnared in the cumbersome machinery of theatrical productions, their aesthetics, and their politics. (*El Teatro Campesino*, 94)

22. Ybarra-Frausto, "I Can Still Hear the Applause," 50.

23. See Ramírez, *Chicanas/Latinas in American Theatre*, 141.

24. See Broyles-González, *El Teatro Campesino*, chapter 3.

25. Teatro Chicana's work is collected in Laura E. García, Sandra M. Gutiérrez, and Felicitas Núñez, eds., *Teatro Chicana: A Collective Memoir and Selected Plays*, Chicana Matters Series (Austin: University of Texas Press, 2008).

26. See Yvonne Yarbro-Bejarano, "Chicanas' Experience in Collective Theater," *Women and Performance* 2, no. 2 (1985):45–48; and Broyles-González, *El Teatro Campesino*, for a more detailed discussion on women's participation in teatro during the 1960s and 1970s, especially in El Teatro Campesino. See also Yarbro-Bejarano, "*Teatropoesía* by Chicanas in the Bay Area," 80.

27. Yvonne Yarbro-Bejarano, "The Female Subject in Chicano Theatre: Sexuality, 'Race,' and Class," in *Performing Feminisms: Feminist Critical Theory and Theatre*, ed. Sue-Ellen Case (Baltimore: Johns Hopkins University Press, 1990), 138.

28. Yarbro-Bejarano, "*Teatropoesía* by Chicanas in the Bay Area," 78.

29. Ibid., 79.

30. Ibid., 82.

31. Estela Portillo Trambley's anthology *Sor Juana and Other Plays* (Ypsilanti, MI: Bilingual Press/Editorial Bilingüe, 1983) contains a queer play titled *Day of the Swallows* (written in 1971), which is considered the first of its kind for incorporating lesbian identity issues in the Chican@ cultural context. Despite its homophobic treatment of the lesbian theme, *Day of the Swallows* was a precursor to Moraga's work, who cites the play's influence in her own writing.

32. Elizabeth Ramírez offers an in-depth discussion of these playwrights in her book, *Chicanas/Latinas in American Theatre*, chapter 5.

33. Alicia Arrizón, *Latina Performance*, 73–74.

34. Most of the characters who speak Spanish in these plays have an informal acquisition of the language; therefore, the author has written certain words and phrases in colloquial and phonetic forms of this language (what some mistakenly refer to as archaic). We, the editors, respect the author's decision to represent her characters' language as she desires. Thus, what might seem like spelling errors to a formally trained bilingual reader are indeed instances where colloquialisms, linguistic games, or phonetic representations exist.

Bibliography

Anzaldúa, Gloria E. *Borderlands/La Frontera: The New Mestiza.* 4th ed. San Francisco: Aunt Lute, 2012.

Arrizón, Alicia. *Latina Performance: Traversing the Stage.* Unnatural Acts: Theorizing the Performative. Bloomington: Indiana University Press, 1999.

Broyles-González, Yolanda. "Performance Artist María Elena Gaitán: Mapping a Continent Without Borders (Epics of Gente Atravesada, Traviesa, y Entremetida)." *Frontiers: A Journal of Women Studies* 24, nos. 2–3 (2003): 87–103.

———. *Lydia Mendoza's Life in Music/La Historia de Lydia Mendoza: Norteño Tejano Legacies.* American Musicspheres. Oxford: Oxford University Press, 2001.

———. *El Teatro Campesino: Theater in the Chicano Movement*. Austin: University of Texas Press, 1994.

Cantú, Norma E. "The Offering and the Offerers: A Generic Illocation of a Laredo Pastorela in the Tradition of a Shepherds' Play." PhD diss, University of Nebraska–Lincoln, 1982.

Cervantes, Lorna Dee. *Emplumada*. Pitt Poetry Series. Pittsburg, PA: University of Pittsburgh Press, 1981.

Chávez, Denise. "Novena Narrativas y Ofrendas Nuevomexicanas." In *Chicana Creativity and Criticism: New Frontiers in American Literature*, 2nd ed., edited by María Herrera-Sobek and Helena María Viramontes, 149–63. Albuquerque: University of New Mexico Press, 1996.

Escalona, Beatriz. "La Chata Noloesca." Four scrapbooks. The San Antonio Conservation Society Archive, San Antonio, TX.

Flores, Richard R. *Los Pastores: History and Performance in the Mexican Shepherd's Play of South Texas*. Washington, DC: Smithsonian Institution Press, 1995.

García, Laura E., Sandra M. Gutiérrez, and Felicitas Núñez, eds. *Teatro Chicana: A Collective Memoir and Selected Plays*. Chicana Matters Series. Austin: University of Texas Press, 2008.

Grise, Virginia. *blu*. Yale Drama Series. New Haven, CT: Yale University Press, 2011.

———, and Mayorga, Irma. *The Panza Monologues*. Austin: University of Texas Press, 2014.

Hudes, Quiara Alegría. *Water by the Spoonful*. New York: Theatre Communications Group, 2012.

Huerta, Jorge. "Concerning Chicano Theater." *Latin American Theater Review* (Spring 1973): 13–20.

———. "Chicano Teatro: A Background." *Aztlán* 2, no. 2 (1972): 63–78.

———. *Chicano Theater: Themes and Forms*. Ypsilanti, MI: Bilingual Press, 1982.

Kanellos, Nicolás. *A History of Hispanic Theatre in the United States: Origins to 1940*. Austin: University of Texas Press, 1990.

———. *Mexican American Theater: Legacy and Reality*. Pittsburgh, PA: Latin American Literary Review Press, 1987.

———. "Two Centuries of Hispanic Theater in the Southwest." In *Mexican Theatre: Then and Now*, edited by Nicolás Kanellos, 17–36. Houston: Arte Público, 1983.

López, Josefina. *Real Women Have Curves*. Woodstock, IL: The Dramatic Publishing Company, 1996.

Manuel, Carlos, ed. *Vaqueeros, Calacas, and Hollywood: Contemporary Chicano Plays*. Tempe, AZ: Bilingual Press/Editorial Bilingüe, 2013.

Marrero, María Teresa. "Out of the Fringe? Out of the Closet: Latina/o Theatre and Performance in the 1990s." *TDR: The Drama Review* 44, no. 3 (2000): 131–53.

Martínez, Elizabeth Coonrod. *Josefina Niggli, Mexican American Writer: A Critical Biography*. Albuquerque: University of New Mexico Press, 2007.

Moraga, Cherríe. *Giving Up the Ghost: Teatro in Two Acts*. Los Angeles: West End Press, 1986.

———, and Gloria Anzaldúa, eds. *This Bridge Called My Back: Writings by Radical Women of Color*. Watertown, MA: Persephone Press, 1981.

Ramírez, Elizabeth C. *Chicanas/Latinas in American Theatre: A History of Performance*. Bloomington: Indiana University Press, 2000.

Sanchez-Scott, Milcha. *Roosters*. New York: Dramatists Play Service, 1988.

Sandoval, Chela. "U.S. Third World Feminism: The Theory and Method of Oppositional Consciousness in the Postmodern World." *Genders* 10 (Spring 1991): 1–24.

Sandoval-Sánchez, Alberto, and Nancy Saporta Sternbach, eds. *Puro Teatro: A Latina Anthology*. Tucson: University of Arizona Press, 2000.

Shaw, George Bernard. *Back to Methuselah*. In *Bernard Shaw: Complete Plays with Prefaces*. New York: Dodd, Mead and Company, 1963.

Steinbeck, John. *The Grapes of Wrath*. New York: The Viking Press, 1939.

Trambley, Estela Portillo. *Sor Juana and Other Plays*. Ypsilanti, MI: Bilingual Press/Editorial Bilingüe, 1983.

Urquijo-Ruiz, Rita E. *Wild Tongues: Transnational Mexican Popular Culture*. Chicana Matters Series. Austin: University of Texas Press, 2012.

———. "Staging the Self, Staging Empowerment: An Overview of Latina Theater and Performance." In *Inside the Latin@ Experience: A Latin@ Studies Reader*, edited by Norma E. Cantú and María E. Fránquiz, 151–72. New York: Palgrave MacMillan, 2010.

Villarreal, Edit. *My Visits with MGM*. In *Shattering the Myth: Plays by Hispanic Women*, edited by Linda Feyder, 143–200. Houston: Arte Público Press, 1992.

Wood, Silviana. *Una vez, en un barrio de sueños* . . . In *The Chicano/Latino Literary Prize: An Anthology of Prize-Winning Fiction, Poetry, and Drama*, edited by Stephanie Fetta, 165–73. Houston: Arte Público Press, 2008.

Yarbro-Bejarano, Yvonne. *The Wounded Heart: Writing on Cherríe Moraga*. Chicana Matters Series. Austin: University of Texas Press, 2001.

———. "The Female Subject in Chicano Theatre: Sexuality, 'Race,' and Class." In *Performing Feminisms: Feminist Critical Theory and Theatre*, edited by Sue-Ellen Case, 131–49. Baltimore: Johns Hopkins University Press, 1990.

———. "*Teatropoesía* by Chicanas in the Bay Area: *Tongues of Fire.*" *Mexican American Theatre: Then and Now*, edited by Nicolás Kanellos, 74–90. Houston: Arte Público Press, 1989.

———. "Chicanas' Experience in Collective Theater." *Women and Performance* 2, no. 2 (1985): 45–48.

Ybarra-Frausto, Tomás. "Rasquachismo: A Chicano Sensibility." In *Chicano Art:, Resistance and Affirmation*, edited by Richard Griswold del Castillo, Teresa McKenna, and Yvonne Yarbro-Bejarano, 155–62. Los Angeles: Wight Art Gallery, University of California, Los Angeles, 1991.

———. "I Can Still Hear the Applause. La Farándula Chicana: Carpas y Tandas de Variedad." In *Hispanic Theatre in the United States*, edited by Nicolás Kanellos, 45–61. Houston: Arte Público Press, 1984.

ONE

Una vez, en un barrio de sueños ...

(Once Upon a Time, in a Barrio of Dreams ...)

A Trilogy of One-Act Plays

The Actos

Introduction. Los sueños que compartimos (The Dreams That We Share)
I. El Militante y la Señora Martínez (The Militant and Mrs. Martínez)
II. ¿Y qué tiene que ver un turkey con Veracruz anyway? (So What Does a Turkey Have to Do with Veracruz Anyway?)
III. El Dragonslayer

Synopsis

Una vez, en un barrio de sueños . . . consists of an introduction ("Los sueños que compartimos [The Dreams That We Share]") and three one-act plays, or actos, and it may be produced as a full-length play or as separate one-acts. The actos share the bittersweet themes of dreams that are never fulfilled or realized, dreams that are put on a "layaway plan," and dreams that come true.

The first acto following the introduction is "El Militante y la Señora Martínez (The Militant and Mrs. Martínez)," which is about the friendship that forms between a nonviolent poet nicknamed "el Militante" by the barrio residents, and Mrs. Martínez, an old widowed woman who has never opened the door to her house to anyone before.

The second acto, "¿Y qué tiene que ver un turkey con Veracruz anyway? (So What Does a Turkey Have to Do with Veracruz Anyway?)," is about a janitor who, after seeing the classic Mexican film *Macario*, wants to fulfill his dream to visit Veracruz. His practical, unromantic wife would rather buy a washing machine for their happy-hour-loving daughter.

The final acto, "El Dragonslayer" is about a dream shared by the barrio's neglected kid and the neighborhood grouch. It is a Chicano "Jack and the Beanstalk" tale. The grouch teaches the boy to love to read, and together they plant a puny tomato plant that is threatened by rain, hail, hot sun, dogs, delinquent glue-sniffers, and finally . . . a giant green tomato hornworm!

Cast

Please note that many of the characters in each of the actos are simply identified as BARRIO RESIDENTS, STUDENTS, or ALL, and a core group of eight to ten actors can double roles as needed; they will serve as a motley barrio Greek chorus, except when portraying the following principal characters: EL MILITANTE, SEÑORA MARTÍNEZ, GILBERTO, RUTHIE, DEBBIE, FEDERICO, and DON ALBINO.

LOS SUEÑOS QUE COMPARTIMOS

BARRIO RESIDENTS, *a collection of up to ten residents. They are identified in the script as Fearful, Hopeful, Hungry, Creative, Pilot, Poetic, Practical, Questioning, El Terco, and Philosopher but may be combined based on the number of actors available.*

EL MILITANTE Y LA SEÑORA MARTÍNEZ

EL MILITANTE, *a nonviolent poet*

SEÑORA MARTÍNEZ, *an old widowed woman*

BARRIO RESIDENTS *and* GOSSIPS, *a core group of eight to ten actors who will share lines and stage space. They are numbered in the script but lines may be redistributed as needed.*

FRIENDS, *six friends of el Militante. They can be played by the Residents or Gossips or by more or fewer actors, as needed.*

¿Y QUÉ TIENE QUE VER UN TURKEY CON VERACRUZ ANYWAY?

GILBERTO RAMÍREZ, *the night janitor at a community college. He is in his early fifties and wears a gray uniform.*

MISS VÁSQUEZ, *a young, very pretty teacher*

STUDENTS, *various ages, dressed in the latest fashion. They will play different roles as indicated.*

MACARIO'S WIFE, *played by one of the Students during the movie*

MACARIO, *played by one of the Students during the movie*

RUTHIE RAMÍREZ, *Gilberto's wife, obsessed with youth and beauty*

DEBBIE RAMÍREZ, *Gilberto and Ruthie's daughter, the single mother of two kids*

KIDS, *Debbie's young children, around six or seven years old*

TOUR GUIDE, *any age, looks and speaks in a very officious manner*

VERACRUZANOS: GRINGO CUSTOMER, FLOWER VENDOR, LOVER, WAITER, *and* TOURIST, *each can be played by one of the Students*

OLD MAN, *gives Gilberto advice in Nogales, Mexico*

EL DRAGONSLAYER

FEDERICO NARICES DE PERICO, *the barrio's neglected kid*

COMADRES CHISMOLERAS, *gossipers*

    COMADRE ANITA SIN CARNITA

    COMADRE ELENA SIN AVENA

    COMADRE SOFÍA SIN COSTILLA

DON ALBINO CARA DE PEPINO, *the neighborhood grouch*
SCHOOL KIDS, *male and female*
EDDIE SPAGHETTI, *a bully*
TONY BALONEY, *a bully*
RAMÓN JAMÓN, *a bully*
LA JEFITA, *Federico's mother*
THREE YOUNG MEN
THREE YOUNG WOMEN
PRISON GUARD
TEACHER, *male or female*
SCHOOL KIDS
DOÑA REBECCA PATAS SECAS, *Don Albino's wife; only her hands are seen*
MANUEL CARA DE PASTEL, *helpful neighbor*
DOÑA MARÍA OJOS DE SANDÍA, *helpful neighbor*
DOÑA ANDREA PANZA DE JALEA, *helpful neighbor*
DOÑA FAUSTINA PATAS DE GALLINA, *helpful neighbor*
TOMATO HORNWORM, *green, may be male or female*

Technical Notes

The actors and the director need to develop voices, gestures, walks, and other personality traits that will distinguish and individualize the roles. The COMADRES CHISMOLERAS, when chanting in unison, should utilize various melodic rhythms—such as operatic, Gregorian chant, choral, rap, etc.—to suit the particular mood. For example, when they are chanting "Benditos sean los dulces nombres del cielo," they should sound like a Gregorian chorus.

The director or collective has much freedom in selecting stage movement, business, exits and entrances, character development, music, props, voice changes, etc., but should keep in mind the surrealistic quality that the play demands.

Also, please note that the playwright has attempted to re-create the voices of the Chicano working class with authenticity and respect; therefore, the syntax and pronunciations should remain without change. The dialogue is a blending of both Spanish and English, with Caló, code-switching, and Spanglish. The actos "El Militante y la Señora Martínez" and "¿Y qué tiene que ver un turkey con Veracruz anyway?" contain adult language; however, "El Dragonslayer" is perfectly suitable for children.

Please keep in mind that this is a comedia, and the more absurd or silly, the better. And above all, have fun.

LIGHTS

Fairly simple with minor cues for the beginning and end of the introduction and the three actos, the dances, and the final scene. SPOTS will be needed for the TOMATO HORNWORM dance and death scenes.

SOUND

Consists mainly of music cues for dancing, transitions, and special effects.

SET

The set consists of flats painted in neutral shades of beige, tan, and light blue, resembling a southwestern sunset. There are four doors on door-frames across the stage. The top half of each door would be screened, but the screens have been ripped out, leaving the edges of the screen hanging, so the BARRIO RESIDENTS, STUDENTS, and COMADRES CHISMOLERAS, etc., can all casually stick their heads out when giving lines.

At the top of each doorframe is a rolled-up canvas that has drawings of Aztec or Mayan pyramids, gods, etc., but please note that these drawings will not be revealed until near the end of the third acto.

Near the doorframes are some scraggly geranium plants and yerba buena in brightly colored giant coffee cans (Mexican and American brands) and some dried-up tumbleweeds. There are old tires, three large boulders, small piles of dirt, and one larger pile of dirt, as well as some garbage strewn around. There is no furniture except for one rocking chair that is behind a short porch rail, and six or eight wooden boxes that are used as chairs, tables, desks, "cars," etc.

Please note that the set does not change throughout the play.

COSTUMES

Since the style of the plays is a combination of various elements of commedia dell'arte, Carpas, fantasy, magical realism, and burlesque, the costumes, makeup, accessories, and props will be comic and exaggerated unless indicated otherwise.

The TOMATO HORNWORM's costume will be the most demanding. It should be a green bodysuit with a padded back and tail. The tail may be up to three feet long with horns at the end, and it should be wired to make it stand up.

The women will wear loud floral housedresses, funky wigs or giant hair-rollers, platform high heels, shower thongs, or fuzzy slippers. The men will wear mismatched plaids or striped shirts and pants, loud ties, patent leather shoes, wigs, and moustaches and beards. Costume changes are minimal; the actors simply add accessories such as bandanas, scarves, robes, etc., as needed for each of their characters. Only the principal characters (listed above) will dress just a bit more realistically than the others. All the costumes and accessories may be readily found at a well-stocked second-hand store or mom's cuartito de cochinero.

PROPS

Very large and unrealistic, such as the flyswatter, coffee cans holding plants, etc. The tomato plant must slowly grow from the pile of dirt. This may be done either with a rope pulley to lift the plant from above or by pushing the plant up from the floor. The tomatoes are the size of big grapefruits. They are very light in weight, covered with red satin material, and hung with hooks similar to Christmas tree ornaments.

INTRODUCTION

Los sueños que compartimos (The Dreams That We Share)

PLACE: *A barrio in a small town somewhere in the Southwest.*

TIME: *Any.*

MUSIC: *A very lively polka is playing on the radio.*

SOUND EFFECTS: *Lots of morning noise indicating a barrio waking up—dogs barking, trash cans being emptied by city trucks, roosters crowing, toilets flushing, etc.*

LIGHTS: UP.

[*The* **BARRIO RESIDENTS ENTER** *and* **EXIT** *as they clean and sweep the yard, water the plants, and discuss their dreams.*]

FEARFUL BARRIO RESIDENT: Last night, I had this dream again—el mismo sueño de siempre. It's always the same one. I'm running away from something, but I don't know what. I have this feeling in my chest, heavy, and I can't breathe, and I try to say something, scream, but nothing comes out. It's like I'm drowning. It hurts. Right here. [*Touching his heart*] Aquí siento un dolor bien pesado.

HOPEFUL BARRIO RESIDENT: Not me. Yo siempre me sueño en un stage, como que me van a dar un prize. Un Pulitzer, o un Nobel. Or, you know, like an Oscar in Hollywood. I'm dressed up a todo dar, and everybody's waiting to see if I've won, and finally they call my name and then everybody's clapping for me. ¡Qué curada, me la rayo!

HUNGRY BARRIO RESIDENT: I think I always go to bed hungry 'cause I'm always dreaming that I'm casi starving. Y luego, in my dreams, I'm eating and eating and eating. Burritos, tacos, steak . . . Mi favorite es cuando estoy como en un summer camp. You know the ones, where some organization sends poor kids for two weeks? Con muncha, muncha comida. And milk. There's this machine, and you pull a lever y sale la lechi—free, all the milk you could drink. Free.

CREATIVE BARRIO RESIDENT: I have the best dreams—better than anyone else's. I dream in Technicolor, and it's like a movie. Or a soap opera on TV. I go to bed thinking: what's gonna happen next? You know, like what's the next chapter? Sometimes, I even dream cartoons. Me la rayo, cartoons like my favorites, *Looney Toons* or *Tom and Jerry*.

PILOT BARRIO RESIDENT: Lots of times I dream I'm flying, you know? Sometimes I fly just like Superman, arms out straight, but other times I run and get momentum and then I push myself up off the ground and fly with swimming strokes, except that the water becomes air. There's lots of different ways to fly in your dreams. I like to fly right here, over our houses, and sometimes you're all in my dreams, too, and you look up and see me flying, so I wave to you. Sometimes you wave back, sometimes you don't. They say it's delusions of grandeur, but I don't care. In all my dreams, I like to fly.

POETIC BARRIO RESIDENT: A mí los sueños me hacen sentirme como un poeta, you know? Yes, a poet, because our dreams really are like poems. Son fragmentos de algo evasivo como el viento. Fragments from the past, blurred images. Like undeveloped negatives—¿ustedes me entienden, verdad?

PRACTICAL BARRIO RESIDENT: No, pero you should always write down your dreams. The minute you wake up, develop those negatives. There's even a special little pen you can buy with a battery and a flashlight so you can see what you write in the dark. That way you don't forget or miss anything.

QUESTIONING BARRIO RESIDENT: They say that dreams are the collective unconscious, which is something I'll never understand. And that we can't dream what we haven't seen or experienced. But I swear I've had weird dreams with people I've never seen. Maybe it's como dicen los indios ... that the dreams son los espíritus de los muertos.

EL TERCO BARRIO RESIDENT: I never dream. Never. I don't care what anybody says. Yo nunca sueño. Jamás sueño. Never.

PHILOSOPHER BARRIO RESIDENT: Pues yo digo, y no me quiero maderear, you know, con cosas psychological or philosophical, pero yo digo que nuestros sueños forman nuestras vidas. It's our dreams that shape our lives. And that's all I have to say on this matter, so take it to the bank, Frank.

LIGHTS: DOWN *and* UP *quickly.*

END OF INTRODUCTION

ACTO I

El Militante y la Señora Martínez (The Militant and Mrs. Martínez)

TIME: *1970, the year of the Chicano Moratorium in L.A.*

PLACE: *Same as in introduction.*

LIGHTS: *Flashes of* LIGHTNING.

SOUND: *Sounds of an approaching chubasco, a monsoon storm; distant* THUN-DER *rumbles.*

[EL MILITANTE, *a man in his early twenties wearing fatigues and a red ban-danna headband, sits and writes poetry. A* HELPFUL BARRIO RESIDENT *sits next to him, giving his unsolicited input. Two other* BARRIO RESIDENTS *are each holding the ends of a clothesline that contains all-black dresses, slips, and thick nylons, held on by clothespins.* EL MILITANTE's *poem and the* BARRIO RESIDENTS' *gossip blend together.*]

EL MILITANTE [*reading his poem*]: "Qué hermoso se pone el cielo cuando va llover—"

HELPFUL BARRIO RESIDENT: Yeah, sure, hermoso, to you maybe. But to me, right before the chubasco, the sky isn't so hermoso. It's more like the color of dirty water. The plain blue sky turning into . . . very drabby colors, like when the dirtiest clothes are thrown into the last load in the washing machine . . . brown, gray, black.

EL MILITANTE: "—colores pardos . . . café, plomo, negro."

BARRIO RESIDENT 1 [*holding clothesline*]: Negra, toda la ropa de la Señora Martínez es del color negro. Why does she always dress in black? Ya nadie se viste de luto. It's too old-fashioned—just go to any funeral nowadays, and you'll see people wearing every color. Even red!

BARRIO RESIDENT 2 [*holding other end of clothesline*]: Bueno, es cierto que está bien guardar el luto, but not for such a long time. How long has it been since Don Fernando died?

EL MILITANTE [*writing*]: "Colores brillantes . . . amarillo, anaranjado, rojo . . ."

HELPFUL BARRIO RESIDENT: Yes, it's true that there's brilliant colors. You just have to look for them . . . there's yellow, orange, red.

BARRIO RESIDENT 3 [*entering*]: Ándale pues, poeta sin escopeta, give us a metaphor, a simile!

EL MILITANTE: Let's see. Before the storm, brilliant colors exploding across the sky . . . as if an artist, "como si un pintor . . . ¿borracho?"

BARRIO RESIDENT 3: Like a drunken artist, yeah!

BARRIO RESIDENT I [*answering question*]: I can't even remember when Don Fernando died. She's been widowed for years. But she could wear un vestidito pinto now, or at least a gray dress, ¿no crees? Why does she insist on wearing only black?

EL MILITANTE [*reading*]: "Como si un pintor borracho, tambaleando con su caballete . . ."

HELPFUL BARRIO RESIDENT: Yeah, I like that. I can see it: a drunken artist, like un Van Gogh, maybe? Staggering around the clouds without his ear but with his easel . . . [*To* EL MILITANTE] Síguele, ¿qué más?

EL MILITANTE: "Brincara por las nubes . . ."

HELPFUL BARRIO RESIDENT: Would leap among the clouds—

EL MILITANTE: No, not leap. Jump. It has to be "Brincara por las nubes."

HELPFUL BARRIO RESIDENT: Okay. Jump. Leap. Same difference.

EL MILITANTE: "Chapoteando sus pinturas . . ."

BARRIO RESIDENT 3: Splashing his paints, that's what chapoteando means. Hey! Did you know that the Spanish alphabet has a whole section just for the *ch*'s? All separate from the *c*'s? My favorite words are there.

EL MILITANTE: "Hasta que las primeras gotas de agua caen y el olor de adobe mojado camina por las calles de mi barrio."

HELPFUL BARRIO RESIDENT: "Until the first drops of rain fall on the ground, and the smell of wet adobe wanders through the streets of my barrio." Yeah, yeah. I can see what you're saying. I can see the smell moving, you know? Just like those in a cartoon that move like a snake. Olores serpentinos. Go ahead, write that down.

[SOUND: *Very loud* THUNDER.]

EL MILITANTE: Thanks, I like that. [*Writing*] "Y el olor de adobe mojado camina por las calles de mi barrio como una serpiente en un cartoon" . . . Oops! Don't know what that is in Spanish. I'll work on it more later.

[**EL MILITANTE** *gathers his papers and books and* **EXITS.**]

BARRIO RESIDENT 1: Well, to continue with la Señora Martínez todavía vistiéndose de luto, I say that going around dressed in black takes away your . . . ¿cómo se dice "ánimo" in English?

BARRIO RESIDENT 2: ¿Ánimo? There's no such word in English. Animation, maybe? Animosity?

BARRIO RESIDENT 1: Spirit! That's the word for "ánimo." Wearing black takes away your spirit. Honest. Anyway, it's too damn hot to wear black. That's why black cars don't sell, you know that? It's 'cause the color black absorbs more heat.

BARRIO RESIDENT 2: Never mind the black dress. The worse is that she's always locked up inside her house. She never goes outside, except to water her plants or hang clothes. Y con trabajos nos da las "buenas tardes."

[*Very loud* **THUNDER** *sounds and* **LIGHTNING** *flashes.*]

[**SRA. MARTÍNEZ**, *an elderly woman in her late sixties,* **ENTERS** *quickly and removes her clothes from the clothesline. She is dressed in black.*]

BARRIO RESIDENTS [*in unison, pointedly*]: Buenas tardes, Señora Martínez.

SRA. MARTÍNEZ [*shyly, keeping head down*]: Buenas tardes.

[*She sits and folds her clothes as* **BARRIO RESIDENTS** *talk about her as though she wasn't there. They prepare for the upcoming storm, tying things down, moving things inside, etc.*]

HELPFUL BARRIO RESIDENT: I wonder why she won't talk to anybody?

BARRIO RESIDENT 1: ¿Quién sabe? But that's not all. Did you know that she locks herself in with lock and key and won't open the door to anyone?

BARRIO RESIDENT 2: Sí, es cierto. The other day, the mailman came y le tocó y tocó la puerta, and she never opened the door for him.

BARRIO RESIDENT 1: I bet you he had a registered letter for her from her son in California.

HELPFUL BARRIO RESIDENT: You mean el hijo who never comes to visit her?

BARRIO RESIDENT 1: Well, maybe he doesn't, pero dicen que siempre le manda money orders pa' su birthday y Mother's Day. Y Christmas.

BARRIO RESIDENT 2: Pues, money order or not, she still didn't open the door.

BARRIO RESIDENT 3: Well, listen to me, el otro día que se me ploguió el toilet, fui pa' su casa to ask her if she would lend me her water hose so I could put it through la pipa on top of the roof—la tripa mía no alcanzaba—and she wouldn't open the door to me either. And she knew very well that there I was, working my ass off in the heat of the sun, climbing the roof like a monkey, and she still didn't open the door.

HELPFUL BARRIO RESIDENT: Maybe she was asleep.

BARRIO RESIDENT 3: No estaba durmiendo. When I got tired of knocking, I started to go ask Don José to lend me his hose, but then I gave a quick turn towards her window, like this, and I saw her wachándome from behind the curtain. And she saw me and moved back, pronto, asina.

BARRIO RESIDENT 2: Well, why won't she open the door?

BARRIO RESIDENT 3: ¿Quién sabe? [*Making a "crazy" gesture of circles beside his head*] I guess she must be loca.

[SOUND: *Very loud* THUNDER.]

BARRIO RESIDENT 1: ¡Ya viene la agua! Chihuahua, voy a tener que encaramarme en el techo como chango to cover the holes pa' que no se liqueye.

[*Note: "liqueye" is a Spanglish word formed from "leak."*]

[ALL *except* SRA. MARTÍNEZ EXIT, *scurrying, mucha bulla, bulla, yelling to offstage kids, etc.*]

SRA. MARTÍNEZ [*to audience*]: ¿Abrir la puerta? ¿Pero por qué he de abrirle la puerta a nadie? Yo estoy muy conforme, solita, con las puertas cerradas. Yo no molesto a nadie y nadie me molesta a mí. Así debe ser. Es mejor así—con las puertas cerradas. Las puertas abiertas siempre dejan entrar las malas noticias. No, es mejor tener las puertas bien cerradas, siempre bien cerradas.

[EL MILITANTE ENTERS, *carrying a clipboard.*]

EL MILITANTE [*to audience*]: Doors! I hate doors. If it was up to me, there wouldn't be any doors. Doors, fences, or walls. Como dijo Robert Frost: "Something there is that doesn't love a wall." I agree. And wouldn't you know it? That's all I do. Knock on doors all day long. Pleading, asking, begging: Please sign this petition. Please march with us on Sunday. Please donate food for the copper strikers. Don't buy scab lettuce.

[*Beat.*]

Anyway, como pregunta Frost: "What am I walling in or walling out?"

[EL MILITANTE *sits on a box next to* SRA. MARTÍNEZ, *back to back.*]

SRA. MARTÍNEZ: ¿Y entonces por qué, le abrí la puerta al greñudo? En primer lugar, no le iva abrir la puerta porque creí que solo era la lluvia, los truenos.

[EL MILITANTE *stands up.*]

EL MILITANTE [*to audience*]: See, I'm wet. Water's dripping down the back of my neck, you know? And I could feel it sloshing around in my boots each time I took a step. And I knew that the old lady, Mrs. Martínez, wouldn't open the door. She never had before. But my car died on me—wires got wet probably—so [*knocking on door*] I knocked and knocked.

SRA. MARTÍNEZ [*standing up and going to door*]: Fui a la ventana, detuve la cortina así [*pantomiming peeking from her curtain*] y vi que era un muchacho greñudo, tocando mi puerta bien fuerte. Pobrecito, estava todo mojado como un ratón 'hogado.

EL MILITANTE [*catching her in the act*]: Hey! The curtain moved.

[*Both face each other. He waves to her, smiling. She is very startled and guilty.*]

SRA. MARTÍNEZ: ¡Y me vio! Tenía una sonrisa. Y luego se movía muy extraño. Yo no sabía que era lo que el muchacho estaba haciendo. Ah, sí. Era pantomima.

[EL MILITANTE *pantomimes that he is drowning, sinking, holding nose, going down for the third time, etc.*]

SRA. MARTÍNEZ [*figuring out pantomime*]: ¡Que . . . se estaba . . . ahogando! [*Laughing*] Pues, pobrecito, le abrí la puerta y lo dejé entrar a mi casa.

EL MILITANTE [*surprised*]: Hey! She let me in.

[SRA. MARTÍNEZ *gives him a black towel from her pile of folded laundry.*]

EL MILITANTE: She gave me a towel to dry my hair. And she gave me a cup of coffee while I waited for Pelón to give me a ride.

[*Both sit.*]

We talked. [*Pointing, as if to pictures*] Are those your grandkids?

SRA. MARTÍNEZ: Sí, viven en California.

EL MILITANTE: California? Have you ever been there?

SRA. MARTÍNEZ: No, ¿y tú?

EL MILITANTE: No, but I plan to go one of these days.

SRA. MARTÍNEZ: Mis hijos quieren que me suba en un avión y vaya a verlos, pero le tengo mucho miedo a los aviones.

EL MILITANTE: Me, too. I'm terrified of flying—and for no reason. I'd rather go in my old car.

SRA. MARTÍNEZ: ¿Pero qué no dices que está quebrado?

EL MILITANTE: Oh, sí, it's always desconchiflado for something or other, but right now I think the wires got wet. It'll be running okay by tomorrow. It has some bad habits, but it never fails me.

[SOUND: *Car honks offstage.*]

EL MILITANTE: There's Pelón now. [*Standing*] Señora Martínez, muchas gracias por el café.

SRA. MARTÍNEZ: De nada. Buenas noches y mucho cuidado.

EL MILITANTE: Buenas noches. [*To himself, softly*] She's nice but she sure likes to talk.

[*He* EXITS.]

SRA. MARTÍNEZ: Qué simpático el muchacho. ¡Ay, pero cómo le gusta hablar!

[*She* EXITS, *and* BARRIO RESIDENT 4 ENTERS.]

BARRIO RESIDENT 4: And that's exactly how the friendship between el Militante y la Señora Martínez started.

[*Other* BARRIO RESIDENTS ENTER. *They are numbered here as* BARRIO RESIDENTS 5, 6, *and* 7, *but they can be played by any of the residents from the previous scene (*HELPFUL BARRIO RESIDENT *and* BARRIO RESIDENTS 1, 2, *and* 3) *or by more or fewer actors as needed.*]

BARRIO RESIDENT 5: A que no se imagina, comadre, pero el Militante is always at la Señora Martínez's house. No sale de ahí.

BARRIO RESIDENT 6: ¡Ajá! I know. And have you seen them? He comes over and picks her up, and off they go in his broken-down car. Where could they be going?

BARRIO RESIDENT 5: Pues solo Dios lo sabrá. Maybe he's got her marching with him, you know? At all those protest marchas that he's always organizing? Maybe she's even carrying one of his signs? [*Pantomiming marching*] ¡Huelga! ¡Huelga! ¡Sálganse de los files! ¡Huelga! ¡Huelga!

[ALL BARRIO RESIDENTS *laugh.*]

BARRIO RESIDENT 7: Pues no me lo van a creer, but the other day, I saw them leaving the library with a stack of books this high. You know how el Militante's always reading? Well, if you ask me, I think he's got her reading now.

[*As the* BARRIO RESIDENTS *give their following lines,* EL MILITANTE *and* SRA. MARTÍNEZ *pantomime actions.*]

BARRIO RESIDENT 4: Pues sí. Y el otro día, he came over wanting me to sign some petition for I don't know what, y se la firmé—what else could I do? There I was, digging the ditch to the toilet, so I couldn't hide from him. And then, he sat down—right on the ground—and read his poetry to me! I just kept on digging . . . What else could I do?

BARRIO RESIDENT 5: And the other day, when I went to make a delivery at the university, I saw the two of them there, ¿tú sabes? When that famous poet came? I don't remember his name, but he's got a long beard, and he's always getting his ass thrown in jail. Anyway, there they were, el Militante y la Señora Martínez. And I saw with my own eyes el Militante take off his jacket and put it on the ground so that la Señora Martínez could sit on it because the grass was wet.

BARRIO RESIDENT 6: That's nothing. The other day que fui a la corte to pay los parking tickets de la Gorda—remember that fountain in front of the courthouse that used to have fish? Well, they all died, but anyway, it's still there so everybody throws pennies and makes a wish, and I saw them eating a hot dog they bought from that blind guy that sells them there. And then el Militante made a wish and threw a penny, and then he wanted la Señora Martínez to make a wish, too, but she wouldn't, pero you know how persuasive el Militante can be, so she finally threw a penny into the fountain, made a wish, and then he hugged her.

BARRIO RESIDENT 5: Ay, qué cute.

BARRIO RESIDENT 7: Well, I don't care what anybody says, I think he's always up to no good. Stirring up trouble.

BARRIO RESIDENT 6: Me too. Ever since he got out of school—

BARRIO RESIDENT 7: Got out? Lo corrieron, you mean. For making trouble. Wasn't that the time he got all the students to walk out of their classes and march to the army recruiting office?

BARRIO RESIDENT 6: I remember that time. El Militante andava protesting quién sabe qué chingadera. Maybe que era contra la war in Vietnam—dice que they're killing too many mexicanos and negros, algo de la population versus the percent de muertos.

BARRIO RESIDENT 5: And what makes him think that the government's gonna pay any attention to what he says?

BARRIO RESIDENT 7: Pues te digo que está loco. They threw him in jail, and the minute he got out, he was out marching again. [*Glancing offstage*] Shhh, ahí viene.

[ALL *pretend to be busy.* EL MILITANTE *and* SRA. MARTÍNEZ *cross stage, mingling and greeting the* BARRIO RESIDENTS *with familiarity, asking for their signatures and to join them in a march. Some sign petition, some don't.*]

EL MILITANTE [*starting a chant*]: ¡Raza sí, Vietnam no!

SRA. MARTÍNEZ [*joining* EL MILITANTE's *chanting*]: ¡Raza sí, Vietnam no!

[*The* BARRIO RESIDENTS, *more in jest than with seriousness, join them and even start to march around, with low energy at first until the energy, momentum, and volume pick up, and* ALL BARRIO RESIDENTS *march and clap in unison and* EXIT, *still chanting and marching.* SRA. MARTÍNEZ *and* EL MILITANTE *sit while* SRA. MARTÍNEZ *sews a button on* EL MILITANTE's *fatigue jacket.*]

SRA. MARTÍNEZ: ¿Y no le tienes miedo a la policía?

EL MILITANTE: They already beat me once. See? [*Showing her a scar on his head*] A pig hit me when we were protesting at the university.

SRA. MARTÍNEZ: ¿Qué hiciste? Tenías que haber hecho algo para que la policía te golpeara.

EL MILITANTE: I didn't do anything! I sat down in the middle of the street—just sat there, like they trained us in passive resistance—and when they were putting me in the squad car, he hit me with his pistol.

SRA. MARTÍNEZ: Pues ten mucho cuidado, muchacho. [*Helping him put on jacket*] Te pueden lastimar. Tú eres solo uno, y ellos son muchos más.

EL MILITANTE: Don't worry about me. I've got too much to do in so little time . . . that's what keeps me going, keeps me alive. Besides, if I was too careful and lived with fear, I would never do anything, ¿qué no?

SRA. MARTÍNEZ [*standing behind him, hands on his shoulders*]: Siempre ten cuidado.

EL MILITANTE [*turning to face her*]: Okay. Vamos, because tonight I think we're gonna have a nice, big crowd, after that last bombing in Vietnam.

SRA. MARTÍNEZ: Ojalá, muchacho, ojalá. [*To herself*] Pobrecito, nunca viene nadie a esas meetings.

[*They both* EXIT, *and two* BARRIO GOSSIPS ENTER *and do busywork. They can be played by new actors or by any two* BARRIO RESIDENTS *who previously appeared onstage.*]

BARRIO GOSSIP 1: Oiga, comadre, no me lo va creer, pero la Señora Martínez is becoming a militant, too.

BARRIO GOSSIP 2: Sí se lo creo, comadre. ¿Pues que no la vi marchando y gritando lo de Vietnam?

BARRIO GOSSIP 1: Pues not only marching, comadre, but they told me that the other day, when she had to go to the grocery store, and El Militante's car was broken—

BARRIO GOSSIP 2: Siempre está quebrado ese carro bombo.

BARRIO GOSSIP 1: Sí, siempre. Anyway, la señora had to take the bus—

BARRIO GOSSIP 2: So, Tencha, what does that have to do with her becoming a militante?

BARRIO GOSSIP 1: Ay, comadre, wait for los chicharrones, you never let me tell you anything.

[*Two* BARRIO RESIDENTS ENTER. *They are numbered* BARRIO RESIDENTS *3 and 4 here but can be played by new actors or any of the previous* BARRIO RESIDENTS *who appeared onstage.*]

BARRIO RESIDENT 3 [*speaking while entering*]: Sí, espérate, I want to hear this, so don't interrupt her anymore. You know that no one can tell a chisme like Tencha can.

BARRIO RESIDENT 4: Sí, la Tencha gets the chisme right off del meritito grapevine.

BARRIO RESIDENT 3: Straight from the horse's mouth, ¿verdad, Tencha?

BARRIO RESIDENT 4: ¡La Tencha es la championa del mitote!

[ALL *cheer.*]

BARRIO GOSSIP 2 [*slightly miffed*]: Ay, pues it's that she takes too long to get to the point. Go on, comadre, la Señora Martínez went on the bus and—

BARRIO GOSSIP 1 [*pleased, telling the story to all who gather around her*]: Pues, you know that bus driver that's always in a bad mood? Barking at everybody? [*Mimicking*] Move on back! You gotta have the exact change! You have to pull the cord before I get to your stop! Woof, woof!

BARRIO RESIDENT 4: You mean Narcizo el cacarizo with the pockmarked face?

BARRIO GOSSIP 1: No, no, ese es el que tiene la ruta de la Broadway.

BARRIO RESIDENT 2: ¿La puta de la Broadway?

[ALL *laugh, and dirty-mouthed* BARRIO RESIDENT *thinks he's pretty clever.*]

BARRIO RESIDENT 4: ¡Ruta, ruta! The route, baboso, malhablado. Siempre sales con tus pend—

BARRIO RESIDENT 3: Ay, pues, comadre, which one is the bad mood driver?

BARRIO GOSSIP 1: Never mind which one, comadre, it's not important *which* bus driver it was; what is important is what la Señora Martínez *did* on the bus. *That* bus driver never ever leaves you right at your bus stop, no matter when you pull the cord—he just decides to leave you where nomás le da su chingada gana, and then you have to walk back or forward.

[ALL *recognize driver and tell their experiences with him, bulla, bulla.*]

BARRIO GOSSIP 2: I know who he is. The other day he almost left me under the freeway bridge, and I pulled the cord way before he passed Davis School—

BARRIO GOSSIP 1: Aha! That's the one. Well, la Señora Martínez was on the bus, coming back from Safeway's, carrying a bag of groceries—

[SRA. MARTÍNEZ ENTERS, *crosses with bag, sits on box, and pantomimes the action being described by* BARRIO GOSSIP 1.]

—and she pulled the cord un bloque before her stop, and what do you know? The bus driver went miles past her stop! And not only that, but he stopped right in front of a giant puddle!

BARRIO RESIDENT 4: There's been a lot of rain—yo les apuesto que se va flood el río. Pero no le hace, my chili and tomato plants need water.

BARRIO RESIDENT 3: No cabe duda, ese driver es un buen pendejo.

BARRIO GOSSIP 1: Entonces . . . [*Checking to see if she has everyone's attention; she does*] La Señora Martínez . . . went right up to the driver—

SRA. MARTÍNEZ: Señor, aquí *no* es mi parada—y además, ¿qué no ve que ahí hay un charco de agua? Hágame el favor de llevar este camión precisamente en donde usted debe de parar para que yo pueda bajarme sin ningún peligro.

BARRIO GOSSIP 1: —and ordered him to back up to her stop.

BARRIO RESIDENT 3 [*amazed*]: Really? ¡Qué nervio!

BARRIO GOSSIP 1: Never mind the nerve, comadre. ¡Se armó un escándalo! [*Relating with great relish and energetic movements*] El terco del bus driver insisted that she had to get off right where he had stopped, and she refused because there was that big puddle of mud in front of her. [*Continuing the story without losing her place*] Y luego, la Señora Martínez told him—

SRA. MARTÍNEZ: Señor, quiero que ahorita mismo me dé su nombre, el número de su licencia y el número de este camión—

BARRIO GOSSIP 1: —for his name, his license number, and the license of the bus he was driving—

SRA. MARTÍNEZ: —porque si no se devuelve y me deja en donde debe usted de parar, yo no me voy a apear y lo voy a reportar a la compañía de camiones porque es usted muy mal-educado con los pasajeros—

BARRIO GOSSIP 1: —and she told the driver that she was going to report him to the bus company because he was very rude to the people.

[ALL RESIDENTS *smack their lips admiringly.*]

BARRIO RESIDENT 3: Pues y luego, ¿qué paso?

BARRIO GOSSIP 1: Well, what do you think? The driver backed up, and just before la Señora Martínez got off the bus, she turned and told all the other passengers—

SRA. MARTÍNEZ: Todos ustedes tienen todo el derecho de exigir buen servicio porque todos ustedes pagan muy buen dinero por este servicio.

BARRIO GOSSIP 1: —that they had the right to demand good service for the money they paid.

ALL [*ad-libbing, murmuring, agreeing, etc.*]: Pues sí, la Señora Martínez is becoming a militant—no doubt about it.

BARRIO GOSSIP 2: Shhhhh! Ahí vienen los *dos* militantes!

[ALL *quiet down, somewhat guilty, and continue working, as* EL MILITANTE ENTERS, *and he and* SRA. MARTÍNEZ *cross and sit.*]

SRA. MARTÍNEZ [*embroidering or sewing*]: ¿Y tú? ¿Eres solo? ¿No tienes familia?

EL MILITANTE: I have a few relatives here and there, but I don't see them too much. They say I'm too crazy. You know, for protesting everything all the time. So I guess you could say I'm alone. ¿Y usted?

SRA. MARTÍNEZ: ¿Yo? Bueno, todos mis hijos viven en California y desde que se casaron casi no vienen. Dicen que hace mucho calor, que todo está muy seco, y que hay mucho polvo por acá, que no hay playas, que mi casita les da muchas alergias.

[*Beat.*]

Tienen toda la razón.

EL MILITANTE: So that's why they never come to visit you?

SRA. MARTÍNEZ [*somewhat defensively*]: Sí vinieran, pero mi hijo Benjamín no puede dejar su trabajo, y mi hija Angelia no le dan vacaciones en el mismo tiempo que le dan a su esposo, y los nietos ni quieren venir. Siempre dicen, "There's nothing to do there!" Así es. Pero me llaman por teléfono en Navidad y en el Día de las Madres. Y me mandan money orders para que me compre mis regalos. Pero yo no necesito nada. ¿A que no crees? Tengo todos los money orders guardados. ¿Y sabes para qué?

EL MILITANTE: No, why do you save the money orders they've sent you?

SRA. MARTÍNEZ: Tengo todos los money orders para cuando muera yo así podré tener una misa cantada.

EL MILITANTE: ¿Misa cantada? What's that? A mass with singing? Aren't they all the same—I mean, the funeral services?

SRA. MARTÍNEZ: No, no todas las misas son igual. Algunas son bien sencillas. Y cortas. Pero yo quiero una misa muy bonita. Y esas cuestan mucho dinero, pero como mis hijos no vienen a verme, pues entonces por lo menos pueden pagar por el entierro que quiero, ¿no crees?

EL MILITANTE: Well, I don't know about no misa cantada 'cause I don't even go to church, but since we're on the subject, I don't really care 'cause if I'm dead, I'm dead, right? But what I would really like for my funeral would be some mariachis playing the song "Sonora querida" for me.

SRA. MARTÍNEZ: "¿Sonora querida?" ¿Por qué? ¿A poco eres de Sonora?

EL MILITANTE: Nope, soy un U.S. citizen, but if I had been born in Mexico, I would've wanted it to be in the state of Sonora. Mi abuelita was from Magdalena, Sonora.

SRA. MARTÍNEZ [laughing]: ¡Pues bonitos funerales vamos a tener! ¡Yo con mi misa cantada y tú con tus mariachis!

EL MILITANTE [singing]: "Sonora querida, tierra consentida—"

SRA. MARTÍNEZ [joining in]: ". . . de dicha y placer . . ."

[Both EXIT, singing, and the BARRIO RESIDENTS continue.]

BARRIO GOSSIP 1: Bueno, lo justo es justo. And I've been thinking about what the crazy el Militante says about Vietnam, and you know? Comadre, it's true. If you read the paper, you can see right away that more mexicanos y negros are getting killed . . .

BARRIO RESIDENT 3: Chicanos, comadres, that's what they're calling themselves nowadays, not mexicanos.

BARRIO GOSSIP 1: Bueno, I don't like to use that word. Somos americanos. It's just the pachucos who call themselves Chicanos, and you know what I think of [*sneering at the word*] pachucos.

BARRIO GOSSIP 2: Pues dicen que el Militante and a bunch of his friends are going to a moratorium in Los Angeles to protest the war in Vietnam.

BARRIO GOSSIP 1: ¿Y qué es eso de moratorium?

BARRIO GOSSIP 2: I don't know what it is, but you know how el Militante talks . . . Did you see him on TV the other night? Big words. And you know what else? He really knew his numbers: how much each tank cost, how many innocent children were getting killed. He's not crazy, nor dumb—he knows what he's saying.

BARRIO RESIDENT 4: Yo sé. And they say he's going very well-prepared to that thing—la Moratorium—and that he's going to present some . . . resolutions that are real important.

BARRIO RESIDENT 3: Not to change the subject, comadre, but have you noticed how expensive everything's getting?

BARRIO GOSSIP 1: Well, that's it, too. El Militante says that the prices are going up because of the war in Vietnam.

BARRIO GOSSIP 2: Watch it, comadre, you sound like el Militante now.

BARRIO GOSSIP 1: Pues, I don't know, but I'm beginning to agree with him. ¿Y sabes por qué? Porque los que siempre se chingan son siempre los pobres, ¿verdad?

BARRIO GOSSIP 2: It's true. Pero comadre, next thing you know, you'll be marching in the streets también!

BARRIO GOSSIP 1: No, comadre, the only place I'll be marching to is the kitchen before Chapo comes home and marches me to the stove a patadas with his boots!

[ALL EXIT *as* SRA. MARTÍNEZ ENTERS *and sits.* EL MILITANTE ENTERS *and stands behind her, holding chrysanthemums behind his back.*]

EL MILITANTE: Guess what I have for you! Give up? [*Coming around and handing her the flowers*] Clavelitos for the lovely lady.

SRA. MARTÍNEZ [*laughing and taking the flowers*]: Gracias, pero estas flores no son clavelitos—son crisantemas, muchacho.

EL MILITANTE: No son crisantemas, son *clavelitos* porque me los clavé.

[*Note:* EL MILITANTE's *line above is playing with the word "clavel," meaning "carnation," and "clavar," meaning "to steal" in barrio Caló.*]

[*Beat.*]

SRA. MARTÍNEZ: ¿Ya vas a California?

EL MILITANTE: Sí, señora, we just need a few more things to pack. We're packed like sardines, but we'll be okay.

SRA. MARTÍNEZ: ¿Salen hoy en la noche?

EL MILITANTE: Sí, señora. We want to cross the desert at night and get into L. A. in the early morning, rest, and go to the Moratorium.

SRA. MARTÍNEZ: Lleven bastante agua y mucho cuidado. Y ojalá que no se te quiebre el carro en el camino.

EL MILITANTE: I hope not. Pelón gave me extra oil. We're all set. We're just waiting for the compañeros from New Mexico. Do you want me to bring you something from Califas?

SRA. MARTÍNEZ: ¿Califas? ¿Pero qué manera de hablar es esa? Se dice California—nada de "Califas."

[*Beat.*]

A mí no me tienes que traer nada, solo quiero que regreses sano y salvo.

EL MILITANTE: Give me your name and address, and I'll send you a postcard if we get a break. And if I can get to the beach, I'll bring you some sand and shells from the Pacific Ocean!

SRA. MARTINEZ: Pues, ¿para adónde vas? [*Writing her name and address on a small piece of paper*] ¿Qué no todos los pueblos en California tienen playa?

EL MILITANTE: Not all of them. I'm staying with one of my cousins who lives near Whittier Boulevard . . . I think that's probably close to the ocean.

SRA. MARTÍNEZ [*giving him the paper*]: ¿Cerraste tu casa bien? ¿Con candado?

EL MILITANTE: Locked my house? Nah, ¿pa'que?

SRA. MARTÍNEZ: Pues, no vaya ser que alguien entre y te robe tus cosas.

EL MILITANTE: I don't even have anything worth stealing. Except for my books. And if anybody wants to steal my books—well, let them. I just hope that if they steal them, they'll read them.

SRA. MARTÍNEZ: Bueno, ojalá que todo les vaya bien en California. Ten mucho cuidado. [*Caressing his face*] Y que Dios te bendiga y te cuide.

[EL MILITANTE *hugs her briefly. He salutes, smiles, and joins his* FRIENDS, *etc., who* ENTER *with the* RESIDENTS (*here labeled* HELPFUL BARRIO RES- IDENT *and* BARRIO RESIDENTS 1, 2, *and* 3), *preparing for the trip, bulla, bulla.* SRA. MARTÍNEZ *remains sitting with her flowers.* EL MILITANTE *and six* FRIENDS *put together the boxes and form a "car." Like the* RESIDENTS, *the* FRIENDS *can be played by new actors or by any* RESIDENTS *from the previous scenes, using more or fewer actors, as needed, regardless of how they are labeled here.*]

BARRIO RESIDENT 1: Can you imagine? El Militante va irse hasta Califor- nia en su carro bombo.

[*As* RESIDENTS *speak, they hand items to* FRIENDS *sitting in the "car."*]

BARRIO RESIDENT 2: Well, dicen que le dio un tune-up, y que he changed the oil. It should be okay now.

HELPFUL BARRIO RESIDENT: Everybody del barrio helped him get ready for this trip. I lent him my jumping cables.

FRIEND 1: I lent him some baling wire—well, you never know when you might need baling wire, ¿qué no?

BARRIO RESIDENT 3: I gave them a piece of nylon rope, you know, to replace a busted fan belt.

FRIEND 2 [*checking contents of box*]: Pliers, monkey wrench, three quarts of oil.

HELPFUL BARRIO RESIDENT: And here's a five-gallon jug of water, in case they run out of water in the middle of the desert.

BARRIO RESIDENT 1: Patches, in case they get a flat.

FRIEND 2: This is VERY important: a piece of red cloth, for a busted taillight.

BARRIO RESIDENT 1: And in this empty can of MJB coffee, throw in all the extra nuts, bolts, and screws. [*Joking*] And don't forget a hose for siphoning gas.

ALL [*teasing about stealing, ending up in jail, etc.*]: Uh, los van a hechar al bote.

BARRIO RESIDENT 3: And stop and see my tía in Garden Grove, ahí tienen su casa—don't forget.

HELPFUL BARRIO RESIDENT: And take these burritos for the trip. They're made with tortillas from El Zarape Market; you know that they don't make them this good in California.

BARRIO RESIDENT 3: No, they're too modern in California.

ALL [*making the sign for "huevones" or "lazy"*]: Sí, son muy modernos por allá.

[EL MILITANTE *joins his six* FRIENDS *in the "car."* RESIDENTS EXIT.]

[MUSIC: *Joyful.*]

FRIEND 1 [*to audience*]: We formed a caravan, and going down was a blast. We ate all the burritos before we even got to Marana! But we still had all kinds of canned stuff—Vienna sausages, crackers, corned-beef hash, peaches—you name it, we had it.

[ALL *ad-lib, bulla, bulla, eating, passing food around, etc.*]

FRIEND 2: What we didn't pack ourselves, someone from the caravan would share . . . vatos from Texas, New Mexico . . .

FRIEND 3: We could spot each other from the bumper stickers, y se formaba una gritería . . .

[FRIENDS *riding in the "car" put their fists up and yell, "Viva la Raza!" Their eyes move as though following a car that is passing them.*]

FRIEND 4: We'd meet at the rest stops and eat and talk strategy before we even got to L.A.

FRIEND 6: You know, we'd been charged up with high energy . . . I mean, you could feel the unity, like electricity—we were all puros carnales.

FRIEND 1: I'm not saying we didn't argue. Have you ever gotten la raza together without arguments?

FRIEND 2: Remember, teníamos coraje, pero siempre we'd manage to agree on munchas cosas—we had good strategy, good resolutions. Some of us even ditched the caucuses and went to a nearby beach. I don't know the name, but we got to wet our feet at least.

[MUSIC: *Somber.*]

[*Mood changes, and as six* FRIENDS *speak, they will move away from "car" until only* EL MILITANTE *is left sitting alone.*]

FRIEND 5: But coming back was different—quiet. No one wanted to talk after what had happened. We really didn't know what happened. It was all too fast. The "riots." Ruben Salazar getting killed. And we were too tired.

FRIEND 1: I still don't know what happened. I was right there—in the middle of everything—and I still don't know what happened. Cops everywhere. Whole families running. Shootings.

[*Pause.*]

FRIEND 2: Coming back, no one was talking much. No eating, singing, jiving like on the way down. We just took turns driving, sleeping. And *he* was even more quiet than us.

FRIEND 3: The only time I remember him talking was when he turned to us de repente . . .

[EL MILITANTE *turns head as though talking to the others in car.*]

. . . with that crazy, shy smile he had, and said—

EL MILITANTE: You know, the tragedy of all this is that ten or fifteen years from now, no one's gonna remember what happened back there— why we were there, why people got killed, not even who Ruben Salazar was.

FRIEND 4: And no one answered him. [*Reflectively*] Maybe he was right about nobody remembering, but who knows?

FRIEND 5: We just kept driving.

FRIEND 6: It was hot—really hot. The sun was just going down when we saw the steam coming out of the radiator, and we knew we had to stop . . . quick.

FRIEND 1: The service station looked deserted . . . with dirty pumps, broken windows, even tumbleweeds. It looked like those service stations in those movies about radioactive ants or rabbits after the atomic bomb testing—you know the movies I mean?

FRIEND 2: I was standing there with the hood up, waiting for the radiator to cool down, and he got out and stretched, walked around.

[EL MILITANTE *stands, stretches, walks around.*]

I guess that's when the old man came out of the station, yelling something about the water.

FRIEND 3: He didn't even hear the old man. He had turned his back and had reached for something—I don't know what—under the car seat.

[EL MILITANTE *reaches under car seat.*]

FRIEND 4: That's when the old man yelled again.

OFFSTAGE: What the hell do you think you're doing?

[EL MILITANTE *turns, wrench in his hand. Slow* FREEZE.]

FRIEND 5: And that's when the old man shot him.

[SOUND: *Offstage gunshot.*]

[SRA. MARTÍNEZ *stands up at the sound, dropping the flowers.* EL MILITANTE *falls slowly.*]

FRIEND 6: Afterwards, the old man was crying, shaking. Saying he hadn't meant to kill him. Pero estaba escamado. He was scared after seeing all about the "riots" on TV and then seeing . . . us.

FRIEND 1: El Militante told me una vez that a poet—maybe Neruda?— had said that death came like a broom, sweeping everybody.

[ALL FRIENDS EXIT, *and* SRA. MARTÍNEZ *crosses to* EL MILITANTE *and sits next to him.*]

SRA. MARTÍNEZ [*to audience*]: Yo savía que él havía fallecido. Lo savía antes que llegara la policía a decírmelo. Encontraron mi nombre y domicilio en su bolsa en aquel papelito que yo le di. Por eso vinieron a decirme de su muerte porque creían que yo era algún pariente. Yo no sé que les dije a la policía, pero firmé un papel que decía que yo me encarcaba de sus cosas y de su entierro. Yo pagué por su funeral con los money orders de mis hijos, y *sí* tuvo los mariachis que él quería.

[*Beat.*]

Me dieron su ropita, y ahí, en otra bolsa, encontré un botecito de tabaco con la arena de la playa que él me había prometido traer de California.

[SRA. MARTÍNEZ *reaches into* EL MILITANTE*'s fatigue jacket pocket and takes out a tobacco can that's filled with sand. As she continues, she lets the sand run slowly through her fingers and onto the floor.*]

Yo no quiero llorar. No quiero que nadie me vea llorar. Casi ni lo conocía.

[*Beat.*]

Y si yo no le hubiera abierto la puerta, no tuviera yo 'orita este dolor.

[**ALL** *doors slam shut.*]

LIGHTS: DOWN.

SOUND: *"Sonora querida" plays very softly, unobtrusively.*

LIGHTS: OUT.

END OF FIRST ACTO

ACTO II

¿Y qué tiene que ver un turkey con Veracruz anyway?
(So What Does a Turkey Have to Do with Veracruz Anyway?)

SETTING: *In a classroom in a community college and in a living room.*

LIGHTS: UP.

MUSIC: *"Veracruz."*

[GILBERTO, *the night janitor at the community college, is dancing dreamily with his push-broom. He is in his early fifties and wearing a grey uniform.*]

MUSIC: *Lowers, and then* OUT.

[*The* STUDENTS ENTER *and sit at desks, bored. Note that they may be played by more or fewer actors as needed.* GILBERTO *sweeps fast.* MISS VÁSQUEZ, *a young, pretty teacher,* ENTERS. GILBERTO *starts to leave but is stopped by* MISS VÁSQUEZ.]

MISS VÁSQUEZ: Oh, good! Buenas noches, Señor Ramírez. I'm so glad you're still here. Please don't leave yet—I'm going to need your help with the projector.

GILBERTO [*pleased to no end*]: Oh, yes, Miss Vásquez, I know everything there is to know about the projector.

MISS VÁSQUEZ: Great. I won't be long.

[MISS VÁSQUEZ *turns to* STUDENTS *and gives the assignment while* GILBERTO *listens to her, fascinated. At times she will pantomime writing on a chalkboard, and when she speaks, she likes to stress words and frequently uses her fingers as "quotation marks" with clicks from her mouth as she stresses words.*]

Okay, right after the movie ends, I want you to start writing your *objectives*. Objectives can be goals, ambitions, or even *dreams*. Be daring. Write something exciting—something you've *dreamed* of but have never done. Then list the *obstacles* or *barriers* to your reaching your objective. The third section should consist of *viable solutions*—ways to overcome the barriers—and the final section is short: *attainment* or *nonattainment* of your *defined objective*. This assignment is due Monday. [*To audience*] And I'll bet myself a steak dinner someone's going to ask—

STUDENT 1: Miss, what if you don't have an objective?

MISS VÁSQUEZ: Make one up.

STUDENT I [*showing off*]: You mean, like if my objective is to get me a girlfriend, and my obstacle is pimples on my face, then is my viable solution to cut off my head?

[ALL STUDENTS *laugh*.]

MISS VÁSQUEZ: Yes, and that would then be the nonattainment of your objective. [*Tossing head*] Obviously.

[*Snaps fingers and clicks tongue.* FREEZE.]

STUDENTS [*mimicking fingers and clicks*]: Obviously.

[STUDENTS FREEZE *in exact pose as* MISS VÁSQUEZ, *who breaks* FREEZE *and crosses to* GILBERTO.]

MISS VÁSQUEZ: Señor Ramírez, ¿me puede hacer un favor?

GILBERTO [*slightly flustered*]: Sí, Miss Vásquez, cómo no. [*Tucking in his stomach*] Lo que usted diga.

[MUSIC: *Bullfighting entry song.*]

[GILBERTO *follows* MISS VÁSQUEZ, *walking much like a proud bullfighter at the plaza de los toros.*]

[MUSIC: OUT.]

MISS VÁSQUEZ: It's this movie that keeps breaking, and there's no one in audiovisual at this hour to fix it. We need to finish it for next week's assignment.

GILBERTO: What movie is it?

MISS VÁSQUEZ: *Macario*. It's a great movie—have you seen it?

GILBERTO: *Macario?* No, I don't think so. I haven't seen a movie from Mexico since I was a kid. Not since they shut the Plaza Theater on Congress.

MISS VÁSQUEZ: Well, it's a film classic—one of my favorites—but it's in pretty bad shape. Either that, or it's the projector at fault. Do you mind taking a look?

GILBERTO [*confidently*]: I'll fix it for you.

MISS VÁSQUEZ: Gracias.

[MISS VÁSQUEZ *returns to her desk and* FREEZES.]

GILBERTO [*to audience*]: Me chingo. "I'll fix it for you." What do I know

about projectors? [*Praying while working on the projector and film*]
If there's a God up there that helps bigmouthed buffoons like me,
please help me now. Don't let Miss Vásquez find out that I can't fix
it. If you help me fix it, I promise to go to church next Sunday with
Ruthie and the kids. Or for sure I'll send Ruthie because *she* likes
to pray. [*To* MISS VASQUEZ] There, Miss Vásquez, I fixed it.

[MISS VÁSQUEZ *breaks* FREEZE.]

MISS VÁSQUEZ: Class. [*Giving a "teacher" signal, two claps*] Class.

[STUDENTS *break* FREEZE.]

Class. Mr. Ramírez has graciously fixed the projector for us, so we
can continue watching *Macario*. Remember to pay close attention
to the leading male actor, Ignacio López Tarso, as Macario, and
especially to his character's motivation and objectives—this will
tie in with your writing assignment. You will be *tested*.

[STUDENTS *groan loudly, then settle down to watch the movie.*]

[*To* GILBERTO] Mr. Ramírez, why don't you stay and watch the
movie with us? You'll like it.

[*Two of the* STUDENTS *role-play* MACARIO *and* MACARIO'S WIFE, *with
strong campesino accents.*]

MACARIO'S WIFE: Macario, ¿no vas a comer?

MACARIO: No. No quiero comer. Toda mi vida me la he pasado con hambre. Tú, yo, y mis hijos nos pasamos la vida muriéndonos de hambre. ¿Y no viste ayer los guajolotes?

GILBERTO [*to a* STUDENT]: What turkeys?

STUDENT 2 [*annoyed*]: Los turkeys de los ricos del pueblo. That dude,
Macario, when he was delivering the wood in town, he saw a bunch
of turkeys going into the ovens to be roasted.

GILBERTO: I must've missed that part. So that's why he wants to starve to
death? 'Cause he saw the turkeys? I don't get it.

ALL STUDENTS: Sshhhh! We can't hear.

MACARIO: Yo ya no me voy a morir de hambre poco a poco. Ya no vuelvo a
comer nada hasta que me muera de hambre de una vez . . . o hasta
que me pueda comer un guajolote entero . . . yo solo sin darle un
pedazo a nadie. Ni a ti, ni mis hijos . . . nomás para mí . . . solo para

mí. Quiero comérmelo hasta que esté llenito, repleto, con el sabor del guajolote en toda mi boca. ¿Me entiendes lo que yo quiero? Yo quiero un guajolote entero y solo para mí.

GILBERTO: I get it now. This Macario has been starving all of his life, and now he wants to eat a whole turkey all by himself, without sharing it with anyone—not with his wife and not even with his kids. He wants to eat a whole turkey until he's stuffed. Makes perfect sense to me.

ALL STUDENTS [*standing up, sarcastic*]: Wow! The janitor has grasped the theoretical concept of instant gratification.

[ALL STUDENTS FREEZE.]

GILBERTO [*insulted, deciding to leave the classroom*]: Miss Vásquez, the projector's fixed for now, but if it breaks again, I'll be around here—just call me.

MISS VÁSQUEZ: Gracias, Señor Ramírez. What did you do to fix it?

GILBERTO: Nomás lo teipié.

[*Note: "teipié" means "taped" in Spanglish.*]

MISS VÁSQUEZ: ¿Teipié? Pero, Señor Ramírez, ¿qué palabra es esa?

[*She* FREEZES *with face contorted at* GILBERTO's *Spanglish.*]

GILBERTO [*to audience*]: Me chingo. Metí la pata otra vez. Teipié. There's no such word. What will Miss Vásquez think of me now? Soy un burro, pocho, maleducado. She speaks such pretty Spanish. Softly. Like music. How do you say "tape" in Spanish, anyway?

[*A loud* BELL *rings, and* ALL FREEZE.]

[*Breaking freeze*] That night I wanted to tell Ruthie about the movie.

[RUTHIE ENTERS, *stands as though looking at herself in mirror, checking for defects.*]

She was hiding in the bathroom. She thinks I don't know what she does in there, but I know. She colors her gray hair, plucks her eyebrows, and does her exercises.

[ALL *break* FREEZE *and do jumping jacks with* RUTHIE, *counting out loud. Stop and* FREEZE.]

RUTHIE [*Breaking freeze, massaging her neck and face*]: No quiero hacerme vieja. Por eso hago mis exercises y compro the best face creams, like Oil of Olay at Walgreens, pero siempre estoy agarrando muchas arrugas por el sol. And Gilberto doesn't understand, doesn't help me. Bueno, él es hombre, and men don't have to worry about wrinkles. When they get wrinkles, they're "character lines," pero cuando una mujer se arruga, es pa' la chingada, and good-bye to her youth.

GILBERTO: Ruthie, remember que te dije que I had to buy me some horse-shoes pa' jugar con los guys from work?

RUTHIE [*with hair clips in her mouth*]: MMMmmm.

GILBERTO: Well, I don't have to buy them anymore porque aquí los tengo! [*Holding up* RUTHIE's *underwire bra*] Mira, I just cut this in half and take off the material y [*pretending to throw like a horseshoe*] tengo mis horseshoes.

[STUDENTS *break* FREEZE.]

STUDENTS [*pantomiming throwing horseshoes*]: RINGER!

[STUDENTS FREEZE.]

RUTHIE: No seas simple, Gilberto.

GILBERTO [*sitting next to* RUTHIE]: ¿Sabes qué vi esta nochi en la class de la Miss Vásquez?

[*He* FREEZES.]

RUTHIE [*standing up, irritated, speaking to audience*]: Ya va otra vez. Miss Vásquez this, Miss Vásquez that!

[STUDENTS *mimic her faces.*]

I can just see her. Bien jovencita, without a single wrinkle, un cuerpecito de Victoria's Secret model, and with plenty of money. Teachers make good money. And why is it that if Gilberto has to clean the entire junior college, he's always in *her* room? I would like to confront Gilberto, sacar las garritas al sol . . .

[STUDENTS *break* FREEZE.]

STUDENTS [*wagging fingers, saying no*]: Nah, ah, ah.

[*They* FREEZE.]

RUTHIE [*sitting down*]: Pero como dice la therapist en TV. You shouldn't let your husband know you're jealous. [*Turning to* GILBERTO *with a sweet smile*] No, Gilberto, sweetie, what did you see in Miss Vásquez's class?

GILBERTO: Era un mono about this real poor woodcutter named Macario. And he had a bunch of kids and they were all starving. One morning he couldn't even eat his tortilla and beans because his little kids were staring at his food. And the whole town is getting ready for some Día de los Muertos fiesta—like Halloween here, but with calavera candies and sweetbread—and this Macario sees the biggest roasted turkeys, and you know what he decides? He decides to starve himself to death, because he wants a turkey. And listen to this—he doesn't want to share the turkey with his kids or his wife. He wants to eat it all by himself . . . Oye, Ruthie, have you ever wanted something that bad?

[NOSY STUDENT *breaks* FREEZE *and lunges forward to hear, hand on ear.*]

NOSY STUDENT: Eternal youth?

RUTHIE: No, and if I did, it sure wouldn't be for a pinchi turkey!

NOSY STUDENT [*horrified*]: ¿Pinchi turkey?

[NOSY STUDENT FREEZES *again.*]

GILBERTO: See how you are. Nobody can talk to you.

RUTHIE: ¿Y tú? Siempre tienes que salir con tus pendejadas.

GILBERTO: ¿"Pendejadas"? You call having a dream a pendejada?

RUTHIE: If it's for a turkey, then yes, it's definitely a pendejada.

[*Three* STUDENTS *break* FREEZE *and become* GILBERTO *and* RUTHIE's *daughter* DEBBIE *and her two* KIDS.]

KIDS [*protesting as they're dragged by* DEBBIE]: We don't want to stay with Nana and Tata. They don't even have MTV. It's too boring!

DEBBIE: 'Amá! ¿Me puedes cuidar los kids? I'm going out with Sandra.

KIDS, RUTHIE, AND GILBERTO [*in unison*]: Babysit?!

[*The* KIDS, RUTHIE, *and* GILBERTO FREEZE.]

DEBBIE [*to audience*]: I hope she says yes. I'm so bored. All I do is work and take care of the kids. And please don't let my dad get started on me. He was right: "Don't get married so young, learn to type, finish school, travel."

[GILBERTO *and* RUTHIE *break* FREEZE.]

GILBERTO: Of course I was right. But did she listen to me? Does anyone ever listen to me?

DEBBIE: No. So here I am, divorced and with two kids. [*To* RUTHIE] Mom, please say yes. I've got to get out of the house . . . alone.

RUTHIE: Sí, Debbie, 'stá bueno. Déjalos.

[STUDENTS *break* FREEZE.]

STUDENTS [*as cheerleaders*]: Babysitter, babysitter, boom, boom, boom.

[STUDENTS FREEZE.]

DEBBIE: And they haven't eaten dinner—could you make them something?

RUTHIE: Sí, m'ija. 'Orita les hago French fries, sopita de fideo, y chocolate milkshakes.

DEBBIE: I'll be back early. I'm just gonna have dinner with Sandra.

[STUDENTS *break* FREEZE.]

STUDENTS [*making drinking motions, still cheering*]: Happy hour, happy hour, chugalug!

DEBBIE: And if I'm late, could they sleep over, and I'll pick them up tomorrow—early?

NOSY STUDENT [*moving forward to hear response*]: Uh oh, now she's gone too far!

RUTHIE: Sure, m'ija. Did you bring their pajamas?

STUDENTS [*forming chorus line and kicking*]: After party, after party, here we go!

[STUDENTS FREEZE.]

DEBBIE [*exiting*]: Oh, Mom, one more favor . . . My washing machine broke again. Will you wash my dirty laundry? I left it there on the porch.

RUTHIE: Sí, Debbie. I'll wash your laundry, don't worry.

[STUDENTS *break* FREEZE.]

STUDENTS [*pantomiming movement*]: BINGO! This is the way we wash her clothes, wash her clothes, wash her clothes . . .

DEBBIE [*arrogantly, to audience*]: You see? My mom always says yes to anything I ask her. [*To* STUDENTS] Let's go party!

[MUSIC: *Contemporary.*]

[DEBBIE *and* STUDENTS *dance as they move away from* GILBERTO *and* RUTHIE. *Then they* FREEZE.]

RUTHIE [*taking kids and sitting them down*]: Vengan, I'll make you something to eat.

GILBERTO [*sarcastically*]: Visita again?

KIDS: Hi, Tata.

GILBERTO: And I bet you haven't eaten, right?

[KIDS *shake head no.*]

RUTHIE: Déjalos, Gilberto, son chiquitos.

GILBERTO: Pero nomás a eso vienen, a comer.

RUTHIE: So what if they do? I work, too—don't I?

GILBERTO: Don't get mad. I was just kidding. [*Snuggling*] ¿Te acuerdas de la noche que nos conocimos? That night we first met in San Diego? I went to the dance, and I saw all the pretty girls sitting there, pero de todas ellas, tú eras la más bonita, with that gardenia in you hair.

NOSY STUDENT [*breaking freeze and sighing*]: Una gardenia en tu pelo.

RUTHIE: And you were wearing your charcoal suit, maroon shirt, spit-shined French-toe shoes.

[GILBERTO *wipes his shoe on back of pants.*]

GILBERTO [*taking her in his arms and dancing with her slowly*]: And we danced and danced.

[MUSIC: *Any danzón.*]

[STUDENTS *break* FREEZE *and dance.*]

Remember? They were playing danzones from Veracruz. By that skinny guy—what's his name?

RUTHIE: Agustín Lara. He married María Félix, the most beautiful woman in all of Mexico.

GILBERTO: But not as beautiful as you.

NOSY STUDENT: Wow! ¡Qué madera!

GILBERTO: María Félix, yeah. What a beauty. [*Reminiscing*] Cuando yo era chavalito, I used to save all my money to go to las vistas at the Plaza Theater. Yo iba todos los sábados. Nomás costaba un daime. Then a quarter.

[**STUDENTS** *act out the movie scene that* **GILBERTO** *is describing.*]

I remember this mono con Agustín Lara playing the piano en un cabaret, crazy in love with some movie star like Ninón Sevilla who wouldn't give him the time of day. She'd walk into the cabaret wearing a tight black satin skirt with a slit up her thigh, smoking a cigarette. Damn, she was sexy! And then she'd walk up to Agustín Lara and lean against the piano, smoking and blowing the cigarette smoke right into his face, waiting for that gangster—what was his name? And as soon as the gangster walked in, with his bigote and a sneer, anda vámonos—Ninón Sevilla would forget Agustín and go with the gangster.

[*The* **MUSIC** *stops and the* **STUDENTS FREEZE** *in dance positions.*]

Ruthie, we haven't gone out dancing in a long time. Let's go tonight, ¿vamos?

RUTHIE [*enthused*]: ¡Sí, vamos!

[*She starts to walk with him.*]

NOSY STUDENT [*breaking freeze*]: ¿Y los kids? ¿Quién va cuidar a los buquis?

RUTHIE [*stopping and turning*]: We can't, Gilberto.

GILBERTO: Pues no, tienes que babysit.

RUTHIE: Some other time—next Saturday, for sure. C'mon, kids.

[**RUTHIE** *starts to* **EXIT** *with* **KIDS**.]

GILBERTO [*decisively*]: Yo quiero ir a Veracruz.

RUTHIE: ¿Qué? What did you say?

ALL [*except* RUTHIE]: Veracruz! He said he wants to go to Veracruz!!!

[*Marimba* **MUSIC** *starts playing, and the* **STUDENTS** *become the* **VERACRUZANOS**, *promenading in plaza as vendors, lovers, bulla, bulla, etc.*]

TOUR GUIDE: Veracruz es el puerto más grande y más antiguo de México y ha jugado un papel muy importante en la historia de México desde la llegada del conquistador Hernán Cortés hasta la Revolución de mil novecientos diez. Veracruz es el puerto principal de entrada de los puertos del este y del golfo, y es conocido por sus tabacos y puros, platillos deliciosos, mariscos y café.

GRINGO CUSTOMER [*rattling a spoon in his glass*]: Waiter, waiter! [*To his*

friend] That's how you order. [*Rattling again, practicing his Spanish*]
Mesero, un café con leche, por favor.

FLOWER VENDOR [*repeating*]: Rosas, gardenias, jazmines, rosas, gardenias,
jazmines.

LOVER: ¿Sabías? Veracruz es para los enamorados.

WAITER: Step right in. ¡Aquí tenemos todo para su deleite—shrimp cock-
tail, una cerveza, coctel de abulón, ceviche, pescado zarandeado,
cerveza y más cerveza, pase usted, camarón al mojo de ajo, música!
Ande, pase usted, para servirle.

TOURIST: My favorite day in Veracruz is Thursday, when the military band
plays right here at the Palacio Municipal and the little fat guy goes
wild playing that instrument . . . the . . .

ALL: ¡El güiro!

[MUSIC: UP. *Still marimba.*]

[ALL *dance and then* FREEZE.]

[RUTHIE *breaks* FREEZE.]

RUTHIE [*to* GILBERTO]: Gilberto, honey, we have to buy Debbie a new
washing machine.

GILBERTO: A new washing machine? Pero, Ruthie, esta vacation quiero ir
a Veracruz.

RUTHIE: Veracruz? But I want to take the kids to Disneyland.

GILBERTO: Que los lleve la Debbie.

RUTHIE: No, no, se le pierden en Disneyland. You know how scatter-
brained she is—for sure she'll lose them. Besides, Veracruz is too
far. Who's gonna take care of the house, my plants, the dog? Who's
gonna babysit Junior?

GILBERTO: Junior doesn't need a babysitter. Ruthie, he's twenty-four. Anyway, all he does is play the video games—he won't even know we're
gone.

RUTHIE: It's too expensive. No tenemos dinero.

GILBERTO: Sí, tenemos. We just got the income tax check.

RUTHIE: But the Mexicans there don't even like us. They say that we're
pochos and that we don't even speak proper Spanish. That we
don't speak Castellano . . .

GILBERTO: Never mind that Castellano—I don't even know that pinchi viejo. Anyway, la Miss Vásquez says—

[DEBBIE ENTERS, *running*.]

DEBBIE: ¡¡'Amá!! ¡¡'Apá!! I want to buy me a car.

RUTHIE: A car, Debbie? Pero you need una washing machine more than you need a *car*.

DEBBIE: Yo no quiero una washing machine—I want a car. I'm sick and tired of always having to ask for a ride. Or the bus. I want a car. Mom, can't you see? I just want my freedom again.

GILBERTO: You're very selfish, Debbie. Don't you see how much work your mother does for you? She's right: you need a washing machine more than a car.

DEBBIE: You just don't understand.

[*She turns her back to* GILBERTO *and* RUTHIE, *pouting*.]

RUTHIE: Pobrecita.

GILBERTO: Pobrecita, nada. Vámonos a Veracruz, Ruthie. Let Debbie take care of herself! You're spoiling her just like Junior. Let's go to Veracruz.

RUTHIE: But viejo, I have to help Debbie buy her washing machine.

GILBERTO: Let her buy it herself. She's got a good job. She's just taking advantage of you 'cause you do everything for her—

DEBBIE [*turning around to face them with car keys dangling from her hand*]: ¡'Amá! ¡'Apá! Come and see! I got me a new car!

[STUDENTS break FREEZE. *Ad-lib, bulla, bulla, excited*.]

ALL: ¡Vamos a ver el carro nuevo de la Debbie!

[ALL EXIT *following* DEBBIE *and quickly* ENTER *from opposite side, surround the "car," kicking tires, etc*.]

NOSY STUDENT [*admiring the car*]: ¡Qué bonito! How's the mileage?

DEBBIE: Bueno, let's find out. How 'bout going for a ride?

[ALL *get in car*.]

[*To her* KIDS] No, ustedes no. Stay with your grandma. [*Pushing* KIDS *toward* RUTHIE *and waving*] Bye, m'ijos! We'll be right back. Mind your nana. And your tata.

[STUDENTS *also wave good-bye.* ALL FREEZE. KIDS *howl.*]

RUTHIE: C'mon, m'ijos. You can watch cartoons.

[*Cartoon* MUSIC *begins to play, and three* STUDENTS *act out a "Three Stooges" routine for* KIDS.]

GILBERTO [*to* RUTHIE]: ¿Vistes? La Debbie got herself a new car and she's off with her friends, and here you are, stuck with her kids, como siempre. Why can't she take care of them herself?

RUTHIE: So what? She's my daughter and they're my grandkids, and I'm gonna always be here to help her.

GILBERTO: ¿Sabes algo, Ruthie? It seems like I've spent my whole life working like a donkey, but there's gotta be more to life than breakfasts at Village Inn. Ruthie, vámonos pa' Veracruz.

RUTHIE: Veracruz? Now? Are you crazy? Is that what the turkey got you thinking about? 'Stás loco. Let me buy Debbie a new washing machine and maybe we can go later.

GILBERTO: No, I have this feeling that if I don't go now, I'll never go. And I'm gonna die without ever going to Veracruz. Let's go, Ruthie.

RUTHIE: No puedo.

GILBERTO [*taking her hand and sitting down next to her*]: Ruthie, let me tell you something I've never told anyone before.

[*Beat.*]

One time I had to go make a delivery in Nogales—on the Mexican side, Sonora—and I parked the truck on the American side and walked across. So there I am, walking with this big box, and I got lost. I couldn't find the elementary school that was supposedly on the main street. I asked and asked for directions, and they kept telling me I just needed a few more blocks, past this or those "semáforos" or "semófaros" or "samóferos." Sepa la chingada what that word was. Anyway, just when I'm ready to drop from the heat, this little old man that had been watching me calls me over.

[OLD MAN *with cart* ENTERS.]

He was selling fruit cocktails in a cart filled with ice, and he invited me for a beer.

[OLD MAN *takes a beer and gestures to* GILBERTO *to come over.*]

[*Crossing to* OLD MAN *and still telling* RUTHIE *his story*] He had it under the ice, you know. So we drank the beer, and the old man— he was somewhat like a philosopher—liked to talk.

[*Beat.* GILBERTO *and* OLD MAN *pantomime drinking beer and talking.*]

He said it was my fault that I stayed lost because I was too proud to ask what the word was.

[OLD MAN *points upward as if to a signal light and laughs.*]

OLD MAN: ¡La palabra que buscas es semáforos! ¡Semáforos, muchacho!

GILBERTO: Signal lights! That was the word I didn't know, and that's why I couldn't find the school.

RUTHIE: Gilberto, what's the point? Just what does all this have to do with anything? Is this gonna be another senseless story just like your turkey and Veracruz one?

GILBERTO: I'm getting to that, Ruthie. See, I was there some time with him, talking, drinking beer. And I finally had to leave, and you know what we had talked about? Dreams. And none of those fancy words like Miss Vásquez. Just plain dreams. He said we all live with one dream—it could be crazy or it could be practical, but still it was a dream. Our very own dream. And that we work like burros just so we can get to reach that dream some day. Sometimes the dream doesn't turn out the way we thought it would, and sometimes it does. But—and this is the most important thing—if you don't reach for your dream, for whatever reason, then you're just a—

OLD MAN [*very simply*]: Pendejo.

[OLD MAN EXITS *with his cart.*]

GILBERTO [*crossing to* RUTHIE]: Mira, Ruthie, that Macario guy didn't want to give his wife any turkey, but I want you to share my dream. I want you to go with me to Veracruz. Ruthie, the train leaves Nogales at five o'clock. We can make it. Let's just pack a few things. Leave the kids with Junior. He won't even notice that we're gone. Ándale. [*Firmly*] I want to go to Veracruz with you, but if you won't go, I'll go alone.

[*He walks away from her, stops, and turns to her.*]

RUTHIE [*undecided*]: Gilberto . . .

[RUTHIE *looks at* KIDS, *pauses, crosses to* KIDS, *and sits down between them.*]

GILBERTO [*extending his hand out to her*]: Vamos, Ruthie. Vamos conmigo a Veracruz.

[GILBERTO *and* RUTHIE *make slight reaching movements, but they do not complete these movements. They* FREEZE.]

MUSIC: *"Veracruz,"* UP *and* OUT.

LIGHTS: OUT.

END OF SECOND ACTO

ACTO III

El Dragonslayer

LIGHTS: UP *slowly.*

SOUND: *Radio giving morning news.*

[LAS TRES COMADRES CHISMOLERAS—ANITA SIN CARNITA, SOFIA SIN COSTILLA, *and* ELENA SIN AVENA—*are at their respective doors. Some of the* SCHOOL KIDS *are playing on* DON ALBINO CARA DE PEPINO's *rocks.* DON ALBINO CARA DE PEPINO, *wearing railroad coveralls and cap, and a red bandanna around his neck, is asleep in his rocking chair, and* FEDERICO NARICES DE PERICO, *a dusty, dirty little boy wearing dirty torn jeans and a T-shirt, is kneeling on the floor and playing with his wilted leaves.*]

MUSIC: DOWN.

[ALL BARRIO RESIDENTS *chatter, joke, etc. No one talks to* FEDERICO *or* DON ALBINO CARA DE PEPINO. *The* MUSIC *stops abruptly, and then changes to theme from* The Good, the Bad and the Ugly. EDDIE SPAGHETTI, TONY BALONEY, *and* RAMÓN JAMÓN ENTER. *They are wearing pants, flannel shirts, shades, and huge bandannas as headbands. These bandannas must be a neutral (that is, non-gang) color, such as orange or purple. They carry one gigantic boom box, which is playing loud rap music.* ALL BARRIO RESIDENTS *hush and stop their activities. They move away fearfully and slowly, as when the villain in a Western drama appears.*]

LAS TRES COMADRES [*in unison*]: Benditos sean los dulces nombres del cielo. [*Identifying the newly entered three with fear*] Son el Eddie Spaghetti, el Tony Baloney y el Ramón Jamón.

[*As each is named, he steps forward and makes a mocking bow.* EDDIE SPAGHETTI, TONY BALONEY, *and* RAMÓN JAMÓN *go straight to* FEDERICO, *stomp on his leaves, and* EXIT, *laughing like hyenas.* FEDERICO's JEFITA ENTERS. *She carries a long cigarette holder and constantly puffs at it. She pulls* FEDERICO *up by his ears or hair.*]

LA JEFITA: ¿Ya ves? You got beat up again. Y es tu culpa porque you never defend yourself.

FEDERICO: Pero, 'Amá, yo no—

LA JEFITA: ¡Cállate! Te digo que *tú* tienes la culpa.

[*She* EXITS *grumbling and repeating this line.*]

LAS TRES COMADRES AND SCHOOL KIDS [*in unison*]: Sí, Federico, it's all your fault. Tú tienes la culpa. [*Louder*] ¡TÚ TIENES LA CULPA!

[**DON ALBINO** *wakes up from the noise, and sees* **SCHOOL KIDS** *jumping on his rocks.*]

DON ALBINO [*standing up and yelling at them like the Tasmanian Devil, sputtering ad-libbed curses*]: Buquis demonios, traviesos, quítensen de mis piedras . . .

[*The* **SCHOOL KIDS** *and* **LAS TRES COMADRES EXIT** *noisily.* **DON ALBINO** *goes back to sleep.* **FEDERICO** *stands alone. He walks across the stage slowly, looking around. He looks at the audience.*]

FEDERICO [*to audience*]: Yo vivo en el barrio más pobre y más miserable, in a desert where the sun has shriveled the honeysuckle vines and nothing dares to grow here, nomás uno o dos árboles polvorosos de piocha. Only one or two dusty chinaberry trees dare to grow here.

ANITA SIN CARNITA [*sticking her head out of door 1 and yelling*]: Federico Narices de Perico, stop dreaming! I know you haven't eaten yet, so come and have a burrito with us. Ya déjate de 'star soñando con la boca abierta. ¡Te van entrar moscas!

FEDERICO: Dreaming? I'm not dreaming—I'm telling the truth.

ELENA SIN AVENA [*sticking her head out of door 2*]: Comadre Anita, buenos días. ¿Qué hizo pa'l breakfast?

ANITA SIN CARNITA [*proudly*]: Chorizo con huevos, refried beans, handmade tortillas—

SOFIA SIN COSTILLA [*sticking her head out of door 3*]: Handmade tortillas? ¡Mentiras! I saw you buy them at Safeway's, Comadre Anita. Remember? I was with you.

ANITA SIN CARNITA: No son mentiras, Comadres Anita y Elena. [*To* COMADRE ELENA] Mire, comadre, even if the tortillas were made on a machine, someone's hand had to push the buttons, ¿qué no?

ELENA SIN AVENA [*somewhat doubtfully*]: Ajá . . .

ANITA SIN CARNITA: ¡Pues ahí 'stá, comadre! Entonces mis tortillas están "handmade," ¿qué no? Nomás que it wasn't MY hands!

[**LAS TRES COMADRES** *laugh at joke.*]

[*To* FEDERICO] So, dreamer, come and have un burrito de chorizo.

FEDERICO [*angrily*]: I said I'm not dreaming! How can anybody have any dreams in this stupid barrio anyway?

[LAS TRES COMADRES *push the doors and step out, hands on hips, in unison.*]

LAS TRES COMADRES [*in unison*]: And why not?

FEDERICO: Because—here your dreams get stepped on.

ANITA SIN CARNITA: Stepped on?

FEDERICO: Sí, pisoteados.

ELENA SIN AVENA: ¿Cómo que pisoteados? ¿Cómo? Explícate, Federico. Tell us.

FEDERICO [*thinking hard*]: It's like . . . Como . . . [*Walking around and using his hands to point and describe*] Like . . . Como . . . You know, when it finally rains here—a real hard chubasco? And then it stops raining, and the hot sun dries up the wet ground?

[LAS TRES COMADRES *nod yes.*]

The dirt starts to dry up, la tierra se seca, and it curls up into different shapes. Y se seca más y más, and the edges dry up more and start to lift up. And when I step on them, they make a crackling sound . . . like cornflakes.

LAS TRES COMADRES [*in unison*]: Cornflakes?

FEDERICO: Si, like cornflakes pisoteadas. That's exactly what my dreams are in this forsaken barrio. They're stomped-on cornflakes.

[FEDERICO *starts to* EXIT *stage right.*]

LAS TRES COMADRES [*taking their right hands off their hips and pointing at* FEDERICO]: WAIT!

[*Still pointing, they march to him and stop.*]

ELENA SIN AVENA: Dices bien, Federico Narices de Perico. But your dreams are just beginning, and already you say they're like cornflakes. Well, our dreams—when we had them—have all turned into dust.

[*In one quick movement,* LAS TRES COMADRES *pivot, put right hand on hips again, and stretch their left arms in sweeping motion to stage left.*]

In this barrio, there are only old, old men. [*Pointing to* DON ALBINO] Puros viejos. Sí, asina como Don Albino Cara de Pepino, who sits all day with his eyes closed like a Mesozoic reptile waiting to kill flies.

SOFIA SIN COSTILLA: Viejos olvidados. They are forgotten old men who spend their days sitting outside, unafraid of the burning sun because their skin has already turned to shoe leather. Translate, Anita.

ANITA SIN CARNITA: Los viejos se pasan los días afuera sin temor al ardiente sol, porque la piel de los viejos está seca como el cuero de un zapato viejo.

ELENA SIN AVENA: So the viejos sit outside all day, waiting for nothing to happen, sunning themselves, like lazy lizards on cemetery tombs.

LAS TRES COMADRES [*in unison*]: Como lagartos perezosos en las tumbas de un panteón.

[*Three* YOUNG WOMEN ENTER *stage left. They are wearing identical stylish clothes and blonde wigs. They pose, looking extremely bored.*]

ANITA SIN CARNITA: The young women se quedan adentro todo el día, afraid of the drying sun, hasta en la tarde, when they draw on pretty faces con makeup del Avon ...

[*The three* YOUNG WOMEN *put on makeup.*]

... and dress in real pretty dresses from Lerner's, and they promenade afuera como token-takers in a cabaret.

[*Sensual* MUSIC *plays. The* YOUNG WOMEN *walk around the stage and return to bored pose.*]

ELENA SIN AVENA: There are no young men here.

[*Three* YOUNG MEN ENTER *stage right. They are handcuffed with their hands behind their backs, and they are wearing orange coveralls with the word "PRISON" stenciled on the back. They cross the stage slowly and stop with their heads down.*]

SOFIA SIN COSTILLA: All of our men are either in prison, or they've disappeared to California, or they've been turned into welfare checks. Translate, Anita.

ANITA SIN CARNITA: Ay, do I have to? Ya me cansé.

[*The other two* COMADRES *glare her down.*]

Okay, okay, pues. Aquí no hay hombres jóvenes. Todos están en la prisión, se han desaparecido a California, o se han convertido a cheques del gobierno.

SOFIA SIN COSTILLA: And we spend our lives watching telenovelas that *almost* make us cry.

[*The theme from a popular telenovela plays.* LAS TRES COMADRES *whip out their handkerchiefs from inside their bras and daintily wipe both eyes. They cross their arms and watch the telenovela unfold in front of them. The* YOUNG MEN *and* YOUNG WOMEN *become couples, and they "act" in identical manners, as though the* COMADRES *are watching three identical television sets.*]

YOUNG MEN: Vanessa, soy un cobarde. Soy un canalla; no merezco tu amor.

YOUNG WOMEN: No digas eso, Bryan. Te perdono tu infidelidad porque sé que todo lo que hiciste fue por el amor que me tienes.

YOUNG MEN: Entonces . . . ¿me perdonas?

YOUNG WOMEN: Sí, te perdono porque te amo con todo mi corazón.

YOUNG MEN: No tengo derecho de pedirte que me esperes, pero . . .

YOUNG WOMEN: Bryan, yo te amo, pero no me pidas que . . .

[*A* PRISON GUARD ENTERS. *He is dressed like a Keystone Kop, walking like Charlie Chaplin and swinging a billy club.*]

PRISON GUARD [*giggling*]: Visiting hours are now over.

[*The couples give lingering looks and* FREEZE. *The* YOUNG MEN EXIT *stage right with the* PRISON GUARD. *The* YOUNG WOMEN *sob melodramatically and* EXIT *stage left, running. The telenovela theme plays and is abruptly cut off by the sound of a commercial for Café Combate, or something familiar to TV viewers.*]

LAS TRES COMADRES [*in unison*]: Sí, es cierto, nos pasamos la vida viendo las telenovelas que ya *casi* nos hacen llorar.

[*In identical movements, they wipe their eyes daintily again and* EXIT *through their doors.* FEDERICO *watches them leave.* DON ALBINO *is looking at* FEDERICO *very intently, but when* FEDERICO *turns toward him, he pretends to be asleep.* FEDERICO *crosses slowly to center stage and stops. He takes a pointed stick from his back pocket and looks around to see if anyone is looking; he almost catches* DON ALBINO *watching him, but* DON ALBINO *again pretends to be asleep.*]

FEDERICO [*to audience, pretending to make furrows in the ground with the pointed stick*]: Someday . . . I would like to have a small garden . . . no, a *big* plantation. Y yo fuera un ranchero muy rico. I would plant rows and rows of . . . something.

[*He takes out some wilted leaves from his pocket and "plants" them.*]

    I would grow chili, maíz, calabacitas, oranges, apples, avocados . . .

[**DON ALBINO** *opens his eyes and listens as* **FEDERICO** *very tenderly "plants" the wilted leaves. He is too absorbed to see* **EDDIE SPAGHETTI, TONY BALONEY,** *and* **RAMÓN JAMÓN ENTER** *with a boom box, which is playing very loud* **RAP MUSIC. LAS TRES COMADRES** *quickly appear at their doors, very agitated at the loud music.*]

LAS TRES COMADRES [*in unison*]: Benditos sean los dulces nombres del cielo.

[**LAS TRES COMADRES EXIT** *quickly.* **EDDIE SPAGHETTI, TONY BALONEY** *and* **RAMÓN JAMÓN** *strut across stage and spot* **FEDERICO** *daydreaming. They stop and check him out. They move closer to him and see his "plants." They put down their boom box.* **FEDERICO** *looks up and is frightened; he crawls away from them.* **EDDIE SPAGHETTI, TONY BALONEY,** *and* **RAMÓN JAMÓN** *gleefully stomp* **FEDERICO'***s "plants" until* **DON ALBINO** *stands up and cusses gibberish at them, enraged.*]

DON ALBINO [*ad-libbing expletives*]: Buquis malcriados, váyanse a sus casas . . .

[**EDDIE SPAGHETTI, TONY BALONEY,** *and* **RAMÓN JAMÓN** *pick up their boom box and* **EXIT,** *laughing like hyenas again.* **FEDERICO** *looks at* **DON ALBINO;** *neither speaks.* **FEDERICO'***s* **JEFITA ENTERS.** *She grabs* **FEDERICO** *by his ear and pulls him roughly to his feet.*]

LA JEFITA [*nagging in a shrill voice*]: How many times have I told you not to get into fights? Nunca me haces caso. I'm gonna call the juvie, ya verás . . .

FEDERICO [*trying to explain*]: Pero 'Amá, yo no hice nada—

LA JEFITA: It's your fault, Federico, es tu culpa.

[*Both* **FREEZE. ALL OTHERS ENTER** *in a conga line;* **DON ALBINO** *watches.*]

ALL [*singing as they enter*]: Tú tienes la culpa; tú tienes la culpa. Tú tienes la culpa; tú tienes la culpa. Tú tienes la culpa; tú tienes la culpa.

[*They step on each syllable and give a kick with alternating feet on the last syllable of the word "culpa." The conga line snakes around the doors, and when it passes by* **LA JEFITA,** *she joins the conga line, and they* **ALL EXIT,** *dancing and chanting.* **FEDERICO** *remains in* **FREEZE.** *Polka or corrido norteño* **MUSIC** *plays, and then a very loud school bell rings.* **SCHOOL KIDS ENTER** *running. They sit on the floor next to* **FEDERICO** *and form a straight line. They are slightly disruptive.*]

LAS TRES COMADRES [*at their doors, in unison*]: ¡Federico Narices de Perico! ¡Despierta, ya comenzó la escuela!

[FEDERICO *breaks* FREEZE *and joins* SCHOOL KIDS. *The* TEACHER ENTERS, *dressed very formally, wearing glasses, and holding a book under his/her nose. The* SCHOOL KIDS *immediately sit up straight and pay attention.*]

TEACHER [*droning, slow-motion unintelligible drivel*]: Blah, blah, blah . . .

[*The* SCHOOL KIDS *yawn widely like crocodiles and fall asleep. The* TEACHER *continues.*]

FEDERICO [*to audience*]: I hate school. I really hate school.

ELENA SIN AVENA [*at her door*]: ¿No te gusta la escuela? Well, too bad Federico, 'cause the law says you have to go to school.

SOFIA SIN COSTILLA [*at her door*]: I don't blame you, Federico Narices de Perico—I used to hate school, too. ¿Se acuerdan, comadres? ¿Cómo hicíamos "play hookie"?

LAS TRES COMADRES [*in unison*]: Ay, pues, who doesn't hate school?

FEDERICO [*trying to explain*]: Well, maybe I don't really *hate* school. I just mostly hate to have to wear zapatos again after running around all summer without shoes. Y me gusta geography. But I hate all the other stuff we have to study. What good is it?

ELENA SIN AVENA: A mí también me gustaba geography. And Federico, you wanna know why you like geography?

FEDERICO: Why?

[DON ALBINO *sits up and listens.*]

LAS TRES COMADRES [*in unison*]: Because in geography class, you can see other worlds, other lands, other people, and, in your mind at least, Federico Narices de Perico, you can escape from this barrio.

DON ALBINO: What?! What did you say, viejas chismoleras?

ANITA SIN CARNITA: Que en la clase de geografía, el Federico Narices de Perico puede ver otros mundos, otras tierras y otras gentes, y en su mente, por lo menos, se puede escapar de este barrio.

DON ALBINO: ¿Escaparse de aquí? ¿De este barrio? How absurd! No one can escape from this barrio. Not even las cucarachas.

[*He whacks the porch rail with his gigantic flyswatter and kills a fly. There is the* SOUND *of a loud* WHACK! *when he does this.*]

SCHOOL KIDS [*waking up, yelling*]: ¡¿Cucarachas?!

[**SCHOOL KIDS EXIT** *running. The* **COMADRES EXIT** *inside. The* **TEACHER** *looks up from his/her book, looks around and sees that he/she is alone, and* **EXITS**, *a bit embarrassed.*]

DON ALBINO [*brushing the dead fly off his porch rail with his flyswatter*]: E pluribus unum.

[**DON ALBINO** *sits in his rocking chair, rocking slowly, eyes closed.* **FEDERICO** *gets up and walks slowly to one of the big rocks, squats down, and touches it, studying it intently.* **DON ALBINO** *opens his eyes and sees* **FEDERICO** *with his rock.*]

DON ALBINO [*yelling and sputtering like the Tasmanian Devil, ad-libbing curses*]: Oye, ¿tú? . . . !!

FEDERICO [*turning to* DON ALBINO *calmly*]: Who, me?

DON ALBINO [*still angry*]: Yes, [*ad-libbing expletives*] you . . . ! ¿Qué estás haciendo con mis piedras?

FEDERICO: I'm studying them.

DON ALBINO [*surprised by* FEDERICO'*s brashness*]: What? ¿Las estás estudiando? And what makes you think you know anything about *my* rocks?

FEDERICO: Estas piedras vinieron de un volcán. I know that they're volcanic rocks.

DON ALBINO: Volcanic? A ver—prove it to me.

FEDERICO [*pointing*]: See these holes? Cuando el volcano exploded a long, long time ago, the melting lava hit the cold air, and the hot gases inside the lava bubbled up and burst, creating these holes.

DON ALBINO [*with heavy Italnian accent*]: Ben travato, linguini.

[**FEDERICO** *looks puzzled.*]

¿No me entiendes?

FEDERICO: No.

DON ALBINO: Es italiano. Ben travato means that what you've just told me is bien pensado, plausible. And plausible means possible, and linguini es mi favorite pasta. Capici, Alfredo fettucini?

FEDERICO: No me llamo Alfredo; me llamo Federico. Are you Italian?

DON ALBINO: No, no, yo soy mexicano, just like you. But I know many, many languages from this book.

[DON ALBINO *reaches over the side of his rocking chair and picks up a giant book with the title* Dictionary of Foreign Phrases.]

FEDERICO [*reading title*]: Dictionary of Foreign Phrases.

[*He is impressed.*]

Can you say something else in Italian? Can you say something about volcanoes? About Vesuvius? Está en Italia, ¿qué no?

DON ALBINO [*pleased with* FEDERICO]: Vesuvius? Certainly. Está en Naples. [*Clearing his throat and gesturing with his arms like an accomplished orator*] Vedi Napoli e poi mouri!

FEDERICO: Wow!

DON ALBINO: That means "Go see Naples and then die."

FEDERICO: Die?

DON ALBINO: Sí, pero lo que de veras quiere decir es que Napoli is so beautiful that once you see it, nothing can compare to its beauty, so you may as well die because you'll never see anything as beautiful again, capici?

FEDERICO: Sí. [*Going to book and reading slowly*] Vedi Napoli e poi mouri. I can speak Italian!

DON ALBINO [*calling to his wife inside*]: Rebecca! Give this boy some cookies para que ya se vaya a su casa.

[DOÑA REBECCA CARNE SECA *hands* DON ALBINO *some cookies through the torn screen. Only her arm and hand are seen.* DON ALBINO *gives* FEDERICO *the cookies and watches him eat them.*]

DON ALBINO: I like you. Puedes venir a visitarme después de la escuela, and you can tell me all the things that you study, and I will teach you all the foreign languages that I know. Is it a deal?

[*He puts out his right hand to shake.*]

FEDERICO [*shaking his hand*]: Yes, it's a deal.

DON ALBINO [*standing up*]: Entonces . . . [*Fiercely, like a samurai warrior*] Sayonara!

FEDERICO [*mimicking him*]: Sayonara!

[FEDERICO *starts to* EXIT.]

DON ALBINO [*chuckling to himself*]: And don't you ever touch my rocks again.

[FEDERICO EXITS *happily, eating cookies. Happy polka* MUSIC *plays.*]

ANITA SIN CARNITA [*at her door, to audience*]: Y así fue que empezó el friendship de Don Albino Cara de Pepino y Federico Narices de Perico.

SOFIA SIN COSTILLA [*at her door*]: Federico visited Don Albino Cara de Pepino every day after school.

[FEDERICO ENTERS *running to* DON ALBINO, *and both converse and read the* Dictionary of Foreign Phrases *quietly.*]

ELENA SIN AVENA [*at her door*]: Y ahora que Federico had someone to talk to, someone who listened, who answered his questions. He started to like school, and geography became Don Albino Cara de Pepino's favorite subject also.

ANITA SIN CARNITA: Intercambiaban information muy seria al the beginning of each visit, pero después, mientras comían Danish rolls con peanut butter and honey ...

[DOÑA REBECCA *hands them goodies through torn screen door.*]

... the talk would turn to silly, funny things.

DON ALBINO [*telling a story*]: ... y luego, from way up in the clouds, the magic flying carpet stopped flying, y el bad boy fell to the earth and he didn't get his three wishes because he was not a good person.

[DON ALBINO *and* FEDERICO *both laugh. Pause.*]

Y tú, Federico, if you had tres deseos, what would they be?

FEDERICO: *Three* wishes? I only have *one* wish, and that's to beat the heck out of el Eddie Spaghetti, Tony Baloney, and Ramón Jamón.

DON ALBINO: Esos tontos buscan sus sueños en los tubos de goma. They search for their dreams in tubes of glue, pobrecitos. You should feel pity for them.

FEDERICO: Pity? As soon as they see me, they come and beat me up, and I want to beat them up, too. Especially el Eddie Spaghetti 'cause he's the one that gives them the order to beat me up.

DON ALBINO: Ah, yes, el Eddie Spaghetti. Él es tu bête noire, isn't he?

[FEDERICO *looks confused.*]

> Bête noire. Did you forget our French lesson already? Parlez vous français, s'il vous plaît?

FEDERICO: Oui, monsieur, but I forgot what bête noire means . . .

DON ALBINO: C'mon, Federico, acuérdate. Bête . . .

FEDERICO: No me diga—I remember now. Bête noire means "black beast"!

DON ALBINO: Sí, exacto. But that's only part of the meaning. Bête noire *does* mean the "black beast," but it also means that it's something that we're afraid of.

FEDERICO: Afraid?

DON ALBINO: Sí, mucho miedo y es algo que tenemos que conquistar.

FEDERICO: Conquer? Are you saying that I have to conquer Eddie Spaghetti?

DON ALBINO: Sí, because if you don't conquer the black beast, you will always live with that fear.

FEDERICO: But Eddie Spaghetti's bigger and stronger than I am. Y el Tony Baloney y el Ramón Jamón le ayudan.

DON ALBINO [*nonchalantly*]: Sí, pues, entonces ni modo.

FEDERICO [*changing the subject*]: Dígame, Don Albino Cara de Pepino, what are your three wishes? ¿Usted tiene tres deseos?

DON ALBINO: Oh sí, yo tengo tres deseos. [*Demonstrating dreamily*] I wish that I could fly en el cielo like a bird, that I could swim underwater like a fish sin un oxygen tank, that I could play the piano like a concert pianist, and that I could plant a seed aquí in this barrio and watch it grow.

FEDERICO: Pues *nothing* grows here. Besides—that's four wishes, and you only said three.

DON ALBINO: Sí, yo sé, yo sé. Tengo cuatro deseos. Pero mira, if you can wish for three, why not four? Or five? Or even one hundred wishes? The important thing is to work for your wishes, no matter how many or how impossible they may seem, ¿no crees?

FEDERICO: Okay, entonces my second wish after beating up Eddie Spaghetti would be to travel all over the world, to all the places we've studied in geography.

DON ALBINO [*wistfully*]: And would you return? Here? To this barrio, to
. . .

FEDERICO: Sí, Don Albino Cara de Pepino. Yo regresaría a este barrio—
and to you, mi amigo. And don't ask me for a *third* wish 'cause I
only have two.

ANITA SIN CARNITA [*at her door*]: Bueno pues, Don Albino Cara de Pepino
had to be satisfied with Federico's two wishes, pero—

ELENA SIN AVENA [*at her door*]: —since beating Eddie Spaghetti presented insurmountable fears, Federico concentrated en su segundo
deseo—

SOFIA SIN COSTILLA [*at her door*]: —and since no one knew more about
foreign lands than Don Albino Cara de Pepino, los dos se pasaban
horas planning Federico's itinerary.

[DOÑA REBECCA *hands them a world globe through the torn screen door.*]

DON ALBINO: Y aquí, [*pointing to a place on globe*] en Argentina, what are
you going to do?

FEDERICO: I'm going to sit around a bonfire con los gauchos de las pampas
and eat beefsteaks—mucha carne asada—over hot burning coals.

DON ALBINO [*spinning the globe and pointing*]: ¿Y aquí, en Japón?

FEDERICO: In Japan, I'm going to go to restaurants, ahí merito al lado
del agua, and I'm gonna pick my fresh fish or lobster right from
the water, and I'm gonna eat it crudo con soy sauce, just like the
Japanese!

DON ALBINO [*spinning the globe again and pointing*]: And in Europe? Los
museos, the churches—

FEDERICO: Voy a comer pastries con custard inside y chocolate on the outside, sitting at a sidewalk café, al fresco, watching the people stroll by.

DON ALBINO: Comiendo, siempre comiendo. You only think of the eating.
How starved you must be, muchacho!

FEDERICO: That's what I want to do in each country that I visit. Quiero
comer y comer todo lo que vea, and when I come back, that's what
I'll remember. The food.

DON ALBINO: Bueno, mañana you can tell me more, Federico. Even if it's
just about eating. Auf Wiedersehen.

FEDERICO: Auf Wiedersehen.

[*He* EXITS.]

ANITA SIN CARNITA: Y así se pasaban el tiempo, learning foreign words, planning Federico's trips—

ELENA SIN AVENA: —hasta que un día Federico stood in front of Don Albino Cara de Pepino holding a cut-in-half milk container con three puny plants inside.

[**FEDERICO ENTERS.**]

SOFIA SIN COSTILLA [*sniffing air*]: ¡Ay, comadre, se me queman los frijoles!

[*She* EXITS.]

ANITA SIN CARNITA: My beans are burning, too!

[*She* EXITS.]

ELENA SIN AVENA [*to audience*]: Well, *my* beans aren't burning 'cause I'm making Rosarita refried beans!

[*She giggles and then* EXITS.]

DON ALBINO: A ver, a ver. Let me see what you have there, Federico. [*Pinching a leaf and smelling it*] Tomate. The word comes from the indigenous Nahuatl. Tomatl. Remember cuando estudiamos los pueblos indígenas de México?

FEDERICO: Sí, señor. I wrote a report on the Mayas and Aztecas for my social studies class.

DON ALBINO: And you received an A, ¿verdad? The indigenous people sembraban tomates even before Christ was born. Y los Europeans thought tomatoes were poisonous. Idiotas.

[*Beat.*]

¿Vas a sembrarlas?

FEDERICO: Will they grow?

DON ALBINO [*annoyed at the stupid question, answering after a pause*]: That's entirely up to you.

[*Waves flyswatter to indicate that the visit is over, but* **FEDERICO** *doesn't want to leave.*]

FEDERICO [*hesitantly*]: I *do* want to plant them—will you help me? ¿Me ayuda?

DON ALBINO [*resistant*]: No, no. It takes too much work to grow anything here. Tú bien sabes que nothing grows here. You even said so yourself, ¿te acuerdas? When I made that fourth wish? Pues, you're right. How can anything grow here? The caliche in the worthless soil, el ardiente sol, the sun that shows no mercy, la gente que no le importa nada, uncaring people, the dust . . . Chihuahua . . . it's useless to try. ¿Para qué?

FEDERICO: No, it's not useless. ¿Por qué no me quiere ayudar? Please, help me. Together we can make them grow. Nomás dígame qué tengo que hacer, and I'll do what you tell me. Why won't you help me?

DON ALBINO [*hesitantly*]: Bueno, I'll help you, but it will take a lot of work. Mucho trabajo. Will you be able to do it?

FEDERICO: Oh sí, sí. Just tell me how, and I'll do it. I know I said that nothing ever grows in this barrio, but we can try, ¿qué no?

DON ALBINO: Sí, muchacho, podemos hacer try.

[**BOTH** *shake hands on deal.*]

FEDERICO: I used to plant wilted chinaberry leaves, ¿se acuerda? But I've never planted anything real.

DON ALBINO: Ni yo—tú vas a ser el primero.

FEDERICO: I'm gonna be the first what?

DON ALBINO: Nada. Never mind.

FEDERICO [*resolutely*]: Don Albino Cara de Pepino, I swear that you and I will eat tomatoes from these plants.

DON ALBINO: Careful, Federico. Ten cuidado. An oath is sacred. Recuerda: un juramento es sagrado. Ahi veremos if we get to eat your tomatoes—we'll see. [*Hitting porch rail with flyswatter for emphasis*] We'll see.

FEDERICO [*to audience*]: If I had known what I would be facing in the future with the stupid tomatoes, I never would have made that juramento.

DON ALBINO: Primero, Federico, necesitamos tierra buena del río bajo los árboles de mesquite.

FEDERICO [*running all over the stage as he follows* DON ALBINO's *orders*]: Manuel Cara de Pastel, can you lend me your wagon?

MANUEL [*stepping out of door 1*]: What for, Federico Narices de Perico?

FEDERICO: So I can get some good dirt from under the mesquite trees next to the river, across the freeway.

MANUEL: Okay, pues, but you better not let it get smashed by a semitruck, ¿me oyistes?

[*He hands* FEDERICO *his wagon and* EXITS.]

FEDERICO [*at door 2*]: ¿Doña María Ojos de Sandía?

DOÑA MARÍA [*at door*]: ¿Qué quieres, buqui mocoso?

FEDERICO: Can you lend me your shovel, ¿por favor?

DOÑA MARÍA: Take it, buqui inservible, but you'd better bring it right back as soon as you're done with it.

[*She gives him shovel and* EXITS.]

FEDERICO: Okay! [*Running to door 3*] Doña Andrea Panza de Jalea, can you lend me your water hose, please?

DOÑA ANDREA: Sí, take it, buqui travieso, but don't let Eddie Spaghetti, Tony Baloney, or Ramón Jamón steal it from you.

[*She gives him the hose and* EXITS.]

DON ALBINO [*with milk container in hand*]: A ver, a ver, Federico. Ahora, let's plant our tres matitas de tomate.

[*He goes to mound of dirt and kneels to plant.*]

LAS TRES COMADRES [*at their doors and in unison*]: Y así fue, que con la ayuda de algunos del barrio, Federico y Don Albino Cara de Pepino sembraron las tres matitas de tomate. In English: and that's how it happened, that with the help from some persons in the barrio, Federico and Don Albino Cara de Pepino planted the three tomato plants.

ANITA SIN CARNITA: But it was more with Don Albino Cara de Pepino's help, his consejos y patience that the plants thrived.

SOFIA SIN COSTILLA: Pero siempre, there were a lot of problems—two of the plants died the very next day.

DON ALBINO [*to* FEDERICO]: No te preocupes, Federico. Anyway, the weakest plants would've had to be pulled out.

FEDERICO: ¿Por qué, Don Albino? Why couldn't the three plants grow together?

DON ALBINO: Because one plant needs to get all the strength from the soil, muchacho. The other two would've just sapped it all and then none of the three would grow—that's just how it is.

ELENA SIN AVENA [*at her door*]: Pasaron las semanas y siempre había nuevos problemas con la planta de tomate.

FEDERICO: Don Albino Cara de Pepino!!! The tomato plant has little bugs, munchos animalitos.

DON ALBINO: Son pulgones, aphids. To get rid of them, wash the leaves carefully with soap . . . con el jabón Tide.

[FEDERICO *washes leaves.*]

ANITA SIN CARNITA: The plant recovered from los animalitos aphids, pero luego it developed un fungus infection—

SOFIA SIN COSTILLA: —and Federico panicked, and instead of going to Don Albino Cara de Pepino—

ELENA SIN AVENA: —he ran to Doña Faustina Patas de Gallina—

DOÑA FAUSTINA: Mira, Federico Narices de Perico, for the fungus, lo mejor es agua remojada en cigarros.

FEDERICO: Water soaked in cigarettes?

DOÑA FAUSTINA: Aha.

[*She* EXITS.]

ELENA SIN AVENA: Federico went home and collected all of his mother's cigarette butts and soaked them in an empty Pepsi-Cola bottle and watered his plant.

LAS TRES COMADRES [*in unison*]: The plant almost died!

DON ALBINO: ¿Tabaco? ¡Vieja ignorante! ¿Qué sabe la Doña Faustina Patas de Gallina de plantas anyway? All she has is plastic geraniums in those coffee cans. Tobacco? That's the worst thing you can do to tomatoes! Mira, Federico, what you need is bleach—

FEDERICO: Bleach?

DON ALBINO: Sí, como Clorox. Una cucharada grande, one tablespoon, to one quart of water, and wash the leaves gently, lava cada hoja suavemente. That will protect our ripening tomatoes.

[LAS TRES COMADRES *step out of their doors and go toward the plant.*]

LAS TRES COMADRES [*laughing*]: Ripening tomatoes? ¿A cuáles "ripening tomatoes?"

[*They* **EXIT** *through their doors, still laughing.*]

DON ALBINO: No les hagas caso, Federico. Las tres comadres mitoteras don't know anything.

FEDERICO: Pero las comadres mitoteras tienen razón, Don Albino Cara de Pepino. There's no "ripening tomatoes."

DON ALBINO: Ah, not yet, Federico, but soon, espérate a los chicharrones, we'll have them. Mira. [*Taking him closer to the plant*] You see? Fíjate bien.

[**SPECIAL EFFECT CUE**: *The plant slowly grows to about two feet.*]

FEDERICO [*inspecting the plant, amazed*]: I see little flowers, Don Albino Cara de Pepino. Are they gonna change into tomatoes?

DON ALBINO: Sí, Federico, muy pronto vas a ver unos tomatitos.

FEDERICO [*impatiently*]: When, Don Albino Cara de Pepino, ¿cuándo?

DON ALBINO: Calmantes montes, alacranes pintos, pájaros volando y un caracol en la frente.

FEDERICO [*thoroughly bewildered*]: Huh?!

LAS TRES COMADRES [*at their doors, attempting to translate but getting mixed up, in unison*]: Patience, patience, Federico, spotted scorpions, birds flying, and a seashell on your forehead . . . Whatever.

DON ALBINO: Calmantes montes, Federico. You have to be patient.

[**DON ALBINO** *goes to sleep.*]

ANITA SIN CARNITA: Never mind the calmantes montes—what is important to note is that Federico's troubles had just begun, and there would be times when he would feel like pulling the plant out by its roots and letting it die in the hot Arizona sun.

ELENA SIN AVENA: But he was afraid of Don Albino Cara de Pepino and the look he would surely give Federico if he let the plant die.

SOFIA SIN COSTILLA: Remember, Federico had made an oath.

LAS TRES COMADRES [*in unison*]: Sí, y un juramento es *sagrado*.

[*They* **EXIT**.]

FEDERICO [*to audience*]: Oh sure, an oath is sacred, but Don Albino Cara de Pepino doesn't have to do anything to keep la mensa plant alive, does he?

[LA JEFITA ENTERS, *smoking, Pepsi in hand and complaining full speed as* FEDERICO *tends to his plant.*]

LA JEFITA: You're spending all your time with that stupid plant, Federico. Te la pasas espantando los pájaros that want to eat the white blossoms. You have to protect it from all los perros de la vecinda that want to lie down on the cool, moist dirt. The hot sun's wilting all the leaves. Tienes que venir de la escuela every lunch time nomás pa' ponerle the piece of canvas you had to borrow from Manuel Cara de Pastel's father. Y de pilón, yesterday, we had a hailstorm that almost knocked off whatever tomatoes the stupid plant had. [*Turning to exit, stopping, and turning to continue*] Y estás gastando muncha agua, did you see how high the water bill was this month? And if the stupid tomato plant dies after all this, it will all be your own fault.

[ALL ENTER *and form conga line behind* LA JEFITA *and sing and dance as they did before.*]

ALL: Tú tienes la culpa, tú tienes la culpa.

[*They* EXIT.]

LAS TRES COMADRES [*at their doors, in unison*]: And despite all this, the plant kept growing. Y a pesar de todo esto, la planta siguió creciendo.

[SPECIAL EFFECTS CUE: *Plant grows slowly higher and higher to almost six feet.*]

ANITA SIN CARNITA: Pero, un día, Federico was sitting on the ground, admiring his plant, cuando all of a sudden le salió the ugliest, fattest, green gusano!

[SPOT LIGHT: *A green* TOMATO HORNWORM *dances out from behind the leaves. Ravel's "Bolero" begins to play.* FEDERICO *and* TOMATO HORNWORM *dance.* FEDERICO *is timid, afraid, and the* TOMATO HORNWORM *is seductive, menacing. The* TOMATO HORNWORM EXITS, *leaving a frightened, cowering* FEDERICO.]

FEDERICO [*running to* DON ALBINO *and shaking him*]: Don Albino Cara de Pepino! Wake up, Don Albino Cara de Pepino!

DON ALBINO [*waking up, startled*]: ¿Qué pasó? ¿Qué te pasa, muchacho?

FEDERICO [*barely catching his breath*]: Un gusanote, Don Albino Cara de Pepino. Our tomato plant has a big fat green worm!

DON ALBINO: ¿Un gusanote grande, gordo y verde?

[FEDERICO *nods yes.*]

> ¿Y la cola? Did you see its tail?

FEDERICO: Oh sí, Don Albino Cara de Pepino, le vi la cola.

DON ALBINO: ¿Y tenía cuernos en la cola?

FEDERICO: Yes, it had horns on the tail.

DON ALBINO: Ah, sí, it's the Tomato Hornworm. O como decimos en Latino: ¡el gusanitis verditis con cuernitis en la [*pronouncing this to rhyme with "eetis"*] colitis! [*Laughing at his own joke*] It's not poisonous, pero you have to kill it before it lays eggs on the leaves. Y si no lo matas, the plant will disappear right in front of your eyes. Lo tienes que matar. You must kill it!

FEDERICO: Kill it? [*Gulping*] With my hands?

DON ALBINO [*sarcastically*]: Or with your feet. ¿Qué? Are you afraid? ¿Le tienes miedo?

FEDERICO [*lying*]: No . . . oo . . . oo.

DON ALBINO: Anda pues, pronto, go kill it. Como dicen los franceses: la mort sans phrases. La muerte sin una palabra. Death without a word. ¿Qué? Did you forget another French lesson?

FEDERICO: No. Parlez vous français?

DON ALBINO: Oui. Bueno, ve.

[DON ALBINO *settles down on his rocking chair and promptly falls asleep.*]

FEDERICO [*with strong resolve*]: I *will* kill the green tomato hornworm.

[LAS TRES COMADRES ENTER *and prepare* FEDERICO *for battle. They give him a bent, dirty garbage can lid as a shield, a wooden fence stake as a sword, and a bucket as a helmet. A stirring march plays, then* EDDIE SPAGHETTI, TONY BALONEY, *and* RAMÓN JAMÓN ENTER *with their giant boom box between them. The march stops abruptly and loud rap is played. The three stand with a menacing pose.*]

LAS TRES COMADRES [*in unison*]: ¡Benditos sean los dulces nombres del cielo!

[LAS TRES COMADRES EXIT. EDDIE SPAGHETTI, TONY BALONEY, *and* RAMÓN JAMÓN *set down the boom box and strut/dance across stage toward tomato plant. With identical synchronized slow-motion moves, they raise their feet to stomp on the plant. The march music plays again.*]

FEDERICO: Stop!

[EDDIE SPAGHETTI, TONY BALONEY, *and* RAMÓN JAMÓN FREEZE.]

> [*Strongly*] ¡Quítense de mi planta!

[*The three break* FREEZE, *turn and walk menacingly toward* FEDERICO.]

EDDIE SPAGHETTI: This *your* plant?

FEDERICO: Sí.

TONY BALONEY: Well, ese, we don't like it.

RAMÓN JAMÓN: So we're gonna stomp it down.

[*He turns toward the plant.*]

FEDERICO: Oh no, you're not. That's my plant, so get away from it . . . NOW!

[FEDERICO's *shout wakens* DON ALBINO, *and he rises slowly from his rocking chair and watches them intently.*]

EDDIE SPAGHETTI: And if we don't, ese? ¿Qué vas hacer?

TONY BALONEY AND RAMÓN JAMÓN: Órale, what are you gonna do . . . punk?

[FEDERICO *hesitates. He looks at* DON ALBINO, *who gives a nod and a "go ahead" signal.*]

FEDERICO: If you don't get away from my plant . . . I'll fight you.

EDDIE, TONY, AND RAMÓN [*in unison*]: Órale pues, ponte.

LAS TRES COMADRES [*at their doors, in unison*]: Uhhhh, el Federico Narices de Perico por fin se va defender.

[ALL OTHERS ENTER *and group themselves around* FEDERICO *and the* THREE *to watch the fight. There is a brief choreographed fight, almost dance-like as* FEDERICO *beats up* EDDIE, TONY, *and* RAMÓN, *who* EXIT *with their tails between their legs.* FEDERICO *starts to cross toward* DON ALBINO *when* LA JEFITA ENTERS.]

LA JEFITA [*starting her usual harangue at* FEDERICO]: ¿Cuántas veces te he dicho not to go around fighting? Es tu culpa que you always end up getting beat.

FEDERICO: But not this time, 'Amá. I finally beat them.

LA JEFITA [*somewhat illogically*]: Pues por eso te digo, no andes peleando—you'll hurt someone. Y luego, ¿qué voy hacer si me hacen sue? Todo esto es tu culpa, Federico. It's your own fault.

[*She starts to* EXIT, *and the longer conga line forms behind her.*]

ALL [*singing in the conga line*]: Tú tienes la culpa, tú tienes la culpa.

FEDERICO [*forcefully*]: No! It's not my fault!

[*Conga line stops with kick in midair and turns to him.*]

No es mi culpa. You're always saying everything is my fault, but it's not. They were going to kill my tomato plant, and I couldn't let them do that. Do you understand? So stop saying it's all my own fault.

[LA JEFITA *is openmouthed and speechless as she looks at the others for their support, but they are in total agreement with* FEDERICO, *so she starts to* EXIT *right near the plant. The* TOMATO HORNWORM ENTERS. LA JEFITA *steps back, almost in a faint, but someone catches her. Some martial* MUSIC *begins to play.* ALL *move back as* FEDERICO *picks up his "sword," and he and the* TOMATO HORNWORM *dance a stylized dance until* FEDERICO *stabs the* TOMATO HORNWORM. *The* TOMATO HORNWORM *lurches around the stage in very dramatic agony and finally* EXITS *and dies offstage.* ALL *gather around* FEDERICO *and the plant.*]

LAS TRES COMADRES [*in unison*]: Nothing else happened to the tomato plant, y pronto, la planta estaba llenita de tomates.

[ALL *step away from the plant and the plant now magically has many giant red tomatoes hanging on it!*]

ANITA SIN CARNITA: Eddie Spaghetti, Tony Baloney, and Ramón Jamón never came near the plant OR Federico again.

ELENA SIN AVENA: Y llego el día que Federico finally went to Don Albino Cara de Pepino—

SOFIA SIN COSTILLA: —with two of the largest, reddest tomatoes.

DON ALBINO [*very proudly holding up the two tomatoes*]: Estos tomates tienen que ser los tomates más hermosos que yo he visto en mi vida. Have you ever seen any tomatoes more beautiful than these, Federico?

FEDERICO: At Safeway's, maybe?

DON ALBINO: No, no, no, muchacho! Those don't count. Don't you know that they spray the fields with poisons? And that they cut the tomatoes when they're still green, and they put them into train cars and inject them with chemicals to make them red. Es para matar un cristiano, no, te digo, *these* are the most beautiful.

FEDERICO: Dice bien, Don Albino Cara de Pepino, estos son los tomates más hermosos que yo he visto en mi vida.

[FEDERICO *sits down next to* DON ALBINO. *They eat tomatoes slowly.*]

ANITA SIN CARNITA: Federico and Don Albino Cara de Pepino each ate their tomato slowly, savoring the taste.

ELENA SIN AVENA: Lentamente, saboreando el sabor del tomate.

SOFIA SIN COSTILLA: It was the best tomato Federico had ever eaten in his entire life. They did not speak for a long time, and then Don Albino Cara de Pepino sighed and asked Federico something.

DON ALBINO: Ahora, Federico, dime, what will you see—o mejor dicho, ¿qué vas a comer?—what will you eat when you get to México, the first country you now plan to visit?

[DON ALBINO *leans back, eyes closed, but listening intently.*]

FEDERICO: In Mexico . . .

[*The* COMADRES *step out and unroll the canvas on their doors. They secure the bottoms of the canvas, and the paintings of the pyramids, gods, etc., can be seen.*]

> . . . Yes, in Mexico City—¿usted sabe, Don Albino Cara de Pepino, that's Tenochtitlán?—I'll visit the Museo de Antropología, Chapultepec, el Palacio de Bellas Artes . . .

[ALL *move closer and sit down, forming a tight circle, and they listen.*]

> . . . and I'll go to Teotihuacán, the city of the Aztec gods, and see las pirámides del sol y de la luna . . .

LAS TRES COMADRES [*in unison*]: Federico and Don Albino Cara de Pepino dreamed, los dos soñaron, y era un sueño tan hermoso que lo compartieron con todos nosotros. They shared their dream with us, and we *all* dreamed the beautiful dream together.

MUSIC: *Triumphant, or indigenous, Aztec.*

LIGHTS: DOWN *and* OUT.

END OF THIRD ACTO

TWO

Amor de hija

(A Daughter's Love)

Synopsis

Amor de hija is a story that encompasses four generations: there is Tata Arcenio and Nana Cuquita, their daughter Consuelo (Connie) and her husband Rogelio (Roy), their grandchildren Junior, Kathy, and Danny; and their great-grandchildren Heather and the newborn baby. The protagonist is Consuelo, a forceful and confident woman in her mid-forties who is discovering new freedom now that her children are grown and on their own. The construction company that she owns with her husband is doing well, and she no longer has to work full-time as the company's bookkeeper; instead she now works part-time out of her home. Her life changes abruptly when Tata Arcenio dies suddenly on Nana Cuquita's sixty-fifth birthday. The death affects Nana Cuquita profoundly, and she begins to deteriorate physically, mentally, and emotionally.

When it becomes evident that Nana Cuquita is suffering from memory loss, possibly Alzheimer's disease or another form of dementia, Consuelo—as the eldest daughter—must become responsible for her mother. As Nana Cuquita's illness worsens, the roles of Consuelo and her mother are reversed. Nana Cuquita becomes childlike, and Consuelo has to take care of all her needs. This role-reversal causes even more conflict when Rogelio, who is going through some kind of midlife crisis, deeply resents Consuelo's new obligations. Rogelio looks for—and finds—the attention he wants in his new receptionist, an ambitious and calculating single woman in her early thirties. This makes Consuelo feel very jealous, threatened, and vulnerable, and she is pulled by her instinctual and emotional drives, which are sure to doom her marriage. Consuelo is finally forced to choose between her mother and her husband, and her decision *almost* rips the marriage apart. It is only with the strong familial bond forged by Nana Cuquita before her illness that the family survives at the end.

Cast

CONSUELO MADRIGAL, *in her mid-forties*

ROGELIO MADRIGAL, *Consuelo's husband, in his mid-forties*

DOÑA MARÍA DEL REFUGIO (NANA CUQUITA), *Consuelo's mother, age sixty-five, has a beautiful singing voice*

DON ARCENIO (TATA ARCENIO), *Nana Cuquita's husband, in his late sixties, handsome, and distinguished. The same actor may also play Young Arcenio at the end.*

KATHY, *Consuelo and Rogelio's oldest daughter, a single parent in her mid-twenties*

HEATHER, *Kathy's daughter, a very smart six-year-old*

JUNIOR, *Connie and Roy's oldest son, a recent college graduate in his early twenties*

DANNY, *Connie and Roy's youngest son, age nineteen or twenty and newly married*

NORMA, *Danny's eighteen-year-old wife*

LA RECEPTIONIST, *a single woman in her early thirties, never named*

COMADRE ROSIE, *Consuelo's sister-in-law, who is married to Consuelo's brother Demetrio. She dresses to fight her age.*

COMPADRE DEMETRIO, *Consuelo's older brother and Junior's godfather. He is in his late forties and dresses cowboy style.*

PRAYER LEADER

COOK, *a chef at Junior's peña*

ANGÉLICA MARTÍNEZ, *a raffle winner at the peña*

YOUNG NANA CUQUITA, *wears a cherry-colored dress with white collar*

YOUNG TATA ARCENIO, *wears a guayabera shirt*

EVERYBODY, *party-goers, cook, gossipers, etc., for* IMÁGENES *and any necessary set changes during scene transitions*

Technical Notes

TIME

1990s, but historical references such as presidents' names, dates, and countries may be updated to the present, and local references such as bars, stores, etc., may be changed to fit other locations of play.

PLACE

A Southwestern town such as Tucson, Arizona, or San Antonio, Texas.

SET

Very simple set, with platforms and ramps of varying heights and ten or twelve boxes for individual or group seating. These boxes may be used separately as chairs or they may be joined to form tables, file cabinets, a refrigerator, the coffin, etc. The boxes' colors are neutral browns, beiges, tans, etc., on some of the sides, and brilliant reds, yellows, blues, etc., on other sides, so they can be changed depending on mood or setting of each scene.

The different stage areas are defined by lighting and/or music and colors. Set changes are done by "dancers" or "workers" who may or may not dance as they change set.

COSTUMES

Contemporary dress, usually in bright colors, except in the funeral IMA-GEN. They should be very easy to change between scenes as needed.

MUSIC

As indicated on IMAGEN and transitions, preshow and intermission music should be old, scratchy-sounding records. Some of the songs within actions are "Las mañanitas," a Mexican "happy birthday" song, which seems to be public domain, with unknown songwriter(s) and many different verses; "Sin ti," which was a hit by Los Panchos in the 1950s, written by Pepe Guizar; "Solamente una vez," which was composed by Agustín Lara in the 1940s (the English translation is "You Belong to my Heart" by Bing Crosby); "Júrame," which was composed by María Greber in 1926; "Toda una vida" by Oswaldo Farres; and "Naranjas dulces," which is in the public domain. Other songs may be selected as suggested within script.

IMÁGENES

These are visual images that Consuelo associates with her emotional distress. They are very stylized and choreographed with surrealistic quality. The IMÁGENES are very dependent on light, music, and other actors' responses or reactions and end in FREEZE. If necessary, the director may change blocking and order of FREEZES, LIGHTS, and MUSIC cues.

LANGUAGE

The dialogue is bilingual (Spanish and English). TATA ARCENIO and NANA CUQUITA speak only Spanish but understand English. CONSUELO, ROG-ELIO, and JUNIOR speak and understand both Spanish and English and code-switch frequently. DANNY, NORMA, KATHY, and HEATHER speak only English. CONSUELO and COMADRE ROSIE sometimes use the formal (usted) and sometimes informal (tú).

ACT I

Introduction

MUSIC: *Romantic, contemporary.*

LIGHTS: UP.

IMAGEN: *Máscaras en el espejo (Masks in the Mirror).*

[CONSUELO ENTERS *and sits downstage center, and with very stylized movements, she pantomimes applying makeup, brushing hair, etc.* ROGELIO ENTERS *and places his hands on* CONSUELO's *shoulders. She looks up and both smile at each other with tenderness.* FREEZE.]

Scene 1

TIME: *7:00 p.m.*

PLACE: CONSUELO *and* ROGELIO's *home.*

LIGHTS: UP *on all stage areas.*

MUSIC: *Riotous polka.*

[*A surprise party is in full swing before* NANA CUQUITA, *the guest of honor, arrives.* EVERYBODY—*relatives and friends—is drinking and dancing.*]

HEATHER [*to* CONSUELO]: Grandma Connie, when are my Nana Cuquita and Tata Arcenio coming to the party?

CONSUELO: Soon, I hope. Your Uncle Junior's bringing them; they think he's treating them to hot dogs at El Güero Canelo, but—

HEATHER: I know! It's a surprise birthday party for my nana! How old is my nana?

CONSUELO: Sixty-five.

HEATHER: Sixty-five! That's old! Were there dinosaurs when my Nana Cuquita was born?

CONSUELO [*laughing*]: No, I don't think so, and don't you dare ask her that!

KATHY [*yelling over*]: Mom! Dad! Hurry up if you want us to practice "Las mañanitas" before they get here. Hurry!

ROGELIO [*impatiently grouping relatives*]: Hey! Stop drinking all the tequila. C'mon, we don't have a lot of time. Comiencen. [*Singing*]

"Estas son las mañanitas que cantaba el Rey David, a las mucha-chas bonitas se las cantamos así. Despierta—"

KATHY: But, Dad, I don't know the words.

ROGELIO: "Mi bien despierta." [*Speaking in tune as though he is still singing* "Las mañanitas"] That's why you were supposed to rehearse yes-terday! "Ya los pajarillos cantan—"

CONSUELO: Start again, honey.

ROGELIO [*still singing*]: "—La luna ya se metió . . ."

CONSUELO [*to* COMADRE ROSIE *and* COMPADRE DEMETRIO *and* OTHER *party members who are entering*]: Pasen, pasen. Come in. ¡Comadre! ¡Compadre! ¡Qué bueno que vinieron! Roy, honey, ven a saludar. [*To* COMPADRES] Roy wants us to learn this song before my Mom and Dad get here. "Las mañanitas."

COMADRE ROSIE: "Las mañanitas?" I already know it! [*Singing*] "Qué linda está la mañana en vengo a saludarte."

[OTHERS *join in.*]

"Venimos todos con gusto y placer a felicitarte."

ROGELIO: Hey! Not everybody's singing. Compadre, ¿por qué no está cantando?

COMPADRE DEMETRIO: Porque no sé las palabras, compa.

ROGELIO: You don't know the words to "Las mañanitas?" Everybody knows it.

COMPADRE DEMETRIO [*sheepishly*]: Pues yo no, compadre. ¿Cómo va? A ver, hum me a few bars.

COMADRE ROSIE: Bars? ¿Ya ve, comadre? ¿Cómo cuando se trata de bars *eso sí sabe?*

ROGELIO [*to* CONSUELO]: Honey, what happened to the copies you were supposed to make for everybody?

CONSUELO: ¡Las copias! Ay, Roy, I forgot. [*To* COMADRE ROSIE] Vamos, comadre, por las copias.

COMADRE ROSIE: ¿Adónde, comadre?

CONSUELO: A mi oficina.

COMADRE ROSIE: Ay, no, comadre. It's too far to your office.

CONSUELO: Didn't you know, Rosie? [*Proudly*] *Aquí* está mi oficina.

COMADRE ROSIE: ¿Aquí?

CONSUELO: Sí. I made Danny's room into my office. C'mon.

[*Others tease* CONSUELO: *"O-O-Oh, tiene su office en la casa," etc., and* CON-SUELO *and* COMADRE ROSIE *walk over to "office" area.*]

CONSUELO [*showing* COMADRE ROSIE]: ¿Ya ve, comadre? Aquí tengo todo. Roy brought the files from the office y me compró un new computer so I can do everything right here without even leaving the house.

COMADRE ROSIE: You don't have to go to the office anymore?

CONSUELO: Well, I still have to go when I have to pick up the time cards and to leave the workers' checks on payday. Or when I want to drag Roy out to have lunch with me. The work was too slow—ya sabe cómo es el construction, and here I can do the work in half the time and still have time for other things.

COMADRE ROSIE: ¡Qué suave! I wish I could work at home. [*Quickly*] I mean, for *pay.*

CONSUELO: No, no se crea que tan suave. Sometimes I think that I work el doble. Pero, you know, Rosie? It feels so nice to be alone, to be my own boss. I really enjoy my freedom. I put the CDs on, have a cup of herbal tea, read, water my plants, and I lounge around—

COMADRE ROSIE: —Naked! Uhh, that's what I would do, comadre, if I stayed home.

CONSUELO: ¡Ay, Rosie, no te aguantas! What I was gonna say is that I lounge around in my pajamas all day like a lazy cat!

COMADRE ROSIE: Pues siempre que suave poder trabajar en su casa. ¿Y qué hace mi Compadre Rogelio without you?

CONSUELO [*laughing*]: Oh, he manages. He just hired a receptionist. [*To herself*] Ay, ¿Cómo se llama? [*To* COMADRE ROSIE] You know, to answer the phone, take work orders for the crew, just simple stuff 'cause she's barely learning English. [*Getting the copies*] Here's the copies, comadre.

[*She starts to walk back to the party.*]

COMADRE ROSIE [*stopping* CONSUELO]: Oiga, comadre; ¿está . . . sexy?

CONSUELO: Sexy? ¿Quién?

COMADRE ROSIE: La receptionist, Connie. ¿Está sexy?

CONSUELO: Not really. In fact, está poco feíta. Pero muy simpática. I can't describe her—she's not really pretty, but she has a real nice way about her.

COMADRE ROSIE: Nice? ¿Cómo qué?

CONSUELO: Bueno pues, pone atención cuando uno le habla. I've talked to her on the phone and she really listens to you . . . she's nice.

COMADRE ROSIE: Pero fea.

CONSUELO [laughing]: Ay, Rosie, I didn't say that!

COMADRE ROSIE: Bueno, pues, feíta y sexy.

CONSUELO: I didn't say that either!

COMADRE ROSIE: Yo sé, yo sé. But if you ask me, parece una buena mosca muerta, so watch out, comadre, *those* are the worst!

[*Both laugh and they return to the party area and pass out the copies of the song to everybody.*]

EVERYBODY [*reading and singing*]: "El día en que tú naciste, nacieron todas las flores, y en la pila del bautismo cantaron los ruiseñores. Quisiera ser solecito para entrar por tu ventana y darte los buenos días acostadita en tu cama."

[*As soon as they sing the word "cama," the group breaks up and ad-libs, telling jokes about beds, water beds, etc.*]

ROGELIO [*annoyed at lack of seriousness*]: All right—someone's flat. ¿Quién está cantando flat?

COMADRE ROSIE: Pues, la Kathy, who else?

KATHY [*indignantly, looking down at her breasts*]: I am not flat.

COMADRE ROSIE: You've all heard of the eighteen-hour bra? Pues, la Kathy usa el *half-hour* bra!

[ALL *laugh and tease* KATHY: *"No le hagas caso, Kathy . . ."*]

ROGELIO: Okay, that's it! If you're not gonna be serious, I'm just wasting my time. Forget it.

[CONSUELO *comes and stands next to* ROGELIO.]

CONSUELO [*forcefully to* EVERYBODY]: Hey! Roy's put in a lot of work into this, and now I want every single one of you to behave and show him some respect, ¿me oyeron?

COMPADRE DEMETRIO: Ándenle pues, vamos a portarnos bien. Okay, Roy, dale gas.

EVERYONE [*singing*]: "Quisiera ser un San Juan, quisiera ser un San Pedro, pa' venirte a saludar con la música del cielo. Volaron cuatro palomas por toditas las ciudades y por ser día de tu santo te deseamos felicidades. ¡Con jazmines y flores este día quiero adornar, hoy por ser día de tu santo te venimos a cantar!"

HEATHER: Here comes my nana and my tata!

[ALL *run to peek, but* ROGELIO *stops them in their tracks.*]

ROGELIO: Places, everyone, places. Remember, my suegra is a very special lady, and we're gonna sing "Las mañanitas" perfectly. No quiero que la rieguen. Per-fec-to. [*Remembering*] Ah, y nada de "sapos verdes to you," ¿me oyeron? ¿Listos?

COMPADRE DEMETRIO: "Sapos verdes to you, sapos verdes to you—"

[ROGELIO *glares at* COMPADRE DEMETRIO, *who instantly gets serious.* NANA CUQUITA *and* TATA ARCENIO ENTER *with* JUNIOR. NANA CUQUITA *and* TATA ARCENIO *stand at center stage surrounded by* EVERYBODY.]

EVERYBODY: Surprise! Happy Birthday! [*Ad-libbing, exchanging hugs and kisses, singing loudly*] "Estas son las mañanitas que cantaba el Rey David, a las muchachas bonitas se las cantamos así. Despierta—"

IMAGEN: *El amor para mi madre (The Love for My Mother)*

[*Singing continues, lower, and* CONSUELO *moves away from the group and watches intently as the group sings.* TATA ARCENIO *looks lovingly at* NANA CUQUITA.]

LIGHTS: *Slow* DOWN.

EVERYBODY [*singing softly*]: "Despierta mi bien, despierta, mira que ya amaneció, ya los pajarillos cantan, la luna ya se metió . . ."

[ALL FREEZE.]

LIGHTS: DOWN *and* OUT.

END OF SCENE 1

* * *

Scene 2

TIME: *Late at night. The party's almost over.*

PLACE: *Still at* ROGELIO *and* CONSUELO'*s home.*

MUSIC: *Party polka.*

LIGHTS: UP.

[EVERYBODY'*s eating cake, drinking, joking, etc.* DANNY *and* NORMA ENTER *with their crying baby. The baby can be a doll and the baby's crying can be recorded sound effects.*]

CONSUELO: Danny! Norma! It's about time! The party's almost over! I thought you guys weren't coming.

NORMA: It's baby Danny—he hasn't stopped crying since Danny got home from work.

DANNY: And he threw up, Mom.

ROGELIO: Does he have a fever?

NORMA: No, he just cries. Should we take him to the doctor?

CONSUELO: Yes, if he's throwing up.

ROGELIO: A la mejor está empachado.

NORMA: Empachado? [*With English pronunciation*] What's that?

CONSUELO: It's when something sticks to the . . . tripas. [*To* ROGELIO] ¿Cómo se dice "tripas," honey?

ROGELIO: Tripe.

NORMA: Tripe? Like in menudo? Yuck, I hate menudo.

ROGELIO: Did you give him bubblegum?

DANNY: Dad, how could we give the baby *bubblegum?*

ROGELIO: Well, you never know with you kids nowadays.

DANNY: We didn't give him bubblegum—besides, the doctors don't even believe in [*also pronouncing it with an English accent*] empachados anymore.

ROGELIO: No te creas, Danny. Remember, Connie, aquel foreman que tenía last year? He couldn't work for over a month, and the gringo doctors couldn't figure out what was wrong with him. He almost died. ¿Qué comió que se empachó? Sardines?

CONSUELO: No sé, Roy. [*Taking the baby from* NORMA] But I know they didn't give the baby sardines. Let's take him to my bedroom. It's too noisy here. [*To* DANNY] Si sigue malito, we'll go with you to the doctor's.

[CONSUELO *and* NORMA *go to "bedroom" area.*]

NORMA: I get so scared when I don't know why he's crying.

CONSUELO: I know. And they can't tell us what's hurting them. Pobrecito.

NORMA: Do you think it's serious?

CONSUELO [*feeling baby's forehead*]: He doesn't seem to have a temperature, but it could be an ear infection.

[*Baby cries louder.* NORMA *takes baby from* CONSUELO *and pats his back frantically.* NANA CUQUITA ENTERS.]

NANA CUQUITA: ¿Y qué tiene el niño?

NORMA [*distraught*]: He's destripado, Nana!

NANA CUQUITA: ¿Destripado?

NORMA: Yes, something's stuck to his menudo, Nana, but I swear we didn't give him sardines!

NANA CUQUITA [*perplexed*]: Ay, Consuelo, ¿qué me dice?

CONSUELO: We think the baby's empachado, y lo vamos a llevar al doctor.

NANA CUQUITA: A ver, dame al niño. [*Taking the baby and checking him over in a very efficient, experienced manner; to* CONSUELO] Más bien tiene cólico. ¿Tienes manzanilla?

CONSUELO: No, but my neighbor does. She's always drinking it for her nerves. [*Explaining as an afterthought*] She's from Mexico—they like to use herbs for *everything*.

NANA CUQUITA: Pues mándale pedir un tantito para hacerle un té al niño.

CONSUELO: Norma, go next door to Doña Rosalía and ask her for a little manzanilla for the baby.

NORMA [*hesitantly*]: Man-zan-i-ya?

NANA CUQUITA [*grumbling a bit*]: ¡Ay, Dios mío, estas criaturas que no saben hablar la lengua cristiana!—

CONSUELO [*interrupting and defending* NORMA's *lack of Spanish*]: Pero lo entiende muy bien, Mom. [*To* NORMA] Go on, Norma. Después we'll get some manzanilla at Food City so you can always have some on hand for the baby. [*To* NANA CUQUITA] Voy a hervir l'agua.

[CONSUELO *and* NORMA EXIT.]

NANA CUQUITA [*talking to herself as she tends to the baby*]: Esta juventud de hoy en día no saben nada. Ni se cuidan en la dieta. Salen del hospital en la mañana y ya pa' la tarde andan de compras en el Kmart, o peor, bailando cumbias en el casino. ¿Adónde dejé mi bolsa? [*Looking around and calling out*] ¿Arcenio, bajaste mi bolsa del carro? [*Finding her purse*] Ah, aquí está. [*Taking a bottle of olive oil out of her purse and pouring a bit into her palm as she talks*] Un tantito de aceite de olivo, aceite de comer, pa' todo sirve. [*Rubbing palms together to warm up oil*] Calientito pa' no asustarlo. [*Rubbing it on baby's stomach*] Pobrecito, tiene el estomaguito bien duro. [*Checking baby's feet*] Y los piecitos bien helados. Le va a entrar frío al inocente. [*Bundling up baby*] Así, bien envuelto como un tamalito de frijol.

[NORMA *and* CONSUELO ENTER.]

CONSUELO: Ya está hirviendo el agua, Mom. ¿Cuánta manzanilla le echo?

NANA CUQUITA: ¿Qué ya se te olvidó? [*Giving directions*] Mira, échale un puñito. Pero que lo haga [*pointing to* NORMA, *who's checking out her fingernails*] ella. [*To* NORMA] Mira, pon atención. [*Taking some manzanilla from the baggie*] Echa esta manzanilla al agua, y cuando se ponga el agua color amarillito, apágale la lumbre. Espera un ratito que se enfríe un poco. Cuélasela a su botella y agrégale un tantitio de azúcar. No mucha, tantitito pa' que no le dé lombrices o diabetes.

NORMA [*checking with* CONSUELO, *repeating slowly*]: I put this stuff into the boiling water, wait till it turns yellow, turn it off, let it cool, pour into my baby's bottle, and add sugar—

NANA CUQUITA [*interrupting*]: *Poquita* azúcar.

NORMA: *Little* sugar. Will this work?

NANA CUQUITA [*with authority*]: Santo remedio.

NORMA [*still not sure; to* CONSUELO]: But will it work?

CONSUELO: Of course it'll work. Mom did it for all of us when we were little. Then she did it for all my kids. Including Danny, ¿verdad, Mom?

NANA CUQUITA: Sí. Y el Danny era el más chillón. Chillón y travieso de pilón. ¡No se aguantaba! [*Laughing*] Y la Kathy no se diga. [*To* NORMA] Ve pues, muchacha.

[**NORMA EXITS.**]

[*To* CONSUELO] Consuelo, todos tus hijos eran bien chillones y traviesos. Menos el Junior. Él siempre ha sido un muchachito muy bueno.

CONSUELO: Oh, Mom, you're just saying that cause Junior's always been your favorite grandchild. Su favorito.

NANA CUQUITA: No digas eso. Uno siempre quiere a todos sus nietos igual.

CONSUELO: Maybe. But Junior's the one who looks the most like Dad— por eso lo quiere más.

NANA CUQUITA: Te digo que a todos los quiero igual.

[*Pause.*]

Bueno, es cierto que el Junior le da un parecido a tu papá, pero no por eso es mi favorito, yo lo quiero porque siempre es muy considerado conmigo. Qué lástima que no pudo venir a mi fiesta.

CONSUELO [*shocked*]: Mom! Junior's the one that brought you and Dad to the party. How could you forget?

NANA CUQUITA [*worried*]: Consuelo, no sé que tengo, pero cada día parece que se me olvidan más las cosas. Si no fuera por tu papá—

[**NORMA ENTERS** *with baby bottle.* **NANA CUQUITA** *takes the bottle, checks for warmth on her wrist, and gives it to baby.*]

Pobrecito, estaba cansado de tanto llorar. [*Rocking baby and singing*] "Lulu que lulu que San Camaleón; de debajo de un hueco salió un ratón, mátenlo, mátenlo, cachorrón—"

NORMA: He's asleep. [*Taking baby*] Thank you, Nana. I hope you can teach me all your home remedies. And the song, too. How does that one go? "Lulu, que lulu . . ."—que what?

NANA CUQUITA: Que San Camaleón.

[**NORMA** *sings, and* **CONSUELO** *and* **NANA CUQUITA** *return to the "living room" area, where the party is still in full swing. Polka* **MUSIC** *or corrido plays and couples dance riotously.* **TATA ARCENIO** *dances with* **NANA CUQUITA;** **ROGELIO** *with* **CONSUELO; COMPADRE DEMETRIO** *with* **COMADRE ROSIE,** *etc. Song ends and* EVERYBODY *prepares to leave. They say good night and hug, kiss, etc.*]

TATA ARCENIO: Esperen, una canción más. Pero que la cante Cuquita.

EVERYONE [*ad-libbing, urging*]: Sí, sí. Que cante.

TATA ARCENIO: "Sin ti," Cuquita. Canta "Sin ti."

CONSUELO: That's Dad's favorite song. Sing it for him, Mom.

NANA CUQUITA [*unsure*]: Pero ni me acuerdo ya de las palabras, hija.

TATA ARCENIO: ¿Cómo que no te vas acordar? [*Starting to hum and sing*] "Sin ti, no podré vivir jamás . . ."

[NANA CUQUITA *sings, and* EVERYBODY *groups around her.*]

NANA CUQUITA: "Sin ti, no podré vivir jamás, ni pensar que nunca más estarás junto a mí. Sin ti, qué me puede ya importar si lo que me hace llorar es estar lejos de ti . . ."

[*As* NANA CUQUITA *sings,* EVERYBODY *pairs off again and now dances romantically.* CONSUELO *and* ROGELIO *dance very closely, and it is obvious to all that they are sharing a moment of love and tenderness.* NANA CUQUITA *ends song.* EVERYBODY *applauds and gets ready to leave again. More ad-libbed hugs, kisses, etc.*]

    ". . . Sin ti, no hay clemencia a mi dolor, la esperanza de los dos te la llevas por fin, sin ti, es inútil vivir, como inútil será, el quererte olvidar . . ."

EVERYBODY [*singing the last verses to "Las mañanitas"*]: ". . . De tanto cantar y cantar, ya me duele la garganta; pues que aquí no saben dar esa agüita que ataranta. Ya viene amaneciendo ya la luz del día nos dio. ¡Levántate de mañana, mira que ya amaneció!"

[*Party-goers* EXIT.]

ROGELIO [*to* CONSUELO]: ¿Tenemos que llevar a tu Mom and Dad a su casa?

CONSUELO: No, honey. Junior's taking them home.

ROGELIO: ¿Y adónde anda el Junior pues?

CONSUELO: Afuera in the garage. He's getting some of his books. Quién sabe qué me dijo de un book drive for campesinos in Nicaragua or Guatemala. I didn't hear him with all the noise.

ROGELIO: Good. Que bueno que regale algunos libros. Está lleno el garage—nunca quiso venderlos. Now I'll have a chance to clean out the garage.

NANA CUQUITA: Bueno, pasen buenas noches y muchas gracias por todo, hija.

CONSUELO: De nada, Mom. There's some cake left—do you want to take some with you?

TATA ARCENIO [*quickly*]: Sí, Consuelo, yo quiero cake pa' comérmelo mañana con mi cafecito.

NANA CUQUITA: No, no. No le des, Consuelo. Tu papá no debe comer nada dulce.

TATA ARCENIO: No es cierto, Cuquita. El doctor dice que *sí* puedo comer dulce. [*To* CONSUELO] Es *ella* quien me quita de comer lo que me gusta.

NANA CUQUITA: Porque sé que te hace daño. No le des cake, Consuelo.

[**JUNIOR ENTERS.**]

JUNIOR: Ready?

NANA CUQUITA: Sí, Junior, vamos.

TATA ARCENIO [*whispering to* CONSUELO]: Guárdame un pedacito de cake, y mañana vengo a tomar un cafecito contigo.

[*He hugs* CONSUELO.]

NANA CUQUITA [*walking away*]: ¡Apúrate, hombre! Tengo frío.

TATA ARCENIO: ¿Y yo que soy? ¿Tu calentón?

NANA CUQUITA: Pues sí, ven.

TATA ARCENIO [*pleased*]: Ay, qué mujer. ¿Ven? No se acuesta sin mí. [*Going to* NANA CUQUITA] ¿Verdad, mi amor?

[*He hugs* **NANA CUQUITA** *and begins to walk with her, then stops.*]

¿Y tu bolsa? ¿Llevas tu bolsa?

NANA CUQUITA: ¡No! ¡Se me olvidó! [*Starting to get agitated, looking around*] ¿Adónde la dejé?

TATA ARCENIO [*to* CONSUELO]: ¿Y la bolsa de tu mamá, Consuelo? Esta mujer 'onde quiera la deja.

[**CONSUELO** *looks around and finds the purse.*]

CONSUELO [*handing the purse to* NANA CUQUITA]: Here, Mom. What would you do without Dad?

TATA ARCENIO: Se pierde, Consuelo, se pierde. ¿Verdad, María del Refugio? ¡Te pierdes sin mí porque tú eres mi reina y yo soy tu rey!

NANA CUQUITA [*humoring him*]: Sí, mi rey. Me pierdo sin ti.

[NANA CUQUITA *and* TATA ARCENIO EXIT *with* JUNIOR. CONSUELO *starts to clean up the party mess.*]

ROGELIO: Déjalo, Connie. You don't have to clean all this tonight. You have all day tomorrow to do it.

CONSUELO: Oh, no. I don't want to face *this* tomorrow. Mira, go bring me a garbage bag, and I'll just throw all the paper stuff and empty the ashtrays.

[ROGELIO EXITS, *and* JUNIOR ENTERS *running, out of breath, frightened.*]

JUNIOR: Mom! Hurry, algo le pasó a mi grandpa! I think he's having a heart attack!

[ROGELIO ENTERS, *and* CONSUELO *runs to him. He holds her tenderly, suspecting the worse.* ROGELIO, CONSUELO, *and* JUNIOR FREEZE.]

IMAGEN: *Dolor (Pain).*

[*Soft organ music plays. A plain coffin with floral spray on top is set downstage left.* NANA CUQUITA *is kneeling in front of coffin.* OTHER *friends and relatives* ENTER, *and they hug* NANA CUQUITA *and give her their condolences:* "Mi sentido pésame," "La acompaño en su sentimiento," *etc., and kneel behind* NANA CUQUITA. EVERYBODY *prays "Ave María" following the prayer leader.*]

PRAYER LEADER [*with a very clear, strong voice*]: "Dios te salve, María, llena eres de gracia, el Señor es contigo. Bendita tú eres entre todas las mujeres y bendito es el fruto de tu vientre, Jesús."

ALL: "Santa María, madre de Dios, ruega por él y por nosotros pecadores, ahora y en la hora de nuestra muerte, amén."

PRAYER LEADER: "Dadle Señor, el descanso eterno y luzca para él la luz perpetua. Que descanse en paz. Amén."

ALL: "Así sea."

[EVERYONE *except* NANA CUQUITA, ROGELIO, *and* CONSUELO EXIT. ROGELIO *is downstage right with his arm around* CONSUELO, *and* NANA CUQUITA *is standing alone downstage left.* CONSUELO *removes* ROGELIO's *arm, goes to* NANA CUQUITA, *and hugs her.* ROGELIO *just looks at them. They* FREEZE.]

LIGHTS: OUT.

MUSIC: *Organ or guitar.*

END OF SCENE 2

* * *

Scene 3

TIME: *Morning, two months after* TATA ARCENIO's *funeral.*

PLACE: NANA CUQUITA's *home.*

[NANA CUQUITA *is sitting, folding* TATA ARCENIO's *clothes, and packing them into a cardboard box. There are piles of shoes, clothing, etc., and many other cardboard boxes strewn around.* CONSUELO ENTERS *and kisses* NANA CUQUITA.]

CONSUELO: Hi, Mom. How are you? [*Looking around*] What are you doing?

NANA CUQUITA: Empacando esta ropita de tu papá. Se la voy a dar al Goodwill o al Salvation Army—no me acuerdo a quién llamé. Le ha de servir a algún pobre, ¿no crees?

CONSUELO: Sure, Mom, I'm sure someone could use them. Want me to help you?

NANA CUQUITA: Sí, cómo no.

[CONSUELO *begins folding clothes with* NANA CUQUITA.]

Mira, en esta caja, sus suits, pantalones; en esa, sus zapatos. Tu papá era una rata—todo guardaba, pero se la voy a dar al Goodwill o al Salvation Army. Ay, ¿a quién llamé?

[*Pause.*]

Le ha de servir a algún pobre, ¿no crees?

[CONSUELO *stops folding abruptly and stares intently at* NANA CUQUITA, *as she realizes that* NANA CUQUITA *has asked her the exact question already.*]

CONSUELO: Mom, are you all right? ¿Se siente bien?

NANA CUQUITA: Sí, ¿por qué me preguntas?

CONSUELO: Nomás quería saber.

[*Pause.*]

Está sola aquí. ¿Por qué no me telefonea?

NANA CUQUITA: ¿Por qué te he de andar molestando?

CONSUELO: You're not bothering. I told you that now that I'm working at home me puede hablar a cualquier hora.

NANA CUQUITA: A mí no me gusta andarle dando guerra a nadie. Ya te he molestado bastante. Me has llevado a la clínica, a pagar las cuentas, al mandado. Yo sé muy bien que dejas tu trabajo por andar conmigo.

CONSUELO: But, Mom—

NANA CUQUITA [*slightly irritated*]: Consuelo, no soy chiquita. Me puedo cuidar muy bien.

CONSUELO: I know, Mom. I just meant for other rides, you know, si se le ofrece algo más de la tienda. I don't like you walking around alone.

NANA CUQUITA: Bueno, bueno. Déjame trabajar en paz. Yo no quiero que nadie se ande preocupando por mí. Estoy fuerte y saludable.

CONSUELO: But I want to help you, Mom.

NANA CUQUITA: Bueno pues, lleva esas cajas a la sala. Van a venir los del Goodwill o el Salvation Army por ellas. ¿Estás segura que venden la ropa que uno les da? ¡A la mejor se quedan ellos mismos con todo!

[**CONSUELO** *crosses with a box, and* **NANA CUQUITA** *follows her to another area.*]

CONSUELO: Are you giving away *all* of Dad's things?

NANA CUQUITA: No, solo la ropa. ¿A quién de la familia le puede servir? Esos libros son pa'l Junior; que no se te olviden; él se los pidió a tu Papá la otra noche en la fiesta, antes que . . .

[**NANA CUQUITA** *trails off, not wanting to say the word* "*muriera.*"]

CONSUELO [*picking up a souvenir near one of the boxes and reading the inscription*]: "Recuerdo de Veracruz." This is pretty, Mom—you're not giving this away, are you?

NANA CUQUITA: ¡Oh no! Fíjate que se me había olvidado que lo tenía arrumbado en el closet hasta que lo encontré esta mañana. Yo ni sabía que todavía lo tenía después de tantos años. Tu Papá me dio este recuerdo cuando fuimos a Veracruz.

CONSUELO [*giving her the souvenir*]: When were you and Dad in Veracruz?

NANA CUQUITA [*thinking*]: Ay, Consuelo, cómo crees que me voy acordar cuando andábamos por allá si ni me acuerdo qué día es hoy.

CONSUELO: It's Wednesday, Mom.

[NANA CUQUITA, *forgetting* CONSUELO, *starts to reminisce with a faraway look.* CONSUELO *listens to her intently, without interrupting her. At times* NANA CUQUITA *repeats or gives partial sentences or phrases. Soft marimba* MUSIC *plays.*]

NANA CUQUITA: Este regalo me lo compró Arcenio cuando caminábamos por todo el malecón. Bien bonito, las marimbas por todos lados. Pescado zarandeado. Caldo de jaiba. Mariscos. Bien bonito. Me acuerdo que me lo compró una tarde que paseábamos por el malecón, me dijo, "¡Para que siempre te acuerdes de Veracruz!" Era una tarde muy bonita, y yo llevaba un vestido color guinda, con cuellito blanco. Hacía un viento muy fuerte, y el viento me subía el vestido, y yo me lo detenía así. [*Holding her dress down*] ¡Y Arcenio, como siempre, se hacía el payaso y se reía!

[NANA CUQUITA *stops talking and recognizes* CONSUELO. *Pause.*]

CONSUELO: Do you miss him?

[NANA CUQUITA *doesn't answer.* CONSUELO *goes to her and hugs her.*]

I miss him, Mom. I miss him very much.

[*Pause.*]

Lo extraño tanto que a veces se me olvida que ya no está con nosotros. Y lo espero que venga a tomar café conmigo y nunca llega.

[*Pause.* CONSUELO *changes the subject.*]

¿Quiere ir a cenar con nosotros?

NANA CUQUITA: Ay, no, está haciendo mucho frío para andar saliendo a ninguna parte.

CONSUELO: It's not cold. C'mon with us. Roy's having a small office party for the crew. They finished some contract in record time, so they're celebrating. Vamos, Mom.

NANA CUQUITA: Consuelo, yo no tengo ganas de andar entre la gente.

CONSUELO: Well, then, come and spend the night with us. ¿Qué va a hacer aquí sola?

NANA CUQUITA: Puedo ver mi telenovela. Vieras que bonita está. Y triste.

CONSUELO: You can watch it en mi casa también.

NANA CUQUITA: Ya te dije que no quiero molestarlos. Además, a Rogelio le gusta ver sus juegos de fútbol. Mañana mejor, ven por mí mañana.

CONSUELO: All right, but call me if you need anything before then. Okay? Promise?

NANA CUQUITA: Bueno, bueno, te hablaré.

[CONSUELO *starts to cross with* NANA CUQUITA. JUNIOR ENTERS.]

JUNIOR: Hi, Mom. Buenas tardes, Nana.

[*He hugs and kisses both his mom and grandmother.*]

I came for the books Tata gave me.

NANA CUQUITA: Ahí están, m'ijito. Ah que tu tata, no lo vas a creer pero hasta tiene libros desde cuando él iba a la escuela. ¿Te imaginas? Y tuyos también, Consuelo. Fíjate nomás, desde que ibas a la escuela Davis.

JUNIOR: Great, Nana—we can use every book we get.

NANA CUQUITA: ¿Y qué vas a hacer con tanto libro, muchacho?

JUNIOR: Son para un book drive para los campesinos en Nicaragua.

[*He picks up the box and starts to* EXIT, *but then stops.*]

Oh, Mom—Dad says to stop and get some ice for the crew before you get there.

CONSUELO: Ice? Okay. Oh, heck, I still have to go home and pick up the salsa and potato salad.

JUNIOR: No, Dad said never mind. The receptionist already took care of all that.

CONSUELO: She did?

[CONSUELO *crosses to one of the boxes and distractedly touches some of her dad's things.*]

JUNIOR: Pues ya me voy, Mom. Bye, Nana.

[*He kisses them both and* EXITS. *Pause.*]

NANA CUQUITA: ¿Pues cuándo van a venir los del Goodwill? Ya se está haciendo tarde y yo no les voy abrir la puerta si vienen ya noche.

CONSUELO: It's not that late, Mom. I'll wait with you.

NANA CUQUITA: ¿Y Rogelio? Y te está esperando con el hielo. Anda, ve. Los del Goodwill pueden venir otro día.

CONSUELO: No, Mom, I'll wait with you. Roy can send the receptionist for the ice.

NANA CUQUITA: ¿Estás segura?

CONSUELO: Yes, I'm sure.

[*There is a loud knock offstage.*]

OFFSTAGE: *Goodwill!*

LIGHTS: DOWN.

MUSIC: *Lively corrido—"El ausente" or something similar.*

IMAGEN: CONSUELO *and* NANA CUQUITA *fold clothes very slowly, and Goodwill workers, wearing coveralls or sweats,* ENTER *and very efficiently pick up boxes and* EXIT. *The last worker takes an article of clothing from* CONSUELO's *and* NANA CUQUITA's *hands and* EXITS. NANA CUQUITA *and* CONSUELO FREEZE, NANA CUQUITA *empty-handed and* CONSUELO *holding the Veracruz souvenir.*

IMAGEN: TATA ARCENIO ENTERS, *crosses to* NANA CUQUITA, *stands behind her, places his hands on her shoulders, and sings softly: "Toda una vida me estaría contigo. No me importa en qué forma, ni dónde, ni cuándo, pero junto a ti . . ." He forgets the words, so he hums until he remembers and continues: ". . . no me cansaría de decirte siempre, pero siempre, siempre, que eres en mi vida ansiedad y angustia, y desesperación . . ."*

LIGHTS: DOWN *and* OUT.

END OF SCENE 3

* * *

Scene 4

TIME: *Late afternoon, some months later.*

PLACE: *Rogelio's office.*

MUSIC: *Modern.*

[ROGELIO *and* LA RECEPTIONIST *are working at their box-desks.*]

LA RECEPTIONIST [*to* ROGELIO]: I've finished filing last week's invoices—is it okay if I leave now?

ROGELIO: ¿Pues, qué hora es, anyway?

LA RECEPTIONIST: Poco después de las cinco. ¿Ya casi termina?

ROGELIO: No, no, I still have a lot of paperwork to finish.

LA RECEPTIONIST: Can I help?

ROGELIO: No, thanks. Nomás es un cochinero con los contracts del city. You have to fill out more and more forms for each job now. Remember that job we did last week?

LA RECEPTIONIST: The sidewalk by the swimming pool at Oury Park?

ROGELIO: Sí, we did the sidewalk, *plus* the driveway. Bueno pues, that contract was from both city and county funds, pero otro pedacito vinía de federal funds. So, I have to send in all these forms.

[*Pause.*]

Has Connie called?

LA RECEPTIONIST: No.

ROGELIO: When she calls, tell her the time cards are almost ready for her but not to bother coming for them. I'll take them to her later.

LA RECEPTIONIST: Maybe I can help you with the time cards.

ROGELIO: That would be great! It'll save Connie some work. And she needs all the help she can get—she's been so busy with her mom.

[**ROGELIO** *crosses to* **LA RECEPTIONIST**'*s desk and leans over her shoulder as he explains the time cards and other paperwork to her.*]

Mira, the workers fill out their own time cards, y luego los foremen las hacen check y ponen sus initials aquí. Yo hago check las horas de los foremen y pongo mis initials aquí. Then you just have to follow esta pay scale, put in the amount, and Connie cuts their checks.

LA RECEPTIONIST: Parece ser fácil.

ROGELIO: Yeah, it's easy, but you have to pay attention cuando cambean los wages from regular to differential.

LA RECEPTIONIST: Differential? ¿Qué es eso?

ROGELIO: La difference que le pagamos con estos contratos. Just follow the schedule of pay. Si es "regular," you pay "regular," y si es "differential," you pay "regular" plus the difference from this schedule.

LA RECEPTIONIST: Okay, let me try—it doesn't seem difficult.

[*She moves closer to* ROGELIO, *their heads together.* CONSUELO ENTERS. *She is surprised and annoyed at their closeness but recovers.*]

CONSUELO: Hi, honey.

[LA RECEPTIONIST *moves away quickly with a sly smile and then goes to work briskly on the time cards.*]

ROGELIO: Híjole, Connie. Why didn't you call first?

[*He crosses to her and gives her a husbandly peck.*]

CONSUELO: I wanted to surprise you. [*Giving* LA RECEPTIONIST *a dirty look*] And it looks like I did. [*Changing tactics; sweetly*] Roy, honey, why don't you go with me now? Let's go in my car. How about dinner? My treat.

ROGELIO: I can't—ya tengo la troka loaded up.

CONSUELO: I'll bring you back in the morning. [*Pulling him*] C'mon, vamos.

ROGELIO: No, I have to take the truck home porque el job site está en Green Valley, so it's silly for you to have to bring me all the way back here when I can just take the truck home. You go home, or visit your mom un ratito. Just give me time to finish here, and call me when you're ready, and I'll drop whatever I'm doing and go home for you. Dinner's on me, okay?

[*They both cross.*]

I promise. Just call me. ¿Qué quieres? Chinese? Italian? Tex-Mex?

CONSUELO [*stopping almost offstage*]: Okay. I guess I'll go see my mom and see if she needs anything. But be ready to leave by six—promise?

ROGELIO: I promise. Just call me.

CONSUELO [*remembering suddenly*]: Oh, las time cards! Dame las time cards de una vez.

ROGELIO [*guiltily*]: Eh, eh-h-h. Don't worry about the time cards, honey.

CONSUELO: But it's Wednesday, Roy.

ROGELIO: Sí, yo sé, pero I'm teaching the receptionist how to get them ready for you. You know, las horas y el pay schedule. If she finishes them today, I'll take them to you.

LA RECEPTIONIST [*quickly and proud of herself*]: Ya las terminé.

[*She hands the time cards to* ROGELIO.]

ROGELIO [*impressed*]: Wow! That was fast! Y apenas acabo de enseñarle, Connie.

CONSUELO [*taking time cards from* ROGELIO]: A ver, maybe I should take them now that I'm here already. [*Checking time cards*] This is incorrect. She's overpaying Eddie. [*Giving time card to* ROGELIO] See? He's not an apprentice yet; he's still a laborer.

LA RECEPTIONIST: No, he's not—he completed his apprentice term five days ago, so he's due journeyman pay from that day on.

ROGELIO: That's right. Y el menso foreman no lo marcó. Good thing you caught it porque si no, se nos viene encima la union como un león. [*To* CONSUELO] She's smart, honey. I just barely explained the time cards to her right before you came in. How long did it take you to catch on?

CONSUELO: I caught on sooner than you think.

[*She* EXITS.]

ROGELIO [*puzzled*]: ¿Y a ella qué le picó?

[LA RECEPTIONIST *shrugs, but she knows.* ROGELIO *returns to his work area, and both work quietly until* ROGELIO *stands up and stretches.*]

LA RECEPTIONIST: Oh, oh. Parece que me estoy embarullando un poco con la time card de Fernando.

[*He crosses to* LA RECEPTIONIST.]

ROGELIO: He's a new worker y siempre hace un cochinero con sus horas. Leave it for Connie.

LA RECEPTIONIST: I can figure it out. Then I'm going to study the contracts.

ROGELIO [*teasing*]: Se me olvidó. You want to be a lawyer.

LA RECEPTIONIST: Sí, y quiero aprender todo lo que pueda aquí.

ROGELIO: Pues, it's almost five o'clock. I'm not a slave driver. Te han de estar esperando. ¿Qué va decir tu . . .?

LA RECEPTIONIST: No hay ningún "tu." [*Taking out an orange from her lunch bag*] Voy a comerme mi naranja, read the contracts y estudiar un poco. [*Peeling orange*] You can leave.

[**ROGELIO** *doesn't move.* **LA RECEPTIONIST** *cuts a section of the orange and holds it out to* **ROGELIO** *in a teasing and challenging way.*]

¿No gusta?

[**CONSUELO ENTERS** *at the exact time that* **LA RECEPTIONIST** *is offering* **ROGELIO** *the piece of orange.*]

CONSUELO: Honey, I . . .

[**ROGELIO** *and* **LA RECEPTIONIST FREEZE.**]

MUSIC: *Jazzy striptease*

IMAGEN: *Celos (Jealousy).*

[**CONSUELO** *stands and watches* **LA RECEPTIONIST** *feed* **ROGELIO** *sections of the orange in a very teasing, seductive manner: licking juice off her fingers, running her tongue over her lips, sucking her finger, wiping juice from* **ROGELIO**'s *mouth, etc.*]

END OF SCENE 4

* * *

Scene 5

TIME: *Late afternoon, months later.*

PLACE: **CONSUELO** *and* **ROGELIO**'s *home.*

[**CONSUELO** *is doing paperwork and* **NANA CUQUITA** *is reading but moving nervously, agitated.* **CONSUELO** *looks up but continues working.*]

NANA CUQUITA: ¿Consuelo?

CONSUELO: Yes, Mom?

NANA CUQUITA: ¿Te fijaste bien si apagué todas las luces de mi casa?

CONSUELO: Yes, Mom, I saw you turn off all your lights.

NANA CUQUITA: ¿Y la estufa? ¿No dejé nada en la estufa?

CONSUELO: No, Mom, I checked—there was nothing on the stove.

NANA CUQUITA: ¿No se te hace que está haciendo frío? ¿Irá a helar a la noche?

CONSUELO: No, Mom, it won't freeze tonight. [*Joking*] Anyway, tenemos bastantes cobijas.

NANA CUQUITA: Pero mis matitas, Consuelo. No quiero que se me vayan a helar mis plantas.

CONSUELO: Ahorita van a dar las news, and we can see how cold it'll get tonight. If we have to, mandamos al Roy o al Junior to go cover your plants, all right?

NANA CUQUITA: Mejor llévame a mi casa.

CONSUELO: But Mom, you're spending the night with us. Mañana tiene un appointment con el doctor.

NANA CUQUITA: Pues, no quiero dormir aquí. Yo tengo mi casa—no hay por qué andarlos molestando.

CONSUELO: You're not bothering anyone. And we now have a room for you.

NANA CUQUITA: Pero te hice que te salieras de tu oficina. Tan bonita que la tenías arreglada, y luego vengo yo y te saco de ella.

CONSUELO: No, you didn't. Anyway, the light's better here in the living room.

NANA CUQUITA: Pero te molesto con la televisión.

CONSUELO: No, you don't. I don't even hear the TV when I'm working.

NANA CUQUITA: A la mejor por eso no viene Rogelio del trabajo, porque sabe que estoy yo aquí de estorbo.

CONSUELO [trying to be patient]: Mom, stop saying that! Rogelio had to work late. [Hearing offstage noise] Mire, ahí viene Rogelio.

[JUNIOR ENTERS with a box of books.]

JUNIOR: Hi, Mom, Grandma. Where's Dad?

NANA CUQUITA: Tu papá no viene porque sabe que yo estoy aquí.

CONSUELO: That's not true, Junior. He's working late.

JUNIOR: Again? You guys are gonna get rich with all the overtime.

CONSUELO: Rich? Are you kidding? [Sarcastically] La que se va get rich es la receptionist. She's helping him, or that's what he's calling it.

[Pause.]

¿Qué andas haciendo?

JUNIOR: I came for more books.

NANA CUQUITA: Que bueno que viniste, Junior. ¿Me puedes llevar a mi casa, por favor? Tu mamá no quiere llevarme.

JUNIOR: Sure, Nana, I'll give you a ride. Just let me load up these books first, okay?

NANA CUQUITA: ¿Y qué haces con tanto libro, muchacho?

JUNIOR: ¿No se acuerda, Nana? Los estoy juntando para los campesinos en Nicaragua.

NANA CUQUITA [slightly bewildered]: ¿Nicaragua? ¿Vas ir a Nicaragua, Junior?

[She EXITS before he can answer her.]

CONSUELO: She does that all the time. She'll ask something and leave without waiting for an answer. M'ijo, she worries me. She's forgetting more and more things, keeps asking the same thing over and over, and I find her staring into space for hours.

JUNIOR: She's probably just thinking about Grandpa.

CONSUELO: Maybe so, but I'm still worried about her. Especially when she's alone at her home. Junior, she needs me.

NANA CUQUITA [entering]: ¿Junior? ¿Eres tú? ¿Cómo estás? Cómo hace que no venías, carajo.

JUNIOR: Ya me saludó, Nana. ¿Sabe algo? Si no tiene memoria, se la llevan a la cuckoo house.

CONSUELO: Junior! Don't say that!

JUNIOR: De veras, Nana. ¿Qué día es hoy?

NANA CUQUITA [unsure]: ¿Jueves? No, ¿lunes?

JUNIOR: ¿Ya ve? Hoy es martes.

NANA CUQUITA: Yo sé que hoy es martes. Y a poco nomás porque no recuerdo el día de la semana ya estoy . . . ¿cómo dijiste? Cuckoo?

JUNIOR: No, pero es lo primero que le preguntan en la cuckoo house. Eso y los presidentes. ¿Quién es el presidente?

NANA CUQUITA [stalling]: ¿De qué país?

JUNIOR: De USA.

NANA CUQUITA: Todo mundo sabe que el presidente es Reagan.

JUNIOR: ¿Está segura?

NANA CUQUITA [*unsure*]: Sí . . . ¿o ya se murió?

JUNIOR: No, you're right, es el Reagan. Okay, you've passed the president test, but you're also asked to count by nine, backwards, from one hundred—

NANA CUQUITA: ¿Que cuente qué?

JUNIOR: Let's see if I can say this in Spanish. [*Explaining slowly*] También le piden que cuente de cien para abajo, pero en los nueves. Mire, cien menos nueve, noventa y uno, menos nueve, ochenta y dos, menos nueve, setenta y tres, menos nueve—

NANA CUQUITA: Déjate de nueves. Mejor los presidentes, Junior. Esos sí los sé—pregúntame de los presidentes. A tu mamá que le pregunten de los nueves.

CONSUELO [*doing paperwork but listening, looking up*]: I'm not crazy—not yet anyway.

JUNIOR: Bueno, Nana, los presidentes. Who was the president *before* Reagan?

NANA CUQUITA [*intently*]: ¿Antes de Reagan? A ver.

[*Pause.*]

　　　　¿El Nixon?

JUNIOR: No, Nana, not Nixon. Mejor empiece backwards. Who is the president that you most remember?

NANA CUQUITA [*proudly*]: Pues Roosevelt. Franklin Delano Roosevelt.

JUNIOR: And after him?

CONSUELO: That's too hard for her, Junior.

JUNIOR: No, it's not, Mom. It's good for her. She needs things like that to make her mind remember. [*To* NANA CUQUITA] After Roosevelt?

NANA CUQUITA: Truman.

JUNIOR: See, Mom? [*To* NANA CUQUITA] Nana, think of all the presidents after Truman—

NANA CUQUITA: ¿Qué?

JUNIOR: Usted piense de todos los presidentes después de Truman, en orden, mientras yo le hablo a un amigo. [*To* CONSUELO] I'm desperate for someone to do something for me at the peña we're having next week.

CONSUELO: I can help you—what do you need?

JUNIOR: A poet, músico, anything for entertainment.

CONSUELO: Oh, *that*. I thought you wanted help with the food. How about your Nino Demetrio?

JUNIOR: He already agreed to play. But I still need more performing artists. It's a three-hour event, at least. [*Getting his phone, dialing, and speaking with appropriate pauses for responses*] Cricket? Junior here. ¿Sabes de la peña que we're having at the centro? Sí, los chilenos van a tener empanadas, pollo con something or other, y los salvadoreños van a servir pupusas. No problem, lo que necesito es alguien en el entertainment. Ajá, ellos no pueden, ya les hablé también. Déjate de la comida, necesito un poeta, sí, sí, pero otro que no sea tan serio. ¿Y canta? ¿Y de qué me sirve si no vive aquí? Bueno, me hablas. Thanks. Bye. [*To* CONSUELO] Cricket can't help me either.

[JUNIOR *keeps dialing other numbers.* NANA CUQUITA *starts to hum "Solamenta una vez" somewhat distractedly.* JUNIOR *notices that she's humming and gets an idea.*]

¿Abuelita?

NANA CUQUITA [*determined to be correct*]: Después de Truman fue Eisenhower . . . ¿y luego Nixon?

JUNIOR: No, not Nixon. He's later, I think.

NANA CUQUITA: ¿Entonces Kissinger? A ver, muchacho, dame uno de esos libros.

JUNIOR [*handing her a book and teasing her*]: Uhhh, Nana, you're going to the cuckoo house!

CONSUELO: Junior! Don't say that!

JUNIOR: Mom, I'm just kidding. [*To* NANA CUQUITA] Nana, ¿quiere ir—

NANA CUQUITA: No, no, yo no quiero ir a la cuckoo house.

JUNIOR: Never mind la cuckoo house. ¿Quiere ir conmigo a una peña la semana que entra?

NANA CUQUITA: ¿Peña? ¿Qué es eso?

JUNIOR: Nos estamos juntando todos los trabajadores del book drive en una fiestecita. Va haber comida, música, poesía, baile, teatro. ¿Vamos?

NANA CUQUITA: Y tú, Consuelo, ¿vas ir? No quiero quedarme sola.

JUNIOR: Yeah, Mom, that's a good idea. You and Dad can go, too. I'll come and pick up Nana.

CONSUELO: You didn't get to the point, Junior.

JUNIOR: I know—I'm working up to it. [*To* NANA CUQUITA] ¿Grandma, me puede hacer un favor? ¿Quiere cantar en la peña?

NANA CUQUITA: ¿Qué peña?

JUNIOR: La que va a ir conmigo, Nana. ¿Quiere cantar una canción?

NANA CUQUITA: ¿Pero qué voy a cantar, Junior? No tengo ganas de cantar, y menos de andar en fiestas—

JUNIOR [*quickly*]: No es fiesta, Nana. Es muy seria la cosa. Y muy importante. Le juntamos libros a los campesinos de Nicaragua y nos vamos a reunir para empacárselos. Y usted puede cantar una canción. Por favor, Nana. Please?

[**ROGELIO ENTERS.**]

ROGELIO: Buenas noches.

[*He crosses and* EXITS *before anyone can talk to him.*]

JUNIOR: Please, Nana. Just one song.

NANA CUQUITA: Pero, m'ijito, ni me acuerdo de las palabras.

JUNIOR: Just pick an easy song. Una muy fácil. Please. Esa que estaba humming 'orita, Nana.

[*He hums "Solamente una vez."*]

NANA CUQUITA [*pausing, and then singing*]: "Solamente una vez, amé en la vida. Solamente una vez y nada más. Una vez nada más en mi huerto brilló la esperanza, la esperanza que alumbra el camino de mi soledad . . .

[*She falters, forgetting the words.* CONSUELO *crosses to her and sits next to her, holding* NANA CUQUITA's *hands, and helps her with the words.*]

CONSUELO [*singing*]: "Solamente un vez se entrega el alma, con la dulce y total renunciación—"

NANA CUQUITA AND CONSUELO [*singing together*]: "Y cuando ese milagro realice el prodigio de amarse, hay campanas de fiesta que cantan en el corazón."

JUNIOR [*clapping*]: See, Mom? She can do it. ¿Abuelita, verdad que usted puede cantar en la peña?

NANA CUQUITA: ¿Qué peña?

[*Pause.*]

JUNIOR [*picking up his books*]: Nana, you practice this song all week, okay? [*To* CONSUELO] Don't worry, Mom, she picked a real easy song. Even I know it. Uhhh, wait till I tell Cricket! Nana, you'll be the star at the peña!

NANA CUQUITA: ¿Pero, qué peña, muchacho?

[JUNIOR EXITS, *singing,* "Solamente una vez, amé en la vida, solamente una vez, y nada más . . ." NANA CUQUITA *watches* JUNIOR EXIT, *and then she* EXITS *quickly to her room. Then* ROGELIO ENTERS, *freshly showered, jacket in hand.*]

ROGELIO: Need anything from the store?

CONSUELO: No, honey, why?

ROGELIO: I'm going to the Shanty for a beer with the guys, and I can bring you anything you want when I come back.

CONSUELO: Pero sí aquí tienes beer, Roy. No tienes que ir a ninguna parte—besides, it's very late.

ROGELIO: Ahorita vengo. Nomás voy a shoot some pool con los guys.

CONSUELO: Why, Roy? Why can't you stay home? Sales todas las noches. ¿Por qué no te puedes quedar conmigo?

ROGELIO: No comiences, Connie. Besides, ¿qué voy hacer aquí contigo? You're no fun, nomás te la pasas trabajando.

CONSUELO: But I'm doing the paperwork for *you,* for our company.

ROGELIO: Pues no es mi culpa que you're so far behind. Nomás te la llevas all over town con tu mom, y ya no tienes tiempo para mí.

CONSUELO: That's not fair. You know that I have to take care of her. She needs me.

ROGELIO: Pues, I need you, too. It's been months since we've done anything together. Alone, just the two of us.

CONSUELO: Don't be a baby. ¿Qué quieres que haga? She's my mother.

ROGELIO [*yelling*]: And I'm your husband! Or did you forget that?

CONSUELO [*yelling back*]: But she's my mother!

ROGELIO: She's also Demetrio's mother. Why does it have to be *you* that has to do everything for her?

CONSUELO [*in a tired, weary voice*]: I told you—because I'm her daughter.

ROGELIO: Well, I told you I'm going out.

[*Pause.*]

Do you want to go with me?

[CONSUELO *crosses to him.* NANA CUQUITA ENTERS, *very agitated and nervous.*]

NANA CUQUITA: Me hubiera ido con el Junior. Pero, ¿por qué no me fui con el muchacho ya que él estaba aquí?

ROGELIO: Go with me, Connie. She can watch her telenovelas—she'll be all right.

NANA CUQUITA [*confused, sitting down*]: ¿Qué me preguntó de los presidentes? ¿Es el Reagan, verdad? Primero Roosevelt, luego Truman, Winston Churchill, Nixon, Roosevelt, Carter, Reagan, uno de los Kennedys . . . ¿a cuál Kennedy?

[*Pause.*]

CONSUELO [*looking at* NANA CUQUITA *with sympathy*]: I can't go with you, Roy. I can't leave her alone. Anda, Roy, you go.

[ROGELIO, *clearly annoyed,* EXITS. NANA CUQUITA *keeps repeating names.* CONSUELO *crosses to her and holds her tenderly.*]

NANA CUQUITA: De seguro era Roosevelt, un Kennedy, *otro* Kennedy, Roosevelt, Kennedy . . . el de los cacahuates . . .

LIGHTS: DOWN.

MUSIC: *Soft.*

IMAGEN: CONSUELO *sits across from* NANA CUQUITA, *and they look into each other's eyes. They "mirror" each other's movements as they touch face, hair, etc. It is as though they are seeing each other in the other's face.* FREEZE.

END OF ACT I

INTERMISSION (OPTIONAL)

ACT II

Scene 1

TIME: *One week later, evening.*

PLACE: *At the peña.*

MUSIC: *Lively cumbia or protest song.*

SETTING: *The set has been preset with stacks of books, about ten cardboard boxes, packing tape, paper plates, cups, etc.* EVERYBODY *is dancing, sitting, eating, packing books into boxes, etc. The song ends, there is applause, and then* EVERYBODY *returns to packing. The packing is an assembly line process with the* WORKERS *who pack books into boxes, tape, address, etc. The boxes move from* RIGHT *to* LEFT, *and the entire packing process moves in a very organized, choreographed rhythm. Occasionally a* WORKER *will call out "Box!" or "¡Caja!" for either an empty box or a filled box to be taken out.*

JUNIOR [*as master of ceremonies*]: Let's hear it for the músicos! ¡Se aventaron!

[EVERYBODY *cheers.*]

¿De adónde viene esa canción? ¿Colombia? ¿Venezuela?

MÚSICO [*joking, naming a popular bar hangout*]: Del Sky Villa!

[EVERYBODY *laughs.*]

JUNIOR: Okay, we're almost done with the packing y va a seguir la fiesta hasta que nos corran. Y una special surprise, mi abuelita Cuquita les va a cantar una classic.

[EVERYBODY *cheers. One of the* WORKERS *crosses to* JUNIOR *and whispers something.*]

Oh, sí, we want to thank todos los cooks.

[JUNIOR *points toward the kitchen area, and* EVERYBODY *applauds.*]

Que salgan los cooks, c'mon take a bow.

[*A shy* COOK *sticks his head out of the kitchen area and bows.*]

COOK: Todavía tenemos mucha comida.

JUNIOR: You heard that? There's more food. Don't forget it's for a good cause. Now that we have all these books, we need money for the shipping and transport, so buy another plate.

[COMPADRE DEMETRIO *crosses,* EXITS.]

There goes my nino—thanks, Nino! Hey, everybody! My nino's starting his landscape business, so if you need a tree, he's the man to see. Wow! Cricket! I just made a poem. Danny, where's the box? We're gonna draw the name for the handmade Chilean wall-hanging. A ver, ¿quién se la ganó?

[DANNY *gives* JUNIOR *the box with raffle tickets.*]

Heather? Come up and pull out the lucky name.

[HEATHER *crosses to* JUNIOR *and some yell, ad-libbing,* "Fixed, not fair, Junior chapucero," *etc.*]

Híjole, how can it be fixed? I didn't even buy a ticket for the raffle.

[EVERYBODY *boos.*]

Gimme a break. Quiet, quiet. Okay, Heather, pull out a name.

[HEATHER *pulls out a ticket stub from box and hands it to* JUNIOR.]

JUNIOR [*reading name*]: Angélica Martínez. Angélica, are you here?

[ANGÉLICA *crosses to* JUNIOR. EVERYBODY *cheers.*]

Congratulations, Angie.

ANGÉLICA: Thanks, Junior.

EVERYBODY [*yelling*]: Speech, speech!

JUNIOR: A few words, Angie.

ANGÉLICA [*clearing throat*]: I'm very happy to see everyone here tonight, and I want to thank everyone who worked on the book drive, but I want to remind everybody that the work's not done: next month we begin our medical supplies drive, so Junior, I want to donate my prize to that drive.

[EVERYBODY *cheers.*]

JUNIOR [*joking*]: Okay, everybody else that's won a prize, bring it back— we need it for the *next* raffle!

ANGÉLICA: ¡Y que siga la lucha!

EVERYBODY: ¡Hasta la victoria!

JUNIOR: Okay, atención, quiet everybody. Here's the treat que les prometimos. Mi abuelita les va cantar. Les presento a mi grandma, Doña María del Refugio, quien nos va cantar—que canción, ¿Nana?

[NANA CUQUITA *whispers title.*]

"¿Júrame?" Okay, una canción del recuerdo, an oldie but goodie.

[ALL *applaud.*]

CONSUELO [*hurrying to* JUNIOR]: No, Junior—that's too hard. She'll forget the words.

[JUNIOR's *now the harried master of ceremonies, so he brushes aside* CONSUELO's *worry.*]

JUNIOR: She can do it, Mom.

NANA CUQUITA [*singing "Júrame"*]: "Todos dicen que es mentira que te quiero, porque nunca me habían visto enamorada. Yo te juro que yo misma no comprendo el por qué me fascina tu mirada. Cuando estoy cerca de ti y estoy contenta, no quisiera que de nadie te acordaras. Tengo celos hasta del pensamiento que pueda recordarte de otra persona amada. Júrame, que aunque pase mucho tiempo, no olvidarás el momento en que yo te conocí. Júrame, pues no hay nada más profundo, ni más grande en este mundo que el cariño que te di. Bésame, con un beso enamorado, como nadie me ha besado desde el día en que nací. Quiéreme, quiéreme hasta la locura, y así sabrás la amargura que estoy sufriendo por ti."

[EVERYBODY *applauds, mingles, talks, etc.* LA RECEPTIONIST ENTERS, *wearing a modest red dress, and stands there, looking around.*]

CONSUELO [*jabbing* COMADRE ROSIE *and whispering*]: That's her, Rosie. Don't look now, pero esa es la receptionist.

COMADRE ROSIE: ¿Esa es, Connie?

[COMADRE ROSIE *turns her head quickly and gives* LA RECEPTIONIST *a once-over.*]

Wow! I knew it! Está sexy la mosca muerta.

[CONSUELO *and* COMADRE ROSIE *turn away and try to look busy.* LA RECEPTIONIST *crosses slowly to upstage work area.*]

[MUSIC: *Same jazz from orange-eating* IMAGEN.]

[LA RECEPTIONIST *stops.* ROGELIO *sees her.* ROGELIO *and* LA RECEPTIONIST's *eyes meet.* ROGELIO *starts to cross to her, stops abruptly, looks around somewhat guiltily, sees a box filled with books, picks it up, and crosses to* LA RECEPTIONIST. *They both* EXIT. CONSUELO *and* COMADRE ROSIE *do not see this.*]

JUNIOR [*bringing* NANA CUQUITA *to* CONSUELO]: See, Mom? I told you not to worry. My nana can still belt out a song.

CONSUELO [*looking around*]: Junior, have you seen your dad?

JUNIOR: Yeah, I just saw him with my nino—

CONSUELO [*asking* OTHERS]: Have you seen Roy? No han visto a Rogelio? [*Moving around*] Roy? Roy?

LIGHTS: DOWN *and* UP.

MUSIC: *Lively polka.*

IMAGEN: *A mí no me gusta el chisme, pero . . . (I don't like to gossip, but . . .).*

[*The* WORKERS *continue to work as before, but the work takes on surrealistic quality with both slow and fast motion. In a very tight choreography, the* WORKERS' *movements and dialogue will mingle with shouts of "¡Caja!" or "Box!" as* CONSUELO *weaves around them and listens to their gossip that is told in "groups" and in past tense. The* GOSSIPERS *can be any number and the lines should be divided up evenly based on the number of actors available. The dialogue should be seamless, with one* GOSSIPER *from Group 1 moving to Group 2 and another from Group 2 to Group 3 and so on as they spread rumors through the peña.*]

Group 1

GOSSIPER: A mí no me gusta el chisme, pero la otra noche, en la peña, ¿vieron a la secretaria de Rogelio?

GOSSIPER: Ay, no la vi, ¿cuál era?

GOSSIPER: ¿No la vio? Era un escándalo. Llegó sola, entro así [*walking*] con un vestido rojo, desgotado hasta aquí, [*pointing to cleavage*] y desde lejos llamaba a Rogelio.

GOSSIPER [*scandalized*]: ¿Lo llamaba?

GOSSIPER: Sí, pero no con la boca.

GOSSIPER: Entonces pues, ¿cómo lo llamaba?

GOSSIPER: Con los ojos. [*With a sexy pose and fluttering eyelashes*] Así lo llamaba: ven, Rogelio, ven, ven.

Group 2

GOSSIPER: Oiga, pero yo nunca los vi juntos.

GOSSIPER: ¿A quién?

GOSSIPER: A la secretaria y Rogelio.

GOSSIPER: Pues ahí está.

GOSSIPER: ¿Qué está?

GOSSIPER: Pues que están guilty. Si fueran nomás amigos—que no lo son—o que fueran nomás el boss y la secretary, se hablaran, bailaran, you know. Pero como son *más* que amigos, se tienen que hacer como que ni se hablan, and they have to stay far away from each other, pa' que no los hagan suspect. ¿Me entiendes?

GOSSIPER [*unsure*]: Sí, te entiendo.

Group 3

GOSSIPER: I don't like to gossip, but I think that something's going on with Roy and his new receptionist. Did you see them at the peña the other night? She had this red dress cut to [*pointing to cleavage, much lower than the first gossiper*] here.

GOSSIPER: No, I didn't see them. What were they doing?

GOSSIPER: Nothing. But like they say: where there's smoke, [*giving an exaggerated wink*] there's fire.

Group 4

GOSSIPER: A mí no me gusta el chisme, pero así son *todos* los hombres. Animales. Y Rogelio tan serio, tan calladito, ¿quién lo iba a pensar?

GOSSIPER: Los calladitos son los peores. Pero los pobres son humanos. ¿No vio el vestido que traiba la secretary? It was cut low—hasta [*pointing even lower*] aquí. Si se hubiera agachado, se le hubiera visto el ombligo.

Group 5

GOSSIPER: ¿Y la Connie qué dice?

GOSSIPER: ¿Pues qué va a decir? No sabe nada. Como dicen: la wife is the last one to know.

GOSSIPER: Pobrecita.

GOSSIPER: Sí, but don't forget, uno no sabe what goes behind closed doors. A la mejor Rogelio tiene motivo para andar messing around.

GOSSIPER: Sí, tiene motivo porque I heard que la Connie es bien mulita.

GOSSIPER: Pero es bueno ser mulita. Ella es muy buena trabajadora; she helped Roy make the company what it is today. I remember when they only had the one truck, and she used to take the kids to school while Roy and the crew were pouring the cement, and then she'd come back with the lunches for Roy and his workers, and—

GOSSIPER: Por eso mismo. You can't be a martyr. Anyway, she should've known that Roy was messing around. The signs were clear; she just didn't see them.

GOSSIPER: What signs?

GOSSIPER: When he started going to work all dressed up, showered and shaved with that Royal Copenhagen shaving lotion all over his body . . .

[EVERYBODY *focuses on the men, who pantomime dabbing shaving lotion on face, armpits, etc.*]

. . . but you want to know what the most obvious sign is?

GOSSIPER [*eagerly*]: What?

GOSSIPER: Chewing gum. If your husband starts mascando chicle, más claro no canta un gallo.

[EVERYBODY *focuses on the men, who pantomime chewing gum.*]

Group 6

GOSSIPER: ¿Verdad, que cantó bien bonito Doña Cuquita en la peña?

GOSSIPER: ¡Oh, sí! Pero dicen que Doña Cuquita no quedó igual desde que murió Don Arcenio. Pobrecita, tantos años juntos, no se halla sin él. 'Onde quiera andaban los dos juntos. Eran partners.

GOSSIPER: ¿Pues, cómo se va hallar sin él? Y ahora dicen que se le está yendo la mente. Se sienta así, viendo quién sabe qué, hablando sola, a veces la ven afuera en pajamas, cantando. Dicen que hasta platica con Don Arcenio. Y es por eso que la Connie la tiene que andar lideando como si Doña Cuquita fuera una baby.

GOSSIPER: Pues si la Connie tiene que cuidar a su mamá, con *más* ganas va a andar alborotado el Roy. Men cannot stand not being the center of the universe.

GOSSIPER: Pero la otra noche en la peña se portó muy bien la señora. Dicen que she even sang a real pretty song. Anyway, allí andaba la recepcionist, con un vestido rojo, cortado atrás hasta aquí. [*Turning and pointing to lower back*] Ya mero se le veía la crack.

GOSSIPER: Shhh, ahí viene la Connie.

CONSUELO [*again asking* OTHERS]: Have you seen Roy? ¿No han visto a Rogelio? [*Moving around*] Roy? Roy?

EVERYBODY [*in unison, with sympathy*]: Pobrecita.

LIGHTS: DOWN *and* OUT.

MUSIC: *Cumbia.*

END OF SCENE 1

* * *

Scene 2

TIME: *Some months later, early morning.*

PLACE: CONSUELO *and* ROGELIO's *home, in "kitchen" area. It is raining outside.*

[CONSUELO *and* COMADRE ROSIE *are sitting at the "table," drinking tea.* CONSUELO *is helping* COMADRE ROSIE *with paperwork.*]

COMADRE ROSIE: Thank you, comadre. Demetrio really needs help to get his landscape business going.

CONSUELO: No problem, Rosie. I'm glad to be of some help—just tell my brother to keep better records.

COMADRE ROSIE: I will. I wish I could help him more, but I don't know diddly-squat.

CONSUELO: Yes, you do! I love the logo you designed, and you're such a great "people person," you'll get plenty of clients. Just watch— before you know it, you and my brother will have that business going full steam. *Everyone* will be buying your trees.

COMADRE ROSIE: And *you* can run the business, just like you did—oops.

[*Awkward pause.*]

Oiga, comadre, ¿usted cree que mi compadre anda . . . messing around?

CONSUELO: No sé, Rosie, pero ya no quiere salir de la oficina; he's always working late. Y cuando él finally comes home, si le pregunto algo, se enoja y se va. I don't know what to do. He won't talk to me, Rosie.

COMADRE ROSIE: Así son todos los hombres, comadre.

CONSUELO: But Roy was never like that. I really don't know what it is. At first it was just little things, pero it's getting worse. Y maybe que así era antes, and I just didn't notice. Pero since my dad died and I've had to spend so much more time with my mom, como que se encela, like he resents my being busy with her.

COMADRE ROSIE: ¿Pues qué quiere?

CONSUELO: Dice que no sabe qué quiere. I thought that con los kids married or living on their own, we'd—you know, be alone, do things together, travel. We have the money; the company's doing well. Pero with my mom alone now, I can't just pack up and go with him nomás porque él quiere. Anyway, ya ni parece que quiere ir conmigo a ninguna parte. I guess he just got tired of me always saying, "No puedo dejar a mi mom sola." ¿Sabe, comadre? Sometimes I think he wants to leave me.

COMADRE ROSIE: No! Mira, Connie, take my advice. Todos los hombres son babies. They have to feel needed.

CONSUELO: But I *do* need him!

COMADRE ROSIE: Sí, pero you're very strong. You take care of things y nunca andas chillando.

CONSUELO: Well, Roy has always admired my strength.

COMADRE ROSIE: Sí, pero son pa' la fregada. Quieren que uno sea fuerte, pero también que los necesiten. Que los chipileyen.

CONSUELO: ¿Chipileyen? How?

COMADRE ROSIE: Así. [*Talking baby talk*] ¿Papito, estás cansado? ¿Te quito los papos? Ven, chéntate—

CONSUELO [*disbelieving*]: ¿Chéntate?

COMADRE ROSIE: Ajá. You have to baby them, pero también you have to be sexy. Mire, [*pulling her blouse off her shoulder*] así.

CONSUELO: Ay, comadre, I don't know … It sounds too complicated, too—

COMADRE ROSIE: I'm telling you, Connie, if Roy's messing around, and you want to keep him, you need to arm yourself with an entire arsenal—

CONSUELO: Rosie, you make it sound like I'm a fighter in one of those wars that Junior's always wanting to join.

COMADRE ROSIE: Pues, that's exactly what it is. A war to keep your husband—you have to do whatever it takes.

CONSUELO: But what if I don't do anything?

COMADRE ROSIE: He'll leave you, comadre. He'll leave you.

[CONSUELO *and* COMADRE ROSIE *counter cross and* EXIT. KATHY ENTERS, *dragging her daughter,* HEATHER.]

KATHY: Mom! [*To* HEATHER] Where is she? I told her I was bringing you over.

HEATHER [*whining as* KATHY *removes her raincoat*]: Why do I have to stay here? Why can't I go to school?

KATHY: Because they won't let you in without the paper from the doctor saying you got all your shots. Anyway, you'll have fun—Nana Cuquita's visiting Grandma.

HEATHER: Nana Cuquita's no fun. She doesn't even know who I am.

KATHY: Sure, she does. She just forgets now and then.

HEATHER [*messing with paperwork on the desk*]: Does Nana Cuquita live here now?

KATHY: No, I said she was visiting. Don't touch Grandma's papers; your hands are wet.

HEATHER: No, they're not.

KATHY: Well, then they're dirty.

HEATHER: No, they're not.

KATHY: I said don't touch Grandma's papers. She told me that the last time you were here, you got into all of her stuff from Dad's work.

HEATHER: She said I could play with the stapler and Scotch tape.

KATHY: Yes, but she didn't say you could polish your nails with the Wite-Out and staple all the pages in Grandpa's *TV Guide*, did she?

[CONSUELO ENTERS.]

CONSUELO: Déjala, Kathy. [*To* HEATHER] Hi, Heather. Is your mom giving you a hard time again?

HEATHER: Yes, Grandma. She says I can't play with any stuff in your office.

CONSUELO: Oh, sweetheart, yes, you can.

KATHY: Mom!

CONSUELO: Pues, how else is she going to learn to be an executive administrator? ¿Verdad, Heather? What do you want to be today?

HEATHER: The boss, Grandma—just like you! When I give you an order, you have to do what I say. Anything.

CONSUELO: Anything?

HEATHER: Yes, anything I say. Promise?

CONSUELO: Anything like what?

HEATHER: Like if I say, "Grandma Connie, time to stop working and time to go to Reid Park."

KATHY: Young lady, you're going back to school as soon as I get the doctor's form. You're not gonna run around anywhere with your grandma.

CONSUELO: Oh, Kathy, let her play. [To HEATHER] But your mom's right, honey. We can't go anywhere today because your Nana Cuquita's visiting.

HEATHER: We can take her with us!

CONSUELO: We'll see. [To KATHY] She doesn't want to go anywhere—says it's too cold. She doesn't want to do anything.

KATHY: Is Dad staying home today?

CONSUELO: No, he's going in later. It's too wet to take the crew out, so he's going to the office just to catch up on the paperwork.

KATHY: Paperwork? Aren't you doing it?

CONSUELO: Yes, but he's been teaching the receptionist a lot of my work. And she's really smart—besides, I'm too busy with your nana now.

KATHY: Is she better now?

CONSUELO: Yes, a little. She's eating a little more now.

KATHY: Is she still sleeping?

CONSUELO: Are you kidding? She gets up at four!

KATHY: At four! What can she possibly do at four?

CONSUELO: Oh, she finds things to do. She reads, putters around, cleans my kitchen all over again and again, straightens my desk—drives me crazy!

KATHY: Where is she now?

CONSUELO: Probably out feeding the neighbor's dog. She thinks it's underfed. Drives Doña Rosalía nuts!

KATHY: Well, I have to hurry—I'll get the form at lunch and pick up Heather and take her to school then. Bye.

[*She kisses* HEATHER *and* EXITS.]

CONSUELO: Heather, sweetie, have you had breakfast?

HEATHER: No, and Mom wouldn't stop at McDonald's.

CONSUELO: What would you like?

HEATHER: Umm, Belgian apple waffles with whipped cream.

CONSUELO: ¿Oh, sí? Belgian apple waffles with whipped cream? I've never heard of that.

HEATHER [*laughing*]: I made it up, Grandma! You can make me some French toast, with lots of syrup.

CONSUELO: Okay, I'll make you some French toast, c'mon.

[CONNIE *and* HEATHER *cross to "kitchen" area and are met by* NANA CUQUITA. *She is wet from rain outside.*]

CONSUELO: Buenos días, Mamá.

NANA CUQUITA: Buenos días, Consuelo.

CONSUELO: Mom! Look at you! You're all wet. ¿Qué anda haciendo afuera? Está lloviendo.

NANA CUQUITA [*emphatically*]: No está lloviendo.

CONSUELO: ¿Y entonces cómo trai el suéter tan mojado? [*Scolding her*] Quíteselo, le va a dar pulmonía. ¿Por qué se fue pa' fuera cuando está lloviendo?

NANA CUQUITA: Te digo que no está lloviendo.

CONSUELO [*removing* NANA CUQUITA's *sweater*]: ¿Qué andaba haciendo? Apuesto que le andaba dando comida al perro de la vecina, ¿verdad?

NANA CUQUITA: Pobrecito, lo tienen muerto de hambre.

CONSUELO: That's not true, Mom. La señora no quiere que usted le ande dando comida.

[CONSUELO *begins preparing French toast.*]

NANA CUQUITA: ¿Pues, entonces por qué no le da ella?

[NANA CUQUITA *sits down.*]

CONSUELO: She does, and he's on a special diet, so stop feeding him. [*Looking at* NANA CUQUITA's *shoes*] Are your shoes wet?

NANA CUQUITA [*a bit angry*]: No, ¡déjame en paz! Te digo que no está lloviendo.

CONSUELO [*trying to pacify her*]: Okay, Mom, está lloviznando. It's just sprinkling, pues.

NANA CUQUITA [*stubbornly*]: Chispeando. Nomás está chispeando.

CONSUELO [*annoyed*]: Lo que sea, lloviendo, lloviznando, chispeando—who cares? I just don't want you getting wet. [*Giving* NANA CUQUITA *another sweater and scolding her as though she were a child*] Tenga, póngase esta que está seca, y no vuelva a salirse pa' fuera, ¿me oyó?

NANA CUQUITA: No me regañes. Eso nomás faltaba, que me regañaras. [*Changing the subject when she notices* HEATHER] ¿Y esta niña quién es?

CONSUELO [*patiently*]: Es la Heather, Mom. Hija de la Kathy.

NANA CUQUITA [*mispronouncing*]: ¿Header? ¿Y por qué no está en la escuela? ¿Cuántos años tiene?

CONSUELO: She's six. Seis. Pero no puede ir a la escuela hasta que la Kathy les lleve un papel del doctor.

NANA CUQUITA: ¿Doctor? ¿Que está enferma? ¿Qué tiene?

CONSUELO: Nothing, Mom. The school just needs proof that she's had all her required shots.

NANA CUQUITA: ¿Shots? ¿Pues qué tiene? ¿Está enferma?

CONSUELO: No, Mom. It's the school's rules.

NANA CUQUITA: ¿Qué escuela?

CONSUELO: Heather's school.

NANA CUQUITA: ¿Qué Header?

CONSUELO [*yelling*]: ¡Esta Header! [*Correcting herself*] Heather! Heather! Her name is Heather!

NANA CUQUITA [*calmly*]: Pues no me grites que no estoy sorda.

CONSUELO [*contrite*]: I'm sorry, Mom. Dispénseme.

NANA CUQUITA [*still grumbling*]: ¡Qué bonito! Ahora sí que se voltearon las cosas. Los hijos le gritan a sus madres; se voltió el palito por el chirrión.

CONSUELO: I said I was sorry, Mom. ¿Quiere French toast?

[**ROGELIO ENTERS.**]

ROGELIO [*cheerfully*]: Buenos días, todos. Buenos días.

HEATHER: Morning, Grandpa.

ROGELIO [*surprised*]: Heather, m'ija! What are you doing here? Why aren't you in school?

HEATHER: 'Cause I didn't get my shots.

ROGELIO [*to* CONSUELO]: ¿Y por qué no agarro sus shots?

CONSUELO [*patiently but starting to get more exasperated*]: She *did* get her shots, Rogelio. But Kathy lost the copy of the doctor's forms, and she had to get another copy today. Are you coming home for lunch?

ROGELIO: What for? It's already late. Mejor llevo algo para comer en la oficina cuando me dé hambre. I'm gonna work late.

CONSUELO [*hiding her anger*]: Again?

ROGELIO [*defensively*]: Sabes muy bien que it's very difficult con las new tax laws. Did you finish the 941s? Los 1099s?

CONSUELO: Not yet, but don't worry—there's not that many left for me to do.

ROGELIO: ¿Por qué no me las das? The receptionist can finish them.

CONSUELO [*beating eggs furiously*]: Te digo que there's not that many left.

ROGELIO: Pues ya mero es the end of the quarter.

CONSUELO: I know, Rogelio, yo sé. Since when do you have to teach me my work?

ROGELIO [*at "refrigerator"*]: ¿Qué pasó con la chicken que quedó anoche?

CONSUELO: It's there.

ROGELIO: No, it's not. Yo la quería for some sandwiches.

CONSUELO: Well, eat out. ¿Qué te cuesta salir de la office?

ROGELIO: I don't want to eat out. I want to eat lunch in my office.

CONSUELO: And why can't you get out of the damn office? Why don't you just move into your office once and for all? Oh, just leave me alone! Ya déjame.

ROGELIO: I'll leave you alone—just give me the chicken.

CONSUELO: Está en el Tupperware. Búscala.

ROGELIO: It's not here. Ven *tú* y búscala.

CONSUELO: *You* look for it—I'm busy. Pareces chiquito, Rogelio.

ROGELIO: *Tú* pareces chiquita. ¿Qué te cuesta levantarte y darme la gallina *tú*?

CONSUELO: Porque no estás mocho, that's why.

ROGELIO: I tell you the chicken's not here. Someone ate it.

CONSUELO: Nadie se la comió. [*Realizing*] ¿Mom, se comió usted la gallina?

NANA CUQUITA [*maybe guilty, maybe not*]: ¿Gallina? ¿Qué gallina?

CONSUELO: La gallina que quedó anoche de la cena.

NANA CUQUITA: Yo no me he comido nada.

CONSUELO: It's okay if you did, Mom. Ah, ya sé. Se la dio al perro de Doña Rosalía, ¿verdad?

NANA CUQUITA: ¿Qué Rosalía?

CONSUELO [*to* ROGELIO]: I'm sorry, Roy. She keeps feeding the neighbor's dog. I can't stop her.

ROGELIO: ¿Y ahora qué llevo de lunch?

[*He crosses to* EXIT.]

CONSUELO: I'll fix something for you and take it to the office.

ROGELIO [*angrily*]: ¿Cómo, Connie, cómo? You're taking care of your mom *and* Heather. Never mind. And don't wait for me for supper—I'm working late.

CONSUELO: Of course you are.

[ROGELIO EXITS. *Awkward pause.*]

CONSUELO: Heather, you play quietly while I finish your grandpa's paperwork. [*To* NANA CUQUITA] Mom, tengo que terminar los papers del income tax de los trabajadores. No se vaya pa' fuera; está lloviendo.

NANA CUQUITA [*noticing* HEATHER *as though for the first time*]: ¿Y esta muchachita, de quién es?

HEATHER: Heather, Nana Cuquita. My name is Heather.

NANA CUQUITA: Header. [*To* CONSUELO] ¿Y por qué no está en la escuela?

Pues, ¿cuántos años tiene, Consuelo?

CONSUELO [*mechanically*]: Es la Heather, la hija de Kathy, mi hija. Tiene seis años y no fue a la escuela porque necesita una forma del doctor para comprobar que ya recibió sus inyecciones que exige la escuela. La Kathy va a ir por la forma a mediodía y luego va a venir por la Heather y la va a llevar a la escuela.

NANA CUQUITA: ¿Qué Header?

[**NANA CUQUITA EXITS** *without waiting for an answer.*]

CONSUELO [*repeating every word*]: Es la Heather, la hija de Kathy, mi hija. Tiene seis años y no fue a la escuela porque necesita una forma del doctor para comprobar que ya recibió sus inyecciones que exige la escuela. La Kathy va a ir por la forma a medio día y luego va a venir por la Heather y la va a llevar a la escuela.

HEATHER: Can I watch cartoons?

CONSUELO: Sure, but it's better if you watch them in Junior's room, okay? And not too loud, in case your nana decides to take a nap since she's surely been up since dawn.

HEATHER: How come she gets up so early?

CONSUELO [*joking*]: Because she had to feed the neighbor's dog your grandpa's chicken.

HEATHER: Is that why Grandpa got mad?

CONSUELO: Yeah, maybe.

[*Pause.*]

Heather, I have to go do something very important, but I have to wait for Junior to come home from work to take care of you and Nana Cuquita.

HEATHER: Where are you going?

CONSUELO [*resolutely*]: To the office to take care of business.

HEATHER: Okay, Grandma, but don't forget—you're the boss.

[**HEATHER EXITS.**]

CONSUELO: Yes, I am.

[**CONSUELO** *starts to dress slowly. She removes her apron, puts on high heels, combs her hair, puts on coat, and gets her purse, as she braces herself for* *confrontation with* LA RECEPTIONIST.]

LIGHTS: DOWN *and* UP.

MUSIC: *A paso doble, e.g., "Silverio Pérez," or a sexy tango.*

IMAGEN: *Las matadoras (The Killers).*

[WOMEN *wearing red dresses and red shawls pose with red roses between their teeth.* LA RECEPTIONIST *is wearing the same dress she wore to the peña. As* MUSIC *plays, the* WOMEN *dance very competitively with bullfighter steps, using their shawls as capes. When the dance ends, the* WOMEN EXIT. LA RECEPTIONIST *is at her "work" area, putting her red rose into a vase.*]

END OF SCENE 2

* * *

Scene 3

TIME: *Same day, late afternoon.*

PLACE: ROGELIO'*s office.*

[CONSUELO ENTERS.]

LA RECEPTIONIST [*very formal*]: Buenos días, Señora Madrigal.

CONSUELO: Buenos días.

[CONSUELO *sits across from* LA RECEPTIONIST.]

LA RECEPTIONIST [*slightly flustered, straightening papers on her "desk"*]: ¿Le puedo ayudar en algo?

CONSUELO: No, thanks, I'm waiting for Roy.

LA RECEPTIONIST: ¿Quiere que le hable por teléfono?

CONSUELO: No, I'll just wait. [*With some sarcasm*] I'm real good at waiting. You didn't know that, did you?

[LA RECEPTIONIST *doesn't answer. An obvious, uncomfortable pause as each tries to check out the other without getting caught.*]

LA RECEPTIONIST: Does Roy—I mean, Mr. Madrigal—does he know you're waiting for him?

CONSUELO: Yes, he does—do you?

LA RECEPTIONIST [*not understanding*]: ¿Perdón?

CONSUELO [*mimicking her*]: ¿Perdón? [*Abruptly picking up a magazine*] ¿Y estos?

LA RECEPTIONIST: Son magazines que trajo mi hermana para los clientes que tienen que esperar.

CONSUELO [*reading titles*]: Good Housekeeping, Better Homes and Gardens, Cosmopolitan.

LA RECEPTIONIST [*disdainfully*]: Son magazines para las housewives. I don't read them.

CONSUELO: No, you don't look the type.

LA RECEPTIONIST [*implying that* CONSUELO *is a housewife*]: Do *you* read them?

CONSUELO [*ignoring her question*]: So, you're not a housewife. What exactly do you do? Do you go out? Do you have friends? Oops, I forgot. You don't speak English that well. ¿Tienes amigas? Una muchacha—young and pretty like you—ha de tener muchos intereses fuera de la oficina, ¿no?

LA RECEPTIONIST [*with her feathers ruffled*]: My English is good enough. I can defend myself in *either* language.

CONSUELO: Defend yourself? But we're not at war, are we?

[*Pause.* CONSUELO *changes the subject.*]

Okay, in English: what do you do for your social life?

LA RECEPTIONIST: My social life? I like movies, eating out, dancing, shopping . . .

CONSUELO: Sounds like you lead a fun-filled life.

LA RECEPTIONIST: Sure, but my work and school are the most important things in my life. Well, at this time, anyway. I started late, so I really have a lot to catch up on.

CONSUELO: What do you study?

LA RECEPTIONIST: Corporate law.

CONSUELO: Corporate law? [*With some sarcasm*] Qué impressive. Y qué ambitious.

LA RECEPTIONIST [*again not understanding*]: ¿Perdón?

CONSUELO [*angrily*]: ¡Perdón! ¡Perdón! ¿Por qué pides tanto perdón?

LA RECEPTIONIST: Dispense, pero no la oyí bien. What were you saying?

CONSUELO: Ambition, hablaba de la ambición. You do know that word, don't you?

LA RECEPTIONIST [*forcefully*]: Yes, I know what ambition means. I know it very well.

CONSUELO: Of course you do.

[*Pause.* CONSUELO *backs off. She begins reading the titles on the magazine covers.*]

"Three hundred and sixty-five ways to cook chicken"—hmmm, Rogelio would like that. He loves his chicken. "Vitamins for your plants," "Is he communicating *his* needs?" "Cancún calls you"—

LA RECEPTIONIST: Cancún? Now, that's a city I'd like to visit. I've always loved the beach.

CONSUELO: Not me. I hate it 'cause the sand gets into everything. Oh, here's a quiz. I used to take them in the doctor's office, you know, before they called my name. Funny, I never had time to finish an article or to check my score. The nurses always call you. Maybe that's my problem, going through life without knowing my score?

LA RECEPTIONIST: Well, I don't know about you, but *I've* always known my score. I mean, on those stupid quizzes. You see, if you know yourself, you just have to read the title, answer one or two of the questions, then read the score at the end. Like I said, if you know yourself, you know your score.

CONSUELO: Well, I've always thought, "Consuelo, there's nothing to stop you from walking back to the reception area and finishing the article or quiz." But no one does that, do they? The receptionist hands you your next appointment card, or you make a payment, or thank the lady, and you walk out. Why don't we ever tell the receptionist, "Wait, I have some unfinished business here"?

[LA RECEPTIONIST *shrugs.* CONSUELO *leafs through more magazines. Pause.*]

Well, well, let's try this one: "What is your generosity quotient?" [*Sarcastically*] Pues, knowing *you*, you should blow the score off the page.

[LA RECEPTIONIST *opens her mouth to speak.*]

Oh, no, please, not another "¿perdón?" Mira, listen—"I'm the type of person who," fill in the blank. Here's a good one. Dice: "You're at a party, in front of you is the cake dish with just *one* slice of cake left. What would you do?" C'mon, complete the phrase. ¿Qué harías con el último pedazo del cake?

LA RECEPTIONIST: ¿Qué party? When I was a little girl, I never got invited to any party.

CONSUELO: Don't be so melodramatic. Besides, it's only an example. You can apply it to other things. It doesn't have to be the last slice of cake at a party, you know.

LA RECEPTIONIST: No, go on with the cake. ¿Qué quiere que diga? That I would leave that last slice of cake for someone else?

CONSUELO: For the hostess, maybe? Or the owner of the cake?

LA RECEPTIONIST: But we can assume that it was the hostess that put out the cake there for everyone to get some, no?

CONSUELO: Then can we assume that the hostess has already had plenty cake to eat? Before the guests arrived?

LA RECEPTIONIST [*laughing*]: Oh, sí, y que está repleta, bursting at the seams!

CONSUELO: I don't understand.

LA RECEPTIONIST: ¿Qué es lo que no entiende? It's your game, isn't it?

CONSUELO [*throwing magazine aside*]: Yes, but I don't want to play anymore.

LA RECEPTIONIST: No, siga.

CONSUELO [*standing up*]: I'm leaving.

LA RECEPTIONIST [*also standing up*]: ¿Y el cake? ¿Quién se queda con el dichoso cake?

CONSUELO: ¿Tú?

LA RECEPTIONIST [*crossing to* CONSUELO *and standing in front of her*]: I don't know if it's me or not. When I told you that I had never been to a party when I was little, I wasn't being melodramatic, era la verdad. Y ahora cuando voy a un party, I seem to get there late. And there isn't even a piece of cake left on that fancy crystal cake dish. Do you understand? Not one piece of cake. I'll complete the phrase, Señora Madrigal: I'm the type of person que lambe las sobras; I'll lick the leftovers. You've seen that kind, the ones who pick up every little crumb with their fingers? That's me. And you, Mrs. Madrigal, are you the type of person who *gives* away that last piece of cake?

CONSUELO: No, I'm not.

LA RECEPTIONIST: ¿No?

CONSUELO: No.

LA RECEPTIONIST: Ah, ya sé. ¿Entonces lo comparte? Mitad y mitad. You're the type of person who *shares* that last piece of cake, half and half. Right?

[CONSUELO *doesn't answer.*]

Am I right, Mrs. Madrigal?

[CONSUELO *crosses slowly to* EXIT. *She stops and turns to* LA RECEPTIONIST.]

CONSUELO: No sé. I really don't know if I could share.

LA RECEPTIONIST [*gathering magazines*]: Wait, this sounds interesting. [*Reading title*] "Does packing your husband's suitcase give you stress?"

[*They* FREEZE.]

IMAGEN: *Huapango de las maletas (Suitcase Shuffle).*

[WOMEN ENTER, *each is carrying a suitcase or a cardboard box, and they dance, exchanging suitcases or boxes, while* CONSUELO *and* LA RECEPTIONIST *watch.* ALL *except* CONSUELO EXIT *with suitcases.*]

MUSIC: *Huapango.*

END OF SCENE 3

* * *

Scene 4

TIME: *Another day, late afternoon.*

PLACE: CONSUELO's *living room.*

[CONSUELO *crosses and meets* JUNIOR, *who* ENTERS *with* NANA CUQUITA. JUNIOR *is carrying* NANA CUQUITA's *suitcases.*]

CONSUELO: Siéntese, Mom. [*To* JUNIOR] Take your nana's things to her room, please.

[JUNIOR EXITS.]

[*To* NANA CUQUITA] ¿Mom, quiere café?

NANA CUQUITA: No, Consuelo, yo no quiero café. Yo me quiero ir a mi casa. Llévame a mi casa.

JUNIOR: I still have some things in the trunk, so I'm gonna have to sneak out, Mom. Keep talking to her.

CONSUELO: What did you get?

JUNIOR: Okay, I've got the bathtub safety rail and a night lamp, and do you want me to go back and get the safety rail for the stairs?

CONSUELO: No, let your dad get it. He said he's putting it in this weekend. That's *if* he doesn't have to work late. Again.

JUNIOR: What about the back porch?

CONSUELO: Your dad's taking care of that, too. He's gonna make a cement ramp with a guardrail so she won't fall.

JUNIOR [*to* NANA CUQUITA]: ¿Ya ve, Abuelita? Yo le voy a comprar un chaize lounge pa' que se siente afuera, como una movie star en Hollywood, con sus shades, un big sombrero pa'l sol, y tomando una Singapore Sling.

CONSUELO: Oh, Junior, no seas tan simple.

JUNIOR: Bueno, pues, ¡nomás tomando una triste limonada! [*To* CONSUELO] Ahorita vengo.

[*He crosses to* EXIT, *and* KATHY ENTERS *with* HEATHER, *who is carrying a small suitcase. Greetings all around.*]

HEATHER: Hi, Tío Junior. Can I go with you?

KATHY: Heather, you don't even know where your tío's going and you want to tag along.

HEATHER: I do know where he's going, huh, Tío? You're going to Nicaragua, and you're going to take me with you so I can learn Spanish.

KATHY: Well, you can learn Spanish right here, young lady.

CONSUELO: Oh, Kathy, let her go with Junior. He's just going outside to get the night lamp and the safety rail that he bought at Home Depot for your nana's bathtub, so she won't fall.

[HEATHER *crosses to* JUNIOR.]

KATHY: But put your things away first.

[JUNIOR *pulls* HEATHER *quickly and* BOTH EXIT.]

Honestly, Mom. She never wants to stay home. The minute she sees someone leaving out the door, she wants to go, too.

CONSUELO: You should talk. I bet you don't even unpack your suitcases before you're off again. Heather takes after you.

KATHY: But it's my work, Mom—and it's not all fun.

CONSUELO: So, where are you off to now?

KATHY: Washington. Washington, D.C.

CONSUELO: Oh, sí, Washington? And it's not all fun?

KATHY: Well, yes, some. But it's meeting after meeting.

CONSUELO: And at night?

KATHY: We do go out. Sometimes. [*Changing the subject*] I know you're very busy taking care of Nana Cuquita—are you sure Heather can stay here? Otherwise, I could take her to Danny and Norma's.

CONSUELO: No, she can stay. Norma has enough with the baby always getting cólico. But she'll have to sleep here on the sofa. She won't mind, will she?

KATHY: She'll love it. She brought her sleeping bag and tent, and she'll probably take up all the space in the living room.

CONSUELO: That's okay. She won't bother anyone.

KATHY: Aren't you doing Dad's work here?

CONSUELO: No, not anymore.

[*Pause.*]

KATHY [*quickly, apparently knowing what's going on*]: I'll be back Monday. Thanks, Mom. Bye.

[KATHY EXITS.]

NANA CUQUITA: ¿Consuelo? Estoy cansada; me quiero acostar un rato.

CONSUELO: Sure, Mom. Venga conmigo.

[NANA CUQUITA *and* CONSUELO EXIT. DANNY *and* NORMA ENTER *with baby Danny in car seat.*]

DANNY: Mom? Mom!

NORMA: Maybe she's not here, Danny.

DANNY: Sure, she's here. You know she has to stay home with Grandma Cuquita.

CONSUELO [*entering*]: Hi, Norma, Danny. [*Seeing baby*] Oh, no, please don't ask me to babysit.

DANNY: No, Mom. We don't need you to babysit today. We're driving to Nogales to visit Norma's family. We want them to see the baby.

CONSUELO: Good, 'cause I've got your grandmother living here now, and Heather's staying for the weekend. Are you driving all the way to Nogales? You know it's raining, so you better be careful.

DANNY: We will. Anyway, we'll be stopping along the way, so don't worry. We just came over to see you before we left.

CONSUELO: Well, I'm glad you did, m'ijo. Pero mucho cuidado. Norma, make him stop if you see him getting sleepy.

NORMA: Oh, I will. I want to stop and stay at a Motel 6!

DANNY: Norma, it's only an hour away.

[DANNY *and* NORMA EXIT. ROGELIO ENTERS *and tries to cross quickly past* CONSUELO.]

CONSUELO: Rogelio, please wait.

ROGELIO: Espérate, I have to clean up, Connie.

CONSUELO: I asked you to please wait. We have to talk.

ROGELIO: Te digo que to esperes. Why can't I walk in here without you nagging?

CONSUELO: I'm not nagging, Roy. We never talk. You're never home. What's wrong?

ROGELIO: And you don't call that nagging?

CONSUELO: Please, Roy. Honey?

ROGELIO: Okay, vamos a hablar, but let me get cleaned up first. Mírame, tengo cement all over my hands and arms.

CONSUELO: This is more important than cleaning off the cement, Roy—

[ROGELIO EXITS. JUNIOR *and* HEATHER ENTER. JUNIOR *starts unpacking his boxes.*]

HEATHER: Help me set up my tent, Tío Junior.

JUNIOR: In a minute, Heather. Let me figure out what I'm doing first.

HEATHER: Grandma Connie, this is going to be our jungle, and we're going to fight the—who, Tío Junior?

JUNIOR [*not looking up from the instruction sheet he's reading*]: The Contras.

HEATHER: The Contras, Grandma. We're fighting the Contras in the revolution.

JUNIOR [*still reading*]: They make everything so hard. Well, let's see—I *think* I can do it.

[JUNIOR *crosses to* EXIT.]

CONSUELO: Sure, m'ijo. If you can fight in revolutions, you can surely install your nana's safety rail.

[JUNIOR *puts on heavily equipped belt with tools and, holding big hammer, salutes and* EXITS, *almost marching.*]

HEATHER: Grandma, I need blankets.

CONSUELO: They're in your nana Cuquita's closet. Go get them.

[HEATHER EXITS. JUNIOR's *hammering can be heard throughout the following dialogue, sometimes softly, sometimes loudly.*]

[HEATHER ENTERS *again.*]

HEATHER [*running, with a blanket in hand*]: Grandma Connie! Nana Cuquita wet her panties!

CONSUELO: What?

HEATHER [*repeating*]: Nana Cuquita wet her panties! She's all wet!

CONSUELO: Oh, no!

[CONSUELO EXITS, *and* ROGELIO ENTERS *from opposite side, carrying a suitcase.*]

HEATHER: Grandpa, can you help me with my tent?

ROGELIO [*pacing nervously*]: Not right now, Heather. I'm busy.

HEATHER [*puzzled*]: What are you doing?

ROGELIO: I'm thinking. [*Changing his mind*] A ver, pues, let me see.

[*He spreads out the blanket.* CONSUELO ENTERS, *drying her hands.*]

CONSUELO: Pobrecita, my mom. She couldn't get into the bathroom 'cause Junior's in there installing her safety rail—

[*She sees* ROGELIO's *suitcase.*]

¿Roy, para dónde vas?

ROGELIO: I need to get away, Connie.

CONSUELO: You need to get away? Where to? [*Referring to the magazine article*] Cancún?

ROGELIO: What?

CONSUELO: Are you going to Cancún with your receptionist, ¿la pinchi guacha?

ROGELIO: She's not a wetback.

CONSUELO: Oh, no? You could've fooled me.

ROGELIO: She has nothing to do with this, so don't start anything, Connie.

CONSUELO: I'm not starting anything. Why can't—

ROGELIO: I'm leaving you, Connie.

CONSUELO: What did you say?

ROGELIO: I said that I'm leaving you.

CONSUELO: Why, Roy? What have I done to you? What have I done wrong?

[**CONSUELO** *tries to grab his arm, but* **ROGELIO** *pulls away from her.*]

ROGELIO: I know this sounds stupid, but it's not you—it's me. I have to get away, Connie. I feel like I'm suffocating, choking. Let me go, Connie. You're making things worse. I'll come back later. We can talk then. All right?

CONSUELO: ¿Qué vas a hacer, Roy?

ROGELIO [*acting dumb*]: Voy a llevar estas cosas que necesito.

CONSUELO: You know darn well that I mean what are you going to do about *us*?

ROGELIO: I don't know, Connie. I need more time.

CONSUELO: More time for what?

ROGELIO: I told you. I need time to think.

CONSUELO: What's there to think?

ROGELIO: About us. You. Me.

CONSUELO: And moving out helps you think?

ROGELIO: No. I mean, no sé que quiero. I need something, pero no sé qué.

CONSUELO: ¿Pues qué quieres? We have the business, the kids are all doing fine. You're healthy, we have the house paid for. What more do you need?

ROGELIO: ¿Qué no me oyiste? Te digo que I don't know what I want.

CONSUELO: Well, I don't need any *thinking*—let me tell you what *I* want. I want you to either stay or you can leave for good.

[JUNIOR's *hammering is louder. One loud hammer blow, then* JUNIOR's *very loud howl of pain from smashing his thumb is heard.* HEATHER EXITS. CONSUELO *starts to laugh softly until* ROGELIO *is annoyed.*]

ROGELIO: ¿Qué tienes? What's the matter with you? Stop it. What's so goddamn funny? Stop it, te digo.

CONSUELO [*rising hysteria*]: Funny? What's funny? I'll tell you what's funny, Roy. Me! ME! I'm funny. Kathy's in an airplane somewhere, going to Washington; Danny and Norma just left on their way to Nogales, and I'm praying that Norma makes him stop at a Motel 6 in half an hour. Junior's in the bathroom hammering his thumbs, working for revolutions, sepa-la-chingada where, and I'm standing here wondering, where can I buy Pampers for my mother? You're standing there with a packed suitcase, and I'm hearing your "it's not you, it's me" bullshit, and you tell me that you're leaving me because you need to *think*—and you're asking me what's funny?

ROGELIO [*shaking his head and picking up his suitcase*]: I'll come back when you're ready to talk.

[ROGELIO EXITS. NANA CUQUITA ENTERS *and crosses to* CONSUELO, *who is fighting tears.*]

NANA CUQUITA: No llores, Consuelo. [*Holding* CONSUELO, *comforting her*] No llores, m'ija. Me vas a hacer llorar a mí. Siempre que te lastimaba algo y llorabas, yo también me ponía a llorar contigo. No llores, hija. Y te cantaba tu canción. [*Starting to sing nursery song*] "Naranja dulce, limón partido, dame un abrazo por Dios te pido . . ."

[*They* FREEZE.]

IMAGEN: *Juegos de mi niñez (My Childhood Games).*

[EVERYBODY ENTERS, *carrying toys, wearing cowboy hats, riding on broom* "horses," and they pair off in couples or get into circles, depending on game requirements. Lots of movement and pantomime.]

Game: "Las calabacitas"

[**ALL** form a circle and go round and round like "Ring Around the Rosy."]

ALL: ¡¡Las calabacitas se queman, se queman, y el que no se abraza se queda de burro!!

[**ALL** hug at the word "burro."]

Game: "Agua té"

ALL [forming two lines]: Agua té, matarile, rile, rile. Agua té, matarile, rile, rile ron. ¿Qué quiere usted, matarile, rile, rile? ¿Qué quiere usted? Matarile, rile, rile, ron.

Game: "Reque, reque"

ALL [paired off in partners, rocking]: Reque, reque, reque ran, la manera de San Juan, pide pan y no le dan. Pide queso y le dan un hueso. ¡Pa' que se rasque el pescuezo!

[**ALL** tickle their partners' necks.]

Game: "Este era un gato"

ALL [paired off in partners and repeating three or four times]: Este era un gato, con las patas de trapo y los ojos volteados al revés. ¿Quieres que te lo cuente otra vez?

Game: "Dos y dos"

ALL [paired off in partners, clapping hands, and repeating]: ¡Dos y dos son cuatro, cuatro y dos son seis, seis y dos son ocho y ocho diez y seis!

Game: "Ahí viene la luna"

ALL [paired off in partners or in a circle]: ¡Ahí viene la luna comiendo la tuna, tirando la cáscara en la laguna!

Game: "Sana, sana"

ALL [in a circle]: ¡Sana, sana, colita de rana! ¡Si no sanas ahora, sanarás mañana!

Game: "Tortillitas"

ALL [paired off in partners, clapping and repeating]: ¡Tortillitas pa' Mamá!

¡Tortillitas pa' Papá! ¡Las bonitas pa' Mamá! ¡Las quemaditas pa' Papá!

Game: "Agua té"

ALL [in a circle, ending chorus]: Agua té, matarile, rile, rile. Agua té, matarile rile, ron. ¡Aquí le traigo a mi hija con dolor de corazón, bailaremos todos juntos con la cola de un ratón!

[EVERYBODY skips offstage, singing softly "Naranja dulce."]

NANA CUQUITA [singing to CONSUELO]: "Naranja dulce, limón partido, dame un abrazo por Dios te pido . . ."

LIGHTS: DOWN and OUT.

END OF SCENE 4

* * *

Scene 5

TIME: Late afternoon, the day before NANA CUQUITA's sixty-sixth birthday

PLACE: CONSUELO's living room.

[HEATHER is playing quietly. ROGELIO ENTERS.]

ROGELIO: Hi, Heather.

HEATHER: Grandpa! [Running to and hugging ROGELIO] Did you come back? Are you staying? I miss you.

ROGELIO: No, m'ija. I just came for a few things.

HEATHER: How come you don't want to live here anymore?

ROGELIO: Cómo preguntas, little bird. Where's your Grandma Connie?

HEATHER: Giving Nana Cuquita a bath; she's always wetting her chones. Do you want me to call her?

ROGELIO: No, that's okay. I'll find her. [Crossing upstage and calling out] Connie! It's me; vine por unas cosas.

[CONSUELO ENTERS quickly, drying her hands with a towel.]

CONSUELO: Heather, go and stay with your Nana. Just watch her. I'll be right there; I just need to talk to your grandpa.

HEATHER: Can I make soap bubbles? Nana Cuquita likes to blow bubbles with me.

CONSUELO: Yes, but keep the water warm, okay? Not too hot and not too cold.

HEATHER: I know! I know! Just like baby Danny's water. Tía Norma showed me.

[HEATHER EXITS.]

ROGELIO: I'll talk to you later, when you're not so busy.

[*He crosses to* EXIT, *but stops just before reaching offstage.*]

HEATHER [*entering*]: Grandma, I think Nana Cuquita wants to get out. There's no more bubbles.

CONSUELO: I'll be right there. Stay with with her.

[HEATHER EXITS, *and* JUNIOR ENTERS, *carrying presents.*]

JUNIOR: Hi, Dad. How are you?

ROGELIO: Fine, m'ijo. I just came to get a few things I need. I don't have time to talk with you right now. Stop by the office, okay?

[ROGELIO EXITS *quickly.*]

JUNIOR: Look, Mom. Le compré a mi abuelita estos regalos para su birthday.

[CONSUELO *doesn't respond.*]

Did you forget? Mañana's her birthday. You forgot, didn't you?

CONSUELO: Junior, my life's falling apart at the seams and you expect me to remember my mother's birthday?

JUNIOR: Sure, why not?

HEATHER [*offstage*]: Grandma! C'mere, Grandma Cuquita's crying.

CONSUELO [*angrily*]: Why not? Why not? [*Crossing stage*] That woman is sitting in the tub, crying, and I have to get her out, dry her, put her in adult diapers, dress her, feed her, change her when she pees or shits, and now you want me to remember her birthday?

[CONSUELO EXITS. JUNIOR *is concerned but decides to sit down and write the birthday card.* CONSUELO ENTERS *with* NANA CUQUITA *and* HEATHER. NANA CUQUITA *is wearing a robe, old slippers, and has a towel around her hair.* CONSUELO *leads her to a chair, removes the towel, and dries and combs her hair.*]

JUNIOR [*quietly*]: Mom, why are you so angry?

CONSUELO: I'm angry, Junior, because you of all people should understand what I'm going through and help me.

JUNIOR: I *do* understand, and I *am* helping you.

CONSUELO: How? By planning a birthday party for her? Don't you understand how hopeless that is? That she doesn't remember anything? Ya no se acuerda de nada, Junior. Nada. Es como una niña. Worse, porque una niña crece, learns, pero ella no. Look at her. Así se pasa todo el día; ni sabe quién soy.

JUNIOR: You don't know that, Mom. You don't know that for sure. Maybe somewhere in her mind, in her memories, she remembers. We don't know—not even the genius doctors know. Mom, yo quiero a mi abuelita, siempre la he querido. You taught me to love, Mom, how can I stop loving her now? [*Crossing to* NANA CUQUITA] Y sí le vamos a hacer un party a mi abuelita. [*Showing* NANA CUQUITA *the present*] Mire, Nana, un present. Y no nos vamos a esperar hasta mañana. [*Unwrapping it and showing her a silk bed jacket*] Que bonita, ¿verdad? [*Putting the bed jacket on her*] ¿Le gusta?

[**NANA CUQUITA** *smiles.*]

See, Mom? That's how I want my nana to remember me. Siempre. Que yo la quiero mucho. [*To* NANA CUQUITA] Mañana es su birthday, y le vamos a hacer un party. ¿Se acuerda last year? Le cantamos "Las mañanitas," y "Sapos Verdes to You," y comimos cake, y le cantó a mi tata Arcenio su favorite song, la Kathy va venir a peinarla, pa' que se vea bien pretty, y la Norma le va bake su cake. It's her first one, so let's hope it comes out okay—

CONSUELO [*softly*]: Junior?

[**JUNIOR** *looks up. Pause.*]

I'm sorry, m'ijo, for what I said. I didn't mean it. I was angry. And tired.

JUNIOR: I know, Mom. But we're gonna help you. We'll work something out between us. [*Handing another present to* CONSUELO] See? This present's from you to Nana. [*To* HEATHER] Ready, Heather?

HEATHER [*hugging and kissing* CONSUELO *and* NANA CUQUITA]: Bye, Grandma. Bye, Nana Cuquita.

[*She starts to* EXIT *with* JUNIOR.]

CONSUELO: M'ijo, dile al Danny que traiga a la Norma early so I can help her with the cake.

JUNIOR: Okay, Mom. [*To* HEATHER] Ummm, Heather, banana nut with cream cheese frosting.

[**BOTH EXIT**, *discussing cakes.*]

CONSUELO [*crossing to* NANA CUQUITA]: Mire, 'Amá, otro regalo.

[*She opens and takes out slippers from the present* JUNIOR *gave her. She kneels and removes the old slippers from* NANA CUQUITA's *feet and replaces them with the new ones.*]

Mire, que bonitas slippers. Pink, my favorite color. ¿Cuál es su color favorito? Ah, yo sé, guinda. I looked it up; guinda is cherry colored. ¿Se acuerda de aquel vestido color guinda? Guinda con un cuellito blanco. You were holding on to your dress, and Dad was laughing, wanting the whole world to see your pretty legs, remember? Remember?

[CONSUELO *puts her head on* NANA CUQUITA's *lap.*]

¿Se acuerda? Lo usó en Veracruz, con mi dad, remember? It was windy, and you held it down. ¿Se acuerda, Mom? You were younger than I am now. Do you remember my dad?

[**LIGHTS** *go* **UP**, *and marimba* **MUSIC** *plays.*]

You were walking up and down the malecón . . .

[**YOUNG ARCENIO** *and* **YOUNG NANA CUQUITA ENTER**, *running, laughing, teasing.*]

Remember how strong the wind was? ¿Se acuerda que fuerte volaba el viento?

[*Offstage a fan blows hard air toward the couple.* **YOUNG CUQUITA**'s *dress flies up, and she tries to hold it down.*]

[*Laughing*] And the wind was blowing your dress! Do you remember what Dad was telling you?

YOUNG ARCENIO: Déjate el vestido, Cuquita. Que lo vuele el viento. [*Playfully*] ¡Que te vea todo el mundo tus hermosas piernas!

[**YOUNG ARCENIO** *pulls* **YOUNG CUQUITA**'s *hands away from her dress.*]

CONSUELO: He wanted the world to see your lovely legs! What did you tell him, Mom?

YOUNG CUQUITA: Arcenio, estate quieto. ¿Qué va a decir la gente?

YOUNG ARCENIO [*putting his arm around* YOUNG CUQUITA]: Que te quiero, eso van a decir. Que hablen, déjalos, que hablen.

CONSUELO: He didn't care what people said. He loved you so much.

YOUNG ARCENIO [*pulling* YOUNG CUQUITA *in close*]: Van a cerrar las tiendas y me falta un regalo más.

YOUNG CUQUITA: Pero si ya llevas tantos regalos, Arcenio; no tienes más campo para otro.

YOUNG ARCENIO: Sí, pero quiero un regalo muy espacial para ti, mi reina.

YOUNG CUQUITA: ¿Especial?

YOUNG ARCENIO: Sí, muy especial. Un regalo que diga, "Recuerdo de Veracruz," para que nunca te olvides de nuestros días aquí en Veracruz.

YOUNG CUQUITA: Jamás olvidaré estos días contigo, mi rey.

YOUNG ARCENIO: Bueno, corre, Cuquita. Corre.

[YOUNG ARCENIO *and* YOUNG CUQUITA EXIT, *laughing.*]

[MUSIC: *Marimba* DOWN *and* OUT.]

[NANA CUQUITA *is crying softly.*]

CONSUELO: You do remember, don't you, Mom? But don't cry. No llore, 'Amá. Si llora, me va a hacer llorar a mí. I love you, Mom. [*Standing up, hugging and rocking* NANA CUQUITA] No llore, Mom, don't cry.

[TATA ARCENIO ENTERS. *He stands behind* NANA CUQUITA *and places his hands on her shoulders.* NANA CUQUITA *reaches up and holds his hands.* CONSUELO *looks at both and moves slightly away from them.* ROGELIO ENTERS. *He stands behind* CONSUELO *and places his hands on her shoulders.* CONSUELO *reaches up and holds his hand. They* FREEZE.]

[EVERYBODY ENTERS, *and* TATA ARCENIO, NANA CUQUITA, CONSUELO, *and* ROGELIO *break* FREEZE.]

EVERYBODY [*singing*]: "Estas son las mañanitas que cantaba el Rey David, a las muchachas bonitas se las cantamos así. Despierta mi bien, despierta, mira que ya amaneció, ya los pajarillos cantan, la luna ya se metió . . ."

LIGHTS: DOWN.

* * *

Finale/Curtain

LIGHTS: UP.

[**EVERYBODY FREEZES** *as if posing for a group photograph.*]

END OF PLAY

THREE

A Drunkard's Tale of Melted Wings and Memories

Synopsis

Nacho "el Borracho" Robles is a paralyzed World War II veteran who lives in a lean-to shed in the backyard of a west-side Tucson barrio sarcastically nicknamed "Hollywood." His landlady, Helen Encinas, a churchgoing spinster, and the deceased Watusi and Artemisa had been Nacho's friends since they were teenagers in the 1940s. They were the four "batos locos" of Barrio Hollywood until Pearl Harbor, and their wild party life continued even when Nacho returned in a wheelchair with Watusi, who suffers from post-traumatic stress syndrome before it's been identified, as his "bodyguard."

Artemisa gets pregnant by a soldier passing through Tucson, and Nacho and Helen baptize her baby Roshanda. Motherhood doesn't stop Artemisa's dancing, but her drunken driving does; she is killed in an automobile accident. Watusi commits suicide by placing himself on the railroad tracks. Helen, refusing to accept any responsibility for Artemisa's death, also refuses to share any memories with Nacho and turns to the church for comfort, while Nacho finds oblivion to his pain by getting senselessly drunk every night, reliving the past, singing, reading old newspaper clippings, and reciting the names of dead comrades with Artemisa and Watusi.

By day, Nacho fixes the barrio residents' small appliances and lives for Roshanda's visits. Roshanda has married Helen's nephew, Hector, and has three small children, and their best friend is Catungas, Watusi's son. Even though Helen and Nacho object strongly, Roshanda, Hector, and Catungas decide to make an old abandoned building into a neighborhood centro, where they can have history, Spanish, and typing classes, as well as daycare, movies, and other activities. They are joined by Moonbeam, a California hippie, and the centro becomes a reality. However, the Movimiento Chicano and FBI meet and collide with their human passions, strengths, and frailties, until another life, another dream may or may not be lost forever.

Cast

NACHO "EL BORRACHO" ROBLES, *a paralyzed World War II veteran, age fifty to fifty-five. He is the barrio drunk and Roshanda's padrino.*
CARLOS ANDRES FLORES, SR. (WATUSI), *a deceased decorated World War II veteran in his early twenties. He is Nacho's best friend.*

ARTEMISA, *died in a car wreck in early 1950s, when she was in her early twenties. She is Nacho's sweetheart and Roshanda's mother.*

HELEN ENCINAS, *faded barrio rose in her late forties. She is Nacho's landlady and Hector's aunt. Since she has saved all her dresses and shoes from the 1940s, she dresses and combs her hair exactly as she did during World War II. Somewhat bitter, she faces stiff competition with Nacho's memories of Artemisa.*

CARLOS ANDRES FLORES, JR. (CATUNGAS), *Watusi's son. He is a close family friend of Nacho, Roshanda, and their families, and roofer by trade. He is in his early twenties and moves clumsily like an overgrown bear cub. He is lovable and lazy but tolerated by everyone. A product of our educational system, he manages to mangle both English and Spanish, speaking puras pendejadas most of the time.*

ROSHANDA, *quick-moving teacher's aide in her early twenties and mother of three—Junior, Diana, and baby Gloria. She resembles Artemisa.*

HECTOR ENCINAS, *mid-twenties, Roshanda's husband, works for the city sanitation department as a garbage collector.*

MOONBEAM, *a typical gringa hippie, who looks to be in her late teens but is actually in her late twenties. She is the gringa villain so vital to Chicano theater, and in this case, is an FBI infiltrator for COINTELPRO.*

CALAVERA, *a Teatro Chicano actor of any age, may be played by Helen or Moonbeam, if she can change costume fast enough, or another actor.*

IRATE NEIGHBORS, *offstage, voices may be recorded or live.*

The CENTRO, *an old abandoned building. Please note that it must be listed on program as part of the cast.*

Technical Notes

Only NACHO can hear and see ARTEMISA and WATUSI (throughout), and ROSHANDA (in act 3, scene 2). HELEN and CATUNGAS will be able to hear them when necessary, but they cannot see them.

MUSIC

Aside from the music indicated, other Spanish or English protest or party music from the 1960s and 1970s may be selected. In addition to the music in act 2, there will be many sounds of activity from within the CENTRO, such as typing, hammering, children singing, etc., to show that the CENTRO has its own energy and vitality.

LANGUAGE

Please note that the playwright has attempted to faithfully reproduce Chicano working-class diction, syntax, Caló, code-switching, and Spanglish. However, to accommodate non-Spanish-speaking audience members, HELEN and NACHO speak more English, rather than the Spanish they would normally speak. Although it may sometimes be necessary to change a word such as "lana" or "jando" to a more familiar, regional word to mean "money" or "dollars," bigger changes may not be made without permission.

SET

It is the backyard of a typical barrio. Only the back walls, windows, doors, and doorsteps are seen. NACHO lives in a lean-to shed at stage right that is connected to HELEN's house. HELEN's house is center stage, and an empty, neglected building is at stage left. A tall, broken-down fence runs between the house and the building, and part of another fence is downstage right next to NACHO's shed and HELEN's small garden patch and clothesline. NACHO has a very cluttered small table at center stage where he repairs small appliances for the barrio residents. NACHO's shed is neat and sparsely furnished with an army cot, crates filled with many books, a table with hot plate and two pans, etc. There is a garbage can near a latched gate at stage left. Parts of the street may be seen through the fences, and there is prickly pear cactus growing on the street side of the fences. NACHO has a tiny bathroom and shower next to his shed, but it is not seen completely. The roof of NACHO's shed is covered with sheets of tin and has various unmatched shoes and other objects thrown onto it. HELEN's house and the empty building have steps that NACHO cannot climb.

The set will remain the same throughout the entire play.

ACT I

Scene 1

TIME: *A hot summer in the early 1970s, late at night.*

PLACE: *A backyard in Barrio Hollywood, Tucson, Arizona. The backyard is dimly lit and bathed in moonlight.*

[NACHO *is sitting in his wheelchair by the garden. He is wearing a scruffy but clean A-shirt, khaki pants, fatigue jacket, and army dog tags.* WATUSI, *dressed smartly in starched army khakis, is standing stage left.* ARTEMISA *and* HELEN *are standing stage right. They are dressed in elegant "chuca" fashion.* NACHO *is lost in his memories from back sometime in the forties, and he is seeing his three friends as they laugh and dance around with each other. Swing* MUSIC *or jitterbug from the 1940s, possibly something by Lalo Guerrero, plays.* WATUSI *holds out his hand to* HELEN, *asking her to dance. She shakes her head no, and* WATUSI *moves into the shadows.* ARTEMISA *twirls away and moves into the shadows to* WATUSI. ALL THREE EXIT.]

[*An instrumental "Stardust" by the Glenn Miller Orchestra plays.* NACHO *is holding a copy of one of Shakespeare's plays and is talking to himself, somewhat drunk.*]

NACHO [*dreamily singing parts of "Stardust"*]: "Sometimes I wonder why I spend the lonely night, dreaming of a song, the memory haunts my reverie, and I am once again with you, when our love was new and each kiss an inspiration." [*Caressing the book*] Shakespeare, quote: "All the world's a stage and all the men . . ." I forget the rest.

[*Pause.*]

Anyway, it's true. "All the world's a stage." And we're all actors in "a tale, told by an idiot, full of sound and fury, signifying nothing." Sound and fury. Faulkner. Or is it a tale told by a drunkard—un borracho, just like me. Well, it's the same thing, no?—drunkard, idiot, es la misma chingadera. [*Going to his shelves near his army cot and getting a metal file box*] Shakespeare again, quote: "To weep is to make less the depth of grief." [*Taking a bottle of wine next to him in wheelchair*] To weep for that catharsis so loved by the Greeks. Nacho, quote: "I'll drink to that."

[NACHO *drinks the remains and tosses the empty bottle carelessly to the side. He wheels himself to downstage right near the fence.*]

[*Singing drunkenly*] "Me voy de soldado raso, voy a ingresar a las filas . . ."

[*He stares intently at a loose fence board, waiting expectantly until he hears soft footsteps. He doesn't move. A hand comes through the fence; it is holding a bottle of cheap wine. The bottle is tossed into the yerba buena plants, and the hand is pulled out quickly.* NACHO *waits a few seconds until he no longer hears the retreating footsteps.*]

[*Saluting smartly*] Gracias.

[*Then he very eagerly gets the bottle, opens it, and drinks with great thirst.*]

" . . . con los muchachos valientes que dejan madres queridas, que dejan novias llorando, llorando su despedida."

[*He takes newspaper clippings from the file box and reads them as he sings incomplete verses of "Soldado raso."*]

" . . . ya volveré de sargento cuando se acabe la bola; nomás una cosa siento, es dejar a mi madre sola . . ." [*Reading*] "Carlos Andrés Flores was awarded the Congressional Medal of Honor and the Distinguished Service Cross for exemplary valor and courage in battle at Rosenkrantz, France, on July 19, 1944 . . ." Carlos Andrés Flores—el Watusi, my best friend.

[*He drinks more wine and continues singing.*]

" . . . y aquí va otro mexicano que va a jugarse la vida, que se despide cantando, que viva la patria mía." ¿Te acuerdas, Watusi? Watusi? [*Very loudly*] Watusi! ¡Ven, Watusi!

[WATUSI *Steps out from the shadows. He is wearing full military dress, and his very curly hair is slicked back under his army cap. His semblance is ghostly, pale.*]

WATUSI: Simón que me acuerdo, Nacho, simón. We were en el train station on Toole Avenue con la marching band del Southern Pacific, las chavalonas kissing us, promising to wait forever—

NACHO: Y la Artemisa was there, too, Watusi, ¿te acuerdas? ¿Con la Helen?

WATUSI: Simón, the two chucas were inseparable. La Helen, who couldn't see my love for her, y la Artemisa, tu sweetheart. Singing in your ear. Off-key, como siempre.

NACHO: "Cuatro vidas." Was that the song, Watusi?

WATUSI: Nacho, Nacho. It can be whatever song you want it to be. These are your memories, remember?

NACHO: Then I want it to be "Cuatro vidas," Watusi. She said it was our song 'cause we were the four locos from Barrio Hollywood. I remember, Watusi. [*Singing*] "Vida, si tuviera cuatro vidas, cuatro . . ."

[*Pause.*]

> [*Somewhat pleading*] Watusi, tell her to come out. To come and sit here with us. To sing with me. [*Calling*] Artemisa, ¡ven! [*Very loudly*] ARTEMISA!

IRATE NEIGHBORS [*offstage, complaining*]: There he goes again—duérmete, Nacho. Deja dormir, con mil chingados; tengo que trabajar mañana. Verás, first he starts with his singing and Artemisa and then his dead soldiers.

NACHO [*ignoring them*]: ¡Artemisa! Ven a cantar conmigo y el Watusi. [*Singing*] "Alma, si te llevas mi alma, contento moriría por ti—"

[**ARTEMISA ENTERS** *from the shadows. She is wearing a 1940s floral blouse, wide-legged pants, and wedged high heels. Her hair is in "chuca" pompadour style, and her semblance is also ghostly, pale.*]

ARTEMISA [*singing*]: "Corazón, en mi corazón te llevas mi alma, mi vida, y mi ser."

[*She stands behind* **NACHO** *and caresses his face as she sings.*]

> "Si tuviera cuatro vidas, cuatro vidas serían para ti."

NACHO: Baila con ella, Watusi. [*Drinking his wine*] I want to see her dancing.

WATUSI [*taking* **ARTEMISA**'s *hand, singing and pulling her to him*]: "Vida, si tuviera cuatro vidas, cuatro vidas serían para ti."

[*They dance as* **NACHO** *watches.*]

NACHO [*calling to* **HELEN**'s *house*]: Helen! Come and sing with them, Helen.

[**NACHO** *starts to go toward* **HELEN**'s *doorsteps.*]

> Helen!

[**ARTEMISA** *stops dancing suddenly and pulls herself away from* **WATUSI.**]

ARTEMISA: No! Nacho, don't call her.

[*She goes to* **NACHO** *and blocks his way.*]

> No la llames. I don't want her here with us; I'll leave if she comes

outside. Make her stay inside. Just us, Nacho, please. Me, you, and Watusi. Nomás nosotros. Please, Nacho, just us.

[*Pause.*]

Watusi?

WATUSI [*knowing what* ARTEMISA *wants*]: Órale, Nacho, read us some more—ándale, carnal, read about los manitos de New Mexico . . .

NACHO [*distractedly*]: They killed all of them in Bataan. [*Mumbling*] The Death March, Wake, Guam, Midway, Corregidor, Guadalcanal . . .

[ARTEMISA *walks slowly to* HELEN's *porch steps and sits down to watch.* WATUSI *goes to* NACHO *and takes the paper clippings from him. He stands at center stage.*]

[*To no one in particular*] Seventeen infantrymen won the Congressional Medal of Honor in World War II and in Korea. Did you know that? Seventeen. Pura Raza.

[MUSIC: *Military band or drum roll every time* WATUSI *gives military information.*]

WATUSI [*reading fragments*]: Company E, the all Mexican American infantry company, Forty-First Regiment of the Thirty-Sixth Division, Texas, landed at Salerno, Italy. Entire company comprised of Spanish-speaking soldiers, mostly from El Paso, National Guard, Camp Bowie—

NACHO: El Pedro Aguilar Despart from Los Angeles, California, was the first Mexican American to be drafted. President Roosevelt himself pulled his number from the national draft lottery. Number one-fifty-eight. Did you know that? [*Louder*] Did you son of a bitches know that?

IRATE NEIGHBORS [*offstage*]: Nacho, ¡cállate el hocico! Deja dormir. Ya comenzó con los chingados soldados.

WATUSI: Staff Sergeant Agustin Lucio from San Marcos, Texas, won the Silver Star, the Bronze Star, and the French Croix de Guerre in the European Theater of Operations—

NACHO: Éramos todos camaradas. Hablábamos español como si fuera "code," y el Beto sabía tocar la guitarra de aquellas, y we'd get together, y yo no sé cómo, the black market or alguna jefita would send chili and frijoles and the cook would fix it. We had to have our chili and beans, como siempre.

WATUSI: Sergeant José M. López from Brownsville, Texas, was awarded the Congressional Medal of Honor; in Krinkelt, Belgium, on December 17, 1944, on his own initiative, he carried his heavy machine gun from Company K's right flank to its left flank in order to protect that flank, which was in danger of being overrun by advancing enemy infantry supported by tanks—

NACHO: Private José F. Valdez, un nineteen-year-old chavalito from Gobernador, New Mexico, was awarded the Congressional Medal of Honor posthumously—that means que le dieron la medalla después que lo mataron—por allá en Belgium, era rifleman de Company B, Seventh Regiment, Third Division. They gave him the medal after he was killed!

IRATE NEIGHBORS [*offstage*]: Nacho, go to sleep con mil chingados!

WATUSI [*reciting without having to read the newspaper clipping*]: Rosenkrantz, Manila, the Philippines, Villa Verde Trail, Okinawa, Ryukyu Islands—

ARTEMISA [*standing up*]: Ya, Watusi, let's go back.

WATUSI: Not yet—he won't let us. Not yet. Espérate, ya mero. [*Continuing to recite*] Through his heroism and indomitable fighting spirit, Sergeant Ismael Villegas, "El Smiley," at the cost of his life, inspired his men to a determined attack in which they swept the enemy from the field.

NACHO: Eran machos. Private Cleto Rodríguez, Congressional Medal of Honor; en San Antonio, they gave him the keys to the city, and they held a Cleto Rodríguez Day in his honor. Y luego los paratroopers, aquí la Raza podía entrar fácil, querían "shorties," pues, el Private Manuel Pérez from Chicago, Illinois—sí, hasta en Chicago, Illinois, anda la Raza. [*Getting very loud*] Otro "posthumously," ¿me oyeron? Posthumously! ¡Los mataron! ¡Los mataron a todos! They all got killed! And you don't even remember them!

IRATE NEIGHBORS [*offstage*]: Nacho, acuéstate y duérmete. Go to bed, Nacho. Call the cops, viejo. He's gonna wake up the baby.

[*A baby cries.*]

¿Ya ves? Nacho, you son of a bitch, shut up! Como chinga con sus dead heroes. Viejo, llama a la chota.

[NACHO *looks around as though hearing the neighbors for the first time. Pause.*]

NACHO: ¿Nacho? Yo no me llamo Nacho. Yo soy Ignacio Robles, hijos de su chingada madre. ¿Me oyeron? Ignacio Robles. Para servirles.

[*He laughs to himself and decides to sing again.*]

[*Note: Very detailed direction is needed to integrate the following to reach a chaotic crescendo:* NACHO's *singing,* WATUSI's *reading and the military* MUSIC *or drums,* ARTEMISA's *singing, and the offstage* IRATE NEIGHBORS. *The pacing and tension should build up slowly with the lines merging, fragmenting, separating, and repeated as objects are thrown on* NACHO's *shed roof, but please note that care must be taken so that the names* WATUSI *is reading can be heard.*]

NACHO [*singing*]: "Me voy de soldado raso, voy a ingresar a las filas, con los muchachos valientes que dejan madres queridas, que dejan novias llorando, llorando su despedida."

WATUSI: Infantry Regiment, Thirty-Sixth Division; Private First Class Ismael "Smiley" Villegas from Casablanca, California; Private First Class David Gonzales from Pacoima, California, Congressional Medal of Honor, posthumously; Private First Class Alejandro Ruiz from Loving, New Mexico. Private Ruiz's heroic conduct in the face of overwhelming odds . . .

[*He crosses to* NACHO, *gives him the newspaper clippings, and then stands next to him.*]

ARTEMISA [*singing*]: "Corazón, en tu corazón te llevas mi alma, mi vida, y mi ser. Si tuviera cuatro vidas, cuatro vidas serían para ti."

[*She crosses to* NACHO *and stands nexts to him.*]

IRATE NEIGHBORS [*offstage*]: Nacho, go to sleep, goddammit! Go to bed, Nacho. Call the cops, viejo. Nacho, you son of a bitch, shut up.

[*A baby cryies loudly.*]

Como chinga con sus dead heroes. Who cares anyway? That war's over.

NACHO [*singing and crying drunkenly*]: "Virgen morena, mi madre te encomiendo, cuídala que's muy buena, cuídala mientras vuelvo."

WATUSI: Staff Sergeant Macario García, Sugarland, Texas, Congressional Medal of Honor; Private First Class Silvestre Herrera, Phoenix, Arizona, Company E, 142nd Infantry Regiment, Thirty-Sixth Division; Sergeant José M. López, Brownsville, Texas,

Congressional Medal of Honor; Private First Class David Gonzales, Pacoima, California, Congressional Medal of Honor, posthumously; Sergeant Alejandro Ruiz, Loving, New Mexico; Staff Sergeant Luciano Adams, Port Arthur, Texas, Congressional Medal
of Honor; Private Joe P. Martínez, Ault, Colorado, Congressional
Medal of Honor . . .

[*Pause.*]

NACHO: They died for you motherfuckers. For you, motherfuckers! [*Waving newspaper clippings in the air and dropping the metal box to the
floor*] You don't even remember them, but they died for you!

[*He tries to pull himself up, holding himself up on the arms of his wheelchair.*
WATUSI *comes to him and holds him up, one soldier holding the other.*]

They died for you! They died for you, motherfuckers! For you!
Motherfuckers!

[**SOUND CUE:** *Loud rifle crack.* NACHO *is shot. He screams.* ARTEMISA *and*
WATUSI *react, and* ALL FREEZE.]

[HELEN ENTERS *at steps. Her face is made-up, and she is wearing fuzzy slippers, chenille robe, and one of those "Save Your Do" chingaderas sold on TV.*]

HELEN: Nacho, are you okay?

NACHO [*breaking freeze and mumbling to himself*]: And you don't even
remember us. [*Repeating this line*] No se acuerdan, no se acuerdan,
no se acuerdan . . .

[ARTEMISA *breaks* FREEZE. *She starts to* EXIT, *stops, and turns. She sees that*
WATUSI *is not following her.*]

ARTEMISA [*forcefully to* WATUSI]: Ya, Watusi, vámonos.

[WATUSI *breaks* FREEZE *and helps* NACHO *sit down. He looks at* ARTE-
MISA *and nods yes. He straightens up, stands at attention, and salutes* NACHO
smartly. He turns to ARTEMISA *and holds out his hand to her. She takes it,
and* WATUSI, *in a graceful, dance-like movement, brings her around behind*
NACHO.]

WATUSI [*softly*]: ¿Qué no oyes que it's no use? They don't remember.

ARTEMISA [*caressing* NACHO'*s face*]: Good night, Nacho.

HELEN [*stepping down*]: Ya, Nacho, duérmete.

NACHO: Helen? ¿Tú sí te acuerdas, verdad? Remember we were all at the train station? The four of us? You remember Artemisa singing? Me and Watusi? You do remember, Helen. Tell me you remember.

[*Pause.*]

[*Starting to sing*] "En tu corazón te llevas mi alma, mi vida y mi ser. Si tuviera cuatro vidas, cuatro vidas serían para ti."

[HELEN *looks at him, fighting tenderness, but does not go to him. There is a pause, and then* MUSIC—"*Cuatro vidas*"—*plays.*]

END OF SCENE 1

* * *

Scene 2

TIME: *Next day, early morning.*

[*The sun is shining brightly. This is the first time that the audience can see the set clearly.* NACHO *is asleep, completely covered with an old olive green army blanket.* HELEN ENTERS *and stands at her doorstep with a laundry basket. She is still wearing her slippers and chenille robe but has removed the hairdo protector. She looks toward* NACHO's *cot and deliberately slams her door shut, kicking it with her foot, and then drops the laundry basket very hard. She is popping her gum furiously as she cleans the yard noisily, hoping to wake* NACHO. *She picks up his metal file box from the ground and slams it on his table.* NACHO *does not respond. She starts to hang clothes, mostly towels, snapping them loudly before pinning them to the clothesline. She leaves some dry towels from the day before on the line.*]

[NACHO *groans and sits up, suffering a super hangover.*]

HELEN [*noticing that* NACHO *has finally heard her*]: ¿Qué celebrabas *this* time? Armistice Day? D-Day? Pearl Harbor? Or were you just celebrating the fact that it was a Wednesday, a weeknight when people who have to work the next day were trying to sleep—

[CATUNGAS *appears at the gate. He is wearing a flannel shirt, khaki pants, and red bandanna as a headband.*]

CATUNGAS [*sounding like Yogi Bear*]: Hey, hey, hey, have no fear, the one and only C. C. Catungas is here.

[*He is trying to open the gate with his left hand but struggles. He finally opens the gate and* ENTERS. *His right hand is bandaged.*]

Helen, sweet Helen, déjalo. [*To* NACHO] Hey, Nacho, te acuerdas que you said I couldn't memorize that poem de la ruca Helen from Greece? Del vato Marlowe?

NACHO: Christopher Marlowe, borrowing a little from Shakespeare and Tennyson.

[NACHO *lies down again.*]

CATUNGAS: Pues now you owe me diez lanas. Listen. [*Kneeling next to* HELEN *and reciting poem*] "Was this the face that launch'd a thousand ships, and burnt the topless towers of Ilium? Sweet Helen, make me immortal with a kiss, her lips suck forth my soul; see where it flies!"

[*Pause.* CATUNGAS *stands up, eyes closed, lips puckered for a kiss.*]

HELEN: Que kiss ni que madre, Catungas. Míralo. Last night se emborrachó and kept the whole barrio awake with his singing—if you can call it that.

CATUNGAS [*to* NACHO]: Nacho, al rato va vinir la Roshanda con tus library books.

[*Note: Don't correct "vinir" to "venir." The spelling is to reflect* CATUNGAS's *pronunciation.*]

HELEN [*irritably*]: Is she bringing the kids?

CATUNGAS: No, mi sister la Molacha is gonna take care of them.

HELEN: Who?

CATUNGAS: La Molacha. My sister that's missing her front teeth—remember her?

HELEN: Yes, you mean Amalia. I can't figure out how you all start out with such wonderful Christian names and end up with those outrageous nicknames. What are your two brothers called? Andrés and Fernando?

CATUNGAS: El Huango y el Chueco.

HELEN: El Huango y el Chueco. I'm not even gonna ask how they got these nicknames.

CATUNGAS: But I'm gonna tell you anyway. El Huango loses all his strength in his neck, arms, and legs sometimes, so he walks like this. [*Showing her*] Y el Chueco has a crooked back, so he walks like this—

HELEN [*sarcastically*]: Well, that should make it easy to remember who's who.

CATUNGAS: Simón. El Chueco's got the pickup 'cause he can drive, y el Huango can't. El Huango's single like me, y el Chueco's married to la Cuata.

HELEN: ¿Cuata? Do you mean one of the twins from Barrio Anita?

CATUNGAS: Simón, no son *identical* twins, pero my jefita says they—

HELEN: Never mind, Catungas, I really don't need to know, but I'm glad your sister's got Rosie's kids because after last night, I don't think I could take their noisy running around out here. I plan to go buy groceries with Hector, nap the rest of the day to make up for my lost sleep, and go to the rosary at seven. [*To* NACHO] ¿Oyistes? Viene la Roshanda. You'd better get up.

[NACHO *sits up again and stares at them blearily.*]

And just wait until she finds out how drunk you got last night.

[NACHO *shudders at the thought.*]

[CATUNGAS *goes to* NACHO *and helps him into his wheelchair.*]

NACHO: ¿Qué te pasó en la mano?

CATUNGAS: Un wetback me la hizo burn con el mop de la brea.

[*He wheels him over to the water faucet, where* NACHO *washes up.* HELEN *continues her nagging.*]

HELEN: Toda la noche se la pasó con sus babosadas, Catungas. He's just lucky no one bothered to call the cops on him.

CATUNGAS [*ignoring her*]: Órale, Nacho, that ruco Marlowe's not the only one that can write poems. Watchen, I wrote a poem about you too. [*Taking out a crumpled piece of paper from his shirt pocket and reciting*] "Helen, oh Helen, Greek goddess of his dreams. In sweet Morpheus's arms let Nacho remain. Let the wine drown out the fallen comrades' screams, so he can sleep and dream of you again."

[CATUNGAS *waits for praise.*]

HELEN [*not one bit impressed*]: Who cares about the dead heroes, anyway? Who cares? And I don't know how he manages to get wine, but I'm gonna find out who's getting it for him, and when I do—

CATUNGAS: Helen, I wasn't finished con mi poem. Wátchate, it gets better: "Dreams without sorrow, dreams without pain, nestled in the fragrance of rose petals in your breasts" . . . I'm stuck aquí, Helen. What word rhymes with "breasts"?

HELEN: Oh, a la chingada con tus poems, Watusi, and Nacho's dreams.

[HELEN *walks up the steps and stops.*]

Y ¿sabes qué? I'm not the Greek goddess in Nacho's pinchi dreams. It's always la—

ROSHANDA [*offstage*]: Nino!

[HELEN EXITS *angrily, slamming door.* ROSHANDA *unlocks the gate and* ENTERS *carrying a stack of books. She is dressed casually in shirt, jeans, and sandals.*]

ROSHANDA: Hi, Nino. Hi, Carlos.

[*She shuts the gate behind her, locks it, and starts to run toward* NACHO.]

NACHO [*pleadingly*]: Roshanda, Roshanda, walk, please—no corras. You're making the earth tremble. Just like my head.

[ROSHANDA *laughingly runs to him anyway. She hugs him, holding him tightly, and is almost ready to spin him in his chair, teasingly, but stops and takes him to the worktable.*]

[*Holding his head*] Ay, borracheras y las crudas, penitencia de mis pecados.

ROSHANDA: Here are the books you wanted, Nino. Hesiod, Homer, Pindar, Aeschylus, Sophocles, and Euripides—again—and more. Greek and Roman legends. [*To* CATUNGAS] Carlos, what happened to your hand?

[*She takes his hand and checks it.*]

NACHO: Some new kid burned him with the roofing tar.

CATUNGAS: Ah, man, Nacho. I wanted to tell Roshanda que pasó.

ROSHANDA: Go ahead, Carlos, tell me how it happened.

CATUNGAS [*explaining*]: Okay. 'Staba en un side job, nonunion—sorry, Roshanda, but it paid buena lana and a chamba's a chamba— anyway, el foreman puso este guachito, un wetback—sorry, Roshanda—un . . . [*pointedly*] *undocumented worker*, bien verde, que no sabía ni madre—sorry—

[ROSHANDA *waves him on to continue his story, still punctuated with his "sorries" as* CATUNGAS *is always trying to be on* ROSHANDA's *good side.*]

—anyway, yo me agacho [*squatting down to demonstrate*] so I can pull the roofing paper, asina y el guachito—undocumented worker, I forget, Roshanda—all he has to do is mapiar la tar that's in the pot, asina. [*Standing and mopping*] But don't forget the tar's boiling, y el pinchi sol—sorry—the sun, está más que one hundred and ten degrees, y nojotros en el techo tenemos close to one hundred and thirty degrees, ¡me la rayo!

[*He puts thumb over index finger to form a cross and kisses it to prove he's telling the truth.*]

ROSHANDA: So you burned your hand with the mop of the boiling tar?

CATUNGAS [*somewhat indignant*]: No, Roshanda! Just as I'm pulling the roofing paper, asina, [*squatting again*] el guachito swings the mop y lo hace land arriba de mi mano, so *he* burned me.

NACHO: And that's exactly what I said, Roshanda, in less than ten words!

ROSHANDA: Pobrecito, Carlos. Is it a bad burn?

CATUNGAS: Simón, pero de volada me llevaron al St. Mary's. Tenía unos big blisters que me dolían un chingo—sorry—y le dije al doctor que me diera something for the pain, so me dio estas pain pills. [*Taking a prescription bottle out of his pocket*] Tienen codeine. Voy a dormir como baby.

ROSHANDA [*putting away the library books*]: Remember, Nino? When Hector, Carlos, and I used to act out your Greek and Roman myths and legends?

NACHO: Oh, yes I do. I remember your favorite part was Icarus. And you always made Hector be Daedulus, and Catungas would never be anything but the king.

CATUNGAS: Simón, I was the best king, ¿qué no, Roshanda?

ROSHANDA: Yes, Carlos. I loved to be Icarus. I'd grab a towel off Helen's clothesline, tie it around my neck like Superman, and fly all over this yard and jump off the steps, remember, Nino?

[CATUNGAS *pulls a dry towel from clothesline and puts it around* ROSHANDA's *neck. She goes to* NACHO. *He knots the towel around her neck.*]

NACHO [*as Daedalus, giving her the warning*]: Icarus, my son, we will fly out of the labyrinth that King Minos has imprisoned us in, but remember: don't fly too high, and don't fly too low. You must stay on the middle course.

[ROSHANDA *swoops around yard.*]

CATUNGAS [*continuing the story*]: But Icarus was young and foolish, and he
flew up higher and higher, wanting to reach the sun . . .

[ROSHANDA *climbs building's steps.*]

. . . and the sun was hot, very hot—

ROSHANDA [*dramatically dropping down the steps*]: And the sun melted the
wax on the feathers, and Icarus fell down to the sea, swallowed by
the water, forever.

[*Pause. She removes the towel from her neck.*]

Oh, I almost forgot, Nino. Hector said to tell you he found more
Steinbeck and Faulkner books in the university trash bins. But you
already have them. Do you want them anyway?

[NACHO *nods yes.*]

HELEN [*sticking her head out the door*]: Catungas, you're wanted on the
phone. Oh, hi, Rosie.

ROSHANDA: Hi, Nina Helen.

CATUNGAS [*acting important*]: ¿Quién es, mi lawyer?

[*He goes to* HELEN.]

ROSHANDA: Lawyer?

CATUNGAS: Simón, voy hacer sue al guachito por un chingo de money.

NACHO: Sue? Pero ellos ni tienen—

[ROSHANDA *puts her hand on his arm as a signal to stop talking.*]

HELEN: Roshanda, go on, ask your Nino what he did last night.

[*She* EXITS, *and* CATUNGAS *follows her and also* EXITS.]

END OF SCENE 2

*   *   *

Scene 3

TIME: *A few moments later.*

[ROSHANDA *is making* NACHO's *bed. Pause.*]

ROSHANDA: Nino, how 'bout a cup of coffee for your favorite godchild? [*Looking at* NACHO *intently*] Headache?

[NACHO *nods yes.*]

Pobrecito mi nino.

[*She quickly sets water to boil on the hot plate. She then takes the towel that's still on her neck, dries his hair, and then combs it.*]

Was it bad? Last night?

[*Pause.* NACHO *does not respond.* ROSHANDA *pours water into cups and sets them on the table and sits down across from* NACHO. NACHO *spoons instant coffee and sugar into the cups. Both take a drink, almost at the same time. Another pause.*]

Nino, you make the best cup of coffee in Tucson.

[NACHO *laughs and pats her hand. He stops suddenly as pain hits him.* ROSHANDA *jumps up quickly.*]

Nino, let me get you your medicine.

[NACHO *shakes his head no.* ROSHANDA *stands behind him and massages his temples until* NACHO *visibly relaxes as the pain leaves him.* ROSHANDA *speaks to him in a soothing, almost hypnotic tone.*]

Ya, Nino, ya. Don't think about the bad things. Remember the good things—please, Nino.

[ROSHANDA *drops her hands to* NACHO's *shoulders and massages them.* ARTEMISA ENTERS. NACHO *stares at her.*]

NACHO: Roshanda, you remind me so much of your mother.

ROSHANDA: You always say that, Nino. Do I look that much like her?

ARTEMISA [*crossing to* ROSHANDA *and looking at her closely*]: Yes, she does, Nacho. She looks just like I did when I was her age.

NACHO: Sometimes.

[ROSHANDA *sits across from* NACHO.]

ARTEMISA: ¿Cómo que "sometimes"? Mira. [*Going to* ROSHANDA *and feeling her hair and face*] She has my hair, my smile. Todo mío—she's all me.

ROSHANDA: Tell me about her. Please, Nino. I want to know everything about my mother.

NACHO: Ay, m'ija, I've already told you everything.

ROSHANDA: Tell me again, Nino.

ARTEMISA [*moving downstage right*]: Dile, Nacho. Tell her the times I'd drive over with Helen and Watusi and pick you up.

NACHO: Your mother drove like a maniac.

ARTEMISA [*mimicking* NACHO]: ¡Artemisa! ¡Nos vas a matar!

[*She laughs.*]

NACHO [*laughing also; to* ROSHANDA]: You know? I think she sweet-talked the guy at the motor vehicle office into giving her a license. Así era, te podía maderear más suave. And then she must've sweet-talked a car salesman in South Tucson 'cause the next day she shows up with this old beat-up Ford—un foringo!

ROSHANDA: Was all this before the war, Nino?

NACHO: After.

ROSHANDA [*surprised*]: You used to go out after the war? But I thought you never left this yard after the war, Nino.

NACHO: Oh sí, in those days I would go out with your mother. I was her chaperone. [*Soft, ironic laugh*] Que chaperone, ¿verdad? El Watusi era mi bodyguard—

ROSHANDA: Watusi?

ARTEMISA [*calling out, laughing*]: Watusi! Ven, make Nacho tell Roshanda about our rides to "A" Mountain—ven, apúrate. [*To* NACHO] He's still trying to sleep off your parranda from last night.

NACHO: Watusi was Catungas's father. Big and strong. El Catungas took after him.

[WATUSI ENTERS.]

WATUSI [*to* NACHO]: I used to pick you up just like a baby, y ay te íbamos pa'rriba. Tell her, Nacho.

[*Pause.*]

But don't tell her the other stuff about me. Not yet.

NACHO [*nodding yes to* WATUSI *and continuing to* ROSHANDA]: El Watusi me subía al Ford, picked me up just like a baby, y ay te ívamos pa'rriba del "A" Mountain, the four of us, sharing two cuartos de cerveza: yo, tu mamá, el Watusi, y la Helen—

ROSHANDA: Helen? She never wants to tell me anything about my mother—

NACHO: Ay, Roshanda, la Helen hoards her memories like she hoards her boxes of Tide soap. I don't know why she's like that, but she must have her reasons, m'ija.

ARTEMISA [*walking toward* NACHO, *angrily*]: You bet she has her reasons. Have you tried asking her, Nacho? Ask her why she didn't drive that night. Ask her!

WATUSI [*stopping her*]: No comiences, Artemisa. [*Placating*] Mira, tu hija, la Roshanda.

ARTEMISA: She's pretty, huh, Watusi?

ROSHANDA: Tell me about my mom, Nino. She loved potato chips—

ARTEMISA AND NACHO [*together*]: Con Red Devil chili.

NACHO: She always carried a bottle of Red Devil hot sauce in her purse. Tenía que ser Red Devil; no other brand would do.

ROSHANDA: Ummmm, I love Red Devil, too! On *everything*—not just potato chips.

ARTEMISA: That's my girl.

NACHO: Your mother loved to dance.

[MUSIC: *Danzón "Juárez"*]

[ARTEMISA *dances in front of* NACHO.]

I would sit at our table and just watch her dance. And she knew it too! Sometimes she would twirl around and give me one of her winks.

[ARTEMISA *twirls and winks.*]

She loved to sing, too. And even when she was going to have you, she kept going to all the dances.

ROSHANDA: Were you mad at her, Nino, for getting pregnant? I mean, without getting married?

NACHO: I could never get mad at your mother. Never. Except for that night when she drove back from Nogales . . . drunk . . . Me and Watusi didn't go.

WATUSI: We didn't go 'cause I got . . . sick . . . that night. I ended up at the vets' hospital, remember? You were there with me, all night, fighting the asshole doctor who wanted to lock me away.

NACHO: I wouldn't have let her drive—I told you she drove like a maniac, and in those days, the roads from Tucson to Nogales were deadly. I never even got the whole story—the bandleader let her drive, I think. Porque la Helen—

[*He stops suddenly as pain returns.* ROSHANDA *moves to get his medicine, but he stops her. Pause.*]

ROSHANDA: Tell me about my dad, Nino. You never want to tell me anything about him. Please. Where was he from? What was his name? Don't you even know that?

NACHO: No.

WATUSI: Tell her how they met. You remember that, Nacho. Era un soldado, like us, on his way back to Texas from DeWitt Hospital en Auburn, por allá en Califas.

NACHO: We were in a bar, and your mother was dancing with this tall soldier.

[MUSIC: *Instrumental section of "Su razón."*]

[ARTEMISA *dances a bit tipsy, dreamily, and pantomimes holding her arms high around her tall soldier's neck.*]

He told everybody he was going to use all mustering pay to open his own garage, but once he saw your mother, he forgot all his plans and started buying everyone drinks. Especially me and Watusi. He wanted to get us drunk.

[*He moves away from the table and gets closer to* WATUSI.]

WATUSI [*pantomiming carrying drinks to* NACHO]: Drink up, partner. Ese pendejo anda tritiandonos just so he can get to dance with Artemisa.

NACHO: La Helen wouldn't dance with Watusi, porque after the war he came back—

WATUSI: Don't tell her about me, Nacho, please—not yet.

[*Pause.*]

NACHO: —no sé. Anyway, Watusi and I were singing right along with the orchestra. "Su razón."

ROSHANDA: Sing it now, Nino.

NACHO [*singing*]: "He perdido para siempre, lo que fuera en mi vida un gran amor . . ." I closed my eyes, Roshanda, and pretended it was me dancing with your mother.

[ARTEMISA *turns to look at* NACHO, *and* NACHO *stares back at her intently.*]

WATUSI AND NACHO [*singing softly*]: "Aquí estoy entre botellas, apagando con el vino mi dolor, celebrando a mi manera, la derrota de mi pobre corazón."

ROSHANDA: That's a pretty song, Nino. [*Singing and translating*] Here I'm sitting between bottles, shutting out my pain with wine, celebrating in my fashion, the defeat of my poor heart—

WATUSI: Y ¿la Artemisa? ¿Se fue con la Helen?

NACHO: And we didn't even see your mother leave with that soldier. Y la Helen, I don't know how she got home that night. Watusi and I waited at the bar until closing time, so drunk we couldn't walk straight.

WATUSI: Pinchi rucas, double crossers. We gotta take a taxi now. [*Checking his pockets for money*] Órale, Nacho, ¿trais jando? Taxi! Taxi!

WATUSI AND NACHO [*singing drunkenly*]: "Y si acaso ya inconsciente, agobiado por el humo y el licor . . ."

[CATUNGAS ENTERS. *He runs and joins* WATUSI *and* NACHO, *and sings with them.*]

NACHO, WATUSI, AND CATUNGAS: " . . . No se burlen si la llamo, si entre lágrimas la lloro, todo tiene su razón."

[HELEN ENTERS *and stands at the doorway.*]

HELEN: Nacho! I'm warning you—don't start con tus chingaderas this early.

[*She slams the door and* EXITS.]

NACHO [*ignoring her; to* ROSHANDA]: We took a taxi back to the barrio that night—y nine months later—you!

[ALL *laugh.* CATUNGAS *grabs* ROSHANDA *and swings her around.*]

CATUNGAS: La Rosie!

ROSHANDA [*protesting, but enjoying the teasing*]: Roshanda! I hate to be called Rosie! My name's Roshanda—tell him, Nino!

END OF SCENE 3

* * *

Scene 4

TIME: *Noon, very hot.*

MUSIC: *"What Does It Take (to Win Your Love)?" by Jr. Walker & the All Stars*

[NACHO *and* ROSHANDA *are reading.*]

ROSHANDA [*seeing* NACHO *flipping pages very fast*]: Okay, Nino, are you cheating? What are you skipping to?

NACHO: No, no, Roshanda, I'm not cheating. I'm just savoring what Steinbeck wrote at the beginning of each chapter in *Grapes of Wrath*, see? You know, a lot of readers just skip these without knowing that they're the best part of the book.

ROSHANDA [*teasing*]: You say that, Nino, 'cause you have all of them memorized by now.

NACHO: No, te digo que they're the best part of the book.

[*Pause.*]

   Well, maybe not the *best* part, but pretty close to it!

[HELEN *and* HECTOR ENTER *at the gate, carrying bags of groceries.* HECTOR *is dressed in gray city sanitation department uniform.*]

HECTOR [*going to* ROSHANDA *and giving her an affectionate kiss*]: Hi, babe. Y ¿el Catungas?

ROSHANDA: Late. I think he was going to the doctor's first. He says his hand's still bothering him.

HELEN: I bet. Nomás se quiere pildorear con el codeine.

[*Pause.*]

   Damn, it's hot.

HECTOR: Hey, Nacho, some television people were in front of the bank across from Lucky's. Know what they were gonna do? Film that sexy blonde from the six o'clock news frying an egg on the *sidewalk*.

HELEN: Ya ni la chingan; el Hector couldn't even find a parking space.

NACHO [*still trying to read*]: Didn't they already do that last year?

HECTOR: Yeah, but the egg didn't fry all the way. Bet it does today, though.

HELEN [*going to* NACHO'S *shed and putting away his groceries on the shelves somewhere over his cot as she speaks*]: Mira, tu Campbell's chicken noodle soup, four for a dollar. Y pa' mí, Chicken of the Sea tuna, three for a dollar. Best Foods mayonnaise, forty-nine cents a quart. You can't beat that, Nacho. Y toilet paper, four packs for a dollar. I got two—one for you and one for me.

NACHO [*giving up trying to read and putting away his book*]: Ay, Helen. I bet you have over fifty cans of Chicken of the Sea tuna and over one hundred packs of toilet paper. Why do you keep buying the same things over and over?

HELEN: And why do you keep reading the same books over and over? It's the same thing. Besides, I only buy things that are on sale and that we need. Like Tide soap. Clorox. And toilet paper. Lots of toilet paper. Well, you never know when you'll need all those things. What if we had an earthquake or a catastrophe? Nuclear war? Look how close those missiles got to us in Cuba. What if Kennedy hadn't stopped the Russians, huh? Where would we have been then?

NACHO: In a fallout shelter, eating tuna sandwiches, with the cleanest asses in Arizona?

HELEN: I'm not standing here one minute more listening to your babosadas.

[*She starts to* EXIT, *and* CATUNGAS ENTERS *at the gate. His hand is still bandaged, and he is carrying a bouquet of half-dead red roses and a small radio with the cord dangling.*]

CATUNGAS: Hey, hey, hey, have no fear, the one and only C. C. Catungas is here, so Helen, my dear, go bring us some beer—

[HELEN EXITS *with a "hmmph!"*]

HECTOR: You're late, Catungas.

CATUNGAS: No te agüites, carnal. I had to go back to the doctor's for more pain pills. [*To* NACHO *as he hands him the radio*] Doña Matilde wants you to fix her radio; she says she can't hear nothing on it.

NACHO: Pues, that's because she's deaf, la pobre. She's the only one who never objects to my late-night serenades. I'll make the volume so loud *she'll* be the one keeping everybody awake!

CATUNGAS [*giving the roses to* ROSHANDA]: For you, Roshanda. El Pelón who works en maintenance at St. Mary's las iva tirar en el garbage, pero they're perfect, ¿qué no?

ROSHANDA: Thank you, Carlos; they're beautiful. Nino, do you have a vase for them?

NACHO [*with sarcasm*]: Sí, m'ija, busca ahí en el "hutch" donde tengo mi china y crystal, enseguidita de los champagne goblets.

ROSHANDA [*unperturbed*]: Oh, Nino. [*Calling out toward* HELEN's *door*] Nina! Do you have a vase we could borrow?

HELEN [*answering quickly, as she's been listening at the door*]: No.

[ROSHANDA *rummages in the garbage can and finds an empty Campbell's chicken noodle soup can.*]

ROSHANDA: Campbell's chicken noodle soup—my nino's favorite.

[*She rinses the can and places the roses in it.*]

HECTOR [*to* ROSHANDA]: ¿Y los kids?

ROSHANDA: Amalia's taking care of them. She's taking them swimming. At Oury Park.

[*She places the roses on the table.*]

HECTOR: Swimming? But our kids can't swim yet.

CATUNGAS: Ni la Molacha! She almost drowned the last time she went swimming. Anyway, está tan gorda que si se dives a cannon ball, saca toda la agua del pool. El otro día, el lifeguard le dijo que nomás juera en los Mondays, when they have to change the water. He said he'd pay her diez lanas—ten dollars for emptying out the pool for him!

ROSHANDA: But Carlos, how can Amalia take care of the kids if she can't swim?

CATUNGAS: Don't worry, Roshanda. Since the time she almost drowned, she just goes to the kids' pool. *When* it has water.

HECTOR: Or *when* it's cleaned up. You know, the kids really need a good swimming pool. The city won't do anything; they don't give a damn. And just wait till it gets hotter . . . Hey, Tía, something sure smells good—what are you cooking?

HELEN [*opening the door and stepping outside*]: Ay, m'ijo, just a guisado with round steak and potatoes. Do you guys want to eat inside or outside?

HECTOR: Just make us some burritos. We're supposed to be cleaning and fixing up the place, but with Catungas burning his hand—

HELEN: What place?

HECTOR [*pointing toward the empty building*]: That place. We rented it.

CATUNGAS: Y lo vamos hacer un centro.

HELEN: ¿Centro? ¿De qué?

CATUNGAS: De nojotros.

HELEN: Wait a minute, Catungas. Hector, what are you going to do?

HECTOR: Tía, we're going to fix up the place, make it into a centro. You know, a place to hang out.

HELEN: Hang out?

ROSHANDA: Not just "hang out." We need a place of our own. For meetings, movies, daycare—you know, a place to bring our kids, bilingual classes, history classes, and tutoring for the school kids—

CATUNGAS: And horses.

ROSHANDA: Don't you see, Nino? We need a place of our very own, and this place is perfect for a centro, and just what we need to organize.

HELEN: Organize? Organize what?

HECTOR: Us, Tía. We need to organize. C'mon, Catungas, we still have to clean it up and paint it. Help me get the stuff out of the car.

[**HECTOR EXITS. CATUNGAS** *follows him with his injured hand raised high in the air, hoping for sympathy but getting none, except from* **ROSHANDA**.]

ROSHANDA: I'll help.

[*They* **EXIT**.]

HELEN [*yelling*]: Hector! Te van hacer fire del city si te metes en political chingaderas. You'd better get back to work y déjate de pendejadas. [*To* NACHO] ¿Qué crees? Can they do it?

NACHO [*shrugging indifferently*]: With their energy, they can move mountains if they want to. But this organizing shit might end up being too much work, verás.

HELEN: Well, they just better not plan on parties. Or loud music. Or marihuana.

NACHO: Déjalos. They're young.

HELEN: I don't care. That's all I needed—a centro! As if we already didn't have enough noise with *you*.

[HECTOR, CATUNGAS, *and* ROSHANDA ENTER, *carrying brooms, mops, buckets, cans of paint, etc.*]

ROSHANDA: Nina Helen, is it okay if we get the water here outside? We don't have enough money to connect the water inside.

HELEN: It doesn't matter to me—use all the water you want. Your nino pays the water bill.

NACHO [*begrudgingly*]: Are you gonna use hot water, too? You know, I don't use a lot of water, just my showers and my plants, but you guys—

ROSHANDA [*buttering him up*]: C'mon, Nino. We won't use a lot of water. Just for drinking and mopping the floor.

[*Pause.*]

Please, Nino.

[*Pause.*]

NACHO: Roshanda, I don't like what you're getting into, m'ija. This centro business *sounds* good, pero it can get you in trouble. I don't want to see you get hurt—

ROSHANDA: Nino, how's giving the kids bilingual classes gonna get me hurt?

[*Pause.*]

Please, Nino.

NACHO [*very reluctantly*]: Bueno, pues, but I'm warning you, Roshanda, if I see my water bill going up—

ROSHANDA: It won't, Nino. [*Kissing his cheek*] I promise.

NACHO [*laughing; to* HELEN]: She's just like Artemisa, ¿verdad?

[HELEN *refuses to answer him.*]

[HECTOR *stretches a long electric extension cord from the building window and brings it toward* HELEN's *door.* ROSHANDA EXITS *into the building with a bucket of water.*]

HECTOR: Tía, can we bring this extension cord into your house?

HELEN: Oh, no, my electric bill's already high enough. Get your own electricity.

HECTOR: We can't—we need a deposit, and we don't have any money. [*To* NACHO] Nacho, can we connect it to yours?

NACHO: That cord won't reach to here. Catungas, pásame el screwdriver.

[CATUNGAS *hands* NACHO *a screwdriver, and* NACHO *continues working on Doña Matilde's radio.*]

HECTOR [*bringing the cord over to* NACHO'*s extension cord that's nailed to the shed's post*]: It'll reach.

[*He's ready to plug it in when* HELEN *objects.*]

HELEN: Oh no, you don't.

HECTOR: But Tía, it's Nacho's electricity.

HELEN: No, it's not. He's plugged into my meter. I let him because he hardly uses any electricity, but you guys are gonna party and waste all my electricity—

HECTOR: No, we're not. C'mon, Tía.

HELEN: No.

NACHO: Let them, Helen. I'll pay for it. Anyway, this damn centro won't even last a month, so stop fighting them.

[HECTOR *plugs in the cord.*]

HECTOR [*yelling to* ROSHANDA]: Try it, Babe!

ROSHANDA [*yelling offstage*]: ¡No sirve!

[*She* ENTERS.]

The light doesn't work.

[HECTOR *keeps working on the plug and cord.*]

NACHO [*to* CATUNGAS]: A ver si no le da un buen choque.

[CATUNGAS *gets up from the table, goes behind* HECTOR, *and pokes him, making an electrical charge noise: ZZZZ!!!* HECTOR *is scared and jumps, then se agüita, and a guilty* CATUNGAS *goes back to the table.*]

CATUNGAS: Since I can't help porque mi mano still hurts, I'm gonna paint the sign for the centro. [*Holding the paintbrush in the air*] What's the name gonna be?

[*There is a long pause as each look at one another, realizing that they hadn't thought of a name for the centro.*]

ROSHANDA: "El Centro de la Raza."

HECTOR: No, "El Centro de Aztlán."

CATUNGAS: ¿Aztlán? ¿Qué es eso?

ROSHANDA: You'll find out at our very first history class!

[*They offer a chorus of possible names: El Centro de la Raza, El Pueblo Unido Center, Centro Quetzal, Centro de la Gente, Centro de los Pobres, Centro del Movimiento Chicano, etc. They can't agree and start to argue.*]

HELEN [*disgusted*]: If you can't even agree on a name, cómo chingados se van a "organize"? [*Sarcastically*] Why don't you name it *Chicano Center?* That's what you're calling yourselves now, isn't it? Chicanos?

[HECTOR, CATUNGAS, *and* ROSHANDA *all look at each other questioningly. Pause.*]

ROSHANDA: Hey, I like that—Chicano Center. Yes! Or, Centro Chicano?

CATUNGAS: El Centro del Pueblo Chicano.

ALL THREE [*agreeing*]: Yeah, sounds good! El Centro del Pueblo Chicano!

[*Pause.* CATUNGAS *tries to get a sense of space needed, like a real artist. Another pause.*]

CATUNGAS: Won't fit.

NACHO: Did I say the centro won't even last a *month?* Well, it looks like it won't even make it for a *day.*

ROSHANDA: The name isn't important, Nina. And Nino, it's what we do that counts, not the name. [*To* HECTOR] C'mon, honey, you're on your lunch break, and this is the only time we have before I go for the kids.

[*Pause.*]

[*To* CATUNGAS] Carlos?

[CATUNGAS *and* HECTOR *pause and look at each other. Then they look at* HELEN *and* NACHO. *There is an unspoken expectancy. Finally,* CATUNGAS *and* HECTOR *begin to pass around the mops, brooms, cans of paint, etc.* ROSHANDA *joins them.*]

[MOONBEAM ENTERS *and stands at the top of the* CENTRO's *steps. She is braless, wearing a very revealing tight tie-dyed top and very short denim cutoffs, with the American flag sewn on the bottom.*]

MOONBEAM [*giving the "peace" sign*]: Hi, I'm Moonbeam. I'm looking for a job—need any help?

[ALL *turn to stare at her. And at that exact moment, Doña Matilde's radio blasts at full volume, a choir singing "Hallelujah," and* HECTOR *and* CATUNGAS *turn to her, openmouthed as though seeing a vision from heaven.*]

END OF SCENE 4

* * *

Scene 5

TIME: *Later that afternoon.*

MUSIC: *Santana's "Abraxas" album, which continues to be heard intermittently throughout this scene.*

[*The* CENTRO *is brightly lit, and the silhouettes of many people walking by or working inside the* CENTRO *may be seen in windows.* NACHO *is sitting in his wheelchair, drinking wine, and* ARTEMISA *is standing next to him.* ARTEMISA *is wearing a maternity smock, and she is about five months pregnant with* ROSHANDA. *She is teasing* NACHO, *wanting him to touch her stomach.*]

ARTEMISA: Touch it, Ignacio; no tengas miedo. It's just a baby.

[*She takes his hand and places it on her stomach. He feels the baby move, and he quickly removes his hand, startled but thrilled.*]

NACHO: ¡Brincó! Artemisa, I felt it jump.

ARTEMISA: That's all she does; she doesn't let me sleep at night.

NACHO: It's the music she's always hearing. She's gonna be pura energy. [*Laughing*] Y ¿cómo sabes que it's a girl?

ARTEMISA: I just know. Ignacio, I'm glad you've agreed to be her padrino. And Helen, too. My two best friends will be my baby's godparents. My compadres.

NACHO: And what will we name her? It better be a beautiful name because I know she's going to be a beautiful baby.

ARTEMISA: My mother's insisting it be a saint's name—you know, from the Mexican bakery's calendar?

NACHO: Have you heard how ugly those saints' names are? On the radio? Día de San Gumersindo, San Gaudencio, San Ciriaco, San Pascasio?

ARTEMISA [*laughing*]: But Nacho, you know how my mother is. She thinks I've disgraced the family, getting pregnant without a husband, so she wants to start my baby off with a solid Christian name— besides, those are boys' names. I told you, my baby's going to be a girl.

NACHO [*continuing with female names*]: Santa Eleuteria, Santa Hermene-gilda . . . Santa Eufemia. All the barrio will be calling her "Eufie."

ARTEMISA: Bueno, bueno, it won't be a saint's name from the calendar. But I want something different. Maybe [*pronouncing it "Dee-ah-nah"*] Diana. Do you like Diana?

NACHO: Diana? That's a pretty name, but it's not so different.

ARTEMISA: It's something she can spell easy, you know, when she goes to kindergarten. Not like mine. I never could spell my name in kin-dergarten. Artemisa. I felt so dumb.

NACHO: I like your name: Artemisa, goddess of the hunt. "Where three roads meet, there she is standing."

ARTEMISA: That's pretty, Nacho. But I want something short. Like Flor. That's only four letters. Or Vida. Don't you like Vida? I do.

[*She starts to hum "Cuatro vidas" softly as she rubs her stomach. Pause.*]

I have another favor to ask you. Well, it's not really *another* favor because if you agree to be her godfather, you also agree to take care of her in case anything should happen to me.

NACHO: Look at me, Artemisa. How can I take care of anyone?

ARTEMISA: Oh, I don't mean always taking care of her. My mother would be sure to do the feeding, clothing, religious upbringing. [*Laugh-ing*] My poor baby! [*Getting serious*] Ignacio, I want you to teach her to fly . . .

NACHO: Fly?

ARTEMISA: Yes, fly . . . teach her to read and to love reading, just like you do. Give her wings, Ignacio—just give her wings. Do you promise?

NACHO: I don't know . . . How can I—

ARTEMISA: Promise, Ignacio, promise.

NACHO: Artemisa, I can only promise to love her, to love her as my own child, and if my love gives her wings—

ARTEMISA: Ignacio, that's good enough—just love her.

[*Pause.*]

How about Alma? That's four letters. [*Singing*] "Alma, si te llevas mi alma, contenta moriría por ti . . ."

[ROSHANDA ENTERS *from* CENTRO *and stands at the top of the steps, fanning her face.* ARTEMISA *and* NACHO *turn to her.*]

NACHO [*to* ARTEMISA]: Rose of Sharon. That's what I want. Rose of Sharon.

ROSHANDA [*crossing to* NACHO]: What, Nino?

NACHO: Your name, m'ija. I wanted Rose of Sharon, from Steinbeck's *Grapes of Wrath.*

ROSHANDA: But I like my name, Nino. And I really hate it when someone calls me Rosie.

[ARTEMISA *stands very close to* ROSHANDA *and plays with her hair.*]

It's so hot in there, at least there's a breeze out here.

ARTEMISA: Nacho, tell her how she escaped getting stuck with an ugly saint's name. Tell her about my mother's fit when we came back from St. Margaret's.

NACHO: Watusi named you Roshanda.

ROSHANDA: Roshanda. I bet that I'm the only one in this barrio—in the entire world, with that name. So tell me the story again, Nino. How did Watusi find this name for me?

[MOONBEAM ENTERS *from* CENTRO *and stands at the top of the steps.*]

MOONBEAM [*calling out*]: Roshanda?

[ARTEMISA *moves in front of* ROSHANDA *protectively.*]

ARTEMISA [*to* MOONBEAM]: I don't like you. There's something dishonest about you.

MOONBEAM: You'd better hurry, Roshanda; Catungas is threatening to put on a show tonight with the dirty poetry he says he's writing for the Coors beer boycott.

ARTEMISA [*going to* NACHO, *frightened*]: Make her leave; she's evil. Don't let her get close to my Roshanda. Nacho, keep her away from Roshanda.

NACHO: I can't, Artemisa, I can't.

ROSHANDA [*referring to* WATUSI'S *naming her*]: Oh yes, you can, Nino. Watusi saw the letters floating from the church ceiling, remember? But I gotta go or Watusi's famous son will empty out what little audience we hope to have tonight. [*Running toward* MOONBEAM]

And the name's Roshanda, Nino—Roshanda. Artemisa's my mom.

[ROSHANDA *and* MOONBEAM EXIT *to* CENTRO.]

END OF SCENE 5

* * *

Scene 6

TIME: *Late at night.*

[ALL *except* HELEN *are sitting outside, lounging around, drinking beer.*]

CATUNGAS [*pretending to be using a microphone from* NACHO'*s junk*]: Testing ... testing ... one, two, three. I am Professor John Sabelotodo, a doctoral candidate from the University of Michigan, and I'm writing my thesis on "the socioeconomic implications and factors that impact and shape the voting pattern of the culturally depraved—"

MOONBEAM [*correcting him*]: Deprived, Catungas—culturally deprived.

CATUNGAS: —same difference—of the culturally deprived Mexican American voter. Roshanda, ¿qué le dijistes al ruco de la university de— Michigan? El que quería saber what gave you pleasure, what gave you pain, were you afraid of dying, did you believe in the future, did you save money in the bank? Remember? ¿Qué le dijistes?

ROSHANDA: Nothing. I just pretended I didn't understand English, just like my nino does when the social worker from the veterans' hospital comes to see him.

CATUNGAS [*insistent*]: C'mon, Roshanda, tell me a simple pleasure, that's all. What makes you happy?

[ROSHANDA *kneels next to a box on the ground and starts to make paper flowers.*]

ROSHANDA: Carlos, you already know what makes me happy. Hector and my three babies.

MOONBEAM: Babies? Just Gloria's a baby.

ROSHANDA: Oh, I know, Moonbeam. But I don't want them to grow up. Junior's going to start kindergarten, and Diana's getting so big. But Gloria, my baby—she refuses to learn to walk, and she's over a year old—and she's so fat! Junior and Diana learned to walk before they were ten months old. But Gloria wants to stay my baby.

[*Pause.*]

I like to give her a bath; she loves the water. And then when I comb her hair—she hates it! So I sing to her. [*Moving her hand as if it were a round moon*] "Ahí viene la luna, comiendo la tuna, tirando la cáscara . . ." And that is when she looks at me with her big brown eyes 'cause she knows I'm getting ready to tickle her . . . "en la laguna!" [*Pantomiming tickling*] So that's when I quickly comb her hair. It's really soft, with just a little bit of curl like Hector's, and I twirl it around my fingers like this, and I comb her bangs to the side—and you, Carlos? What gives you pleasure?

[**CATUNGAS** *steps forward with a chair and straddles it, with the back of the chair to his front. He sits next to* **ROSHANDA**.]

CATUNGAS: Mis lonches. [*Emphatically*] ¡Me la rayo! No me ganan con mis lonches. Los vatos del jale me hacen burla pero se alinean pa' ver que traigo—wanna know mi favorite? Cold pork chop sandwiches. Yeah, pork chops from the night before. La Molacha me hace unos extras pa' mi lunch next day. Ummm, pork chop sandwiches on white bread con mustard. Pura vida.

[*Pause.*]

Pues agarro asina two slices de white bread, les pongo la mustard a cada slice—yes, on each of the two slices, see that way the mustard's on *both* sides of the pork chop. La Molacha le gusta hacer trim la fat de los pork chops pero a mí me gusta just a little bit right near the bone, see? It's that fat that gives it that great flavor, y luego I eat my sandwich con un jalapeño bien crunchy—like the ones que hace la Helen.

[*Pause.*]

[*Calling out*] Helen! ¡Ven y dilos tu simple pleasure!

[**ROSHANDA** *and* **MOONBEAM** *also call her.*]

[**HELEN ENTERS** *at her steps. She is wearing a black crepe dress and high heels and is carrying a black lace shawl and black purse. She gives her lines as she walks down the steps and to the gate.*]

HELEN: I don't have any pleasures; no estén fregando. That's exactly what I told that viejo baboso with his stupid questions. And I was going to give him an interview, you know? But he's sitting there in my living room, looking at my pictures on the wall, and he turns to me and says, "You used to be real pretty." I *used* to be. How do you think that made me feel? Just like those ugly roses Catungas brings from the trash at St. Mary's, that's how. And you're making me late for the rosary.

[*Pause.*]

Praying. That's my simple pleasure. Praying for the souls of the dearly departed.

[*She* EXITS *into her house.*]

HECTOR [*standing up, finishing his beer*]: Órale, pues, the union organizers for the copper strikers are gonna be here tonight. They want help with the strike in Clifton, and we're committed to help get donations. Catungas, we need to borrow el Chueco's truck again for a door-to-door appeal for nonperishable food and blankets.

CATUNGAS: Pues, let's see if we can borrow the truck 'cause my jefita told me that el Chueco's using it to move—again. La Cuata's always spending the rent money—

HECTOR: We really need a truck and your brother's the only one that's got one. Vamos.

CATUNGAS: Espérate, carnal, what is your simple pleasure?

ROSHANDA: You'd better tell him, babe, or you'll never leave.

HECTOR: What makes me happy? Roshanda. And my kids.

CATUNGAS: No, asina no. We all know you love Roshanda and your kids. El ruco wanted something more personal, something that means a lot to you but not too many know about it, tú sabes . . .

[*Pause.*]

HECTOR: I don't remember too much about my jefito now. But I do remember when he'd get ready to go to work. The night before . . . polishing his shoes. And he taught me how to shine mine. Anyway, he told me what his father had told him . . . and what I tell Junior. "No matter how poor you are, your shoes better be shined good." He said that's what the bosses, or people, look at. Your shoes. See? [*Showing his shoes*] Not a scratch. That's why I don't like to dance at these parties here at the centro. 'Cause I don't want anybody stepping on my shoes. You know, I work for the city, picking and hauling stinky trash all day, but I'll tell you one thing: I've got the best-looking shoes in the whole department. Ask anybody, and they'll tell you: Hector Encinas has got the best-looking shoes in the whole department. Your turn, Moonbeam.

MOONBEAM: There's not really much to tell . . . I'm from California. Oh, some small town no one's even heard about. Near Monterey.

[*Pause.*]

Well, I like to walk on the beach. Barefooted. The wind blowing in my face. I like to sit on the rocks and listen to the waves crashing on the rocks near my feet, the ocean spray wetting my face. I like to smell the seaweed on the sand and hear the sea gulls shrieking and fighting for scraps, itty-bitty insects jumping near my bare legs. And best of all, I like to run right along the water. Hard. I run and run, and I wish that I would never have to stop—I run so hard that it hurts me to breathe . . . Then I just stop . . . and walk away.

[*Pause.*]

Yeah . . . just walk away.

HECTOR: Órale, Catungas, let's go.

[HECTOR *and* CATUNGAS EXIT *at the gate.* MOONBEAM *gets a box of paper flowers and* EXITS *to* CENTRO. ROSHANDA *picks up the empty beer bottles and throws them into garbage can. Pause.*]

ROSHANDA [*without turning to face* NACHO, *looking toward the street*]: And you, Nino? What's your simple pleasure?

NACHO: ¿Mi verdadero placer, Roshanda? To sit here, drinking my wine, reading the Greek legends, remembering. Siempre remembering. [*Crossing to* ROSHANDA] And you m'ija? What gives you the most pleasure?

ROSHANDA [*turning to him*]: You heard what I said, Nino. Hector and my babies are my pleasures. [*Turning toward street again*] But I want more, I guess.

[*Pause.*]

See the El Rio Golf Course over there on Speedway?

NACHO: Si, what about it?

ROSHANDA: The grass looks so green. Cool. Why can't we have something nice like that? A clean park, with rolling hills and lots of grass where the kids can play King of the Mountain, with a swimming pool for the little kids, a picnic area, maybe even a library filled with books in Spanish—a real centro where there would be something for everyone.

ARTEMISA [*crossing quickly and standing between them*]: Nacho! Stop her!

NACHO [*looking around, confused*]: Sounds good, Roshanda, pero ese country club belongs to the gringos.

ROSHANDA [*turning to* NACHO, *with determination*]: Nino, you're wrong— it doesn't belong to the gringos, it belongs to the people. Us. It's in the middle of our barrio, but none of us can even get in there. Except as caddies, of course. And look at the dirty parks we have. The grass is all dried up and there aren't even any trees for shade or tables for picnics. The little kids can't even go swimming because the regular pool is too deep for them. The swimming pool water is filthy; it never gets changed. Every time I drive past that golf course, Nino, I get so angry!

WATUSI: Sí, Nacho, stop her—those are dangerous thoughts.

NACHO: Roshanda, m'ija, wait a while. It used to be worse, much worse before the war. But things are changing—

ROSHANDA: No, Nino, they're not changing fast enough. Know what I'm thinking? That I can try to get everyone to go march in front of the golf course and demand that the land it's on be given back to us—

NACHO: March and demand? ¿Estás loca? You can't do that. Someone will get hurt, Roshanda.

ROSHANDA: No one will get hurt, Nino. No one. It'll just be a peaceful demonstration just to get people's attention, that's all. And maybe city hall will really fix up the junky parks we have now, or find some land for us for a brand-new park with everything we need.

ARTEMISA: Do something, Nacho.

NACHO: Ven, Roshanda, let me tell you about your mother. [*Singing*] "Aquí estoy entre botellas, apagando con el vino mi dolor . . ."

[*Pause.*]

ROSHANDA [*softly*]: I'm sorry, Nino, but sometimes memories and remembering is not enough. You have to do more; you have to take action—and no matter what it costs, you have to bring about change.

LIGHTS: OUT.

END OF ACT I

INTERMISSION

[*During intermission, the building is transformed into the* CENTRO *by the* ACTORS *and* STAGEHANDS, *and the audience sees the transformation take place. It now sports newly painted windowpanes and door, huge planters with plants near the door, more plants hanging on macramé planters, children's toys (tricycles, wagons, etc.), and chairs. The sign that* CATUNGAS *was going to paint is hanging lopsided on one nail near the door. It reads "El Centro" with some space left for the name to be completed if the group should ever decide on a name for the centro. They sing "El picket sign" as they work.* ALL EXIT.]

ACT II

Scene 1

TIME: *About a month later, early morning, another hot day. It is the third day of demonstrations.*

[*There is a typing class inside the* CENTRO *and the sound of very slow typing is heard.* NACHO *is repairing a toaster at his worktable, and* MOONBEAM *is across from him, stapling leaflets.*]

MOONBEAM [*grumbling*]: This stapler doesn't even work right. I'm getting a blister right here.

[MOONBEAM *shows* NACHO *the bottom of her palm;* NACHO *is not sympathetic.* NACHO *keeps working and hums under his breath.*]

I've already stapled over a hundred of these leaflets. Think that's enough?

[NACHO *shrugs.*]

Well, it's too hot, and I'm quitting.

[*She doesn't move.*]

NACHO [*singing softly*]: "Aquí el que llega se chinga, dijo la gringa—"

[CATUNGAS ENTERS *through the gate and joins* NACHO.]

CATUNGAS: "Sentadota en la portrona, la muy culona . . ." [*Peeping through window at typing class*] ¡Hijo! Qué recio 'stá typing mi sister, la Molacha. [*Mimicking typing*] Asina. Y la Roshanda parece una professor de la university.

MOONBEAM: You guys better stop.

CATUNGAS [*innocently*]: Stop what?

MOONBEAM: Stop singing that dirty song.

CATUNGAS: How do you know it's a dirty song? Do you speak Spanish?

MOONBEAM: You know I don't speak Spanish.

CATUNGAS: Well then, why don't you take one of Roshanda's classes? The one for kids.

MOONBEAM [*very annoyed*]: I may not know Spanish, but I do know you're calling me a [*pronouncing Spanish words with an accent*] gringa culona.

NACHO AND CATUNGAS [*together, pretending to be shocked*]: No! [*Singing*] "Aquí el que llega se chinga, dijo la gringa, sentadota en la portrona, la muy culona—"

MOONBEAM [*threateningly*]: I hope Roshanda catches you.

[HELEN ENTERS *with a basket of wet sheets.*]

HELEN: Catungas, your lawyer called this morning, and he wants you to call him back.

CATUNGAS [*explaining to* NACHO]: El workmen's compensation no me quiere pay porque they found out I was working on a side job cuando el wetback burned my hand.

NACHO [*sarcastically*]: Well, weren't you planning to sue him for all his money?

CATUNGAS: Sure, but he turned out to be related to me, mi primo on my mother's side, and she swore she'd kill me if I sued a relative.

HELEN: Well, hurry up—you can't keep a lawyer waiting forever.

[*She crosses and hangs white sheets on the clothesline.*]

CATUNGAS: Why not? He keeps me waiting. [*To* NACHO] Ni sirve el abogado—

NACHO AND CATUNGAS [*singing*]: "—¡culo cagado!"

HELEN: Ay, Moonbeam, how can you stand them?

[HECTOR ENTERS.]

M'ijo! You're just in time for lunch, but it's just a sopita 'cause I'm broke.

HECTOR: That's okay, Tía, but I don't have a lot of time anyway. I just came over to help before the march. [*To* MOONBEAM *and* CATUNGAS] What are you guys doing?

MOONBEAM: I'm getting the leaflets ready for the meeting tonight, and Catungas is just singing a dirty song with Nacho.

HELEN: Meeting? Ni viene nadie a sus meetings. Remember last week when that viejo from the university came and gave that boring speech about the conquest of Mexico? No one came. Just Nacho sat there by the window and listened. And that's only because his wine delivery was late.

HECTOR: It'll be different this time.

HELEN: Different? How?

HECTOR: No one wanted to come 'cause they heard it was gonna be a talk on history. And you know la raza when it comes to things like *history*. Anyway, Roshanda says we have to learn our history ourselves. So this time we're gonna show movies and give them popcorn.

HELEN [*sarcastically*]: Popcorn and movies? Oh, yeah, that'll bring them out.

HECTOR: It's Roshanda's idea. She says they'll show up for the movies and popcorn—then we'll sneak in the history. Tía, you're gonna make the popcorn, okay?

HELEN: I'm not making anything.

[*She* EXITS *to her house.*]

HECTOR [*to* CATUNGAS]: We still need to find a screen for the movie. Do you think you can find one?

CATUNGAS: Simón. ¿Y de qué va ser la movie?

HECTOR: *Salt of the Earth*, or something like that. I've never seen it.

MOONBEAM: I have. It's about some miners that go on strike somewhere in New Mexico.

[*Pause.*]

Isn't that guy they're searching for from New Mexico?

[HECTOR *and* CATUNGAS *exchange looks.*]

HECTOR: What guy?

MOONBEAM: Oh, I don't know. I heard something on the news about some fugitive from New Mexico heading to Arizona. Didn't you guys hear about it?

[*Pause. No one answers her.*]

Well, my blister's ready to pop. So here, Catungas, you can finish this stack.

[MOONBEAM *hands* CATUNGAS *a stack of leaflets, and he gets to work unwillingly.* CATUNGAS *jabs* NACHO *and both sing.*]

NACHO AND CATUNGAS: "Aquí el que llega se chinga, dijo la gringa, sentadota en la portrona, la muy culona, cuando llega el abogado, culo cagado, y aquí todo terminó."

[SOUND CUE: *Truck honking in front of* CENTRO.]

ALL, INCLUDING MOONBEAM [*ending the song*]: "Tun, tun."

CATUNGAS: That's el Chueco. He's got his pickup loaded with some boards for some bookshelves that Roshanda wants for her Chicano history class.

[HECTOR *and* MOONBEAM EXIT *to* CENTRO. CATUNGAS *follows them, stops, looks around, winks at* NACHO, *and then runs and gets one of* HELEN's *white sheets off the line. He calls out to the others inside the* CENTRO.]

CATUNGAS: ¡Hey, miren! ¡Aquí 'stá el screen pa'l mono que trajieron los Brown Berets!

[*He* EXITS *to* CENTRO.]

END OF SCENE 1

* * *

Scene 2

TIME: *Same day, noon.*

[*Offstage chants can be heard: "El Rio for the people," "Queremos justicia," "Chicano!" With the response: "Power!" Then singing is heard closer as the marchers enter the* CENTRO *from the street. They are singing "No nos moverán."* NACHO *wheels himself closer to the* CENTRO's *window. There is a very noisy party atmosphere inside as the marchers celebrate.* CATUNGAS ENTERS, *dressed as a caricature of an affluent golfer, and poses ready to hit ball.* NACHO *is at the gate, watching the marchers on Speedway.*]

NACHO [*not wanting to give in to his curiosity at first but finally having to ask*]: Bueno, Arnold Palmer, ¿cómo les fue en la marcha?

CATUNGAS [*walking down the steps and around the stage, hitting imaginary golf balls*]: Four! Five! [*Pretending to ask an invisible caddie*] Iron. Asina se dice, Nacho, iron. La marcha became a take-over, Nacho. There were cops all over the place, in riot gear, ready to shoot. Primero, we were marching peacefully, como quería la Roshanda, pero before you knew it, we marched right onto the golf course! Even into the coffee shop. Y believe it or not, I even got to ride all over the grass en una de esas golf carts!

NACHO: I believe it. Pero la Roshanda—is she all right? She didn't get hurt, did she?

CATUNGAS: Nah, nobody got hurt, 'orita viene. Anda en el radio station, dando un interview. You should've seen her, Nacho, parecía una Trojan warrior from one of your books when we marched down Speedway. [*Changing the subject*] Oye, Nacho, wanna hear some jokes? Okay, what is it when you see a gabacho driving a big white Cadillac?

[NACHO *doesn't know, so* CATUNGAS *gives him the answer.*]

White Power! Okay, what is it when you see a black dude driving a big black Cadillac?

NACHO [*tentatively*]: Black Power?

CATUNGAS: ¡Simón! And what is it when you see a Chicano driving a big brown Cadillac?

NACHO: I know! Brown Power!

CATUNGAS: No ... grand theft auto! [*Laughing uproariously at his joke*] Let me ask you a question. Do you know what Chicanos use for air conditioning in their cars?

NACHO [*warily*]: No, Catungas, I don't know what Chicanos use for air conditioning in their cars—what?

CATUNGAS: They use the four-forty cooling system.

NACHO: Four-forty? ¿Qué es eso?

CATUNGAS: You roll down your four windows and hit forty miles per hour! That's Chicano cooling. Four-forty. ¿No le agarras?

NACHO: Yes, Catungas, I get it. I have one. Do you know why Chicanos don't write grants?

CATUNGAS [*pondering*]: Why don't Chicanos write grants?

[*He stops abruptly as* ROSHANDA *and* HECTOR ENTER.]

ROSHANDA [*to* CATUNGAS]: What are you doing, Carlos? Telling racist jokes again?

CATUNGAS: No, Roshanda, it's your nino—

NACHO: A ver, a ver. You sure look pretty, m'ija; ¿cómo te fue en el interview?

ROSHANDA: I was scared stiff, but the radio announcer was real nice. He talked to me before we went on the air, and he seemed very supportive of the take-over, but he gave a little lecture about the "increasing militancy" and "propensity for violence."

HECTOR: Yeah, he's right, though; there's been too many fights breaking out on the picket lines. And it's people we don't even know, who don't live here in the barrio. What do we do with strangers who just show up saying they want to help and then disrupt the meetings?

ROSHANDA: I don't know, hon. But it's not always just strangers. Even people who started with us on the first march to the golf course are starting to argue over whether we should stick to our demands or take whatever the city offers in negotiations. There's talk of splitting into two coalitions or just quitting.

[*Pause.*]

Anyway, I was still very nervous 'cause I didn't know what he'd ask me once we got on the air. And then the phone wouldn't stop ringing! Everybody was calling. One man called, real angry, and said we were low class, that Chicanos were no better than dogs, that he was proud to be an American, and that if we didn't like it, to go back to Mexico.

CATUNGAS: ¿Y tú qué le dijistes?

ROSHANDA: That we had as much right as anyone to be here, that the Treaty of Guadalupe Hidalgo guarantees our rights to our land, language, religion, and culture. But I didn't have that much time to answer. I'm going again tomorrow. Nino, can you help me with my Spanish? The announcer says I'm doing fine, but I know I'm not. That's something else another angry listener said: that we didn't even know how to speak proper Spanish. That we were "pochos." Oh, and the radio announcer corrected me one time. I was talking away about "las problemas que tenemos en el barrio." And he slipped me this little note correcting me: "los problemas."

CATUNGAS: ¿Los problemas? I always thought it was "las."

ROSHANDA: Me, too . . . Where's Moonbeam? Inside?

HECTOR: Yeah. You'd better have a talk with her. I saw how she almost got you arrested when she was calling the pigs dirty names even after you told everybody to keep quiet.

ROSHANDA: I will. Things are getting pretty tense without her adding to it. Carlos, were you involved in that fight at the end of the line?

CATUNGAS: Me? Chalecos. They were just some assholes from the East Side who came to make trouble. Anyway, I had to hit a couple of them, just to break it up, ¡tú sabes! [*Changing the subject*] And you'd better tell Moonbeam to leave me alone. She just keeps wanting me to dance with her. Y ni sabe bailar la ruca.

NACHO: When have you seen a gringa that knew how to dance? It's not in their blood.

CATUNGAS: Who cares about the blood, Nacho. It's not in their feet! Me la rayo. They all dance on their tippy-toes. Asina. Con las manos up in the air. [*Showing them*] Y ¿sabes qué, Roshanda? No la trasteo.

HECTOR: I don't trust her either.

CATUNGAS: She's bien metichi. Nosey. She's always asking questions about everything. ¿Sabes? She's still asking about the carnal from New Mexico. The one the Feds are looking for.

HELEN [*from inside her house*]: You're just paranoid.

CATUNGAS: Paranoid? Me?

HELEN [*entering through her door*]: Yes, you. From smoking all that marihuana.

CATUNGAS [*strongly*]: Well, I may be paranoid, like you say, but that doesn't mean someone isn't watching us.

HECTOR: Tía, there's no pot.

HELEN: So how come I hear you guys laughing?

[HELEN EXITS, *slamming the door.* MOONBEAM ENTERS *from the* CENTRO. *Loud polka music is heard when she opens the door and stops when she closes the door again.*]

MOONBEAM [*dancing on her toes*]: I want to dance. Who wants to dance with me?

HECTOR [*quickly*]: I'm gonna go buy some ice.

[*He* EXITS.]

CATUNGAS: I'm going with Hector.

[*He also* EXITS.]

ROSHANDA: I have to make the punch.

[ROSHANDA EXITS, *running to* HELEN's. *Pause.*]

NACHO [*quickly finding a book to read*]: Don't look at me; I don't dance.

MOONBEAM: What are you reading? [*Looking at book*] Steinbeck? *Grapes of Wrath.* I had to read that at . . . Berkeley. Twice, as a matter of fact.

[NACHO *lets her ramble.*]

Remember that scene where the waitress sells the kids the candy for less money because she feels sorry for them? Well, I wrote a paper on her character's motivation.

[*She sits down even though it annoys* NACHO.]

I read all of Steinbeck. *Cannery Row, East of Eden, Tortilla Flat.* Did you ever read it? *Tortilla Flat?*

NACHO [*reluctantly*]: Of course I read *Tortilla Flat.*

MOONBEAM: Well, did you like it?

NACHO [*sarcastically*]: Yes, I liked it so much I modeled my life after the winos in it.

MOONBEAM: Winos? Oh, well, my professors explained that they were parodying the Knights of the Round Table. You know, King Arthur and his knights. [*Taunting him*] Who knows, Nacho? You may be a knight in shining armor, ready to rescue damsels in distress.

[*She laughs.*]

[NACHO *wheels himself out and* EXITS *stage right to his bathroom.* MOONBEAM *immediately searches his belongings.* ROSHANDA ENTERS *and quietly looks at* **MOONBEAM** *going through* **NACHO**'s *metal file box until* **MOONBEAM** *notices her.*]

ROSHANDA: What are you doing with my nino's things?

MOONBEAM [*trying to laugh it off*]: This? Nothing. I was just looking for one of his pain pills for my cramps.

ROSHANDA: Put it back. My nino doesn't like anyone going through his things.

MOONBEAM [*waving newspaper clippings*]: Why does he save these? Did he know these soldiers?

ROSHANDA: Some of them. Moonbeam, put it back. Now.

[**MOONBEAM** *puts the box back finally.*]

Anyway, my nino's out of his pain pills, and I'm refilling his prescription tomorrow.

MOONBEAM: Do you know who brings your nino his wine?

ROSHANDA: No. No one knows that.

MOONBEAM: Well, someone leaves him the wine through that broken fence board. Did you know that?

ROSHANDA: How did you find out? And why are you always asking so many questions?

[**NACHO** *has wheeled in silently; he listens.*]

MOONBEAM: I'm just curious, that's all . . . Is that why he drinks? Because all his friends are dead?

ROSHANDA [*looking at her with a somewhat sympathetic look*]: No, Moonbeam, my nino doesn't drink because his friends are dead. He drinks because *he's* alive.

MOONBEAM [*flippantly, as she runs into the* CENTRO]: Same thing.

NACHO [*crossing to* ROSHANDA]: She's right, Roshanda—it's the same thing, la misma chingadera. Her words are just a rearrangement of my words, that's all.

[**ROSHANDA** *turns to* **NACHO** *but doesn't speak.*]

END OF SCENE 2

* * *

Scene 3

TIME: *Same day, early afternoon.*

[*Loud hammering is heard from inside the* CENTRO. *Also, persons inside the* CENTRO *are singing "Huelga en general . . ." An actor in a* CALAVERA *costume and mask and* ROSHANDA ENTER *from the* CENTRO. *Singing continues to be heard intermittently from inside the* CENTRO.]

ROSHANDA: Good. You can rehearse your lines here as long as my nino's not here. I think he's showering right now.

CALAVERA: Your nino lives here?

ROSHANDA: Yeah, right there. And good thing he's not here right now 'cause he wouldn't let you do anything. He's very curious.

[*The* CALAVERA *sits on doorstep with script in hand and lights up a joint.*]

Eh . . . my Nina Helen doesn't let anyone smoke pot on her property.

CALAVERA: Not even outside?

ROSHANDA: No, not even outside.

[CALAVERA *takes very quick drags, puts the joint out carefully with fingertips, and saves it in her pocket.*]

I'll go help the other actors unpack.

CALAVERA: Bring me the flag if you run across it, please?

ROSHANDA: Flag?

CALAVERA: Yeah, the American flag—I need it for my grand entrance. It's folded in a box with my name on it.

[ROSHANDA EXITS. NACHO ENTERS *from his shower room but doesn't see* CALAVERA. *He has just showered. He gets his shaving gear and a mirror that hangs on a nail on a post.* CALAVERA *puts the script aside, stands up, sweeps stage with pointed finger and very dramatically gives her opening line.*]

CALAVERA: La muerte viene . . . viene cantando.

NACHO: Ay, chingado. I knew it, I knew it.

CALAVERA [*noticing* NACHO]: Knew what?

NACHO: No te hagas pendeja. I always knew Death would come singing. But I'm not going; I'm not ready. No, señora, I'm not ready.

CALAVERA [*kidding*]: Señorita, por favor.

NACHO [*disbelieving*]: You're a señorita? ¿A poco?

CALAVERA: You find that hard to believe?

[*Pause.*]

NACHO: Actually no. By the time you come around to a man, all he can think about is praying—and besides, you're too ugly for sex. Which reminds me: let me pray.

[NACHO *closes his eyes, folds his hands to pray, and mumbles. He opens one eye cautiously to see if* CALAVERA *has gone, but she, enjoying the joke, moves closer to* NACHO.]

CALAVERA: You're cute. What's your name?

NACHO: Igna—Hey, if you don't know my name, you're in the wrong house. [*Trying to shoo her away*] ¡Fuera, fuera de aquí! [*Making a cross with his thumb and pointer finger and repeating*] ¡Qué se vaya el diablo y qué venga Dios!

[ROSHANDA ENTERS.]

ROSHANDA: Nino! What are you doing to Kathy?

NACHO [*fearful for* ROSHANDA, *moving quickly between them*]: Vete, Roshanda, vete. Take me, vieja seca, take me.

[CALAVERA *and* ROSHANDA *laugh;* NACHO *is bewildered.*]

Why are you laughing? It's not funny, dammit!

ROSHANDA [*explaining*]: Nino, this is Kathy. She's an actress with a street theater from California. Teatro Unidad.

NACHO: ¿Teatro?

CALAVERA: Yes, we're performing here at the centro tonight. I play the role of La Muerte, among others, and I enter, very dramatically with the American flag ... [*To* ROSHANDA] Did you find it?

ROSHANDA [*handing* CALAVERA *her folded flag*]: Here it is. [*Showing her a piece of paper*] Is this the song we have to learn for tonight?

CALAVERA [*reading paper*]: Yeah, "Yo soy chicano." It's real easy. We needed more copies so la gringa hippie went to make some.

ROSHANDA: You mean Moonbeam? ... She's a real good worker.

[*Pause.*]

What do you do with the flag?

CALAVERA: The acto, the play, begins with these two Chicano brothers lying on the ground in Vietnam, and I enter with the flag and cover them with it.

NACHO: So, are you saying death is inevitable? The end result of any war?

CALAVERA: No! I'm saying that the deaths must stop. Do you know how many Chicanos and black brothers are getting killed in Vietnam?

ROSHANDA: But, Kathy, do you really think that people care? We always seem to be asking—no, begging—people to help us, to march with us. To help us pass leaflets for the lettuce boycott, to collect blankets for the strikers. Anything. But they're indifferent. The other day when we marched down Speedway to the golf course, we needed everyone to help us. Some people did join us, but most didn't. I stopped to talk to one of my friend's family. They were under a mesquite tree, playing cards, drinking beer, and they listened politely. But they wouldn't budge from their poker game. They wouldn't march with us. Not even my friend. And we've been friends since Davis School.

CALAVERA: I know. Sometimes I feel discouraged, too, but we can't stop—

VOICE [*from inside the* CENTRO, *yelling out the cue for* CALAVERA]: ¿Y la muerte viene cantando? Calavera, on stage!

CALAVERA: That's my cue. [*Giving* ROSHANDA *the paper with the song*] Here, maybe you can learn it before the show. That way you can start the singing while we get out of costume.

[*She* EXITS *quickly.*]

NACHO: She runs instead of walks, just like you, Roshanda.

[ROSHANDA *places a towel around* NACHO's *neck, gets a pan of water and* NACHO's *shaving gear, and starts to shave him.*]

ROSHANDA [*teasing him*]: Did she scare you, Nino?

NACHO [*sarcastically*]: No, Roshanda, I see Death standing on the doorsteps pointing her long ugly finger at me every day. [*Mimicking* CALAVERA] "La muerte viene cantando."

[HELEN ENTERS *with a can of air freshener and sniffs the air around her.*]

HELEN: Aha! I knew it! I smell marihuana. [*Spraying the air*] Where are those people from? The actors? From California, I bet. *Todos* los de California son puros marihuanos.

[*She gives one more angry spray and* EXITS, *slamming her screen door.*]

ROSHANDA [*handing* NACHO *the song*]: Here, Nino, hold it for me while I shave you. And don't move. [*Reciting*] "Yo soy chicano, tengo color, americano pero con honor . . ."

NACHO: Very good. Ahora, sing it.

ROSHANDA: But I don't know the tune. [*Reading*] To the tune of "La rielera." What's that?

NACHO: "La rielera?" Uuh, that's an old song—from the Mexican Revolution. Las rieleras were the women who rode the trains, fighting in the Revolución.

ROSHANDA [*impressed*]: Really, Nino? I never knew that. [*Filing that away mentally*] Las rieleras: women who rode the trains and fought in the Mexican Revolution.

[*Pause.*]

Well, hum it, Nino, so I can hear the tune. I'll follow you.

[NACHO *hums and* ROSHANDA *starts to sing the words to* "Yo soy chicano."]

". . . Yo soy chicano, tengo color, americano pero con honor. Cuando me dicen que hay revolución, defiendo a mi raza con mucho valor."

NACHO: "Tengo todita mi gente para la revolución, voy a luchar por los pobres, pa' que se acabe el bolón."

[NACHO, ROSHANDA, *and* ALL *inside the* CENTRO *repeat first verse together.*]

END OF SCENE 3

* * *

Scene 4

TIME: *A few moments later.*

[NACHO *is at his worktable fixing a toaster.* CATUNGAS *is pacing, agitated, picking up objects and placing them down again. He seems impatient and worried but is telling one of his usual long stories to help pass the time.* ARTEMISA *and* WATUSI *are sitting on* HELEN's *steps, silently watching* CATUNGAS.]

CATUNGAS: Yesterday, Nacho, 'staba en un side job, fixing this teacher's roof, and it was hot, so I took a break. Out comes his wife with a pitcher of ice-cold lemonade and she gives me some, and we start to talk . . . about the roof, the weather, tú sabes. Then the teacher comes out y le dice, "Listen, honey—Catungas, what's your sister's name?" And I answer, "Amalia." And he says, "No, her nickname, tell Muffin her nickname." So I say, "Molacha." [*Explaining to* NACHO] You know we've called her "la Molacha" since she fell off a bike and knocked out her two front teeth.

NACHO: Yes, I know. Siéntate, Catungas, por favor. You're making me dizzy.

CATUNGAS [*not sitting down*]: But the teacher doesn't let me explain. He says, "Your other brothers, what are their nicknames?" I know he means el Chueco y el Huango, my younger brothers, pero me hago pendejo. I'll be goddamned if I tell him what's wrong with them. "Honey," he says, "I really should tape record him. For my class." And he laughs and laughs like a cartoon jackass. But you now, that's not so bad. I can take that. But I look at his wife, and she just looks away from me, just looks at the pitcher on the patio table and draws circles on the frost with her finger. That hurts my feelings more than her asshole husband. I don't know why, but it does.

[HELEN ENTERS *at the gate with groceries, crosses, and puts them away on shelves.*]

HELEN: I got you your chicken noodle soup, four for a dollar. Y mira. [*Holding up a can*] Vienna sausage. On sale también. I got some real nice hamburger meat for tonight. [*Starting to exit to her door, but then stopping*] I think I'll make some albóndigas with it. Albóndigas, just like they make them in the state of Michoacán.

NACHO: Sounds good. Are you making tortillas?

HELEN: Well, maybe. If Hector comes over for dinner. He loves my tortillas. Well, that's if Rosie doesn't have him out marching or protesting God knows what. Oh, I better get the yerba buena now.

[*She starts to go past* NACHO *toward garden area.*]

NACHO [*quickly seeing where she's heading to and trying to stop her*]: No, don't put yerba buena in the albóndigas—they don't need it. Just use oregano like everyone here does.

HELEN [*insistent*]: Yes, they do need the peppermint. That's what the people from Michoacán use to make them so special.

NACHO [*blocking her way*]: Catungas can cut it for you. You go inside and start cooking.

CATUNGAS: I'll get it for you, Helen.

HELEN: No, Catungas, the last time you cut the verdolagas for me you cut them out by the roots instead of snipping them off. No, I'll cut the peppermint myself.

[*She pushes* CATUNGAS *aside and goes to the mint that is planted very close to the fence.* NACHO *is resigned and returns to fixing the toaster.*]

HELEN [*giving a triumphant yell and holding up a bottle of cheap wine*]: AHA! I found your stash. [*Walking over to* NACHO *and holding the bottle under his nose*] You were saving it for tonight, ¿verdad?

[NACHO *nods.*]

Well, tough shit, 'cause I'm throwing it away.

[HELEN EXITS *to her house, and* ARTEMISA *and* WATUSI *jump out of her way.* HECTOR ENTERS *with* MOONBEAM *at the gate.*]

HECTOR: ¡Quiubo, Nacho! Ready Catungas? [*Looking around*] Where are the blankets Roshanda's supposed to bring here?

CATUNGAS [*relieved to see* HECTOR]: She's still at Molacha's. Hector, we have a problem.

[ARTEMISA *and* WATUSI *cross to* NACHO, *somewhat protectively.*]

HECTOR: Nacho, cuando venga la Roshanda con las blankets, dile que deje las blankets *aquí*, en el centro y que *no* vaya pa'n que'l Chueco.

MOONBEAM [*suddenly standing up to leave*]: I gotta go.

HECTOR: I thought you were going with us to Clifton.

MOONBEAM: I changed my mind. I gotta catch up on a lot of reading.

[MOONBEAM *crosses to the gate.* ARTEMISA *and* WATUSI *run quickly to the gate to block her leaving, but* MOONBEAM *gets to the gate before they do and* EXITS *quickly.*]

HECTOR: Let's go, Catungas.

[*He and* CATUNGAS *cross to the gate.* HECTOR *stops and turns.*]

Don't forget, Nacho.

NACHO: Forget what?

[CATUNGAS *groans.*]

HECTOR: In case Roshanda gets here before we find her, tell her *not* to go to Chueco's house. Not for anything. Can you remember that?

NACHO: Sure. Tell Roshanda not to go to Chueco's house.

HECTOR: Good. Okay, Catungas, let's go.

CATUNGAS: I don't know if Nacho will remember to tell her.

HECTOR: Don't worry. She's probably still at Molacha's. Let's go catch her there.

[HECTOR *turns to* EXIT, *but he stops when* HELEN ENTERS. *She is carrying a hammer, nails, a small board, and a very determined look.*]

HECTOR: Hey, Tía, need any help?

[CATUNGAS EXITS *quickly before he's asked to help.*]

HELEN: Hell, no. I finally found Nacho's stash, and whoever it is that's bringing Nacho his wine won't be able to do it anymore. I'm boarding up that hole in the fence once and for all.

[*She goes to the fence and pounds board over the hole. Pause.*]

HECTOR: Tía, si viene la Roshanda, tell her to stay away from Chueco's—

HELEN: Hector, I don't have any time to be giving anyone your messages.

[CATUNGAS *is honking his car horn furiously.*]

I'm going to the rosary at seven.

[HECTOR EXITS *without really hearing* HELEN's *answer. She turns to* NACHO *as she continues hammering.*]

Ready for some albóndigas?

[NACHO *is sulking and won't answer her.*]

¿'Stas enojado? Nacho, it's for your own good. I had to throw the wine out. Look at you. You won't take the medicine, but you get drunk every single night. You're killing yourself.

NACHO: Es mi vida, ¿qué no?

HELEN: Your life? What kind of life is it? You haven't been out of this yard in over twenty years—you don't do anything but get drunk.

NACHO: ¿Y qué quieres que haga, Helen? ¿Qué quieres que haga?

HELEN: I don't know. You can do anything! Stop sitting there! Help Roshanda—anything!

NACHO: Help? How? By *marching* with Hector and Catungas at Lucky's? By *walking* from house to house asking for donations? By *running* with Roshanda past the gates at the golf course? That just about covers it, doesn't it? Marching, walking, running. How about crawling, Helen? Do you want me crawling somewhere?

HELEN: STOP IT!

[*She stands up and crosses.*]

NACHO: Take a good look, Helen; I'm crippled.

HELEN [*softly*]: Yes, Nacho, you're crippled. You really are.

[*She goes up her steps and hesitates. She turns to* NACHO.]

What did Hector say about Roshanda?

[NACHO *refuses to answer her.*]

ARTEMISA AND WATUSI [*pacing furiously, trying to pound the message into both* NACHO *and* HELEN]: Hector said, "Don't let her go to Chueco's house—there's danger there! [*Repeating*] Don't let her go to Chueco's house.

[NACHO *starts to look around his things for a hidden bottle but doesn't find one. The scene ends with a frustrated* NACHO *looking helplessly at the boarded hole in fence while* HELEN *glares at him.*]

END OF SCENE 4

* * *

Scene 5

TIME: *Late at night.*

[*The set is dimly lit.* NACHO *is reading a book. He hears movement by the fence and listens intently. The unknown person who delivers his wine is kicking at the nailed board.* NACHO *is gladdened by the kicks, but the board does not give.* NACHO *hears the person leave. He mutters some choice obscenities, then resumes his reading.* MOONBEAM ENTERS.]

MOONBEAM: Good evening, Nacho. What are you reading?

[NACHO *doesn't answer her.*]

Another Steinbeck epic?

[*When* NACHO *again doesn't answer her, she bends her head and reads the title.*]

> *Occupied America: The Chicano's Struggle Toward Liberation.* One of Roshanda's books? Occupied America? We've never been occupied. Have we?

NACHO: Read the book.

[*He offers her the book, but* MOONBEAM *doesn't take it.*]

MOONBEAM: I don't have time for any reading right now.

[NACHO *resumes his reading, ignoring her.*]

> Has Roshanda been here?

NACHO: No.

MOONBEAM [*reaching into her backpack and taking out an expensive bottle of Scotch*]: Well, well, what have we here? Chivas Regal. [*Holding the bottle out to* NACHO] Have you ever had Chivas Regal, Nacho?

[NACHO *visibly perks up, licks his chops, and moves closer to* MOONBEAM.]

> I have. Do you want some? Here, take it. It's a gift—from me to you.

NACHO: "Beware of Greeks bearing gifts."

MOONBEAM: Greeks? I'm not Greek. [*Tantalizingly*] Smooth. Goes down your throat like honey.

[*The following dialogue is like an orchestrated pas de deus of temptation until* NACHO *drinks most of the Chivas Regal.* MOONBEAM *only pretends to drink as she pumps* NACHO *for* CHUECO's *address.*]

> Here, let me pour you a drink. Like it? Have some more. Not so fast. Expensive liquor like this is to be savored. Ummmm. Warm. Okay, Nacho, where does el Chueco live? No more Chivas Regal until you tell me. Where does el Chueco live?

NACHO: El Chueco? Pues, con la Cuata, where else?

MOONBEAM: Not with whom, Nacho, where? He used to live in Barrio Anita, remember? But he just moved, Nacho. Where did he move to?

NACHO: Pour me some more.

MOONBEAM: Not yet. Where does he live now?

NACHO: Who?

MOONBEAM: El Chueco.

NACHO: What chueco?

MOONBEAM: Here, have some more. El Chueco, you know him. He's Catungas's brother. The one that's married to a twin.

NACHO [*suddenly very suspicious*]: Twin? I never said he lived with a twin.

MOONBEAM: So, where does he live?

NACHO [*stubbornly*]: I didn't say "twin." I said "la cuata." So how did you know that "cuata" means "twin" if you don't know Spanish?

MOONBEAM: Dammit, I don't know Spanish!

[*She quickly starts to* EXIT *through gate. She is obviously irritated and mumbling under her breath.*]

Borracho motherfucker. I'm gonna tell them they have to follow her from here, and see if she goes to Chueco's house.

NACHO [*crossing quickly to* MOONBEAM]: Follow who?

MOONBEAM [*turning*]: Nobody. [*Handing him the bottle*] Here, Nacho, kill it. It's the only chance you'll ever have.

[MOONBEAM *laughs and* EXITS *to the* CENTRO, *leaving her backpack behind.* ARTEMISA *and* WATUSI ENTER, *running to* NACHO. *They try to shake him awake, but he is very drunk.*]

NACHO: I didn't tell her, Artemisa. No le dije 'dónde vive el Chueco. I know where Chueco lives, but I never told her. Never. Pinchi gringa, ¿pa' qué quiere saber?

[ARTEMISA *crosses to the backpack.*]

ARTEMISA [*to* WATUSI]: We're too late.

END OF SCENE 5

* * *

Scene 6

TIME: *Same night, sometime later.*

[NACHO *is sitting at his worktable, very drunk, talking to himself.* ARTEMISA *and* WATUSI *are guarding the gate, waiting for* ROSHANDA.]

ROSHANDA [*entering at the gate*]: Hi, Nino. [*Noticing that he's drunk and helping him to bed*] Where's Hector, Nino? Was Hector here? [*Calling out toward* HELEN's *door*] Nina Helen? Did Hector come over? Nina? [*To* NACHO] Nino, listen, did Hector or Carlos come over? I'm supposed to give them some blankets and other stuff for the strikers. Nino, were they here?

NACHO [*mumbling drunkenly*]: El Hector? Sí, aquí estaban el Hector y el Catungas.

ROSHANDA: What did they say? Where did they go? Nino, please try to remember.

NACHO: Remember what?

ROSHANDA: Did they tell you anything? To tell me where they went?

ARTEMISA AND WATUSI [*almost in a wailing singsong*]: Roshanda, they said to stay away from Chueco's. Nacho, she can't hear us. Tell Roshanda to stay away from Chueco's

NACHO: Sí, m'ija. They said to tell you not to go to Chueco's house.

ROSHANDA: Chueco? Uh, you mean Fernando? Carlos's brother?

NACHO: I don't know. I just remember something about Chueco.

ROSHANDA: Are you sure they said *not* to go? I bet they said I'm supposed to *go* to Fernando's.

[*Car horn honks.*]

Uh oh, the kids are honking for me. Bye, Nino—I have to go. If Hector comes over, tell him I went to leave the blankets at Fernando's. Don't forget, Nino.

[*Car horn honks more.*]

[*Calling out to kids as she runs out*] Junior, stop honking the horn! You're gonna wake up the baby! [*Walking toward the gate*] I'm sure he means I'm supposed to go to Fernando's.

[ROSHANDA EXITS *running, leaving the gate open.* NACHO *stares at the gate somewhat befuddled. He suddenly realizes her mistake and wheels himself to the gate.* ARTEMISA *and* WATUSI *follow him.*]

NACHO: Roshanda! Roshanda! Don't go to Chueco's house. Roshanda!

ARTEMISA: Follow her, Nacho, please! Stop her!

NACHO: I can't.

WATUSI: Síguela, Nacho—someone will stop and give you a ride to Chue-co's. Follow her, Nacho.

[NACHO *moves to the gate, but his wheelchair gets stuck, and he is either too drunk to maneuver the wheelchair past the gate or he simply cannot make himself leave the safety of the yard. When he finally reverses the wheelchair, he hesitates.*]

NACHO [*sobbing helplessly, repeating*]: No puedo salir de aquí, no puedo. Roshanda!

[ARTEMISA *and* WATUSI *immediately rush past him and* EXIT.]

END OF SCENE 6

* * *

Scene 7

TIME: *Much later that same night.*

SOUND CUE: *Distant police sirens.*

[NACHO *is sitting at his worktable.* HECTOR *and* CATUNGAS *have blood-stained clothes.* HELEN *is standing at her doorsteps, listening.* CATUNGAS, *in a shocked daze, is sitting at the* CENTRO'*s steps. It is dark inside the* CENTRO. HECTOR *is trying to explain* ROSHANDA'*s death to* NACHO.]

HECTOR: Catungas and I went to Molacha's house, but Roshanda had already left. We should've come back here, but we figured you or Helen would tell her not to go to Chueco's. So we went to Chue-co's for the truck, and Chueco asked us to take the vato from New Mexico to Clifton. Then from there someone else would take him as far as Yuma, I think. Anyway, we had to wait for the vato to pack his stuff. Then Roshanda walks in with the blankets.

CATUNGAS: I yelled at her, "Roshanda, get out of here!" I tell her that I'm hearing these voices telling me there's danger for her, but Roshanda just laughed. Said she's ready to leave anyway 'cause the three kids are asleep in the car and she wants to take them home. She's already at the front door when we hear the pig on the bullhorn: "Come out slowly with your hands up."

HECTOR: I run to her, but she's already out the door. She's stepping outside, with her hands up, walking slowly. The Feds have the house and the street surrounded. Lights, megaphones. Roshanda's walking slowly to the gate now. I swear to you, Nacho, she's walking slowly, when she hears baby Gloria crying. It's like I could read her mind in that instant: the baby's gonna fall off the car seat. Roshanda puts her hands down and . . . runs. Runs to the gate. And that's when they shot her.

[*Pause.*]

[*Standing up*] Right now Tía Helen and I have to pick up the kids at some children's shelter and go make the . . . arrangements.

[*Pause.* HECTOR EXITS *with* HELEN *into her house.* CATUNGAS *and* NACHO *exchange looks.* CATUNGAS *stands up and seems ready to say something, but* NACHO *cuts him off with a hand gesture.* CATUNGAS EXITS *to* HELEN's *house.*]

END OF SCENE 7

* * *

Scene 8

TIME: *Same night, almost dawn.*

[NACHO *is sitting in the shadows quietly, holding* MOONBEAM's *backpack.* MOONBEAM ENTERS *furtively from the gate entrance. She is dressed in striking contrast to the "hippie" Moonbeam, wearing a tailored suit, her hair combed back, heels, and face makeup skillfully and artfully applied. She is carrying a leather briefcase. Trying not to make any noise, she searches for her backpack.* NACHO *watches her, and then turns the light on.*]

NACHO: Looking for this, Moonbeam?

[*He stresses her name and throws her backpack very hard at her. It hits her and falls to the floor.* MOONBEAM *picks it up and turns toward the gate to* EXIT. NACHO *wheels himself very fast to get to her.*]

Why the backpack, Moonbeam? It clashes with your Wall Street image.

MOONBEAM: I came back for something.

NACHO: It must be important enough for you to sneak back here after what you did.

MOONBEAM: It is.

[*She unzips the backpack and takes something out.*]

NACHO: What's that?

MOONBEAM: A county hospital identification bracelet.

NACHO: Yours?

MOONBEAM: No, it's my baby's. [*Putting the bracelet into the briefcase*] I don't go any place without it. She died.

NACHO: Spare me the melodrama.

[MOONBEAM *angrily starts to* EXIT.]

    Why do you do it, Moonbeam?

[MOONBEAM *stops without turning.*]

    Why? And don't give me any of that "It's for my country" John Wayne bullshit.

MOONBEAM [*turning*]: No, I do it for the money.

NACHO [*surprised*]: For the money?

MOONBEAM: It sure beats packing squid in the canneries.

NACHO: Canneries?

MOONBEAM: Yeah, near Monterey.

NACHO: So you really are from California?

MOONBEAM: Oh, yeah, I'm really from California. From that great Steinbeck country you're so crazy about. Remember the Joads from *The Grapes of Wrath*?

[NACHO *nods yes.*]

    Well, that's us, my family. Okies. Me and my nine brothers and sisters. My mother was a skinny, toothless hag before she was even twenty-five—nine of us—she kept losing weight and tooth after tooth with each pregnancy.

NACHO [*sarcastically*]: Well, that explains everything. You betray your friends so you can have perfect teeth.

MOONBEAM: Fuck you. I don't betray anyone; they betray themselves.

NACHO: What do you mean?

MOONBEAM: Do you really think I could do any damage if the Movement was really as strong as it thinks or wants to be?

NACHO: You got Roshanda killed.

MOONBEAM: *Roshanda* got herself killed. Sweet, stupid Roshanda. Idealistic to the end. She didn't have to take the blankets tonight; the strikers could've waited. You did tell her not to go to Chueco's, didn't you?

NACHO [*nodding yes*]: Yes, I told her not to go to Chueco's.

[*Pause.*]

But why was she killed? For collecting blankets?

MOONBEAM: She wasn't supposed to get killed. Just arrested. We wanted to make her look bad.

NACHO: Look bad? Why?

MOONBEAM: Too many people were listening to her. She was good—you heard her on the radio and here at the meetings. I tried to get her arrested, but sometimes she was just too lucky. At the golf course, when I was telling the pigs to fuck off, she almost got arrested with me—but no, she talked to the detective, some Chicano she knew in high school, and he let us go. And tonight, we just wanted her arrested for harboring a fugitive or illegal possession of arms. Anything. I'm telling you, we just had to make her look bad. Nacho, please believe me—the shooting wasn't part of the plan. It just happened.

NACHO: It just happened.

MOONBEAM [*looking at her wristwatch*]: Well, I don't have time for this; I have a plane to catch.

NACHO [*sarcastically*]: I like your watch. What happened to your "it's too establishment" shit?

[MOONBEAM *doesn't respond. She shrugs and crosses to gate.*]

Before you go, Moonbeam, tell me, how much Spanish can you understand?

MOONBEAM [*speaking in perfect, accentless Spanish*]: Bastante. Lo aprendí cuando jugaba con los niños de los campesinos. I'm really quite good with languages. También puedo hablar en filipino—bueno, solo los dialectos Tagalog y Visayen. I'm going to learn Vietnamese next.

NACHO: I'm impressed.

[*Pause.*]

    [*Smiling wryly*] And you even learned the regional usage, so you wouldn't slip up. Like knowing the word we use for twin: cuate. Only us Mexicans or Chicanos around here use the word "cuate" for "twin."

MOONBEAM: Yes, I know. The Latinos around the Bay Area prefer the word "gemelo."

NACHO: That guy that came and gave the lecture about the conquest of Mexico said it was an Azteca word, from the Nahuatl "koatezon."

[*Pause.*]

    Enough on linguistics—go and leave me alone.

MOONBEAM: Well, Nacho, I was just doing my job.

NACHO: You did a fine job, Moonbeam, the multilingual federal whore.

MOONBEAM: I'm an agent, not a whore!

[NACHO *gives her a wry salute and she* EXITS.]

NACHO: Agent, whore. Same thing. Words. Words. Cuate, gemelo.

[*Pause.*]

    It's the same goddamn thing. La misma chingadera, Moonbeam. Stardust. Whatever your name is. [*Taking another long swig and starting to sing part of "Stardust"*] "Sometimes I wonder why I spend the lonely night, dreaming of a song, the memory haunts my reverie, and I am once again with you, when our love was new and each kiss an inspiration." [*Picking up a book and caressing it*] Shakespeare, quote: "That's all there is; there is no more . . ." I forget the rest. [*Starting to sing*] "Me voy de soldado raso, voya ingresar a las filas"—Watusi! ¡Ven, Watusi!

[ARTEMISA *and* WATUSI ENTER *and stand at their usual places, as* NACHO *sings "Soldado raso."*]

END OF ACT II

ACT III

Scene 1

TIME: *Two days later, late afternoon, a beautiful Arizona sunset. It is the night of* ROSHANDA'S *rosary.*

[NACHO *is sitting, doing nothing.* ARTEMISA *and* WATUSI *are nearby, feeling useless.* HELEN, *dressed in her usual black church clothes* ENTERS *from her house and crosses to* NACHO.]

HELEN: You're not going to Roshanda's rosary, are you?

[*Pause.*]

It's just like all the other times. You've never gone to any of the rosaries, funerals, burials. Not even for Artemisa. Or Watusi. I always ended up going by myself. But did you know, that right up to the very end of each rosary, each funeral, each burial, I waited for you to come and sit next to me? I was always so sure you'd show up. I always sat there all by myself, alone. Smelling the chrysanthemums, hearing that awful organ music, greeting old, old, friends telling me—what's that phrase in Spanish? When you give the pésame? [*Answering herself*] "Te acompaño en tu sentimiento." How beautiful that sounds: I accompany you in your sorrow.

[*Pause.*]

But why am I asking you what it is? You wouldn't know, would you? When you're out here, drunk, singing, I'm inside, all by myself, remembering, too. And you know? I feel the same pain you do, Nacho. Because pain is remembering the past. [*Turning to go, then stopping and turning back to* NACHO] You say that I hoard my memories, and I guess it's true. I will never share these memories with you. Never.

[*She starts to* EXIT *and reaches the top of her steps.*]

ARTEMISA [*very suddenly to* HELEN, *forcefully*]: Oh yes, you will, Helen.

[HELEN *stops without turning.*]

WATUSI: Déjala, Artemisa, she can't hear you.

ARTEMISA: I'll make her hear me. [*Crossing to the steps*] Tell him, Helen, tell him the truth about why you won't sit out here with him and share your memories. Tell him, goddamit!

HELEN [*turning, to* NACHO]: You know, don't you? You've always known.

NACHO: No, Helen, I haven't always known. Suspected, maybe, but never sure.

ARTEMISA: Tell him!

HELEN [*holding her head as though to shut out the voice*]: All right, I will! Just shut up!

[*Pause.*]

[*To* NACHO] That night, at the dance in Nogales, Artemisa asked me to drive. We both knew she was too drunk. But I told her no, and I left her. I was angry. Jealous.

NACHO: Jealous? Why?

ARTEMISA [*to* NACHO]: You still don't see it, do you? Tell him, Helen.

WATUSI [*tenderly*]: You don't have to, Helen.

HELEN: Because I was burning with envy. I've always loved you, but you could only love Artemisa. And after the war when you came back—

NACHO: Crippled.

HELEN: —You still loved her, followed her around like that wounded, drooling dog that's always looking for a bone behind El Grande Market. And she knew it. I would see her at the dances, dancing where you would be sure to see her, twirling and winking at you. She never knew how much I hated her then.

ARTEMISA: I knew.

HELEN: So that night, when you and Watusi didn't go with us, I wanted to stay home, too. But Artemisa insisted on going. It was raining. She got drunk, and you weren't there to stop her. I refused to drive, and I left with some friends; she was giving the bandleader, or a musician—I don't remember who—a ride, and he let her drive, and she didn't make a curve, and she—

NACHO: Died from a broken neck.

HELEN: Yes, and it was my fault. Afterward, I felt so guilty, blaming myself. That's why I wouldn't sit out here and talk about the past. I'm sorry, Nacho. I've been sorry ever since, but I couldn't tell you. [*To* ARTEMISA, *softly*] I'm sorry, Artemisa.

WATUSI [*to* ARTEMISA]: Satisfied? [*To* HELEN] How 'bout me, Helen, the other drooling dog?

HELEN: Y el pobre Watusi. One minute he'd be fine, and then he'd be off in his own world, seeing imaginary things floating in the air, or worse, he'd be back in the war, fighting invisible enemy soldiers, dodging invisible grenades, hearing the official commendations for medals he was awarded. All this exploding in his head, giving him those headaches.

WATUSI: Just call it "combat fatigue," Helen. That's what the doctors said. Combat fatigue, a fancy name for a plain crack-up.

[*Pause.*]

Well, Nacho, finish the tale.

NACHO: Yes, Watusi was next. You turned him down, so he marries someone he meets one drunken night, has four kids, and the headaches—the explosions, you said—get worse. So, on another drunken night, he walks to railroad tracks, right next to Van Alstine Street, puts his head down on the tracks, and waits for a train.

HELEN [*to* WATUSI]: I'm sorry. [*To both* ARTEMISA *and* WATUSI] I'm very sorry. [*Crossing to* NACHO, *taking his hand*] Nacho, I'm very sorry for your loss of Roshanda.

[*She turns to* EXIT *but stops. Pause.*]

Nacho, I want to share one memory now. At the church when we baptized Roshanda, remember, Nacho?

[ARTEMISA *and* WATUSI *cross and stand on each side of* NACHO.]

You and I held Roshanda during the baptismal, and at the end, outside St. Margaret's, do you remember what we both said to Artemisa?

[NACHO *nods yes. Pause.*]

Here's another beautiful phrase in Spanish, Nacho. [*Reciting*] "Aquí le entregamos a su hija, que de la iglesia salió con el santo sacramento que del cielo recibió." A beautiful arrangement of words, Nacho.

ARTEMISA [*translating as she crosses to* HELEN, *arms out*]: We are returning your daughter, who has come out of church with the holy sacrament that from heaven she's received.

[*Pause.*]

HELEN: And then we handed Roshanda back to Artemisa.

[*Pause.*]

       Nacho, you have to give Roshanda back to Artemisa again.

[HELEN EXITS *to her house.* ARTEMISA *turns to* NACHO, *but he turns away from her angrily.*]

NACHO: No! You cannot ask me to give her up. Not when she's the only thing I have from you.

[NACHO *wheels himself to the* CENTRO*'s sign and angrily knocks it down.* ARTEMISA *starts to cross to him, but* WATUSI *holds her back.*]

WATUSI: Déjalo, Artemisa.

NACHO [*beginning to sob softly and ending with very painful, almost animal, howls of grief*]: Roshanda. Roshanda. ROSHANDA!!

LIGHTS: DOWN.

END OF SCENE 1

* * *

Scene 2

TIME: *Later that week, the night before* ROSHANDA*'s rosary. It is starting to get dark.*

[*Only the lights in* HELEN*'s house and the* CENTRO *are on now, and* NACHO *is sitting in the dark.* CATUNGAS ENTERS *from the* CENTRO. *His mood is serious, somber, and he is dressed in a dark suit. He is carrying a black jacket on a hanger for* NACHO.]

CATUNGAS [*holding out the jacket to* NACHO]: Listones?

[NACHO *looks up at him but doesn't answer.* HELEN *turns off her light and* ENTERS *at her steps.*]

HELEN [*pointing to the street where moving candles are seen*]: La Molacha and some of Roshanda's other friends are starting a candlelight walk to St. Margaret's. [*Walking down her steps and crossing to the gate*] And after the rosary, they're holding another vigil at the federal courthouse. They're demanding an investigation into the shooting.

[*She opens the gate, and* HECTOR ENTERS *at the gate, dressed in a dark suit.*]

HECTOR: Ready?

[*Pause. There is an uncomfortable silence as no one speaks or knows what to do next.* CATUNGAS *removes the suit jacket from the hanger and walks down the steps, crosses to* NACHO, *and holds out the jacket to him again.* NACHO *looks up.*]

CATUNGAS: Nacho, they're waiting. They want someone to lead the candlelight walk.

[*Pause.*]

    It should be you. You were her nino; she loved you very much.

HELEN: And he loved her, but I know him. He won't go; he'll never change. Much less now that he has *another* reason to sit here and get drunk. Let's go.

[HELEN, CATUNGAS, *and* HECTOR EXIT. NACHO *gets his newspaper clippings and tries to read but stops.*]

NACHO [*rubbing his temples, starting to sing*]: "Aquí estoy entre botellas . . ."

[*He hears laughter, and* ROSHANDA ENTERS *with* ARTEMISA *and* WATUSI. *She is wearing a white lace spring dress, and her hair is combed up in ringlets. She runs to* NACHO.]

ROSHANDA: Hi, Nino!

[ROSHANDA *puts her hands over* NACHO's *and caresses him.* ARTEMISA *and* WATUSI *playfully take* ROSHANDA *and sit her on a stool.* ARTEMISA *starts to insert baby rosebuds in* ROSHANDA's *hair as* WATUSI *watches. They seem to be engaged in happy, gossipy talk, and* NACHO *listens intently.*]

ARTEMISA [*conversing*]: See, Roshanda? It was like this. Your nina Helen and I had a big fight at the dance in Nogales. And comadres are not supposed to fight. It's one of God's rules. That's what my mother always said, and she was an expert on God's rules. There's even an old story, a cuento, about these two comadres who were cutting verdolagas—that's purslane in English.

WATUSI: People around here think it's a weed, but not in Europe, Roshanda. M'ija, in France, when I was in the hospital there, the nurses served me the plain old verdolagas in the fanciest salad I ever had in my life!

ARTEMISA: Anyway, the two comadres got mad about some silly little thing, and they got into a hair-pulling fight. Well, God saw them

fighting, and he punished mankind—mostly verdolaga lovers—
by making them wash and wash the purslane in case one of the
comadres' hair was still in it.

WATUSI: And it's true, m'ija! I remember when mi jefita made verdolagui-
tas con queso, sometimes I *would* find a hair in the purslane, even
after all her washing!

[*They laugh as they help* ROSHANDA *off the stool.*]

ARTEMISA: There! Roshanda, m'ija, you look as beautiful as you did the
day we baptized you. Remember, Watusi?

WATUSI: Simón, Artemisa. [*Pushing* NACHO's *wheelchair around*] Remember, Nacho? Artemisa, la Helen, you, and me. [*To* ROSHANDA] The
four of us took you to St. Margaret's. I hated to go inside a church;
I came back from the war all fucked up—sorry—and smelling the
incense always made me go a little . . . crazy, I guess.

[*The two group themselves around* ROSHANDA, *and they act out the memory
as they talk.*]

ARTEMISA: We four managed to sneak away from my mother, who wanted
an ugly saint's name for you. And your nino wanted something
from some Steinbeck guy and his grapes—

ROSHANDA: Rose of Sharon—that's what my nino wanted.

ARTEMISA: Yeah, Rose of Sharon. But I wanted Rosa. Just four letters,
easy to spell. But your nino thought Rosa was too ugly. He said the
teachers would make it Rose, and the kids would call you Rosie
for sure.

[WATUSI *starts to pace, nervous.*]

So then he wanted Rosenda, Rosalía, Rosana, Rosalba,
Rosalinda—

WATUSI [*throwing a fit*]: Stop! I see all these letters floating around,
up to the altar, floating down, and I grab the ones I can, and I
shake them like dice and throw them down. And I tell your nino,
"C'mere, Nacho, tell me what they spell." And your nino comes
over, looks down at the letters, and spells: R-O-S-H-A-N-D-A.
Roshanda. That's what the letters spelled, and that's how you got
your name.

ROSHANDA: Roshanda. I love my name.

[*Pause.*]

But where did you find the *h?*

WATUSI [*baffled*]: What *h?*

NACHO [*finally laughing*]: There never was an *h*, Watusi. I knew you couldn't spell any of those names, so I made one up for you. And you see, my Roshanda did end up with the most beautiful name in Barrio Hollywood.

WATUSI [*joking*]: She sure did. Bueno, pues, ¿qué esperan que no se encueran? C'mon, Roshanda, let's go kick some ass.

[WATUSI EXITS.]

ROSHANDA: Ready, Nino?

NACHO: Espérate, m'ija. [*Crossing to the* CENTRO *and hanging up its sign again*] Ya vamos, m'ija. I'm ready now.

[*He takes her hand and the two* EXIT.]

LIGHTS: DOWN.

[*The lights inside the* CENTRO *flicker unsteadily at first, but then flicker rhythmically like a heartbeat on a hospital monitor. Offstage marchers are carrying candles, and* MUSIC *can be heard from them outside. The song is "No nos moverán" but with these words: "Unidos en el Centro, no nos moverán . . ."*]

FIN

FOUR

Yo, Casimiro Flores*

(I, Casimiro Flores)

---

* A version of Yo, Casimiro Flores appears in Vaqueeros, Calacas, and Hollywood: Contemporary Chicano Plays, edited by Carlos Manuel. © 2013 Bilingual Press/Editorial Bilingüe.

Synopsis

Yo, Casimiro Flores is a trilingual (Spanish, English, and Yaqui) tragicomedy that takes place in the present, past, and afterlife. It begins during Halloween and Día de los Muertos in a small understaffed, underfunded general hospital in a southwestern town much like Tucson, Nogales, or San Antonio. The second half of the play takes place in the mythical Mictlán, the Aztec place of the dead.

The protagonist, Casimiro Flores, a Yaqui Mexican hospital janitor, is a lonely, bitter man without friends or relatives, who carries the weight of his guilt for his perceived past sin. Twenty years before, he encouraged his girlfriend and three other friends to attempt to cross the U.S.-Mexico border with him. Betrayed by the coyote who took their money, Casimiro's friends are led into an ambush and only Casimiro survives. Blaming himself, Casimiro has literally buried himself for the last ten years in a small, cramped rest area in the hospital basement. His only company is Geraldine, a discarded anatomy class skeleton that stands in a corner, and a usually out-of-focus television set. For the last ten years, he has decorated an altar in honor of his four friends that died, and seeking redemption for the betrayal, Casimiro prays for their forgiveness while he awaits their one-night visit on Earth before returning to Mictlán. He adorns the altar with their favorite foods and drinks, pictures, candles, and cempasúchil, the traditional marigold flowers whose scent helps the dead visitors find their way to Earth and back home to Mictlán.

Bolstered with some toasts of tequila, Casimiro, in a drunken rage, taunts and invokes Mictlantecuhtli, the Aztec god of the dead and the underworld. Mictlantecuhtli, in full dress and regalia, appears and informs Casimiro that the altar and chop suey will not appease Casimiro's guilt very easily. If he really wants forgiveness, Casimiro must take *another* four dead persons from the hospital and help them pass the nine grueling, arduous tasks so they can enter Mictlán. These four are Rocky Road, a "party animal" who, tired of life and affairs with married men, has committed suicide; Mad Dog Sánchez, a neglected, abandoned teen who has been killed in his first "initiation" gang fight; Xóchil, the innocent fourteen-year-old who, thinking of nothing but her upcoming quinceañera fiesta, is shot when she walks into the gang shooting; and Don Prisciliano, the old man who is slowly dying of pneumonia, living in the past and dreaming of his drowned fiancée, until he is finally hurried to his death by an impatient Mictlantecuhtli.

In Mictlán, Casimiro and the four travelers get to meet legendary and cultural icons such as La Llorona, the comic Cantinflas, Selena, and César Chávez, as well as Ehécatl, the god of the wind who can grant wishes. Ehécatl makes them examine their past and the choices they have made, and with very high stakes—a chance to return to the living.

Production Note
The production of *Yo, Casimiro Flores* was made possible by the Guadalupe Cultural Arts Center in San Antonio, Texas, during the Gateways Fall 1997 Creative Performance Residency, a binational (United States and Mexico), multidisciplinary collaboration funded in part by the Ford Foundation and the National Endowment of the Arts. Original music was composed by Raúl González Guzmán from Monterrey, Nuevo León, Mexico.

Any programs or other pertinent mentions must include this credit per the contract with the Guadalupe Cultural Arts Center.

Cast
CASIMIRO FLORES, *an almost-forty-year-old Yaqui*
EL COYOTE, *any age*
FELIPE, *mid- to late teens*
JESÚS, *mid- to late teens*
CARLOS, *mid- to late teens*
MARIEL, *age fifteen*
DON REMIGIO, *a very old Yaqui maestro, strong in appearance and bearing*
HUNTER, *any age*
MICTLANTECUHTLI, *costumed and masked, tall, imposing, ageless*
CALAVERA NURSE, *any age. Her calavera costume is similar to a José Guadalupe Posada caricature. Optional: if funds are available, she may be accompanied by other costumed Calaveras, or a "skeleton crew," who will help dress the set, dance, etc.*
ROCKY ROAD, *age twenty-five*
MAD DOG SÁNCHEZ, *a very thin teenager and wannabe gang member*
XÓCHIL, *a fourteen-year-old girl, soon to be fifteen*
DON PRISCILIANO, *an old man in his seventies*
ALLEGORICAL DANGERS: BLADES, JAGUARS, LIZARDS, ETC.
CANTINFLAS, *need we say more? The actor's homework is to rent and watch his movies.*

LA LLORONA, *any age*
CÉSAR CHÁVEZ, *in his sixties, with a dignified bearing*
EHÉCATL, *costumed and masked, any age*
MARIA ISABEL, *a woman in her seventies*
EL TANQUE, *a very obese teen*
EL PEEWA, *a skinny, runty teen*
RECORDED OFFSTAGE VOICES OF MANUEL, XÓCHIL'S MOTHER, MAD DOG'S
   FOSTER MOTHER, ROCKY'S SUGAR DADDY, and CASIMIRO'S MOTHER
Note: Except for CASIMIRO, most roles may be doubled depending on
   blocking and costume changes.

Technical Notes

The transitional LIGHTS between scenes should be DOWN and UP quickly,
even though the actors may not be completely in place. The MUSIC may
start sooner than is indicated on script. An offstage actor or technician will
be needed for Geraldine's movements. Optional: The FRIENDS' dialogue in
act 1, scenes 2 and 3 may be prerecorded for ethereal effect.

SET

The sets change during acts. In act 1, there are many hospital or office room
dividers in various stages of disrepair and abandonment, overhead water
and heating pipes, plastic bags filled with garbage, several laundry duffel
bags, a few old Halloween decorations, and a RAMP or STEP UNIT, pref-
erably at upstage center, that leads to upstairs. There is a small, cramped
rest area for CASIMIRO's coffee breaks; it includes a small table with a large
bowl of old Halloween candies and the makings for instant coffee, a small
portable TV near an old beat-up recliner chair covered with a zarape blanket, one or two chairs, and a box filled with a photo, pompon, food and
drinks, flowers, candles, etc., for the altar that CASIMIRO will set up on the
table. Geraldine, CASIMIRO's best friend, is a discarded classroom skeleton,
who hangs on a nearby stand, dressed in her vintage Goodwill finery; a cigarette dangles from her upraised hand or from her mouth. In act 2, everything from act 1 is removed, and the setting in Mictlán is rather brown and
desolate. The RAMP now has a carpet runner with an Aztec design. There
are two PLATFORMS with SLOPING RAMPS on each side of the stage, and
possibly some side decorated pillars.

YAQUI LANGUAGE

The Yaqui prayer was given to theater director Jorge Piña and actor Franco Ontiveros by a Yaqui leader in San Antonio. The spelling and pronunciation may need to be checked for accuracy and respectful use.

TIME

The present, during a combined Halloween and Día de los Muertos, but please note that CASIMIRO's nightmare takes place twenty years earlier, somewhere at the border between Mexico and the United States.

ACT I

Scene 1

Casimiro's Nightmare

MUSIC: *Introductory, mysterious, and dreamy.*

LIGHTS: UP. *Soft moonlight on* CASIMIRO *at center stage, shadows of desert cacti.*

[CASIMIRO *is acting out his nightmare. He is dressed in his janitor's uniform with his hospital identification badge over his shirt pocket but is wearing parts of the Yaqui Deer Dancer's costume: a deer head with a red scarf tied across its antlers over a folded white handkerchief, cocoon rattles on his ankles, and a dry gourd in each hand. He is crouched, wary. Indigenous* MUSIC *or "La danza del venado" plays.* CASIMIRO *dances; his movements should be hesitant and unskilled but determined.* EL COYOTE, *wearing border cowboy clothes and a coyote mask,* ENTERS *and joins the dance, stalking* CASIMIRO. *They hear a noise, and* EL COYOTE *hides. The same introductory* MUSIC, *mysterious and dreamy, resumes.* CASIMIRO'S *four* FRIENDS—MIGUEL, CARLOS, JESÚS, *and* MARIEL—ENTER. *They are holding hands, helping each other in the desert darkness, and they are dressed for travel, carrying mochilas with their little clothing and containers of food and water.*]

CASIMIRO [*joining them, urging them to hurry*]: ¡Aquí, Miguel! Apúrate, Carlos. Cuidado con los nopales. ¡Miguel, ayúdale a Jesús! Mariel, dame la mano.

[EL COYOTE *comes out of his hiding place, with his hands out, waiting to be paid his money.* EVERYONE *pays* EL COYOTE. *The four* FRIENDS *sense danger, but* CASIMIRO *reassures them and they follow him and* EL COYOTE. *Unseen by them,* EL COYOTE *gives a signal and quickly hides again.* GUN-SHOTS *are heard.*]

[LIGHTS: *Jumpy and erratic, following the running figures who are trying to hide and escape from the bullets.* CASIMIRO *and his* FRIENDS *run.*]

CASIMIRO [*going toward* MARIEL]: ¡Mariel, corre conmigo!

MARIEL: ¡Casimiro! No puedo ver; [*putting her hand out to* CASIMIRO] ¡dame tu mano!

[CASIMIRO *goes to* MARIEL *and is ready to take her hand, but he hesitates. He moves away from her quickly and hides. Louder* GUNSHOTS *are heard.* CASIMIRO'S FRIENDS *are trapped, cornered. They are shot, and they fall to* the ground, wounded and dying. CASIMIRO reacts but cowardly stays hidden.]

[The MUSIC abruptly changes to something joyous, lively. EL COYOTE and CASIMIRO come out of hiding, and EL COYOTE gives CASIMIRO half the money. They embrace and dance happily, waving the money in air.]

[A loud, sharp DRUMBEAT is heard, and then indigenous MUSIC, blended with violin. DON REMIGIO ENTERS, beating a drum. He is dressed completely in black, with a ragged black poncho over his pants and shirt, and an old, beat-up cowboy hat and boots.]

CASIMIRO: ¡Tata Remigio! [Showing him the money] Mire, ahora sí tengo dinero para—

[DON REMIGIO angrily pushes CASIMIRO's hand aside, and the money falls to the ground. CASIMIRO kneels and starts to pick up the money.]

DON REMIGIO [pointing at EL COYOTE accusingly]: ¡Coyote maldito!

[EL COYOTE slinks away with guilt. DON REMIGIO turns to EXIT.]

CASIMIRO [standing up]: Tata Remigio, espere. [Pleading, almost childlike] No se vaya. Mire, ya mero aprendo su danza. [Starting to dance] Mire, abuelito.

[The MUSIC is indigenous or "La danza del venado." CASIMIRO dances, but DON REMIGIO remains unimpressed, disapproving. The HUNTER ENTERS. He is armed and may be dressed in either military camouflage or a Border Patrol uniform. CASIMIRO continues dancing, and the HUNTER stalks and shoots CASIMIRO.]

[A GUNSHOT is heard, and CASIMIRO starts to fall. FREEZE.]

[MUSIC: UP for the FREEZE, then DOWN and continuing, blending with the drum beating.]

[CASIMIRO falls to the ground. The HUNTER takes the deer antlers as trophy, and EL COYOTE takes the money and the gourds. The HUNTER and EL COYOTE EXIT on very good terms.]

DON REMIGIO [beginning to sing or chant a Yaqui prayer]: Vesate sewau hotekate. Sewa valikai, sewau hotekatee.

[The four FRIENDS rise.]

FRIENDS [in unison, repeating slowly in Spanish as they cross to CASIMIRO]: Ya nos sentamos a la flor; para recibir la flor, nos sentamos a la flor.

[They kneel around CASIMIRO.]

MARIEL [repeating in English as she removes the handkerchief from CASIMIRO's head]: Already we sit down to the flower; to receive the flower, we sit down to the flower.

DON REMIGIO [*still beating drum softly, repeating the prayer*]: Vesate sewau hotekate . . . [*kneeling next to* CASIMIRO] . . . Sewa valikai . . . [*Laying the drum down*] Sewai hotekatee . . . [*Cradling* CASIMIRO's *head on his lap*] Ne Casimiro Flores . . .

FRIENDS [*praying in unison*]: Yo, Casimiro Flores . . .

[*They pick up* CASIMIRO *and carry him to his recliner chair. They remove the cocoon rattles and cover him with his zarape as they continue repeating the prayer. They place an old book in his hands.*]

DON REMIGIO [*louder*]: Ne Casimiro Flores: sewa walikai, sewai hotekatee. [*Giving the drum one last hard beat*] Ne Casimiro Flores:—

LIGHTS: OUT.

MUSIC: UP. "*La danza del venado*" or indigenous with violin. Then OUT.

END OF SCENE 1

* * *

Scene 2

TIME: *Present, immediately after the nightmare.*

PLACE: *Hospital basement.*

LIGHTS: *All* UP *on stage.*

[AMBULANCE OR POLICE SIRENS *are heard in the background, and western television* THEME MUSIC *emanates from the TV set.* CASIMIRO *is sleeping restlessly, mumbling.* MIGUEL, CARLOS, JESÚS, *and* MARIEL ENTER. *They are wearing inexpensive Woolworth's Halloween masks and carrying jack-o'-lanterns for their candy. They are playful.*]

FRIENDS [*in unison*]: Trick or treat, smell my feet, give us something good to eat!

[*They remove their masks and place the jack-o'-lanterns nearby. They look at* CASIMIRO *intently as he tries to wake up from his nightmare. Note: Except in some comedy bits, the four* FRIENDS *will not be seen or acknowledged by* CASIMIRO, *and they can either start or finish his sentence or thought, and they can complete his actions for him.*]

CASIMIRO [*still dreaming*]: Yo, Casimiro Flores . . . para recibir la flor . . .

MIGUEL: Ya, Casimiro, never mind las flores. [*Crossing to* CASIMIRO *and yelling near his ears*] ¡Despierta, Casimiro! It's time to set up our altar! C'mon, wake up! ¡Tenemos hambre!

CARLOS: Déjalo, Miguel. He'll be waking up soon.

[*Sounds of* GALLOPING HORSES *emanate from the television set, then* GUNSHOTS.]

CASIMIRO [*sitting up, half awake and half asleep*]: ¡Mariel! ¡Dame tu mano!

JESÚS [*to* MARIEL]: Pobrecito, he'll never stop dreaming that night.

MIGUEL: La misma pesadilla de siempre, pero tonight at least the nightmare wasn't so bad. Mictlantecuhtli sent Don Remigio to help him.

CARLOS: ¿Don Remigio? ¿El maestro de los Yaquis?

MARIEL: Don Remigio is Casimiro's grandfather; he will be the best guide for Casimiro's journey. [*Crossing to* CASIMIRO, *caressing his brow, and speaking to him softly*] Despierta, Casimiro, despierta.

CASIMIRO [*very loudly*]: ¡Mariel! ¡Dame tu mano!

[CASIMIRO *is awake now. The four* FRIENDS *move away and watch.* CASIMIRO *sits up and tosses the book aside. He turns off the TV, drinks water, and tries to relax.*]

[*To Geraldine*] Ah, Geraldine, my love. Buenos días, nalgas frías. [*Taking her hand and kissing it, then removing her cigarette*] Cuántas veces te he dicho: smoking can kill you.

JESÚS [*nervously, to ease tension*]: You can say that again.

FRIENDS [*repeating admonishment to the audience*]: Smoking can kill you!

[*The* FRIENDS *giggle.*]

CASIMIRO: Oye, sweetheart, ¿sabes qué holiday es esta noche?

FRIENDS [*in unison, teasing*]: It's Halloween! [*Picking up the jack-o'-lanterns and holding them out*] Trick or treat, smell my feet, give us something good to eat!

CASIMIRO [*to Geraldine*]: No, no, Geraldine. Ni Halloween, ni trick or treat.

[*Disappointed, the four* FRIENDS *put the jack-o'-lanterns down and move away very agitated.*]

Anyway, tú sabes que ni vienen aquí los trick-or-treaters. They're afraid porque saben que aquí en el basement del hospital ponen todos los dead bodies conmigo. Pobrecitos, tienen miedo.

CARLOS: ¿Qué pasó, pues? I'm dying of thirst! Why hasn't he set up the altar with my Tecate beer?

JESÚS: ¡Ay, tonto! Ya sabes que every year we have to come all the way from Mictlán to help him set it up.

MARIEL: Pobrecito. Even after all these years, our deaths are still very painful for him.

MIGUEL: Sí, todavía siente mucho dolor por nuestras muertes y se cree culpable por lo que pasó esa noche.

CARLOS: It wasn't his fault! How was he to know that the coyote would betray him?

MARIEL: Okay, it's over; nothing can change the past. Besides, setting up the altar for us every year helps Casimiro with his pain, and that's why we're here tonight.

MIGUEL: Dices bien, Mariel; estamos aquí pa' ayudarle a nuestro amigo.

CASIMIRO [*removing the zarape from the recliner*]: Esta noche, Geraldine, es Día de los Muertos, and it's time to set up my altar again.

FRIENDS [*in unison*]: ¡Órale pues, a trabajar, muchachos!

[*The* FRIENDS *cross to* CASIMIRO *and help him cover the coffee table with the zarape.*]

CASIMIRO [*taking a framed photo from the box*]: Primero, la foto.

[*He stares intently at the photo, in reverie.* MIGUEL, *very nosy, peers over* CASIMIRO's *shoulder.*]

MIGUEL [*to* FRIENDS]: Es la foto que nos tomó Manuel, ¿se acuerdan? Aquel día después del soccer game.

[MIGUEL, CARLOS, *and* JESÚS *quickly pantomime some energetic soccer moves.* CASIMIRO *places the photo on the table and, remembering that day and the soccer game, seems to be seeing his friends when the photo was taken.*]

CASIMIRO: ¡Tenemos que ganarle a Navojoa!

[*He crosses to his* FRIENDS *and joins in soccer moves.* MARIEL *crosses to the box and takes out a bedraggled pompon.*]

MARIEL [*cheering with pompon*]: "¡A la bim, a la bum, a la bim-bum-bah! Nogales, Nogales, ra-ra!"

[*A goal is scored.*]

ALL [*in unison, long and drawn-out*]: G-O-O-O-L!

[*They jump and hug.*]

MARIEL: ¡Vengan, pronto! Manuel nos va sacar una foto.

[JESÚS, MIGUEL, *and* CARLOS *run to* MARIEL *and strike a hugging pose while* CASIMIRO *watches.*]

¡Casimiro! ¡Ven! No vamos a sacar la foto sin ti. Espérate, Manuel. ¡Casimiro! ¡Ven, apúrate!

[CASIMIRO *runs to his friends and gets in the middle of them. He places his arms around* MARIEL *and* CARLOS. ALL *pose seriously.* MANUEL'*s line below can be prerecorded.*]

MANUEL [*offstage*]: Ay, pero no tan serios, you're not at a funeral. ¡Sonrían!

ALL [*smiling and in unison*]: ¡Enchiladas!

[*They* FREEZE. *A* CAMERA FLASH *is seen.*]

LIGHTS: DOWN.

MUSIC: *A corrido norteño.*

END OF SCENE 2

* * *

Scene 3

LIGHTS: UP.

MUSIC: DOWN.

[CASIMIRO *has placed the photo on the table. As he continues to speak and to place the other items on the table, his four* FRIENDS *are still unacknowledged by him, and they will continue to either start or finish his sentence or thought and complete the actions for him.*]

CASIMIRO: Un six-pack de cerveza Tecate para el tragón de Carlos, tequila con sal y limón—

JESÚS: Tequila? He's never put out tequila for us before.

CASIMIRO: El tequila es para *mí.* To celebrate my tenth anniversary working in this hospital. [*Continuing to take out items*] Un bucket de Kentucky Fried Chicken para Mariel y Miguel—

MARIEL: La pechuga es para mí, Miguel, y Casimiro, vale más que sea *extra crispy*.

CASIMIRO: Y como siempre—el chop suey es para Jesús.

JESÚS: ¿Y los egg rolls? Casimiro, you know that I love egg rolls; ¿por qué nunca me compras los egg rolls?

MIGUEL: No seas tan necio; he can't remember everything. Let's help him with the flowers.

CASIMIRO [*snapping fingers*]: ¡Las flores! I almost forgot the flowers. Lots of strong-smelling marigolds—cempasúchiles bien apestosas—

FRIENDS [*smelling the flowers and holding their noses, in unison*]: ¡Fuchi!

CASIMIRO: —so that the muertos can smell them and find their way back to—

FRIENDS: ¡Mictlán!

CASIMIRO: —wherever they go.

[**CASIMIRO** *and his* **FRIENDS** *place bouquets of marigolds in the plastic jack-o'-lanterns and place them in a path leading to the* **RAMP** *at upstage center, and they sprinkle petals all over.*]

CASIMIRO [*taking out four candles*]: And finally, las velas.

FRIENDS [*in unison*]: So that los muertos can see what they're eating!

[*The* **FRIENDS** *giggle and light the candles.* **CASIMIRO** *lies on the recliner, legs crossed, his hands behind his head, pleased with himself as he surveys the altar.*]

CASIMIRO [*to Geraldine*]: Geraldine, mi amor, tú sabes que por more than ten years I've been setting up this altar con las ofrendas for my dead friends, sin saber if I was doing it right or wrong—

CARLOS: ¿Y el libro, pues?

[*The* **FRIENDS** *scatter around, looking for the old book until one of them finds it and hands it to* **CASIMIRO**.]

CASIMIRO: —pero mira, according to this book, tonight estoy haciendo todo bien como se debe de hacer. I found it anoche, right before my last coffee break, en la basura. Maybe one of the new candy stripers threw it away by mistake—

JESÚS: No era "mistake." ¿Te acuerdas, Felipe? Mictlantecuhtli said Casimiro had to read it in preparation for his journey when his heart—

CASIMIRO: Anyway, I started to read it, y lueguito pensé en mi tata Remigio. People used to call him "el maestro" because he knew everything about the Yaqui people.

[*Pause.*]

I'm Yaqui, ¿sabías? [*Reflective*] I thought about all the times he wanted me to learn La Danza del Venado—

MIGUEL: The Deer Dance—es bien difícil. Not just anyone can learn to dance it.

CASIMIRO: It was a manda, a promise he made when I was very sick one time . . . but I couldn't learn it; it was just too hard for me.

MARIEL: Casimiro, una manda se *tiene* que cumplir. You should've learned the dance. If not for you, then for your grandfather, Don Remigio.

CASIMIRO: Anyway, me dio sueño, and I guess I fell asleep. And then I had the same nightmare, la misma pesadía de siempre. But this time, my tata Remigio was in my dream, and I tried to dance.

[*Pause.*]

Mira, Geraldine. Este libro te dice todo de los aztecas.

[CASIMIRO *stands up, crosses to Geraldine, and shows her the book, as the* FRIENDS *cross to him and peer over his shoulder.*]

CASIMIRO [*reading title*]: Peregrinación a Mictlán en el Día de los Muertos.

FRIENDS [*in unison*]: Journey to Mictlán on the Day of the Dead.

[*The* LIGHTS *flicker, and spooky but playful organ* MUSIC, *like "The Monster Mash" begins to play.*]

FRIENDS: Uuuuh, esta cosa se 'stá poniendo bien spooky.

CASIMIRO: Parece que no hicieron pay la 'lectricity otra vez. ¡Qué nuevas!

[*Pause.*]

A ver, a ver, where was I? [*Reading the title again*] Peregrinación a Mictlán en el Día de los Muertos. [*Looking around to see if lights go out again, but they stay on*] Okay, maguey. "Peregrinación" means journey. To Mictlán. Okay, so where's this Mictlán place?

[JESÚS *licks his finger then leafs through pages for him.*]

Ajá, aquí 'stá. [*Reading*] "Mictlán: place of the dead, the dwelling of—"

FRIENDS [*in unison, fearful*]: Mictlantecuhtli!

[CASIMIRO *turns to his* FRIENDS. *Comedy peekaboo bit as he tries to see if he can see them. At one time, he almost sees one who gets scared at seeing* CASIMIRO *seeing him, etc.*]

CASIMIRO [*reading, pronouncing very slowly*]: "Mic-tlan-te-cuh-tli, the Aztec god of the dead!"

[*The* LIGHTS *flicker and the* SOUND *of the same organ, but louder, is heard.*]

[*Looking around*] ¡Ajá! I knew it! No pagaron la luz, Geraldine. Y last week we almost didn't get paid porque el payroll ran out of money. [*Continuing to read*] "Mictlantecuhtli. One of the most powerful of the Aztec gods. Mictlantecu—" [*Looking around*] Nah, I'm not gonna say that name again.

[*Pause.*]

[*Mockingly to* FRIENDS, *mispronouncing*] El Mictlante-cu-*cuy*!

[FRIENDS *jump back, both fearful yet enjoying wordplay.*]

FRIENDS [*in unison*]: Ay, Casimiro, you better be careful! ¡Te va 'garrar el cu-cuy!

CASIMIRO [*getting daring*]: Mictlantecuhtli. El mero chingón de los dioses.

[*Pause.*]

[*Suddenly*] ¡Un brindis! [*Serving himself a shot of tequila; to photo*] A shot of my tequila, mis buenos amigos, con sal y limón, si me lo permiten. Salud, amigos: Jesús, Miguel, Carlos y ... [*tenderly*] Mariel.

[*The four* FRIENDS *quickly serve themselves a shot of tequila and gather around him. The lemon and salt, toasts, clinking of glasses, etc., are done with very synchronized and stylized movements.*]

CASIMIRO [*toasting*]: ¡Salud, amigos!

FRIENDS [*toasting*]: ¡Salud, Casimiro!

CASIMIRO [*serving himself another shot*]: *Otro* brindis.

[*The four* FRIENDS *serve themselves.*]

CASIMIRO [*toasting*]: Salud, amigos; salud, amor y pesetas.

FRIENDS [*in unison*]: ¡Y tiempo para gastarlas!

[ALL *drink a shot of tequila.*]

CASIMIRO [*pouring himself another shot, toasting photo*]: I drink to your happiness and eternal peace.

[*He drinks the shot alone.*]

FRIENDS [*toasting and drinking*]: Un brindis para nuestra felicidad y la paz eterna.

[MUSIC: *Both melancholy and aggressive.*]

CASIMIRO [*becoming bitter*]: Qué dichosos los muertos; they only have to be here for one or two days, then back to Mictlán with the mighty Mictlantecuhtli.

[*He is now drinking the tequila straight from the bottle.*]

JESÚS [*refilling his shot glass*]: Oh, oh, ya está comenzando el rencor.

MIGUEL: Yeah, that's what tequila always does to you. Makes you mean and bitter. Wátchalo.

CASIMIRO [*continuing to drink, with increased aggression*]: So who needs an Aztec god anyway? [*Getting abrasive*] ¿Me oyistes, pinchi Mictlantecuhtli? ¡Tú no compones nada!

CARLOS [*a bit righteously*]: You see? That's why I never drink tequila. [*Drinking tequila anyway*] Yo prefiero mi Tecate.

[*The* FRIENDS *put down shot glasses and move away from* CASIMIRO, *fearfully.*]

CASIMIRO [*putting the bottle down and crossing to center*]: Mictlantecuhtli! I dare you to come and take me and put an end to my miserable existence! [*Putting his arms up in defiant supplication*] Si eres el dios tan poderoso que te crees, ven por mí ahorita mismo. [*Repeating very loudly*] ¡MICTLANTECUHTLI! ¡VEN POR MI!

[*Discordant* MUSIC *is heard. The* LIGHTS *flicker, and the* SPOT *is on Geraldine, who is now moving spasmodically, unseen by* CASIMIRO. *The* SOUND *of a conch shell is heard and then Aztec or indigenous* MUSIC. *The* LIGHTS *go* DOWN *and then* UP *again on* MICTLANTECUHTLI *and* CALAVERA NURSE, *who enter on top of* RAMP. MICTLANTECUHTLI *is standing tall, arms akimbo, in full costume, headdress, and face makeup. He carries a beeper or cellular phone on his waist. The* CALAVERA NURSE *is wearing a nurse's uniform and cap or green hospital operating scrubs and calavera face makeup, and she is holding an urn with burning copal.*]

MICTLANTECUHTLI: Aquí estoy, Casimiro Flores. I am Mictlantecuhtli, god of Mictlán, the land of the dead, or—[*walking down the* RAMP]—as you so eloquently put it—[*stopping midway*]—el mero chingón. A tus órdenes.

[MICTLANTECUHTLI *nods smartly.* CASIMIRO *promptly faints. The* FRIENDS EXIT *quickly.*]

LIGHTS: DOWN.

MUSIC: UP.

END OF SCENE 3

* * *

Scene 4

TIME: *Immediately after.*

LIGHTS: UP.

MUSIC: *Theme from a popular soap opera.*

[MICTLANTECUHTLI *has removed his headdress and is lying down on the recliner, eating the old Halloween candies, and watching TV. The* CALAVERA NURSE *has spread out all of her latest state-of-the-art communications gadgetry: iPod, Blackberry or other cell phone, laptop, portable video camera, etc., all over the basement and is now kneeling over* CASIMIRO, *attempting to revive him.*]

CALAVERA NURSE: Look, Mictlantecuhtli, parece que 'stá reviving. Pobrecito, you really scared him.

MICTLANTECUHTLI [*too engrossed to turn to her*]: ¿Pues quién le manda salir con sus babosadas? Calling me names and daring *me* to come and take him?

[CASIMIRO *sits up and looks intently at the* CALAVERA NURSE. *He doesn't see* MICTLANTECUHTLI *behind him. Pause.*]

CASIMIRO [*stalling*]: Ehhh, trick or treat, right? [*To Geraldine*] Geraldine, can you believe it? We finally got some trick-or-treaters here. [*To* CALAVERA NURSE] No offense, calaca, pero you look kinda old to be out trick-or-treating. Don't get me wrong—Geraldine y yo estamos bien happy to finally see someone down here with us. *Anybody.*

[*Pause.*]

> ¿Quieres candy?

[**CASIMIRO** *stands up, goes to the table, and looks for candies.*]

MICTLANTECUHTLI: I have the rancid candies. [*Extending the bowl to* CASIMIRO] Ten.

CASIMIRO [*afraid to turn around; to* CALAVERA NURSE]: ¿Quién habla? ¿Otro trick-or-treater?

[**MICTLANTECUHTLI** *gets up and stands behind* **CASIMIRO**. *He taps him on the shoulder.*]

MICTLANTECUHTLI: Turn around and face me, Casimiro. Oh, ¿me tienes miedo?

CASIMIRO [*still won't turn*]: ¿Quién eres?

MICTLANTECUHTLI: ¡Ay, Casimiro! What a short memory you have. ¿Qué no te acuerdas que me llamaste? [*Mimicking*] "Mictlantecuhtli, ven por mí." ¿Qué más? Ah, sí. "Mictlante-cu-*cuy.*" Remember? ¡Qué imprudencia! Bueno pues, here I am.

[*He forcefully turns* CASIMIRO *around to face him.*]

CASIMIRO [*stammering*]: N-n-nice c-c-costume.

MICTLANTECUHTLI [*ignoring remark*]: Y la Calavera Nurse is my administrative assistant—a bit inept, pero what can I do? Good workers are so hard to find.

CALAVERA NURSE: My job is to keep track of every single person in the universe. See? [*Showing* CASIMIRO *her gadgetry*] This is for *this* town. Antes, no era tan difícil to keep track of everybody when everybody stayed put en el pueblo 'donde nacieron, pero ahora con el upward mobility, es una chinga keeping it up-to-date. Aquí tengo todos los nombres, con su número, and a brief description. When someone kicks the bucket—o como dicen ustedes, cuando cuelgan los "tenis"—Mictlantecuhtli gets a call on his beeper, and then we come and take the body to Mictlán.

CASIMIRO: I am honored to meet both of you, y les pido disculpa por mi... imprudence, pero you can leave now. Ustedes dos ya se pueden ir.

CALAVERA NURSE: It's not that easy, Casimiro. Once Mictlantecuhtli comes for a body, that's it: no podemos regresar a Mictlán sin el cuerpo.

CASIMIRO: You need a body? Pues, in less than an hour, when the new interns on the midnight shift come on duty, they make so many surgical mistakes que ustedes tendrán todos los cuerpos que quieran. It'll be a busy night, so save me some work and take them!

MICTLANTECUHTLI: Qué listo eres, Casimiro, para intercambiar lo que no es tuyo. Sorry, Casimiro, you called me, begging me to take you. Pues, aquí estoy, and I'm ready to take you with me.

CASIMIRO: Pues, I refuse to go.

MICTLANTECUHTLI [*patiently*]: Casimiro, believe me, just like the book says, soy uno de los dioses más poderosos. I can easily give you a fatal heart attack, end this discussion, and take you to Mictlán.

CASIMIRO [*to* CALAVERA NURSE]: Can he really do that?

CALAVERA NURSE: Aha, he sure can. [*Reading from one of her gadgets, describing* CASIMIRO] "Casimiro Flores, age . . ." [*To* CASIMIRO] Thirty-seven?

[CASIMIRO *nods yes.*]

[*Continuing to reading*] ". . . Employed as janitor in a hospital for ten years; cruzó la frontera en mil novecientos ochenta y ocho with his four friends, Jesús, Carlos, Miguel, and Mariel—

MICTLANTECUHTLI: —and led them straight into an ambush. Write that down.

CALAVERA NURSE [*obeying, writing*]: "—and led them straight into an ambush."

CASIMIRO [*protesting with anger*]: I didn't know that the coyote would betray us! There was nothing I could do but run to save my life. We all had to run; it wasn't my fault. We had all agreed to take our chances in the desert that night. [*Repeating*] It wasn't my fault.

MICTLANTECUHTLI [*crossing to altar*]: Well, maybe not. [*Derisively*] But now, do you really think que un container de chop suey is a fair exchange por una vida de un ser humano?

CASIMIRO: ¡No! No, lo es. But what of the ten years that I've spent here, alone, in this godforsaken basement, sin ningún amigo, with no one to talk to but that stupid skeleton? ¿Eso no cuenta?

MICTLANTECUHTLI: ¡No, eso no cuenta! You've buried yourself in this basement porque eres un cobarde! [*To* CALAVERA NURSE] Add this: "For that betrayal, Casimiro diligently sets up an altar en El Día de los Muertos ..."

[*He picks up the photo and studies it. Pause.*]

Pero, you didn't really think that placing this altar, con las ofrendas, velas y flores, would ease your guilt? ¿Que ese dolor que cargas en tu alma would disappear like magic, con un trago de tequila?

CASIMIRO: Maybe not—la traición no tiene perdón. But there was nothing else I could do, was there?

[**SOUND CUE:** *Beeper.*]

MICTLANTECUHTLI: Parece que ya llegaron tus interns, Casimiro. [*Reading the number on his beeper*] The number's not too clear, pero we may soon have the body you were so ready to exchange for yours.

[**SOUND CUE:** *Beeper.*]

[*Reading beeper*] It's still not clear—someone's still clinging to life; parece ser number five-eight-seven six-six-one-four. ¿Quién es?

CALAVERA NURSE: Five-eight-seven six-six-one-four? [*Reading from her gadget, tense, worried*] Oh, oh, es la Rocky Road.

CASIMIRO: Rocky Road? ¿La nieve?

CALAVERA NURSE: No, no es la ice cream. Así se llama, Rocky Road. Bueno, más bien es un nickname que se puso ella misma—¿y Don Prisciliano? Where is he? ¿Qué no la ve? He's always there—

CASIMIRO: Who's Don Prisciliano?

CALAVERA NURSE: He's an old viejito, a very good friend of Rocky Road's. She lives across from his house in an apartment on the second floor, so he sits outside and keeps an eye on her.

CASIMIRO: Why?

CALAVERA NURSE: Well, to make sure that she's safe. La Rocky Road likes to party, but afterwards she gets very sad and depressed. Suicidal, you might say.

MICTLANTECUHTLI [*with power to see beyond*]: Don Prisciliano isn't looking up. He doesn't see Rocky. Está platicando con Xóchil. She's describing her upcoming quinceañera fiesta to him.

CALAVERA NURSE [*fervently*]: Look up, Don Prisciliano, look up! No le quite la vista a la Rocky.

MICTLANTECUHTLI [*still seeing beyond*]: I see bullets. Wayward bullets and blood running in the street. Parece que es initiation night. I see el Tanque y el Peewa de la pandilla del South Side. Esta noche habrá muchas, muchas balas.

CALAVERA: Xóchil! [*With urgency*] Mictlantecuhtli, you must take Xóchil away from the bullets.

MICTLANTECUHTLI [*angry*]: ¡Sabes bien que no puedo! She cannot escape her destiny.

[*Pause.*]

It's gonna be a busy night, Calavera. Too busy for just the two of us. We'll need help.

[*They exchange meaningful looks, and then they both look at* CASIMIRO. *Pause.*]

CASIMIRO: ¿Qué?

CALAVERA NURSE [*doubtful*]: Mictlantecuhtli, I really don't think that he can—

MICTLANTECUHTLI: Why not? The trip must be made, alone or with company. Either way, he'll have to do it, no? He may as well earn it.

CASIMIRO: Earn what? I'm not working overtime! El bookkeeper ya no quiere authorize nada de overtime.

MICTLANTECUHTLI: Overtime? ¿Y cómo a *mí* nadie me paga overtime, eh?

[*Pause.*]

A while ago you were talking about betrayals and forgiveness, Casimiro. Those are very difficult concepts for me to understand, la traición, el perdón y la redención. How can we correct the mistakes we made in the past?

CASIMIRO: Don't you think I've asked myself that over and over? ¡No podemos cambiar el pasado!

MICTANTECUHTLI: *Yo sí puedo cambiar el pasado.*

CASIMIRO: Can you really change the past?

MICTLANTECUHTLI: Most of the time. But really, it's the future that's a bitch.

[*Pause.*]

You wanted me to come and take you to Mictlán, no? Para mí, eso es muy fácil. I can take you to Mictlán right now, con o sin el perdón de nadie. Or . . .

CASIMIRO: Or what?

MICTLANTECUHTLI: Or you can take four bodies to Mictlán for me and return bien perdonado. A fair exchange, ¿no crees? Cuatro cuerpos por los cuatro amigos que traicionastes.

[SOUND CUE: *Beeper*.]

Entonces, Casimiro, ¿qué va a ser? ¿Tu vida, o ese perdón que buscas?

[*Pause*. CASIMIRO *doesn't answer*. MICTLANTECUHTLI *asks again, louder*.]

Well, Casimiro, what will it be? Your life or that forgiveness you desire?

MUSIC: *Aztec or indigenous*.

LIGHTS: DOWN.

SOUND CUE: *Beeper, louder*.

END OF SCENE 4

* * *

Scene 5

LIGHTS: UP.

MUSIC: *Theme from the* Oprah Winfrey Show.

[MICTLANTECUHTLI *and the* CALAVERA NURSE *are drinking tequila and watching TV, and* CASIMIRO *is packing some of the things he had on the altar*.]

MICTLANTECUHTLI [*to* CALAVERA NURSE]: La Oprah Winfrey, I love her. ¡Qué mujer tan fuerte! She's almost as powerful as I am. She can make miracles happen. Miren, today she's gonna try to turn these ugly ducklings into beautiful women con un "makeover." Lots of luck, Oprah, porque están más feas que mi wife, [*shuddering*] Mictecacíhuatl.

CASIMIRO: Bueno, pues, since I've agreed to take your next four bodies to Mictlán, I think you should explain your beeper system to me mientras que esperamos los cuerpos, ¿no?

MICTLANTECUHTLI [*showing* CASIMIRO *his beeper*]: You see, Casimiro, everything's high technology now. Tú sabes, high tech. Todos tienen sus beepers, ¿no?

[CASIMIRO *nods yes.*]

Pues, yo también, caller ID, call waiting, cellular phones, conference calls, call forwarding, yo tengo todo. So that makes my job much easier. Mira, five-eight-seven, six-six-one-four? Este número es el de la Rocky Road.

CASIMIRO [*reading description from the gadget*]: "Rocky Road, age twenty-five but looks younger—or older—depending on makeup. Somehow manages to live dangerously and to fall in love with rats. Married rats who promise her the world at her feet. She's a "party animal"—dances salsa or punk all night, smokes, drinks tequila, has a black belt in karate, hang glides, bungee jumps—

MICTLANTECUHTLI: Bungee jumps? ¿Qué es eso?

CALAVERA NURSE: Pos jefe, the way I understand it, se suben en un platform—bien alto—y se ponen un harness, un cinturón, yo creo, y luego . . . brincan.

MICTLANTECUHTLI: ¿Brincan? ¿A poco?

[*Pause.*]

Just like the voladores de Papantla, ¿no? [*With sarcasm*] Well, it pleases me that something has endured from the greatness of the Aztecas—even if it's only jumping off high platforms.

CASIMIRO [*curious*]: This Rocky Road sounds like a real interesting person. Me hubiera gustado conocerla.

MICTLANTECUHTLI: Oh, don't worry—you'll be meeting her soon enough. They're bringing her here, to this hospital. [*Musing*] La Rocky Road. [*To* CALAVERA NURSE] Lo que no dice en tu gadget es que she has a special laugh that sounds like bells ringing. And a throaty voice. She likes to give a "dramatic pause," and she makes circling motions with her hand while she searches for just the right word.

CALAVERA NURSE: Asina: "Death is just an . . . [*stopping, making three circling motions*] . . . experience." Pero, this time, you might say she took a [*stretching word*] 1-o-o-o-o-o-o-n-g dramatic pause and died before she found the word she wanted!

[*She giggles at her wit until* MICTLANTECUHTLI'*s glare stops her.*]

MICTLANTECUHTLI: "An experience." Pero no se crean. At the end, they're all afraid. And they all exit kicking and crying. Chillones. Pero como dice mi paisano José Alfredo Jiménez, "La vida no vale nada."

[*Pause.*]

CASIMIRO [*suddenly, to break the silence*]: ¡Un brindis!

[*He quickly pours three shots of tequila.*]

ALL [*toasting*]: ¡A la vida!

[*They all drink the tequila with salt and lemon with very synchronized and stylized movements. They keep drinking and immediately become sentimental drunks.*]

CASIMIRO [*singing*]: "No vale nada la vida, la vida no vale nada . . ."

CALAVERA NURSE [*hugging* CASIMIRO *and singing with him*]: ". . . Comienza siempre llorando y así llorando se acaba . . ."

MICTLANTECUHTLI [*hugging* CASIMIRO *on the other side and also singing*]: ". . . Por eso es que en este mundo . . ."

ALL: ". . . La vida no vale nada."

[*They end the song with more hugs and maudlin statements of love and eternal friendship.*]

[**SOUND CUE:** *Beeper.*]

MICTLANTECUHTLI [*sobering up instantly, checking beeper, reflectively*]: La Rocky. So she finally did it. Vayan por el cuerpo de la Rocky Road; está en el corridor outside the emergency room. Y tú, Casimiro, cuídala. [*Referring to* CALAVERA NURSE] She loves to go into the intensive care unit and play with the heart defibrillators.

CALAVERA NURSE [*still tipsy*]: Oh, sí. I love the intensive care unit, especially when it's full of chief executive officers and bankers. [*Demonstrating*] Agarro los defibrillators asina, place them over the heart como el doctor George Clooney used to do it en *ER* y luego: z-z-z-z-z-z-z-z-zz!

MICTLANTECUHTLI: ¡Vayan! ¡Apúrense! You've wasted enough time already.

CALAVERA NURSE [*saluting like a soldier, but still drunk*]: Adelante, mi comandante. [*Taking* CASIMIRO *by the arm*] ¡Vamos, Casimiro! ¡Por el cuerpo de la encantadora Rocky Road!

CASIMIRO AND CALAVERA NURSE [*embracing, singing, and staggering as they exit*]: "Por eso es que en este mundo, la vida no vale nada."

LIGHTS: DOWN.

SPECIAL EFFECTS: LIGHT *and* SOUND *from* TV.

MUSIC: UP. *Something lively or Oprah's theme.*

END OF SCENE 5

* * *

Scene 6

LIGHTS: UP.

[*Applying what he learned on the* Oprah Winfrey Show, MICTLANTE-CUHTLI *is diligently giving himself a makeover.* CASIMIRO *is standing over a covered body on a gurney. The* CALAVERA NURSE *is standing next to him, holding the old book, and instructing* CASIMIRO *on how to revive* ROCKY ROAD'*s corpse so they can take her to Mictlán.*]

CALAVERA NURSE: Okay, Casimiro, put your hands over la Rocky Road and repeat after me: "Les imploro: al dios Mictlantecuhtli y a la diosa Mictecacíhuatl . . ."

CASIMIRO [*placing his hands over the body and repeating the invocation*]: "Les imploro: al dios Mictlantecuhtli y a la diosa Mictecacíhuatl—"

MICTLANTECUHTLI [*interrupting*]: That's my wife, la Mickey. Hijo, que si me hace nag. All day long: [*mimicking*] "Mictlantecuhtli, go see why Huitzilopochtli and Quetzalcoatl are fighting again; las milpas de aguacate no tienen agua porque Tlaloc trai pleito casado con el señor César Chávez y—

CALAVERA NURSE: "—que Cantinflas se puso de tour guide, pero se la lleva platicando and ends up getting lost. Y que los babies en Chichihuacuaco no tienen Pampers y La Llorona y la Selena—" [*Stopping sheepishly; to* CASIMIRO] Sorry, sigue.

[*She hands the book to* CASIMIRO.]

CASIMIRO [*taking the book from* CALAVERA NURSE *and continuing invocation*]: "To the water gods, Tlaloc and Chalchi . . . salchichas!"

MICTLANTECUHTLI [*correcting him*]: Chalchihuitlicue.

CASIMIRO: Esto es demasiado difícil. I can't even pronounce these gods' names. Chal-chi-huit-li-cue. Why don't you just say "water gods"?

MICTLANTECUHTLI [*angry, explosive*]: ¿Y cómo si puedes pronunciar los nombres de los dioses *aquí*? The powerful gods of capitalism? El poderoso: [*pronouncing as one Aztec-sounding word*] Let's-go-shopping-charge-it-Jerry-McGuire-get-the-money-get-the-money god?

CALAVERA NURSE [*to* CASIMIRO, *placating*]: Go on, los nombres de los dioses get easier the more you say them.

CASIMIRO [*reading*]: "Al dios de las flores, Xochipilli—

MICTLANTECUHTLI: Xochipilli, my favorite. God of the flowers. Did you know, Casimiro, that every flower here on Earth is someone's soul?

CASIMIRO: No, no lo sabía. Pero it makes sense. Somehow. Mi abuelito, Tata Remigio, always talked about a flower world. La sea anía.

[*Pause.*]

[*Reading*] "Y Iztpapalotl—"

MICTLANTECUHTLI: Goddess of the butterflies. ¿Sabías que de ahí viene la palabra "papalote"? Kites. And that our warriors who die in battle return to Earth as hummingbirds or butterflies after traveling with the sun por cuatro años?

CALAVERA NURSE: Mictlantecuhtli, he's never going to finish the invocation si nomás lo estás interrumpiendo.

[**SOUND CUE:** *Beeper.*]

MICTLANTECUHTLI [*reading the number on the beeper*]: Five-seven-eight one-three-one-one. ¿Quién es?

CALAVERA NURSE [*reading from her gadget*]: Es el Mad Dog Sánchez.

MICTLANTECUHTLI: "Mad Dog?" ¿Estás segura que no es el número del dog pound? Muy pronto hasta los perros van a trai sus "beepers." Ya ni la friegan.

CALAVERA NURSE [*defensively*]: Hey, I don't make these names up! Nomás estoy reading what it says here: el Mad Dog Sánchez.

MICTLANTECUHTLI: Bueno, Florence Nightingale, no te agüites. With a name like that, tiene que ser un bona fide gang member, or un otro stupid "wannabe."

CALAVERA NURSE: Neither one. Ni gang member, ni wannabe. Era un "gonna be." He was supposed to prove himself tonight. Pero, he didn't make his initiation. You could say que one of the other gang's members—el Peewa o el Tanque—put Mad Dog to sleep.

[*She giggles.*]

MICTLANTECUHTLI: Vamos por él.

[*He and* CALAVERA NURSE *start to* EXIT.]

CASIMIRO: Hey, wait! ¿Pa' 'dónde creen que van? You can't leave me with ... [*gesturing to the body on the gurney*] her.

MICTLANTECUHTLI: ¿Y por qué, no? She's dead. ¿Qué te puede hacer?

[*Pause.*]

Maybe—if you had met her when she was alive—de seguro que she would've broken your heart, Casimiro. ¿Pero muerta? Here, you can do the invocation without our help.

[MICTLANTECUHTLI *gives* CASIMIRO *the old book.* CASIMIRO *takes it with apprehension.*]

MICTLANTECUHTLI: It's on page two-eighty-seven.

CASIMIRO: ¡No! No puedo y no quiero.

[CASIMIRO *throws the book down, and a horrified* CALAVERA NURSE *quickly picks it up and hands it to* MICTLANTECUHTLI.]

MICTLANTECUHTLI [*unruffled*]: You really don't have any choice, do you? We have to go pick up this "Mad Dog" for you, and you can continue the invocation and bring her back to life ... o te puedes quedar aquí con ella, así—muerta.

[*Pause.* CASIMIRO *takes the book.* MICTLANTECUHTLI *continues, giving instructions.*]

You start by imploring to the gods, you call their names as you called mine, pero no les digas dioses chingones—they're not as tolerant as I am—and then ... you wait.

[CALAVERA NURSE *and* MICTLANTECUHTLI *again start to* EXIT.]

CALAVERA NURSE [*stopping and turning to* CASIMIRO]: Oh, one more thing, Casimiro. Use maracas. The gods love to hear maracas. Cha cha cha.

[*They* BOTH EXIT.]

CASIMIRO [*mimicking*]: "The gods love to hear maracas." ¡Que chistosa! Page two-eighty-seven. [*Finding the page*] Órale, Rocky Road, here it goes. [*Reading*] "Les imploro: al dios Mictlantecuhtli y a la diosa Mictecacíhuatl . . ." [*Looking down at* ROCKY ROAD. *Nothing. Continuing*] "Al dios de las flores, Xochipilli, and to the goddess of the butterflies, Itzpapalotl . . ."

[*Geraldine moves convulsively.*]

Yo, Casimiro Flores, implore you to lift this body . . ."

[*Unseen by* CASIMIRO, ROCKY ROAD *sits up.*]

[*Continuing the invocation*] ". . . and take it to Mictlán, the land of the dead."

[*Pause.* ROCKY ROAD *falls back.* CASIMIRO *looks up from the book and looks at* ROCKY ROAD *lying down. He gives* ROCKY ROAD *a dirty look and crosses to the table and starts to put the rest of his friends' ofrendas back into the box. The photo of his friends is the last item, and* CASIMIRO *holds it, meditatively.*]

[*Turning to* ROCKY ROAD] Mictlantecuhtli said you would break my heart, pero he was mistaken; I don't have a heart. Yo no tengo corazón. ¿Me oyistes, Rocky Road? ¡No tengo corazón!

[ROCKY ROAD, *hearing her name, sits up, sheet to her waist, and looks around.*]

ROCKY ROAD: Ya pues, you don't have to shout! Aquí estoy, mi rey.

[*She jumps off the gurney, flinging the sheet aside. She is wearing a striking outfit of tiger, leopard, or zebra print.*]

[*Directly to audience*] Órale, raza, it's party time! [*Toward* SOUND *booth*] ¡Música, maestro, o me voy!

[MUSIC: *A sensual danzón.*]

[*Putting her hand out to* CASIMIRO, *seductively inviting*] ¿Bailamos, mi amor?

[CASIMIRO *almost faints.*]

LIGHTS: DOWN.

MUSIC: UP.

END OF SCENE 6

* * *

Scene 7

MUSIC: UP. *Danzón continues.*

[ROCKY ROAD *and* CASIMIRO *are dancing.* ROCKY ROAD *is definitely leading.*]

MUSIC: OUT. *Danzón ends.*

[ROCKY ROAD *lets go of* CASIMIRO *abruptly. He almost falls but catches his balance.*]

ROCKY ROAD: Not bad, partner—pero you do need more practice.

[ROCKY ROAD *looks around, sees the tequila, and serves herself a shot, drinking it expertly and with great thirst. She picks up the photo.*]

Cute. Están guapos los . . . chavalones. ¿Quiénes son? Parecen part of a soccer team. Ah, there you are. Te ves bien joven; when was this picture taken? [*Reading the date on the back*] April 1987. How old were you? Fifteen, sixteen? Uuuuh, you've got your arm around someone. ¿Quién es la cheerleader?

[*She shows* CASIMIRO *the picture.*]

CASIMIRO [*tightly*]: Mariel.

ROCKY ROAD [*laughing her tinkling laugh, which annoys* CASIMIRO]: Mariel. Bonito nombre—I like it. Sounds . . . cosmic. ¿Es tu girlfriend?

[CASIMIRO *doesn't respond but takes the photo from her and places it in the box.* ROCKY ROAD *checks out* CASIMIRO.]

¿Y tú? What's your name?

CASIMIRO [*somewhat formally*]: Casimiro Flores, para servirle.

[*He puts out his hand for her to shake, but she ignores it.*]

ROCKY ROAD: Casimiro? Sounds . . . traditional. [*Putting her fingers around her eyes like eyeglasses, teasing*] Ay, Doctor Oculista, *casi* miro, pero *no* miro. ¿Estaré ciega? ¿Qué cree? Do you think that I need glasses?

CASIMIRO: ¿Y a poco crees que tu nombre está muy pretty? Rocky Road. Mejor te hubieras puesto "pistachio nut."

ROCKY ROAD [*ignoring his remark*]: Bueno, si . . . Mariel, no es tu novia, entonces . . . [*Crossing to Geraldine*] Maybe *she* is. [*Facing* CASIMIRO] ¿Cómo se llama mi rival?

[**CASIMIRO** *refuses to answer her.*]

Anda, don't be mad. [*Referring to Geraldine*] No está fea, pero she looks like she's been on a diet too long.

[*Geraldine hits* **ROCKY ROAD** *on her shoulder.*]

Ow! [*To Geraldine*] No es pa' tanto, cara de espanto. [*To* **CASIMIRO**] Parece que 'stá jealous la girlfriend. C'mon, she's gotta have a name. ¿Cómo se llama?

CASIMIRO [*blurting out*]: Geraldine. Nomás Geraldine.

ROCKY ROAD [*laughing*]: Geraldine! Que . . . precious. Well, I hate to kiss and run, pero there's no action here, so ya me voy. [*Crossing to exit*] Arrivaderci.

CASIMIRO [*very quickly*]: ¿Y el kiss?

ROCKY ROAD: Dices bien, no hubo kiss, just a dance and good tequila. Pero eso se remedia . . . easily, ¿no?

[**ROCKY ROAD** *crosses to* **CASIMIRO**, *dips him backwards, and gives him a nice, long passionate kiss. He is too astounded to respond, and he almost falls when she finally lets go of him.*]

There. Para que no digas que no te pagué por el tequila.

[**ROCKY ROAD** *heads toward one of the room dividers, leaving an openmouthed* **CASIMIRO**. *She gets confused when she can't find an exit.*]

Hey, where's the exit? ¿Por 'dónde salgo? Where am I, anyway?

CASIMIRO: En el basement del hospital.

ROCKY ROAD: Hospital?

[*Pause. She starts to remember slowly and crosses to* **CASIMIRO**.]

[*Pointing upward*] Allá arriba 'stá el emergency, ¿no? I remember waiting hours and hours before they finally got around to pumping my stomach, para sacarme las píldoras. [*Realizing*] But it was too late, ¿verdad?

[**CASIMIRO** *nods yes. Pause.*]

CASIMIRO: Why did you take the pills?

ROCKY ROAD: ¿Por qué? Why does anyone take too many pills? [*Crossing to gurney*] Because I wanted to die—I was ready to die. And maybe I thought that the old viejito downstairs would see me in time, and he'd call the paramedics, but this time he didn't look up. [*Climbing* *up on the gurney*] He was enjoying Xóchil's visit; she's forever talking about her quineañera, and he was probably describing all of his usual aches and pains to her.

[*She starts to cover herself with the sheet.*]

CASIMIRO: I still don't understand why you—

ROCKY ROAD: ¿Sabes qué? You're boring me, and if I had wanted to be bored, I wouldn't have taken the pills. Life bored me, okay? So, ya déjame en paz.

[*She lies down and covers her face with the sheet. Pause.*]

[*Uncovering her face and sitting up again*] And one more thing . . . Casimiro, I know for sure that this . . . dump . . . ain't heaven or hell, so don't you dare bring me back, unless you've got a good reason. ¿Me oyistes? A damn good reason.

[*She lies back down and covers her head again.*]

LIGHTS: DOWN.

MUSIC: UP. *Danzón.*

END OF SCENE 7

* * *

Scene 8

LIGHTS: UP.

MUSIC: *Rap.*

[MICTLANTECUHTLI *and* CALAVERA NURSE *wheel in* MAD DOG, *who is covered with a hospital sheet, and place him next to* ROCKY ROAD.]

MICTLANTECUHTLI [*to* CASIMIRO, *referring to* ROCKY ROAD]: ¿Qué pasó? Didn't you try the invocation?

CASIMIRO [*calmly drinking coffee*]: Oh, I got her up all right, pero she got mad y se volvió acostar.

MICTLANTECUHTLI [*to* ROCKY ROAD]: ¿Es cierto, Rocky?

[ROCKY ROAD *nods yes under the sheet.*]

Ay, ¿qué voy hacer contigo? I know you're gonna raise hell in Mictlán if I don't find something to occupy your time there.

[ROCKY ROAD *nods another yes.*]

CALAVERA NURSE: Why don't you introduce her to Selena? Ella siempre está complaining que en Mictlán nadie tiene rhythm y que los concheros need to update their steps—

[SOUND CUE: *Beeper.*]

MICTLANTECUHTLI: You were right, Casimiro; [*reading the number on the beeper*] we'll have our four bodies very quickly.

CALAVERA NURSE: Otro gang member? El Tanque? El Peewa?

MICTLANTECUHTLI [*very sad*]: No. I don't have a complete number yet, pero no es un gang member; it's one of the innocents.

CALAVERA NURSE: Es Xóchil, ¿verdad?

MICTLANTECUHTLI [*nodding yes*]: It won't be long now, le falta poco. [*Getting angry*] Parece que'l mentado Mad Dog wasn't satisfied to seek his death alone, también se lleva a una de las inocentes, one who wasn't even expecting death. [*To* CALAVERA NURSE] Vamos, we don't have much time, pero maybe we can still help.

[BOTH *start to* EXIT.]

CASIMIRO [*stopping them*]: Hey, wait! You can't just keep waltzing in here with dead bodies and leaving them here with me. Este hospital— believe it or not, tiene proper procedures con el required paperwork, processing, death certificates—

[SOUND CUE: *Louder beep.*]

CALAVERA NURSE: ¿Xóchil?

MICTLANTECUHTLI [*without reading beeper number*]: Sí, es Xóchil.

[CALAVERA NURSE *and* MICTLANTECUHTLI *cross to* EXIT.]

CASIMIRO: ¿Y ahora pa''dónde creen que van?

MICTLANTECUHTLI [*softly*]: A recoger una hermosa flor. Xóchil Martínez. [*Rhetorically*] Would you believe it? ¿A flower blossoming *aquí*, entre las espinas de tu barrio? [*Suddenly very angry*] Sí, una flor, cut down by a bullet aimed at this scum: el Mad Dog Sánchez.

[*He pushes the gurney with Mad Dog toward* CASIMIRO *and* EXITS *with* CALAVERA NURSE *following him.*]

LIGHTS: DOWN.

MUSIC: UP.

END OF SCENE 8

* * *

Scene 9

ROCKY ROAD [*sitting up*]: Uhhhh, he sure is mad.

CASIMIRO: I thought you weren't getting up again.

ROCKY ROAD: Te dije que nomás for a good reason, remember? Besides finally getting to meet Selena, yo digo que finding out who got Mictlantecuhtli so pissed off is a damn good reason, ¿verdad? Let's meet el Mad Dog Sánchez! [*Jumping off gurney and ordering*] Levántalo, Casimiro.

CASIMIRO: Oh no, yo no levanto a nadie. Never again.

ROCKY ROAD: Ándale, don't be such a . . . pissant all your life. [*Looking around for the book and finding it*] ¿Qué page?

CASIMIRO [*reluctant but curious*]: Two-eighty-seven.

ROCKY ROAD: Two-eighty-seven? Aquí está. [*Reading*] "Les imploro: al dios Mictlantecuhtli y la diosa Mictecacíhuatl—"

CASIMIRO [*crossing to* ROCKY ROAD]: That's Mictlantecuhtli's nagging wife, la diosa regañona. Can you believe it? She sends Mictlantecuhtli to buy Pampers.

ROCKY ROAD: Good. *All* husbands should be sent to buy Pampers. Shhh. [*Continuing to read*] "Created by Ometeotl, les imploro a los water gods, Tlaloc y—"

CASIMIRO [*pronouncing it expertly to show off*]: Chalchihuitlicue.

ROCKY ROAD AND CASIMIRO [*together*]: "Al dios de las flores, Xochipilli, and the god of the butterflies, Iztpapalotl." We, Rocky Road and Casimiro Flores, implore you to lift the body of Mad Dog Sánchez . . .

[MAD DOG *rises.*]

. . . and lead him to Mictlán!

[MAD DOG *jumps off the gurney. He is dressed in stereotypical "cholo" fashion: plaid flannel shirt, baggy pants, neutral-color headband, shades, etc.*]

ROCKY ROAD AND CASIMIRO [*together*]: We did it!

[*They high-five. Rap* MUSIC *is heard in the background.*]

MAD DOG [*rapping and break-dancing*]: Yo soy el Mad Dog Sánchez, and that's easy to say; me gusta matar people in a major way. Yeah, I know that killing's no game, but here in the barrio, it's the quickest road to fame. Un hero no llora, so don't mention my pain; when you're writing a poem or a very triste canción, just remember my name. Ask me no questions and I'll tell you no lie. I don't know the reason, so don't even ask why; I just know that today el Tanque y el Peewa will have to die!

[MAD DOG *whips out a knife and advances toward* CASIMIRO *and* ROCKY ROAD. CASIMIRO *pushes* ROCKY ROAD *behind him in a protective gesture, but* ROCKY ROAD *steps around him.*]

ROCKY ROAD [*executing fancy preliminary karate steps and yelling*]: Ki-ya! [*She is ready to knock the knife out of* MAD DOG'*s hand.*]

[*They all* FREEZE.]

LIGHTS: DOWN.

MUSIC: UP. *Rap.*

END OF SCENE 9

* * *

Scene 10

LIGHTS: UP.

MUSIC: DOWN.

[CASIMIRO *is reading the old book*, ROCKY ROAD *is pacing impatiently, and the* CALAVERA NURSE *is placing an ice pack on* MAD DOG'*s wrist. He is sitting on the gurney.*]

MAD DOG [*wincing in pain*]: Owwww! That hurts.

ROCKY ROAD: Don't be such a . . . puppy dog. You sound just like the cowardly lion in *The Wizard of Oz*. [*Mimicking*] "Am I bleeding? Am I bleeeding?"

MAD DOG: Lady, you're dangerous; you shouldn't be allowed out on the streets.

ROCKY ROAD: Neither should you—at least, not without your rabies shots. [*To* CALAVERA NURSE] ¿Pues cuándo regresa Mictlantecuhtli? He should've already been back, no? How come you came back by yourself?

CALAVERA NURSE: He'll be here soon. It's just taking him longer porque Xóchil was one of the innocents.

ROCKY ROAD: Innocents? Who are they?

CALAVERA NURSE: Los inocentes son the ones you least expect to die. Or that you think shouldn't die porque they haven't really lived their lives, nor reached their potential. Están floreciendo, dice Mictlantecuhtli.

ROCKY ROAD: Pues, why do they die?

CASIMIRO: Who knows why anybody dies? Maybe es como digía mi tata Remigio cuando no sabía la answer: nomás porque sí. Just because.

MAD DOG: Or like one of my foster mothers always said: "¿Quién te lo manda?" Shit, that would make me mad. No matter what happened to me, she would just say, "¿Quién te lo manda?" She could never explain anything.

CALAVERA NURSE: Oh, sometimes it can be explained. An unknown virus, bad luck, human error, a drunk driver, or—in Xóchil's case— [looking directly at MAD DOG] a stray bullet meant for someone else.

MAD DOG: Hey, it wasn't my fault! El Tanque y el Peewa started to shoot wild—Don Prisciliano tried to stop Xóchil—

CALAVERA NURSE [ignoring him]: And when it can't be explained, there's always the "pobre, ya le tocaba."

ROCKY ROAD: El "ya le tocaba." That sounds so . . . existentialist.

CALAVERA NURSE [continuing to explain]: The innocents are always confused, scared. And angry. Por eso it's taking Mictlantecuhtli so long to bring Xóchil. She's very angry, but he'll calm her down. Van a ver. He has a way with words.

ROCKY ROAD: Well, you'd think that by now, a god as powerful as Mictlantecuhtli—or any other god—would've figured out a way to protect the innocents, no?

[Pause.]

CALAVERA NURSE: Yes, you would think so. Pero nadie puede proteger a los inocentes. Not even a god as powerful as Mictlantecuhtli. [Sensing without seeing] Ya viene Mictlantecuhtli con Xóchil.

[**MUSIC: UP.** *Soft.*]

[**ALL** *stand and turn toward the* **RAMP** *as* **MICTLANTECUHTLI** *leads* **XÓCHIL** *by the hand. She is dressed in a school uniform. A very calm and smiling* **XÓCHIL** *looks around* **CASIMIRO'S** *room.*]

CALAVERA NURSE: ¿Qué les dije? Xóchil ya no está tan enojada como estaba before Mictlantecuhtli had his talk with her.

[**XÓCHIL,** *still smiling beatifically, crosses to* **MAD DOG** *and gives him a resounding slap that knocks him down.*]

Well, I did say *not* as angry, didn't I?

MICTLANTECUHTLI: Sorry, Mad Dog, I did have to promise her that one slap.

[*Pause.*]

Bueno, you have a lot of things to do before you leave—

CASIMIRO: Pero nomás son *tres* cuerpos—didn't you say I had to take four? Where's the fourth body?

MICTLANTECUHTLI [*checking file*]: Ya mero, Casimiro. The fourth body will be here soon enough.

CASIMIRO [*getting suspicious*]: Hey, I'm not gonna be the fourth body, am I?

MICTLANTECUHTLI: No, Casimiro, trust me; you're not the fourth body.

[*Pause.*]

As I was saying, you have a lot of things to do before you leave, pero primero, let's introduce ourselves. Como los gringos en sus meetings: [*with accent*] "Give us your name and tell us a little something about yourself." . . . Ya saben quién soy yo.

[**MICTLANTECUHTLI** *nods to* **ROCKY ROAD** *to begin.*]

ROCKY ROAD: My real name is Raquel Castillo, but I changed it to Rocky Road. Not for the ice cream, pero for my . . . philosophy on life. It's a rocky road—get it?

MAD DOG: Yo soy el Mad Dog Sánchez. And let me tell you right now antes que somebody else decides to give me another karate kick or a slap. I never meant to hurt anyone. I was ready to join the gang nomás to prove que no soy un coward. With my luck, I figured I was gonna get killed before I killed anyone—just like it happened. And if I was gonna get killed, pues at least then maybe someone in the 'hood would write a corrido about me.

XÓCHIL: You went out to shoot someone just so someone could write a corrido about you? Pues why didn't you just go fix a horse race instead? Como en "El Moro de Cumpas"?

MAD DOG: The who?

CALAVERA NURSE: "El Moro de Cumpas." El Moro was a very famous horse from el pueblito de Cumpas, en Sonora. [*Singing and pantomiming riding a horse*] "El diez y siete de marzo, en la ciudad de Agua Prieta, vino gente de 'onde quiera—"

XÓCHIL: I remember that song. It's my dad's favorite corrido because he's from Douglas and that's near Cumpas. His father, my tata, always used to claim that he was there, at the horse race, when the horse, "El Moro," won—or lost, I forget which. But my tata always said he thought that the race was fixed. [*To* MAD DOG] Anyway, I can't believe I'm here, stuck with a bunch of losers, just because you wanted a *corrido* named after you.

MAD DOG: Who you calling a loser? ¿Pues, qué te crees? You and your friends. Stuck up como si you owned the world. I used to watch you, en la elementary, before you transferred to your fancy private school, but you never once looked at me. Un día, we were gonna have a test, y la vieja teacher said we had to use a number two pencil. Pues, I didn't have a pencil—number two or any other number—so I asked you to lend me one of yours and you just looked at me like you were smelling a fart.

[ALL *turn to* XÓCHIL, *who has a fart-smelling expression.*]

Yeah, like that. Just like you're doing now.

XÓCHIL [*quickly changing her fart-smelling expression and smiling sweetly; to* OTHERS]: My name is Xóchil Martínez—

CASIMIRO: Named for the god of the flowers, Xochipilli!

XÓCHIL: No, I wasn't! Me nombraron por la "Panadería Xóchil," where my mom worked when she got pregnant with me and all she did was eat the pan dulce all day. Anyway, as I was saying, my name is Xóchil Martínez; tengo catorce años, pero soon to be fifteen—I'm already planning my quinceañera—

[*Pause.*]

[*Realizing that she's dead*] No, I guess I'm not having a party. I'm fourteen. There, I'm done.

MICTLANTECUHTLI: Bueno. As soon as everyone's here, you will all be heading to Mictlán, place of the dead. Your journey will be long and difficult, pero las ofrendas de su familia y amigos will help you. [*Lecturing*] In our world, how you died determines where you'll end up in Mictlán. Xóchil, you're going to be with the children en Chichihuacuauhco—

XOCHIL: ¡Oh, no! Yo no quiero estar con los niños chillones; I'm too old for that, and besides, I don't want to be stuck babysitting.

ROCKY ROAD AND MAD DOG [*together*]: ¿Y nosotros?

MICTLANTECUHTLI: Ay, Rocky y Mad Dog, todavía no sé where you'll be porque we don't have a place in Mictlán for persons who die como ustedes dos: de puro stupidity.

CASIMIRO: Bueno, let Mictlantecuhtli finish lo que 'stá diciendo, so we can leave. Yo tengo mucho que hacer, and you're holding me up. Mictlantecuhtli, sigue.

MICTLANTECUHTLI: Gracias, Casimiro. Before reaching Mictlán, you must cross nine levels—eight, really, because your life here, on Earth, is the first level. You will encounter many dangers: eight deserts without water, ocho montañas de alturas peligrosas, and you must cross eight rivers. Encontrarán jaguares, wild jungle jaguars, winds as sharp as obsidian knives, flechas que vuelan por el aire, green serpents and lizards, and in Teocoyocualloa, your hearts will be eaten—

[**SOUND CUE**: *Beeper.*]

CALAVERA NURSE [*annoyed*]: ¡Ay! Just when he was getting to the good part! [*Sadistic, demonstrating*] En Teocoyocualloa les arrancan el corazón y se lo comen—

MICTLANTECUHTLI [*reading beeper*]: Eight-nine-three four-three—

CALAVERA NURSE [*interrupting and completing the number from memory*]: Three six. It's eight-nine-three four-three-three-six. [*To* MICTLANTECUHTLI] Es Don Prisciliano, our fourth body.

XÓCHIL: ¿Don Prisciliano? I know him! [*To* OTHERS] He lives down the street from me, and he's always sending me to the tiendita to buy the things he needs. Rocky, you know him, too; he lives across the street from your apartment.

ROCKY ROAD: ¿El viejito que se la pasa siempre sentado afuera? Is that his name, Don Prisciliano? I could always see him from my window. Just sitting there. Watching the world go by. I always had this weird feeling that he was looking out for me, you know, that he worried about me when no one else gave a damn.

CALAVERA NURSE: Pues, it's true; he *was* looking out for you. Don Prisciliano's a very caring person.

MAD DOG: Oh, yeah? He's always hated my guts. When I walk by, he always mumbles in Spanish, "desgraciado pachuco." What's that, anyway?

CASIMIRO [*impatiently*]: Bueno, pues, is this Don Prisciliano the last body we're waiting for?

CALAVERA NURSE: Maybe. Don Prisciliano siempre se anda muriendo—

MICTLANTECUHTLI: But he never dies! Puro false alarms. Los paramedics ya ni quieren ir a su casa.

CALAVERA NURSE: Mictlantecuhtli, it looks very serious this time. Don Prisciliano tiene pulmonía.

XÓCHIL: Pneumonia! No wonder his chest hurt! And that's why he was sending me to the tiendita to buy him some Vicks. Pobrecito. This time he *really* was sick.

CALAVERA NURSE: Aquí está, en el emergency. I don't think he's gonna make it this time.

MICTLANTECUHTLI: Bah. Siempre dices eso, but the old man ya me cansó. Casimiro needs to take four bodies to Mictlán. Aquí ya están tres; Don Prisciliano will be the fourth one.

CALAVERA NURSE: But, Mictlantecuhtli, he's not dead!

MICTLANTECUHTLI: Not yet, pero he will be soon. This time, Don Prisciliano, ready or not, I'm taking you with me!

LIGHTS: DOWN.

END OF SCENE 10

* * *

Scene 11

LIGHTS: UP.

MUSIC: *Something similar to "La danza de los viejitos" from Michoacán.*

[DON PRISCILIANO *is walking with very slow turtle steps down the* RAMP, *pushing a metal walker. He is wearing a hospital gown, slippers, and his old black hat, and a sign stating "Do not resuscitate" is hanging from his neck.* DON PRISCILIANO *finally reaches the bottom and does not see* MICTLANTE-CUHTLI *step up behind him.* MICTLANTECUHTLI *is wearing surgical greens and a stethoscope around his neck.* DON PRISCILIANO *continues to walk around the room, somewhat sneakily, looking out for* MICTLANTECUHTLI, *not knowing that* MICTLANTECUHTLI *is right behind him, matching him step by step.* ALL OTHERS *quietly move in behind* MICTLANTECUHTLI *and also stalk* DON PRISCILIANO *until he is totally surrounded.* DON PRISCILIANO *finally turns and sees* MICTLANTECUHTLI *behind him. He is startled and starts to run slowly up* RAMP/STEP UNIT.]

MICTLANTECUHTLI [*forcefully*]: Not so fast, Don Prisciliano—stop!

[DON PRISCILIANO *stops and walks down.*]

> [*Gently*] ¿Por qué corre? [*Pointing to the sign*] Aquí dice "Do not resuscitate."

DON PRISCILIANO [*looking down at the sign and trying to read it upside down*]: Sí, eso dice . . . Pero . . . [*sheepishly*] I changed my mind.

[DON PRISCILIANO *picks up the ends of his hospital gown, leaps up, and starts to run again, but* MICTLANTECUHTLI *grabs him.*]

MICTLANTECUHTLI: Pues, you've changed your mind too many times before, pero esta vez, lo siento, but you've finally died, and now you're going with me to Mictlán.

[DON PRISCILIANO *gets dejected.*]

> Ande, Don Prisciliano, no se ponga triste. You've been wanting to die for over sixty years, ¡pues hasta que se le hizo! Come and meet the others who are going to Mictlán with you. [*Taking* DON PRIS-CILIANO *to the* OTHERS] Les presento a Don Prisciliano.

DON PRISCILIANO [*talkative, like most viejitos*]: Si, es cierto, hace más de sixty years que mi vida terminó. My fiancée, María Isabel, and I were planning our wedding. We were novios for three years, mientras que yo trabajaba, saving my money for the wedding. Y la noche antes de la boda, we all went swimming a las pompitas, the irrigation canals near Oracle. I kept yelling to her, "¡No te vayas a lo hondo! ¡No te vayas a lo hondo!" You see, she didn't know how to swim, but she wouldn't listen to me. Y se ahogó. Right in front of my eyes, she drowned.

[*Pause.*]

I tried to save her. I wanted to save her, pero no pude.

MAD DOG: And why not?

DON PRISCILIANO: ¡Porque yo tampoco sabía nadar!

MICTLANTECUHTLI: Pero anímese, Don Prisciliano. You'll be seeing your beloved María Isabel very soon. Está en Tlalocan, the land of Tlaloc, the water god.

[*Pause.*]

[*Giving orders as he removes the surgical gown and stethoscope*] Bueno, now you must all make preparations for your journey. You'll need plenty of water, your favorite foods, pots and pans for cooking—¡vamos! ¡Pronto!

[*Lively polka MUSIC is heard. Energy rises as the CALAVERA NURSE equips them for the trip with water, backpacks, etc., very similar to the border desert crossers.*]

DON PRISCILIANO [*modestly putting on a pair of pants behind a chair and complaining*]: Pues yo digo, que no es proper que una señorita, como Xóchil, haga travel sola, sin chaperone, con hombres—

ROCKY ROAD: Oh, Don Prisciliano, don't be so . . . prissy.

DON PRISCILIANO [*stepping out*]: No soy prissy, but in my time—

ROCKY ROAD [*crossing*]: Han cambiado los tiempos since you were engaged. [*She links her arm through his.*]

XÓCHIL [*also crossing to DON PRISCILIANO*]: I've never ever gone on a trip, with or without men, Don Prisciliano. In fact, I never did get to do much of anything. And now, I'm ready to go to this Mictlán place. [*She links arms on his other side.*]

MAD DOG [*crossing next to ROCKY ROAD*]: And I will protect you! And if I can't—I've got this! My good-luck charm!

[MAD DOG *takes out a little toy dog from inside his shirt pocket and places it on the floor. The toy dog has batteries that make him wiggle.*]

CASIMIRO: Good thinking, Mad Dog. The book says que ningún viajero a Mictlán puede caminar sin un perrito amarillo.

MICTLANTECUHTLI: Sí, es cierto. And in case que les dé hambre, you can always make him into taquitos de escuincles!

CALAVERA NURSE: ¡Ajá! ¡Asina se los comían los aztecas!

[ALL *react, horrified.*]

MICTLANTECUHTLI: Just kidding. But it would be one way to finish off that odious dog in the commercial: "Yo quiero Taco Bell!"

MAD DOG [*picking up the dog*]: Well, not this perrito; he's not edible. [*Linking arms with* ROCKY ROAD] Ready?

[*Pause.*]

[MUSIC: *Similar to* The Wizard of Oz *theme.*]

XÓCHIL, ROCKY ROAD, MAD DOG, AND DON PRISCILIANO [*with arms linked, skipping, hopping, and singing in unison to the tune of "We're Off the See the Wizard"*]: Vamos ir a Mictlán, the wonderful world of the dead! The dead, the dead, the dead! ¡Oh Hermoso mundo Mictlán!

[*The four* TRAVELERS EXIT, *dancing up the* RAMP. *The offstage voice of Geraldine says "Bye!!!" And the skeleton waves her hand, then her arms and the rest of her body.*]

CALAVERA NURSE [*to Geraldine*]: Bye!

[CALAVERA NURSE EXITS *up the* RAMP *behind the* OTHERS.]

LIGHTS: DOWN.

MUSIC: UP.

END OF SCENE 11

* * *

Scene 12

LIGHTS: UP.

MUSIC: *Soft, as in the beginning of* CASIMIRO'S *nightmare.*

[MICTLANTECUHTLI *is putting on his headdress, and* CASIMIRO *is getting ready for the trip.*]

MICTLANTECUHTLI: Your friends are waiting for you, ¿listo?

CASIMIRO: No son mis friends; I don't even know them.

MICTLANTECUHTLI: ¿No?

[*Pause.*]

Casimiro, te dije que el perdón y la redención eran conceptos que yo no comprendía muy bien, perhaps forgiveness and redemption are concepts that are too modern for me to understand. También te dije que yo puedo cambiar el pasado—

CASIMIRO: ¡El pasado no me interesa!

MICTLANTECUHTLI: Then why are you forever dreaming of the past?

CASIMIRO: Porque nadie puede dirigir sus sueños. Not even you, the mighty Mictlantecuhtli, can direct my dreams.

MICTLANTECUHTLI [*with sarcasm*]: Well, hello? Who do you think brought your Tata Remigio into your dream last night? I did! And not only can I direct your dreams, I can bring the past to you. Now! Casimiro, listen carefully. Sit down, close your eyes, put your head down, and start counting while your Tata Remigio hides from you.

[**CASIMIRO** *follows his orders.*]

[*Calling out to beyond*] Vamos a su pueblito en México cuando eras un niño, many, many years before the tragedy at the border.

[**LIGHTS: DOWN.** *A conch shell is heard, followed by indigenous* **MUSIC.**]

Casimiro, you're now very young; eres un chamaco, jugando en el monte, entre los nopales. Your grandfather's hiding from you, y tú lo buscas porque te prometió un cuento si lo encuentras. He always has the most fascinating stories for you. Find him!

CASIMIRO [*raising his head, counting as a young child*]: ¡Veinte y ocho, veinte y nueve . . . treinta! [*Runing around*] ¡Tata Remigio! ¡Quiero mi cuento!

[*He runs to slightly offstage and pulls* **DON REMIGIO** *forward.*]

CASIMIRO'S MOTHER [*offstage*]: ¡Casimiro, ya déjate de juegos y cuentos! Tienes que ir a ayudarle a tu padre en el molino.

CASIMIRO [*responding to the* OFFSTAGE *voice*]: I still have time, Mamá! [*To* DON REMIGIO] Please tell me a Yaqui legend. Please, Tata. We still have time antes que entreguen el maíz al molino. Please.

DON REMIGIO: Bueno, hijo. Te platicaré de nuestra religión Yaqui, but then you must go and help your father. You know that he needs your help.

[DON REMIGIO *sits down.*]

CASIMIRO: Sí, Tata Remigio, I will. [*Kneeling on the floor next to* DON REMIGIO] Abuelito, tell me about the seyewailo.

DON REMIGIO: M'ijito, la seyewailo is the Yaqui convergence of time, place, direction, and quality of being—'donde todo de la vida se junta, ¿me entiendes?

CASIMIRO: Sí, Tata, seyewailo also means "the earth covered with flowers," ¿no?

DON REMIGIO: M'ijo, óyeme bien. This is very important. Para llegar a seyewailo, un Yaqui debe ser de buen corazón. With good heart. Some Yaquis have a very special power: seatakaa, the flower body. Solo las personas de buen corazón tienen seatakaa. Only those persons that would never harm another person have this special power.

CASIMIRO [*impatiently*]: Sí, sí, Tata, yo sé. A Yaqui must be with good heart to reach seyewailo—ahora, tell me about the sea ania—

DON REMIGIO: Again? Bueno. La sea ania is the essence of the Yaqui world of flowers. Someplace in the East—en un lugar "beneath the dawn" ahí está nuestra sea anía. And there, toda la belleza natural del Sonoran Desert may be seen. Las flores, el agua, abundancia de todo—pájaros, insects—all the animals live there. And especially the sacred deer—

CASIMIRO: I know! I know! The Yaqui word for deer is "malichi," ¿qué no?

DON REMIGIO [*laughing, proud that* CASIMIRO *remembers*]: Sí, hijo. Malichi. Our sacred deer. [*Starting to sing popular song*] "Soy un pobre venadito que habita en la sea anía . . ."

[*Pause.*]

[*Reflecting*] Casimiro, hijo mío, last year, cuando estabas tan enfermo con una fiebre, I made a promise that I would teach you our Deer Dance and that you would dance it at our ceremonies.

CASIMIRO: Abuelito, teach me La Danza del Venado now; I know I can learn it. I'm ready. Mire.

[CASIMIRO *tries to dance.*]

MICTLANTECUHTLI: Dispense, Don Remigio, but we don't have time. Se nos terminó el tiempo; we must return to the present. Es la hora que Casimiro tiene que caminar hacia Mictlán.

[*A conch shell is heard again, and the* LIGHTS *go* UP. DON REMIGIO *crosses to the* RAMP *and starts to walk up slowly.*]

DON REMIGIO [*stopping midway*]: Ven, hijo mío, I will help you on your journey to Mictlán. You won't see me, but on every step of the way I will be with you, guiding you. [*Putting his hand out to* CASIMIRO] Ven, hijo mío, ven.

[CASIMIRO, *almost trancelike, starts to walk slowly up to* DON REMIGIO.]

Escúchame bien, Casimiro: Life here on Earth is a journey. And you are now embarking on *another* journey—un viaje que sigue un camino muy peligroso. On one side of this road, there is an abyss.

[CASIMIRO *looks to one side of the* RAMP.]

En el otro lado del camino, *otro* abismo.

[CASIMIRO *looks to the other side.*]

You must walk without falling on either side; andando siempre en el mero centro del camino. Always, right in the center.

[CASIMIRO *centers himself and holds out his hand to* DON REMIGIO. DON REMIGIO *pulls* CASIMIRO *to him and embraces him.*]

And at the end of your journey, [*voice breaking*] you . . .

[*Pause.* DON REMIGIO *is unable to continue.*]

MICTLANTECUHTLI: Siga, Don Remigio. And at the end of his journey—what?

DON REMIGIO [*turning to* MICTLANTECUHTLI, *forcefully*]: Mictlantecuhtli, this time he will not fail; Casimiro will fullfill his obligation and his destiny. [*Turning to* CASIMIRO *and placing his hands on* CASIMIRO's *shoulders*] And at the end of your journey, Casimiro, you will dance La Danza del Venado, y cumplirás la manda y tu destino.

LIGHTS: DOWN.

MUSIC: UP. "*La danza del venado.*"

END OF ACT I

INTERMISSION

ACT II

Scene 1

TIME: *Sometime in the beyond.*

PLACE: *Mictlán.*

SETTING: *Mictlán is rather brown and desolate. The* RAMP *now has a carpet runner with an Aztec design. There are two* PLATFORMS *with sloping* RAMPS *on each side of the stage, and possibly some side-decorated pillars. The* ALLEGORICAL DANGERS—BOULDERS, KNIVES, WINDS, JAGUARS, *and* LIZARDS—*are dressed in surrealistic costumes and masks, and they are positioned in place.*

TECHNICAL NOTES: *Act 2 is one long scene and is not divided into scenes in traditional format, but it should have a dream quality of unconnectedness, yet seamless. Please note that the set does not change during act 2. The ending will consist of two parallel scenes taking place at the same time on the* PLATFORMS: *the shooting at the border in 1988, and the gang shooting on the barrio street that took place in the present. Precise coordination of* LIGHTS, SOUND CUES, MUSIC, *blocking, dialogue and repeated lines, pantomime, and* FREEZES *is required and is not always marked in script.*

LIGHTS: UP.

MUSIC: UP. *Aztec, indigenous. Then a soft drum beat during* MICTLANTE-CUHTLI's *monologue.*

[MICTLANTECUHTLI *is standing at the top of the* RAMP *very much as he was in his first entrance in act 1. The* ALLEGORICAL DANGERS *are simply lounging and making very slight, menacing movements. They will be choreographed to follow* MICTLANTECUHTLI's *descriptions.*]

MICTLANTECUHTLI [*directly to audience, almost chanting*]: En Apanohuaia, the water crossing place, los viajeros a Mictlán cruzaron el río, on the back of a dog—[*aside*] believe me, they did. Créanmelo, así pasó—and here you *must* suspend your disbelief. Otherwise you won't believe what follows next.

[CASIMIRO, ROCKY ROAD, MAD DOG, XÓCHIL, *and* DON PRISCILIANO ENTER, *tired and staggering from their arduous trip.*]

Y en Tepectli Monamictlan, the place where the mountains come together, las montañas golpearon a todos los viajeros, the mountain boulders gave the travelers a terrible beating.

[BOULDERS *knock them around.*]

En Itztepetl, the knives as sharp as obsidian blades made them bleed.

[BLADES *cut them.*]

Y en Izteecayan, the wind place, los fuertes vientos brought out the fierce jaguars and green lizards.

[JAGUARS *and* LIZARDS *attack them.*]

Pasaron por Paniecatacoyan, and in Timiminaloayan, they were repeatedly shot by arrows. Y en Teocoyocualloa, the place where one's heart is eaten, their corazones were ripped out—

[ANY *of the* DANGERS *can cut out their hearts.*]

[ALL DANGERS EXIT.]

Hasta que por fin llegaron a Izmictlan Apochcalolca, the place with no chimneys, o simplemente, el lugar sin escape. [*Starting to exit, sternly, but then stopping and turning*] Oh, what the hell. There *is* an escape. But I'll leave that part to my compadres Cantinflas and Ehécatl, god of the wind.

[SOUND CUE: *Final sharp drum beat.*]

LIGHTS: DOWN.

[MICTLANTECUHTLI EXITS. CASIMIRO, ROCKY ROAD, MAD DOG, XÓCHIL, *and* DON PRISCILIANO *are huddled in dead heap on the ground.*]

LIGHTS: UP.

[*They get up slowly, helping each other, and look around, trying to get their bearings.*]

CASIMIRO: Bueno, parece que ya estamos en Mictlán.

XÓCHIL: This is Mictlán? [*Disparagingly*] Ghet-to heaven.

ROCKY ROAD: Well, if it is, it looks like I'll need to take more pills!

DON PRISCILIANO: ¿Casimiro, y ahora qué hacemos?

CASIMIRO: I don't know what *you'll* do, Don Prisciliano, pero *I'm* heading back to the hospital. Mictlantecuhtli just said I had to bring four of you here to Mictlán. Pues aquí están.

MAD DOG: But where's Mictlantecuhtli? Shouldn't he be here? How are we supposed to know where to go now? Didn't he say there wasn't a place for stupid ones like me and Rocky Road?

DON PRISCILIANO: Casimiro, yo no pienso que nomás te puedes ir and just leave us here. Alone.

[ALL *ad-lib, worried and complaining.*]

CASIMIRO: Quiet, everybody! Everyone, stay here, and I'll try to find him.

[*He* EXITS. CANTINFLAS ENTERS *as tour guide.*]

CANTINFLAS [*to* TRAVELERS]: Bienvenidos a Mictlán, my sweethearts.

[*He places arms around* XÓCHIL's *and* ROCKY ROAD's *shoulders in a very familiar manner.*]

> Yo soy su tour guide, so let me give you a brief overview of your new residence, el merito Mictlán.

[LA LLORONA ENTERS.]

LA LLORONA [*crossing, practicing her wailing*]: ¡Ay, mis hijos! Where are my children?

[*She stops, takes a can of hair spray from a shopping bag that she's carrying, and sprays her hair. She continues wailing as she* EXITS.]

> ¡Ay, mi hijos! ¿Adónde 'stán mis hijos?

ROCKY ROAD [*in wonder*]: Wow! So, that's La Llorona. All my life I've been afraid of her and now I finally get to see her.

CANTINFLAS: La Llorona? There's really no reason to be afraid of her; she just has a bad reputation. Como dice el refrán, "cobra fama y acuéstate a dormir." Es la best friend de la goddess Chicomecoatl. Y las dos son bien chillonas. Actually, there's three crybabies. [*Beginning to cry as he gives lecture*] Chicomecoatl was the first of all mothers to die in childbirth, so she's forever wandering, forever wailing for her lost baby and her own life. La segunda chillona es la goddess Cihuacoatl, que siempre se viste de blanco and also roams the Earth, weeping and wailing, predicando guerras y miseria. [*Blowing his nose loudly*] But we should be the ones weeping and wailing, porque fue Cihuacoatl who gave mankind the tools of labor: el azadón and the tumpline—

DON PRISCILIANO: Herramienta para que el hombre trabajara como un buey—

CANTINFLAS [*abruptly continuing his tour lecture*]: Aquí en Mictlán, seguimos el calendario azteca; the year is divided into . . . vamos a ver . . .

[*Taking out a pad and pencil, licking the pencil tip, and writing as he talks*] Eighteen months, each with twenty days, porque mire usted, diez y ocho por veinte, equals three hundred and sixty days, and it's very clear that the year has three hundred and sixty five days, ¿verdad, chato? Sí, pero no. Vea usted, ahí 'stá el detalle, compadre. Sobran cinco días. Entonces, in these leftover five days, useless and inservibles, ahora dígame usted, Don Prisciliano, what do we need these five days for?

[**DON PRISCILIANO** *opens his mouth to answer, but* **CANTINFLAS** *merely takes a deep breath and continues.*]

Es bueno el cilantro, pero no tanto, y no todo en el monte es orégano, ¿verdad? Pues por eso mismo le digo, that's precisely why we have Días de los Muertos. To use up these five leftover days. Pero, luego llegaron los españoles y lueguito metieron la pata, ya los conocen, con sus santos y misas y qué sé yo, y luego los gringos con su "Halloween" y "trick or treat." Bueno pues, lo que se va pelar que se vaya remojando. Caminen, caminen, no se haga bola.

[**CÉSAR CHÁVEZ ENTERS**, *reading his notes and talking to himself.*]

CÉSAR CHÁVEZ: Tenemos que organizar a todos los trabajadores en Tlalocan. We have to demand better wages, an eight-hour day, breaks, clean and sanitary bathrooms . . .

CANTINFLAS: Oh, este es el Señor César Chávez, el presidente de los United Farm Workers, el sindicato de los campesinos unidos. He and I came to Mictlán almost at the same time. Fíjense nomás, when he was alive, he was always organizing, organizing, organizing. Y desde que llegó a Mictlán, ¿qué creen ustedes que se la pasa haciendo? Organizing! He hasn't stopped organizing. Listen to him; está preparando su espeeche para los aguacateros, newly arrived de por allá de Chula Vista, California, y qué bien lo saben son rabble-rousers criados en Oaxaca 'donde allá *sí* conocen sus derechos, not like the mensos en Tlalocan. Pay attention.

CÉSAR CHÁVEZ: Tenemos que organizar a todos los trabajadores en Tlalocan. We have to demand better wages, an eight-hour day, breaks, clean and sanitary bathrooms—

[**XÓCHIL** *moves away from the other* **TRAVELERS**, *moving closer to hear* **CÉSAR CHÁVEZ.**]

Vacaciones con pago, agua fresca, todos los días de fiesta pagados o double pay if they have to work on holidays. ¡Aguacateros, sálganse de los files!

[*He starts to* EXIT.]

XÓCHIL: Mr. Chávez! Please wait—who are the aguacateros?

CÉSAR CHÁVEZ: They are the avocado pickers, m'ija. They have very dangerous jobs, way up in the trees, cutting the avocadoes with sharp knives—vente conmigo; I'll introduce you to them. [*Starting to exit with* XÓCHIL, *then stopping*] Ah, but what's your name?

XÓCHIL: Xóchil Martínez.

CÉSAR CHÁVEZ: Xóchil?

XÓCHIL: Yes, and I've decided that I am named for the goddess of flowers and not for the bakery.

CÉSAR CHÁVEZ [*not really understanding her*]: Qué bueno; you have a beautiful name. Wait until you see the flowers in Tlalocan. They are the most beautiful flowers on Earth—pero we must organize the nursery workers—

XÓCHIL [*stopping in her tracks*]: Nursery? With babies? I distinctly told Mictlantecuhtli that I'm not about to be stuck babysitting in Chichihuacuauhco—

CÉSAR CHÁVEZ: No, no. This is not a nursery for babies; it's a nursery for plants and flowers, and they need tender care just like babies, pero Tlaloc tiene un foreman . . .

[CÉSAR CHÁVEZ *continues talking as he and* XÓCHIL EXIT.]

ROCKY ROAD: Oh, no! Did you hear what he said about the avocado workers? He wants them to go on strike! And if they go on strike, we won't have the guacamole for the Super Bowl, and what's a Super Bowl without guacamole? And I must find Selena and convince her to let me help her choreograph the half-time dance—

[*Her attention is caught by* EHÉCATL, *who* ENTERS *in full costume and mask, carrying his bench and a bag filled with "Powerball" numbered balls. He places his bench down, sits on it, and starts to throw the balls around.*]

MAD DOG: Who's that vato?

CANTINFLAS: Ese "vato" es Ehécatl, god of the wind. Bueno, technically he's another aspect of our great Quetzalcoatl, pero eso es demasiado metaphysical to explain to mere mortals, so never mind.

MAD DOG: What's he doing with those balls?

CANTINFLAS: Picking the Powerball winner. Ehécatl loves to roam the Earth—y aquí en Mictlán—dressed in rags, sentadito en su banco.

MAD DOG: Why does he do that?

CANTINFLAS: If I knew that, no anduviera aquí de tour guide. Pero lo que sí sé, es que if you catch him, he'll grant you a wish and a long life to enjoy it.

MAD DOG AND ROCKY [*together as they exchange looks*]: Un wish?

CANTINFLAS: Ajá, un deseo. [*Continuing as tour guide*] Por aquí tenemos Tlalocan, the land of water, filled with corn, frijol—all kinds of beans—squash, and chili. Chili, pues pa' que les cuento: chili colorado, chili del árbol, serrano, jalapeños, chili piquín, chili poblano—

DON PRISCILIANO: Déjese de chilis, Señor Cantinflas. I'm dying to see my fiancée—bueno, ya murió—and Mictlantecuhtli said that María Isabel, mi novia, está aquí, en Tlalocan, because she died by drowning. [*To* OTHERS] Verán cuando la vean; she's so beautiful and—

CANTINFLAS: ¿Se ahogó? Ah, pues sí, todos los ahogados llegan aquí, a Tlalocan. Y ahí les va algo muy interesante que yo sé que no sabían porque apenas lo supe yo, pero not only do the drowned ones end up here in Tlalocan, but also the ones que les pegó un rayo, or that died from water-related enfermedades like gout o pulmonía y—

DON PRISCILIANO: That's where I'm going; I died of pneumonia. ¿Pues adónde es este Tlalocan? Yo quiero ver a mi novia ahorita mismo. Where is she?

CANTINFLAS: Ay, Don Prisciliano, pues where else do you think she'd be? [*Pointing offstage*] Over there, en aquel swimming pool, taking swimming lessons, pues no faltaba más—sigamos a Chichihuacuauhco, land of infants and children, where el árbol Chichihuacuauhco nourishes them with milk from its leaves. Caminen, caminen, no se hagan bola. Walk this way.

[ALL *except* EHÉCATL *follow* CANTINFLAS, *with comedy bit imitating his famous walk and* EXIT, *except* DON PRISCILIANO, *who stops.*]

DON PRISCILIANO [*to himself*]: Yo no tengo que ir a ningún Chichihuacuauhco; yo voy a buscar a mi María Isabel en la alberca. That
shouldn't be hard; I remember exactly how she looked that night
she drowned. Recuerdo muy bien como se veía, con su bathing
suit—modesto, no desoluto—so beautiful, so young. [*Starting to
sing*] "Coje tu sombrero y póntelo, vamos a la playa, calienta el sol.
Chivirivirí . . ."

[DON PRISCILIANO EXITS. EHÉCATL *glances up and sees that he's now alone.
He stands and picks up his bench and starts to cross stealthily.* ENTERING
from the opposite side from which they EXITED, ROCKY ROAD *and* MAD DOG
sneak up behind EHÉCATL, *match their steps to his, and grab him.* EHÉCATL
puts up a struggle, but he is quickly subdued and forced to sit down on his bench.
MAD DOG *holds him down on one side and* ROCKY ROAD *holds him down on
the other side.* DON PRISCILIANO ENTERS, *sputtering, with* MARÍA ISABEL,
who is wearing a very old-fashioned bathing suit and rubber cap on her head.]

DON PRISCILIANO [*still sputtering, indignant*]: Esta vieja . . . dice . . . que es
. . . mi María Isabel.

ROCKY ROAD AND MAD DOG [*together, introducing themselves but not releas-
ing* EHÉCATL]: Mucho gusto, semos Rocky Road y Mad Dog, a sus
órdenes, Doña María Isabel.

DON PRISCILIANO: ¡No! ¡No! No es mi María Isabel. Esta es una vieja; mi
María Isabel is just seventeen.

MARÍA ISABEL: I *was* seventeen, but Prisciliano, that was over sixty years
ago.

DON PRISCILIANO: Yes, but now you're so . . . old.

MARÍA ISABEL: Well, viejo choro, have you looked in the mirror lately?

[*She* EXITS *in a huff, sputtering insults.*]

ROCKY: Se fue bien enojada, Don Prisciliano.

DON PRISCILIANO [*somewhat remorseful*]: I'm sorry, but did you see her?
My María Isabel was so beautiful, and so—

EHÉCATL: Young?

DON PRISCILIANO: ¿Y a usted quién le dio permiso pa' que se metiera en
la conversación?

MAD DOG [*quickly*]: Don Prisciliano, this is the god Ehécatl. ¿Se acuerda?
The one that the Cantinflas dude told us can grant us one wish.

DON PRISCILIANO: ¿Un deseo? [*Getting an idea*] Hmmm . . .

EHÉCATL: Yes, but only if you let me get up. I'm not going to run away, ¿qué creen? ¿Que soy un leprechaun?

[ROCKY ROAD *and* MAD DOG *release him.*]

DON PRISCILIANO: Señor dios Ehécatl, yo quisiera que—

EHÉCATL: Ay, Don Prisciliano, I'm sorry. I know what your wish is, but I can't grant it. I cannot make your María Isabel young again. Don Prisciliano, todos estos años, you've been in love with a memory, and now it's time for you to fall in love with the present.

DON PRISCILIANO: Y entonces, ¿de qué demonios sirve?

[DON PRISCILIANO EXITS, *grumbling about useless gods.* XÓCHIL ENTERS, *carrying a flower.*]

XÓCHIL [*to* EHÉCATL]: Can you really grant us a wish?

EHÉCATL: Sí, I can grant wishes. Bueno, but only within reason. Pero before you ask me for anything, think about it carefully. Above all, consider your reasons. Ya vieron a Don Prisciliano, his was a purely selfish wish, pero everyone does that, at first. I'll give you some time to reflect on your wish. Piénsenlo muy bien, and one more thing: you must *justify* your wish.

[EHÉCATL EXITS.]

XÓCHIL: Think about it? That'll take forever! Besides what's there to think about? Where do I start? I never got to do *anything*!

ROCKY ROAD: And I already did . . . everything! I don't need a wish.

[*She* EXITS.]

MAD DOG: And everything I did, I did for the wrong reasons.

[XÓCHIL *and* MAD DOG *share brief awkward moment, neither one knowing what to say next. The same* MUSIC *that played when* XÓCHIL *entered in act 1 continues during this dialogue.*]

XÓCHIL: Well, if neither Rocky nor Don Prisciliano want to make a wish, I guess that leaves just you and me, no? But how does this work? Do we really get to wish *anything*?

MAD DOG: Well, remember that Ehécatl said it had to be "within reason" and "justified." You know, like in those social science exercises: you're in a spaceship or a raft in the middle of the ocean, there's seven of you, and you have water for only six persons, and only so much room for things, so do you throw out the prostitute and the matches?

XÓCHIL: Oh, forget about the matches. I never went out on a date, much less a spaceship. [*Playing nervously with her flower*] I never danced with a boy, and you know? I never, ever . . . got kissed.

[*Pause.*]

MAD DOG: We might end up having the same wish. [*Crossing to her*] I never went out on a date, [*taking the flower from* XÓCHIL'*s hand*] or danced with a girl, [*holding her other hand*] or ever . . . kissed . . . [*kissing the flower*] a girl.

[MAD DOG *then brushes* XÓCHIL'*s lips with the flower.* XÓCHIL *takes his hand and* BOTH *look into each other's eyes.*]

Would you vote to throw me off the raft in the middle of the ocean?

XÓCHIL: Depends. Is the ocean filled with sharks?

MAD DOG: Sharks, barracudas, giant squid, piranhas—

XÓCHIL: Piranhas? In the ocean? I thought they were only somewhere in the Amazon—

MAD DOG: Okay, the Amazon. Would you throw me off the raft and keep all the water for yourself?

XÓCHIL [*teasing*]: Maybe.

[MAD DOG *and* XÓCHIL *lower their hands and share a soft kiss.* EHÉCATL ENTERS, *sees them, and sighs.* MAD DOG *and* XÓCHIL *break apart quickly. Pause.* MAD DOG *and* XÓCHIL *exchange looks.*]

MAD DOG AND XOCHIL [*together*]: Dios Ehécatl, we have our wish. We want to—

EHÉCATL [*sadly*]: Sí, yo sé. But your wishes cannot—

[ROCKY ROAD ENTERS, *cutting off* EHÉCATL'*s speech. She has* LA LLORONA *in tow, who is wearing pink plastic rollers in her hair and something obviously borrowed from* ROCKY ROAD.]

ROCKY ROAD: Mr. Ehécatl Quetzalcoatl, I've been networking with this lady, and we need to deal with her . . . depression, low self-esteem, and self-punishment. Sure, she did wrong, pero if even the prisoners on death row can get out on appeals, entonces, ¿por qué esta pobre mujer no? Y nada de . . . Prozac. We've decided that

Chichihuacuahco, where all the babies are at, needs to be reorganized. The children there do nothing but drink milk from that immense ... chichi tree ... Well, you tell him our plans, Chillona.

[ROCKY ROAD *pushes* LA LLORONA *forward.*]

LA LLORONA: Queremos establish un beauty shop for all the working moms and a day-care center para los niños, con música, theater, arts and crafts ... Y vamos a tener poetry readings, plays—muchas cosas—para los aguacateros con el Señor Chávez, y—

[DON PRISCILIANO *and* MARÍA ISABEL ENTER, *holding hands.*]

DON PRISCILIANO: Gran dios Ehécatl? [*Embarrassed slightly*] My wish is . . . to marry María Isabel!

MARÍA ISABEL: I have forgiven his unkind words and have agreed— again—to be his wife.

EHÉCATL: Bueno, let me review your wishes. Raquel Castillo, is this your wish, then—to work with the niños en Chichihuacuahco?

[ROCKY ROAD *nods yes.*]

XÓCHIL: And my wish is that I want to—

MAD DOG: It's the same as mine. We both want to—

EHÉCATL: Wait, Xóchil and Mad Dog. [*To* ROCKY] ¿Estás segura? It'll be a drastic change from your life when your T-shirt's slogan was "Life Is Too Short to Dance with Ugly Men," ¿no te parece?

ROCKY ROAD: Oh, that was the ... shallow Rocky Road. You know, dios Ehécatl? When I was alive I never realized that the best thing, the very best thing about life, is that we can always [*trying to think of the word*] ...

ALL [*impatiently*]: ¡¿Qué pues?!

ROCKY ROAD [*calmly*]: Change. We can always change. And if I had changed my way of living, I guess I never would've taken those pills.

MAD DOG: Our wish is to—

EHÉCATL: ¿Y usted, Don Prisciliano? Your wish is to marry María Isabel and stay here?

DON PRISCILIANO: Sí. Usted dijo bien, I was in love with a memory, pero ya veo que la María Isabel that I knew and loved is still the same one, underneath the old body here.

MARÍA ISABEL: Sí, Prisciliano, and even though our bodies get old and wrinkled, our corazones don't get old.

DON PRISCILIANO: Es cierto; our hearts forever stay young y siempre recuerdan el "first love."

[CANTINFLAS ENTERS *and crosses.*]

CANTINFLAS: Bueno, si vamos a tener una boda y una fiesta, tenemos mucho que preparar. Lo que se va pelar, que se vaya remojando. Vénganse conmigo, Chato y Chata.

[CANTINFLAS EXITS *with* DON PRISCILIANO *and* MARÍA ISABEL.]

ROCKY ROAD: If there's going to be a fiesta, we have to find Selena. She promised me that I could choreograph one of the half-time dances at the Super Bowl. [*To* LA LLORONA, *giving her "bad hair day" tips*] Mira, Chillona, con el humidity que tenemos aquí, necesitas un buen mousse. I know how to make an excellent moisturizer from the nopal, sí, el cactus, es un secreto, pero I'll share it with you, just don't be a crybaby anymore, okay?

[ROCKY ROAD *and* LA LLORONA EXIT. MAD DOG *and* XÓCHIL *exchange uneasy looks.* EHÉCATL *is clearly very uncomfortable.*]

XÓCHIL: It looks as though Don Prisciliano's and Rocky Road's wishes are to remain here, in Mictlán.

[EHÉCATL *nods yes.*]

MAD DOG: Well, that takes care of two of the wishes. What about *our* wishes? You can't keep stalling around—

[CÉSAR CHÁVEZ ENTERS.]

CÉSAR CHÁVEZ: Xóchil! You must come quickly. The meeting you had with Tlaloc's foreman—¿qué le dijiste?—he has finally agreed to start negotiations, and you must be at these meetings to—

[*He starts to* EXIT *with* XÓCHIL.]

XÓCHIL: Wait, Mr. Chávez. Mad Dog, come with us; we need all the help we can get.

MAD DOG [*to* EHÉCATL]: I know there's something wrong here that you don't want to tell us.

CÉSAR CHÁVEZ: Xóchil, we have to go before the foreman changes his mind.

XÓCHIL: Please, Mad Dog, come with us.

MAD DOG: All right, I'll go with you, but I'm not gonna carry no picket sign. That would ruin my image. [*Crossing to them, strutting, and then stopping; to* EHÉCATL] But, I'll be back, and I'm getting my wish.

[XÓCHIL, MAD DOG, *and* CÉSAR CHÁVEZ EXIT. CASIMIRO ENTERS.]

CASIMIRO: Well, that should make it easier for you, no? Solo te quedan los wishes de Xóchil y Mad Dog.

EHÉCATL: Sí, pero there's a problem; they both have the same wish: to return to the living.

CASIMIRO [*impressed*]: Can you do that?

EHÉCATL: ¿Yo? No. Solo Mictlantecuhtli puede regresar los muertos a la vida. And only in very special cases. Es algo muy difícil: it depends on the circumstances, the timing, el . . . sacrificio.

CASIMIRO: Sacrifice?

[SPOTLIGHT *on* MICTLANTECUHTLI. *Drums and a conch shell are heard, followed by the same Aztec or indigenous* MUSIC. MICTLANTECUHTLI *is standing exactly as when he first appeared to* CASIMIRO *in act 1.*]

MICTLANTECUHTLI: Sí, el sacrificio. Before I can return someone who has died back to the land of the living, *another* living being must be willing to die and take that person's place aquí en Mictlán.

CASIMIRO: Die?

MICTLANTECUHTLI [*with sarcasm*]: Sí, dying is usually enough. Una vida por otra vida, you might say. So, ¿qué dices, Casimiro? Would you be willing to give up *your* life for one of your friends? For Xóchil or Mad Dog?

CASIMIRO: ¡Ya te dije que no son mis friends! I only helped them because you made me. I've done what you asked, now let me go back. Es demasiado lo que tú pides. No one can be expected to give up his life for a stranger.

[*He starts to* EXIT.]

MICTLANTECUHTLI: No, I guess not. Not for a *stranger*. Pero entonces, ¿qué tal si la conoces?

[CASIMIRO *stops in his tracks.*]

It's been a long time, Casimiro—twenty years to be exact—but surely you remember . . . Mariel?

[MARIEL ENTERS.]

MARIEL [*calling him to pose for the picture, just as she did before they went to the desert*]: ¡Casimiro! ¡Ven, apúrate! Manuel nos va a tomar una foto.

CASIMIRO: ¡Mariel!

MARIEL [*holding her hand out to* CASIMIRO]: ¡Ven, Casimiro!

MICTLANTECUHTLI [*taunting*]: Anda, ve, Casimiro. Go to her. Take her hand.

[CASIMIRO *starts to go to* MARIEL, *holding out his hand to her.*]

> Ahora sí le puedes dar la mano. After all, it's just for a photo, ¿no? ¿Por qué, no se la diste aquella noche en el desierto?

[CASIMIRO *hesitates.*]

> Take Mariel's hand!

CASIMIRO: No, no puedo. I know what you're asking me to do, but I'm not ready to die for her.

MICTLANTECUHTLI: Casimiro, Casimiro. ¿De veras no ves? You're already dying, Casimiro. ¿Me entiendes? You were dying, there on the recliner, with my book on your chest, y el sueño que tuviste de tu abuelo y Mariel was to be your last dream—all these last years, you've been just like Don Prisciliano, living in the past.

CASIMIRO: Maybe the past is safer.

MICTLANTECUHTLI: Maybe.

[*Pause.*]

> Pero, Casimiro, ¿sabes qué es lo más triste? That you're gonna lay there, dead, día tras día, hasta que someone finally notices that the hospital garbage is piling up, porque nobody will notice that you're gone, Casimiro. Nobody. Oh, but I'm forgetting your sweetheart, Geraldine. Ella sí va derramar muchas lágrimas—

[DON REMIGIO ENTERS.]

DON REMIGIO [*forcefully*]: Mictlantecuhtli! Ya déjalo! No trates a mi nieto como un ratón entre las garras de un gato. You told him that he only had to bring the four bodies to Mictlán; he's done that. Ahora, lo tienes que dejar que regrese.

MICTLANTECUHTLI [*chastened*]: Perdóneme, Don Remigio, dice bien. Go, Casimiro, and get your water and food for your journey back.

[CASIMIRO *starts to* EXIT.]

DON REMIGIO: ¡Hijo! Espera—prove to Mictlantecuhtli and to yourself que *sí* tienes seatakaa, the flower body. Que sí eres de buen corazón; que no eres un cobarde. Help Mariel now, and forever change your past.

[CASIMIRO *stops and turns to* MARIEL, *and gives her a thoughtful look. Pause.*]

CASIMIRO: No, Abuelito. Lo siento, pero yo no tengo seatakaa. Yo sí he lastimado a otras personas. I am not of a good heart.

[CASIMIRO EXITS.]

MICTLANTECUHTLI: I'm sorry, Mariel; you must remain in Mictlán.

[MARIEL EXITS.]

DON REMIGIO [*sad*]: Yo estaba seguro que Casimiro—

MICTLANTECUHTLI: Give up, Don Remigio; he's failed *again*.

DON REMIGIO: No tuve bastante tiempo para prepararlo con solo una noche. Mictlantecuhtli, I need more time!

MICTLANTECUHTLI: But we don't have more time! Ya es demasiado tarde para Mariel, but there's still hope for Xóchil.

DON REMIGIO: Only Xóchil? Are you forgetting that Mad Dog wants to return also? Son *dos* almas, *dos* cuerpos. You need *two* sacrifices.

MICTLANTECUHTLI: Yes, I know, but there's also the special consideration for exceptional bravery. Yo creo que'l Mad Dog—

DON REMIGIO: Mad Dog?

[*Pause.*]

Yes, I see what you're planning. And if Casimiro—

MICTLANTECUHTLI: Forget Casimiro! He's a coward! I'm sending him back to his Geraldine.

[*He starts to* EXIT.]

DON REMIGIO: Casimiro is not a coward!

MICTLANTECUHTLI: ¿No? ¿Qué no lo vio, Don Remigio? Ni el gran amor que le tiene a Mariel fue suficiente.

DON REMIGIO: Mictlantecuhtli, tú nunca has sido cruel. Give him another chance.

MICTLANTECUHTLI: Another chance? ¿Para qué?

DON REMIGIO: Para que por fin encuentre ese perdón que busca.

MICTLANTECUHTLI: You know that the foregiveness he seeks must come from himself.

DON REMIGIO: Nosotros vemos eso, pero él no lo ve. We must help him see this.

[*Pause.*]

MICTLANTECUHTLI: There's only one way left to find out.

[DON REMIGIO, *realizing what* MICTLANTECUHTLI *means, nods his head slowly.*]

DON REMIGIO: Sí, tenemos que volver al pasado; we must return to the past.

MICTLANTECUHTLI: Bueno. We will let the events of those nights reoccur.

[*A conch shell is heard, and then mysterious* LIGHTS *dance across the stage. A blending of previous* MUSIC *is heard; it is almost jarring, as when a sound technician is trying to find a cue.*]

Esta será la última vez que Casimiro podrá cambiar su destino. This will be the last time that Casimiro can change his destiny; there will not be another.

LIGHTS: DOWN *and* UP.

[DON PRISCILIANO ENTERS *with his chair.*]

DON PRISCILIANO [*talking at times to himself and at other times to the audience*]: Sí, I saw everything. Bueno, *almost* everything. I didn't see Rocky take the pills or I would've called the paramedics, although no sé si hubiera servido de nada porque los paramedics don't want to go to my house anymore after all of my false alarms . . . Yo, como siempre, estaba sentado afuera . . . [*pointing and crossing*] ahí. Just watching people go by. Nomás sentado ahí, looking across the street, at a vacant lot, wondering: when did it become a vacant lot? Una vez era un negocio, lots of trucks in and out, mucho ruido . . .

[*He sits down and the* SOUND *of trucks, etc., is heard.*]

Muchos trabajadores—and then one day—nothing.

[*All noise stops abruptly.*]

Not even one brick was left there.

[*Pause.*]

Ayer, primero, Xóchil came down the street.

[**XÓCHIL ENTERS.**]

XÓCHIL [*talking to someone offstage*]: How come I always have to go for his tortillas?

[**XÓCHIL FREEZES.**]

DON PRISCILIANO: I knew that she would stop and talk to me. Siempre que la mandaban a la tiendita de la esquina, y le dijían que se hiciera "hurry up," ella siempre hallaba tiempo para platicar con este viejo. Not like that pachuco, Mad Dog, strutting como un gallito en el gallinero. I'm not sure if Xóchil really liked to stop to talk to me, or if she only did it to make her father mad for making her go to the store all the time. Anyway, I always enjoyed our pláticas even if lately all she does is talk about her upcoming quinceañera, her fifteenth birthday.

[**XÓCHIL** *breaks* **FREEZE** *and crosses to* **DON PRISCILIANO.**]

XÓCHIL [*dreamy*]: For my quinceañera, Don Prisciliano, I'm gonna have fourteen madrinas, and they're gonna each carry a bouquet of white roses with pink and lavender ribbon streamers, my favorite colors—

DON PRISCILIANO [*on his own usual subject, his health*]: Xóchil, m'ijita, todo el día he tenido un dolorcito right here on my chest. It hurts more when I take a deep breath . . . [*breathing deeply*] like this.

XÓCHIL: And their caps come over their foreheads, like this, pointing down, in a triangle, you know, sorta like from Romeo and Juliet's time, with little pearls hanging—

DON PRISCILIANO: Xóchil, dime una cosa: when did that building across the street disappear?

[**MARIEL ENTERS.**]

MARIEL [*leading a cheer with her bedraggled pompon*]: "A la bim, a la bum, a la bim, bum, bah . . ."

[**MARIEL FREEZES.**]

XÓCHIL: Disappear? It didn't "disappear." Don Prisciliano, la tumbaron last year, ¿qué no se acuerda? You sat here every day and watched the wrecking crew from sun up to sun down. Remember?

DON PRISCILIANO: Sí, ya recuerdo. But what I said about the building disappearing, yo sé que it didn't just disappear. Pero tengo miedo que someday alguien va a mirar pa'ca and see this empty chair and wonder: when did that old man disappear?

XÓCHIL: Oh, Don Prisciliano, don't worry; you're not gonna disappear. [*Returning to her usual subject, without dropping a beat*] And I haven't decided if the dresses will have hoops, like in *Gone with the Wind*, you know? But probably not, 'cause all my madrinas say they won't wear them, but I ask them: so whose quinceañera is it, yours or mine?

DON PRISCILIANO [*continuing on his subject*]: Maybe not "disappear," but what if I die someday and nobody even notices?

MARIEL [*breaking freeze and finishing her cheer*]: "Nogales, Nogales, rah, rah rah! [*Jumping up and down*] ¡Ganamos, ganamos!"

[**MARIEL FREEZES.**]

XÓCHIL: You're not gonna die. Besides, if you do, my dad says that nobody's really dead until no one ever thinks of them. So if you die, I'll always think of you when I have to go to the store for my dad's tortillas. I promise. [*Starting to leave*] Con su permiso, do you need anything from the tiendita?

DON PRISCILIANO: Sí, hija. Por favor, cómprame un frasquito de Vicks. No se te olvide. Vicks. I don't want Mentholatum. Tiene que ser Vicks.

[*He stands up to get the money from his pants pocket.*]

[*Danzón* **MUSIC** *is heard, and then* **ROCKY ROAD ENTERS** *carrying a cellular phone and pacing nervously. She carries a large purse on her shoulder as though ready to leave the house.*]

XÓCHIL: Look, Don Prisciliano, up there. See? La Rocky Road. What's she doing?

DON PRISCILIANO [*looking up at* ROCKY ROAD]: Pues, what she's been doing all week, m'ijita. Walking back and forth with that newfangled telephone, waiting for the llamada.

XÓCHIL: Who calls her?

DON PRISCILIANO: Pues, como dicen . . . su "main squeeze."

ROCKY ROAD [*willing the phone to ring*]: Ring, dammit, ring.

[*She* FREEZES.]

DON PRISCILIANO: I think it was someone that used to call her every day, a todas horas, and she'd jump in her car and run all over town with him, probably. Pero luego, las llamadas stopped. Pobrecita.

[*Rap* MUSIC *plays.* MAD DOG ENTERS, *strutting.*]

XÓCHIL [*turning toward* MAD DOG]: Here comes that loser, Mad Dog.

DON PRISCILIANO [*also turning*]: Desgraciado pachuco, perro callejero. Stay away from him, Xóchil.

[DON PRISCILIANO *and* XÓCHIL FREEZE. MAD DOG *gives his monologue as he finishes dressing in a ritualistic manner, similar to a matador, buttoning his shirt, combing his hair, folding handkerchief, putting it on as a headband, putting on his shades, etc., as* ALL *in* FREEZE *positon watch him, hypnotized as spectators seeing a cobra coming out of a basket.*]

MAD DOG [*getting ready to face rival gang*]: After I beat up my foster mother's real kid, the welfare said they were going to have to put me in yet *another* foster home. And nobody ever asked me why I beat up the punk. He used to go into the room and sit across from me, drinking this big glass of ice-cold milk. The rest of us foster kids weren't allowed to get into the milk 'cause it was just *his* milk, she said. Me and the other foster kids could just drink some cheap fruit punch she got with the food stamps.

MAD DOG'S FOSTER MOTHER [*offstage*]: Mad Dog! Vente a comer, and don't you dare say nothing about it just being baloney y papas. Pues, ¿qué crees que el welfare money's for millionaires?

MAD DOG: I bet you've never tasted baloney con papas, tomato sauce, and onions. Tastes like shit. Dog shit.

[MAD DOG FREEZES.]

XÓCHIL'S MOTHER [*offstage*]: ¡Xóchil! ¡Apúrate! Your dad's waiting for his tortillas!

[XÓCHIL *breaks* FREEZE.]

XÓCHIL [*to* DON PRISCILIANO, *repeating previous lines*]: For my quinceañera, I'm gonna have fourteen madrinas, and they're gonna each carry a bouquet of white roses with pink and lavender ribbon streamers—my favorite colors—marching into the church like this . . .

[*She* FREEZES, *and* DON PRISCILIANO *breaks his* FREEZE.]

DON PRISCILIANO: Todo el día he tenido un dolorcito right here on my chest. It hurts more when I take a deep breath ... [*breathing deeply*] like this.

[DON PRISCILIANO FREEZES. EL COYOTE ENTERS. *He is not wearing the coyote mask. He is counting money and talking to an unseen "associate."* DON REMIGIO ENTERS.]

DON REMIGIO [*angry, fist up*]: ¡Coyote, maldito! ¡Desgraciado!

[DON REMIGIO FREEZES.]

EL COYOTE: There's five of them: Casimiro and his four friends; it's not worth the risk to cross with less than ten persons, but I'll make an exception just this once porque ya llevan más de tres años juntando el dinero. Yo le dije a Casimiro que les cobraría "group rate"! Cruzaré los cinco esta nochi.

[EL COYOTE FREEZES. MAD DOG *breaks* FREEZE.]

MAD DOG: So I wrote a letter to my sister, BeeBee, in California, asking if I could go live with her and her husband, Brian. She says they live in some apartments that have a swimming pool for everybody to use. A swimming pool. It took her over two months before she finally answered my letter. "Sorry, but Brian thinks that you'd be a bad influence on our younger kids." Can you believe that? A bad influence? Me?

[MAD DOG FREEZES. *A* TELEPHONE *is heard ringing insistently.* ROCKY ROAD *breaks her* FREEZE.]

ROCKY ROAD [*continuing to pace with the phone but doesn't answer it*]: I know exactly what he's gonna say: [*Quoting her* SUGAR DADDY'S *litany of excuses*] "Sorry, sweetheart, but you know how it is, in-laws came into town, had to take them and wife and kids to Sea World, the baby has a temperature, too much sun, I guess, you understand, don't you? Ah, c'mon, don't be like that ..."

[*She throws the telephone into her purse and* FREEZES. MARIEL *breaks her* FREEZE.]

MARIEL: "Nogales, Nogales, rah, rah, rah! [*Jumping up and down, cheering*] ¡Ganamos! ¡Ganamos!"

[MIGUEL, JESÚS, *and* CARLOS ENTER *and join* MARIEL, *jumping and hugging.*]

¡Casimiro! ¡Ven, apúrate! Manuel nos va tomar una foto.

[**MARIEL** *and the male* **FRIENDS** *group themselves as in the photo on* **CASI-MIRO**'s *altar.*]

> [*Insistent*] Casimiro, ven. No vamos a sacar la foto sin ti. Manuel, espera. ¡Casimiro!

[**CASIMIRO ENTERS** *and crosses to* **MARIEL** *and* **FRIENDS** *and joins them in the pose for the camera. He places one arm around* **MARIEL**.]

MANUEL [*offstage*]: Pero no tan serios, you're not at a funeral. ¡Sonrían!

CASIMIRO AND FRIENDS [*in unison, smiling*]: ¡Enchiladas de pollo!

[*There is a* **CAMERA FLASH**, *and* **CASIMIRO** *and* **FRIENDS FREEZE**.]

[*Note to director: By now* **EVERYONE** *should be in a* **FREEZE** *position. Some, but not all, of the* **FREEZES** *will break with* **SOUND CUES**. *Also, some of the lines are intentionally repeated and out of order, overlapping, fast-paced, and without pauses.*]

XÓCHIL'S MOTHER [*offstage*]: ¡Xóchil! ¡Apúrate! Your dad's waiting for his tortillas!

XÓCHIL [*breaking freeze; to* DON PRISCILIANO, *repeating previous lines*]: For my quinceañera, I'm gonna have fourteen madrinas, and they're gonna each carry a bouquet of white roses with pink and lavender ribbon streamers—my favorite colors—marching in to the church like this—

MAD DOG'S FOSTER MOTHER [*offstage*]: Mad Dog! Vente a comer, and don't you dare say nothing about it just being baloney y papas. ¿Qué crees que the welfare money is for millionaires?

MAD DOG [*breaking freeze, taking his gun out*]: So. Fuck the baloney con papas.

DON PRISCILIANO [*breaking freeze*]: Desgraciado pachuco.

ROCKY'S SUGAR DADDY [*offstage, on telephone, caressingly, sexy*]: Sorry, sweetheart, but you know how it is, in-laws came into town, I had to take them and the kids to Sea World, the baby has a temperature, too much sun, I guess, you understand, don't you? Ah, c'mon, don't be like that—

[*As* ROCKY'S SUGAR DADDY *speaks*, ROCKY ROAD *breaks her* FREEZE *and rummages through her purse, taking out bottles of pills.*]

EL COYOTE [*breaking freeze, gun in hand, defensively*]: Hey! It's a dirty job, but someone's gotta do it.

DON REMIGIO [*breaking freeze*]: ¡Coyote, maldito! ¡Desgraciado!

MAD DOG: I'm going out to waste either el Tanque or el Peewa. Maybe both.

EL COYOTE: Let's go to work, kid.

[EL COYOTE *and* MAD DOG *put their guns into their waistbands in the same movement.*]

EL COYOTE [*crossing to* CASIMIRO, *familiarly*]: ¡Casimiro! Amigo mío.

[*He pulls* CASIMIRO *out of the pose, and the four* FRIENDS *remain in* FREEZE.]

¿Ya tienes el dinero pa' cruzar la frontera esta nochi?

CASIMIRO: Sí, I have the money.

EL COYOTE: Pues, it's about time. Ya llevas más de tres años saving for the trip. ¿Y tus amigos? Did you convince them to cross with you?

CASIMIRO: Sí, there's five of us now. Ellos también tienen el dinero.

EL COYOTE [*aside*]: ¡Qué suerte! [*Putting his hand out for the money*] Cinco pollitos!

DON PRISCILIANO: Xóchil, ya que vas a la tiendita, cómprame un frasquito de Vicks. Tengo un dolorcito right here on my chest. No se te olvide. Vicks. I don't want Mentholatum. Tiene que ser Vicks.

[DON PRISCILIANO *hands* XÓCHIL *the money.* XÓCHIL *and the* EL COYOTE *take the money at the same time.*]

EL COYOTE [*to* CASIMIRO]: Hicistes bien, Casimiro, porque así les cobro "group rate"! It's not worth the risk to cross with less than ten persons, but for you, I'll make an exception this time. Cruzaré los cinco esta nochi. I'm taking a loss, tú sabes, pero como eres un buen amigo mío . . . [*Turning to the four* FRIENDS] A la nochi, muchachos, a los United States of America!

[*The* FRIENDS *break* FREEZE. *They prepare for the desert crossing, putting on preset jackets, mochilas with some clothing, water, etc. Talk turns to food—fried chicken, chop suey, etc.*]

MARIEL: ¡Manuel! Saca *otra* foto, anda, no seas malo. ¡Para ti, pa' que te acuerdes de nosotros!

[CASIMIRO *and* FRIENDS *group themselves again, unsmiling.*]

MANUEL [*offstage*]: Okay, pero no tan serios, you're not at a funeral. Acuérdense que se van hacer ricos en los United States of America.

MARIEL: ¡Tú también, Coyote! ¡Ven!

[EL COYOTE *joins them.*]

MANUEL [*offstage*]: Smile!

CASIMIRO, FRIENDS, AND EL COYOTE: Cheeseburgers!

[*They end with a smiling, silly camera pose. There is a* CAMERA FLASH, *and then* CASIMIRO, FRIENDS, *and* EL COYOTE FREEZE.]

EL COYOTE [*breaking freeze*]: Bueno, vámonos, hay que aprovechar la nochi.

DON REMIGIO: Casimiro, m'ijo, aquí puedes cambiar tu destino. Don't listen to him; quédate en México.

CASIMIRO [*breaking freeze and crossing to* DON REMIGIO]: ¿Quedarme *aquí?* ¿Para qué, Abuelo? So that I can end up like my father? Ni tiene los cuarenta años y ya lo ve jorobado como un viejito de noventa, his back bent from carrying los costales de maíz sixteen hours a day. Y yo y mis hermanos sufriendo hambre—eating week-old tortillas—tengo que irme a los Estados Unidos. I'll find a job, fácil. And I'll send all my money to my father, se lo juro. [*Turning to his four* FRIENDS] We'll all find a job. Esta nochi, nos vamos a los Estados Unidos!

[*A mixed, warped blending of Mexican and rap* MUSIC, *then* OUT.]

LIGHTS: DOWN, *shadows.*

[MICTLANTECUHTLI ENTERS *and stands at the top of the center* RAMP. SPOTLIGHT *on* MICTLANTECUHTLI.]

MICTLANTECUHTLI: Ahora, volveremos a esa noche en el pasado. Don Remigio, empezamos.

[SPOTLIGHT *on* DON REMIGIO.]

DON REMIGIO [*praying*]: Vesate sewau hotekate. Sewa valikai, sewau hotekatee.

[*He starts to beat his drum and crosses to his place at the border shooting. He repeats his line softly as he continues to beat his drum.*]

JESÚS, MIGUEL, CARLOS, AND MARIEL [*breaking freeze, in unison*]: Nomás queremos trabajar.

[*They position themselves as in* CASIMIRO'S *dream and start to move slowly, repeating this line softly.*]

XÓCHIL'S MOTHER [*offstage*]: ¡Xóchil! ¡Apúrate! Your dad's waiting for his tortillas!

XÓCHIL: For my quinceañera, I'm gonna have fourteen madrinas, and they're gonna each carry a bouquet of white roses with pink and lavender ribbon streamers—

[*She crosses to her place in the street for the barrio shooting, and repeats this line softly, blending in with the four* FRIENDS' *line.*]

MAD DOG'S FOSTER MOTHER [*offstage*]: Mad Dog! Vente a comer, and don't you dare say nothing about it just being baloney y papas. Pues ¿qué crees que with the welfare money you can eat like a millionaire?

MAD DOG: All I want is for someone to write a corrido about me.

[*He struts to his place in the barrio shooting and keeps repeating this line, until it blends with the four* FRIENDS' *and* XÓCHIL'S *lines.*]

DON PRISCILIANO: Tengo un dolorcito right here, and it hurts when I take a deep breath.

[*He sits down on his chair and keeps repeating this softly, and it, too, blends in with the others.*]

ROCKY ROAD: Ring, phone, ring.

[*She paces, repeating this line softly.*]

EL COYOTE: Hey! It's a dirty job, but someone's gotta do it, ¿qué no?

[*Gun now in his hand,* EL COYOTE *moves stealthily and positions himself, repeating his line softly.* ALL *should now be in their places for the barrio street shooting and the U.S.-Mexico border shooting.* EACH *is repeating his/her lines softly at the same time, almost chanting or praying as* DON REMIGIO *beats the drum rhythmically. Volume increases.* DON REMIGIO *gives one last loud drumbeat, and* ALL *stop chanting at exact same time.*]

LIGHTS: UP.

DON PRISCILIANO [*standing up suddenly and with energy*]: ¡Xóchil! ¡Cuidado! ¡Ahí vienen otros desgraciados pachuco gang members!

[EL TANQUE *and* EL PEEWA ENTER *strutting, menacing.* EL TANQUE *is huge, and* EL PEEWA *is a skinny runt. They are dressed almost identically to* MAD DOG, *with guns showing at their waists.*]

XÓCHIL: El Tanque y el Peewa!

[*Comedy bit.* EL TANQUE *is on* EL PEEWA'S *left side. On* XÓCHIL'S *line, they look at each other, point to selves, and see that they are not in correct order so they do-si-do and change position so that* EL TANQUE *is now on* EL PEEWA'S *right side.*]

EL TANQUE AND EL PEEWA [*together*]: Hey! Ese, Mad Dog Sánchez!

[MAD DOG *turns to them, defiantly and without fear.*]

MAD DOG: That's my name, don't wear it out.

EL TANQUE: Wrong. It *was* your name—

EL PEEWA: Yeah, era tu nombre, past tense, porque te vamos a hacer into dog food, so now it's [*nervous giggle*] Dead Dog.

[MAD DOG, EL TANQUE, *and* EL PEEWA *take out their guns in one quick movement.* JESÚS, CARLOS, MIGUEL, *and* MARIEL, *moving in the desert, get separated.*]

MARIEL: ¡Casimiro! ¡No puedo ver; dame tu mano!

DON PRISCILIANO: ¡Xóchil! ¡No cruces la calle!

[XÓCHIL *is confused and crosses toward* EL TANQUE *and* EL PEEWA. *She turns to* MAD DOG.]

XÓCHIL: Mad Dog! Look out!

[*There is the* SOUND *of a* GUNSHOT. MAD DOG *is wounded.* XÓCHIL *starts to cross to* MAD DOG.]

DON PRISCILIANO: ¡No, Xóchil, no!

MARIEL: ¡Casimiro, dame tu mano!

[EL COYOTE *aims at* MARIEL, *and* EL PEEWA *aims at* XÓCHIL.]

DON REMIGIO: Casimiro! Take Mariel's hand!

MICTLANTECUHTLI: Mad Dog, you're wounded, but you still have time. [*Commanding*] Sálvale la vida a Xóchil.

[CASIMIRO *starts to cross slowly to* MARIEL, *and* MAD DOG *starts to cross slowly to* XÓCHIL. BOTH *move with almost identical movements.* BOTH *stop.*]

DON REMIGIO [*to* CASIMIRO]: Hijo, prove to Mictlantecuhtli and to yourself que *sí* tienes seatakaa, the flower body. Help Mariel now, con buen corazón, and forever change your past. ¡Casimiro! ¡Cambia tu pasado! ¡Salva a Mariel! Save her, m'ijo!

[CASIMIRO *and* MAD DOG *move closer to* MARIEL *and* XÓCHIL. *At the precise moments that the bullets are shot,* CASIMIRO *and* MAD DOG *reach* MARIEL *and* XÓCHIL; *they both move and* CASIMIRO's *and* MAD DOG's *backs are now next to* EL COYOTE *and* EL PEEWA, *who are aiming and ready to shoot.*]

[*There is the* SOUND *of more* GUNSHOTS. CASIMIRO *and* MAD DOG *get shot at the same time.* XÓCHIL *and* MARIEL *try to support and hold the bodies.*]

MICTLANTECUHTLI: We now have the sacrifices, two souls and two bodies: dos almas y dos cuerpos se han sacrificado.

[SOUND EFFECT: *Conch shell.*]

LIGHTS: DOWN.

[JESÚS, MIGUEL, CARLOS, EL TANQUE, EL PEEWA, ROCKY ROAD, DON PRISCILIANO, *and* EL COYOTE EXIT.]

LIGHTS: UP.

MICTLANTECUHTLI: Mariel, you may return to the land of the living— to that night twenty years ago. You will work in Manuel's camera shop and eventually become a professional photographer there in your pueblito and buy him out.

MARIEL [*slowly letting go of* CASIMIRO *as he falls to the floor*]: Casimiro, you've been too hard on yourself. All these years, blaming yourself for what happened. Tú no sabías que el coyote nos iba a traicionar; besides, it wasn't your fault. We were to blame, too. We were young and caught up in the excitement of crossing the border, and we took that risk.

[*She* EXITS.]

MICTLANTECUHTLI: Xóchil, you will return to the land of the living and take your father his tortillas before his sopita de fideo gets cold, and help your mother with all those silly table decorations you want for your quinceañera fiesta.

XÓCHIL: They're not silly! They're pink and lavender Jordan almonds wrapped in white veil with a good-luck charm.

MICTLANTECUHTLI: And you, Mad Dog Sánchez, stand up!

[MAD DOG *stands up.*]

MAD DOG: I know. You don't have to tell me; I'm not going back. I took that bullet for Xóchil, right?

MICTLANTECUHTLI: No, you're not going back. Only Mariel and Xóchil can return.

MAD DOG: But you said there was no place here in Mictlán for people like me. Stupid.

MICTLANTECUHTLI: Sí, es cierto, te dije que there was no place for you here in Mictlán, but that was before you saved Xóchil. *Now* there is a place for you, a very special place. Ven.

[MAD DOG *crosses to* MICTLANTECUHTLI.]

I want you to know that I'm making a great exception here. [*Removing* MAD DOG's *headband and tossing it aside*] Gang members who kill each other or who kill innocent bystanders do not come to Mictlán, much less to be among the brave guerreros who die in real battle.

MAD DOG: ¿Guerreros? I'm gonna live with the warriors?

MICTLANTECUHTLI: Sí, porque you've done a very heroic act—más o menos—by taking that second bullet aimed at Xóchil, you will now reside in Tonatiuhilhuicac and ride with the sun god, Tonatiuh, on his daily journey across the sky for four years.

[MICTLANTECUHTLI *places a magnificent headdress of sunrays on* MAD DOG's *head.* MAD DOG *preens proudly.*]

XÓCHIL [*looking over her shoulder as she exits*]: Uuhhh, Mad Dog, you look like a god!

MAD DOG: The name's Daniel. Daniel Sánchez.

XÓCHIL: Uuhhh, Daniel Sánchez, you look like a god!

MICTLANTECUHTLI: Después de los cuatro años, you will return to earth as a hummingbird or a butterfly. And then, if you're really lucky, you'll end up in Xóchil's garden!

XÓCHIL AND MAD DOG: Cool.

[XÓCHIL *and* MAD DOG EXIT.]

LIGHTS: DOWN.

MUSIC: *Indigenous, with violin.*

DON REMIGIO [*crossing to* CASIMIRO *and praying as he removes* CASIMIRO's *shoes*]: Vesate sewau hotekate. Sewa valikai. Sewai hotekate ne Casimiro Flores, sewa walikai, sewai hotekatee.

[CASIMIRO *stands up slowly.*]

Ahora, sí, m'ijo, puedes cumplir la manda y bailar La Danza del Venado.

MUSIC: "*La danza del venado.*"

[CASIMIRO *starts to dance—at first slowy, then faster, assured and skillfully.*]

MICTLANTECUHTLI: Already we sit down to the flower, para recibir la flor, we sit down to the flower—

DON REMIGIO [*continuing to pray*]: Vesate sewau hotekate. Sewa valikai, sewau hotekatee.

CASIMIRO: Yo, Casimiro Flores—

MUSIC: UP.

SPECIAL EFFECT: *Thousands of flower petals and blossoms float down over and around* CASIMIRO.

LIGHTS: DOWN *and* OUT.

FIVE

Anhelos por Oaxaca

(Yearnings for Oaxaca)

Synopsis

Anhelos por Oaxaca is the story of Don Felipe and his grandson Rudy. Don Felipe, who is in his mid-sixties, is an impatient, grouchy, retired rail-road worker who lives with his daughter Amelia in Tucson, Arizona. He is very critical of Rudy, who doesn't seem to have any manners or respect for his grandfather, and worse, refuses to speak Spanish even though he understands it. Don Felipe shows a very gruff exterior, and he very casu-ally calls anyone or anything a "cabrón" or other "bad words." Underneath his gruff exterior, however, Don Felipe hides a tender, sensitive side that he has never been able to reveal to anyone. When he receives word from Mexico that his older brother, Antonio, has had a very serious heart attack, Don Felipe impulsively decides to go visit him in Cuilapan, Oaxaca. Ame-lia knows that her father's health and memory are slipping, but since she cannot get off work to accompany him, a very reluctant Rudy is forced to leave his girlfriend, rock concert, and flavored yogurt to go on the train trip with his grumpy grandfather.

Don Felipe has not spoken to his brother since the death of their father forty years prior. Hurt and angry that his father left his ranch in Antonio's name only, Don Felipe decided to come to the United States. He begged his fiancée, Juanita, a flower vendor, to come with him, but she refused to leave her ailing mother and family obligations. Don Felipe left Mexico, went to work for the railroad, married Marta, and had a daughter, Amelia. When his wife Marta dies, Don Felipe brings his twelve-year-old Amelia to visit his dying mother, but he and Antonio do not speak to each other. And now, twenty years later, Don Felipe has a premonition that Antonio may die before they make peace.

In flashbacks, Don Felipe re-creates the angry conversation with his brother, Juanita's refusal to leave Mexico with him, and his imagined last visit with Amelia before his death.

Before they leave Mexico, Rudy helps the Cuilapan baseball team beat their rival Coyotepec, and Don Felipe finally expresses his love for Rudy. Rudy has learned his manners, speaks Spanish, and loves to eat taquitos de lengua, gorditas de flor de calabaza, and even the Oaxacan delicacy, grass-hoppers! On the last day of the visit, the family gathers to send off a very happy Rudy and an ailing Don Felipe. They both promise to return next year. But Don Felipe will die at the Mexican bus station as he waits for his bus to return to the United States. His death, however, is joyful, and his life ends in a surrealistic dance with Juanita, a woman in black, Rudy, Amelia, his relatives, and other passengers.

Cast

With the exception of Rudy and Don Felipe, all other roles may be doubled with layered costumes and different hats, etc., for quick changes. Please note that it is suggested that Young Antonio and Antonio, Juanita and the Flower Vendor, and the Bag Lady and Woman in Black each be played by the same actor.

DON FELIPE, *age sixty-five*
RUDY, *his grandson, age fifteen*
AMELIA, *his daughter and Rudy's mother, age thirty-four*
TEENAGERS at Greyhound bus station
BAG LADY, *age unknown, played by the same actress as Woman in Black*
WOMAN IN BLACK, *age unknown, played by the same actress as Bag Lady*
YOUNG ANTONIO, *Don Felipe's brother, age twenty-six*
PASSENGERS at Greyhound bus station, *all ages*
TRAIN PASSENGERS or VENDORS:
    DON MANUEL, *very informed traveler*
    CANDY VENDOR, *singsongs memorized candy choices*
    FEMALE PASSENGER, *know-it-all interrupter*
    NEWSPAPER VENDOR, *similar to Candy Vendor*
    LOVER BOY, *young male, deeply in love with Lover Girl*
    LOVER GIRL, *young female, deeply in love with Lover Boy*
    YOUNG MAN, *eating and sharing oranges*
    MÚSICO, *musician who asks for requests and sings them*
    GRINGA TOURIST, *loves Mexico, music, and language*
    JUANITA, *Don Felipe's fiancée*
    FLOWER VENDOR, *played by same actress as Juanita*
ANTONIO, *age sixty-seven, Young Antonio all grown up*
ORALIA, *in her mid-sixties, Antonio's wife*
TOÑITO, *in his thirties, Antonio and Oralia's son*
ARMANDO, *age fifteen or sixteen, Toñito's son*
ANGELITA and TEENAGERS in Mexico
PASSENGERS at bus station in Mexico
VARIOUS VENDORS at bus station in Mexico
TOURIST, *male or female, who listens to Rudy's lecture about mole*

Technical Notes

The set is minimal, mostly boxes of various sizes and ramps if available. The time is in the 1980s, and the play covers a passage of ten or so days.

MUSIC

As indicated, or other music may be selected. The music should match the setting or mood: Oaxacan for Don Felipe at beginning, modern for Rudy in United States, norteña on train, marimba in Oaxaca (just because it's Don Felipe's favorite), and Oaxacan at the end.

ACT I

Scene 1

TIME: *Around noon.*

PLACE: *A living room in Tucson, Arizona.*

LIGHTS: UP.

MUSIC: *Introduction to "La danza de la pluma" (Oaxacan).*

[DON FELIPE, *dressed in pants, undershirt, and shoes, is standing over an open suitcase.*]

DON FELIPE [*talking to himself as he checks the contents of his suitcase*]: A ver, a ver. Mis camisas, pantalones, ropa interior, camisetas, calcetines. [*Closing suitcase*] Uno no debe empacar demasiado cuando se va en un viaje. ¿Para qué? Uno siempre puede lavar la ropa sucia en donde quiera que ande. No quiero ir cargado como burro. [*Picking up the suitcase and hefting it to check the weight*] Ummm, está bien, no muy pesado. Así debe ser. Los que no saben, siempre empacan de más, y luego se joden cargándolo.

[*He takes his handkerchief from his back pants pocket and wipes his forehead. He is slightly out of breath.* RUDY ENTERS, *dressed casually and carrying a ghetto blaster playing at full volume. He crosses the stage, ignoring* DON FELIPE *totally.*]

DON FELIPE [*seeing* RUDY]: Buenos días, animal mal-educado. ¡Buenos días!

[RUDY EXITS *without acknowledging* DON FELIPE. DON FELIPE *continues talking to himself.*]

Nadita de respeto. [*Sitting down, grumbling*] Ni un grano de respeto. [*Remembering suddenly*] ¡La caja de los regalos! Ya casi se me olvidaba la caja de los regalos. ¿Pero cómo se me iban olvidar los regalos?

[*He* EXITS, *talking to himself, and then re-*ENTERS *quickly with a small cardboard box.*]

Es lo primero que los parientes allá en México quieren ver. Qué les lleva uno de aquí de los Estados Unidos. Cualquier cosita, nomás que sea algo de aquí. Pues no faltaba más. [*Checking box and taking a pair of binoculars out from their case*] Los miralejos para mi hermano, Antonio.

[*He fiddles with the binoculars and adjusts the knobs. He checks out the room, the floor, and his shoes. He is looking at his shoes intently when* AMELIA ENTERS. *She is wearing a bright chartreuse green dress. She crosses slowly to* DON FELIPE, *who hasn't heard her come in. She stands in front of him as he slowly moves the binoculars up from his shoes to her face.* AMELIA *makes an ugly face into the binoculars and startles him.*]

DON FELIPE: ¡Ay, cabrona, me asustaste!

AMELIA [*teasing him*]: Oh, Dad, you knew it was me. And don't you keep cussing. Remember, they don't let you talk that way at the ranch. Especially my tía Oralia.

DON FELIPE: Sí, yo sé cómo son allá. Pero me asustaste.

AMELIA: I scared you? Why, Dad?

DON FELIPE: Pues, te me pareciste a una campamocha verde y radioactiva.

AMELIA: What's a campamocha?

DON FELIPE: Bueno, también la llaman mantis religiosa.

AMELIA: Oh, you mean a praying mantis?

DON FELIPE: Esa mera, pero ni tan religiosa porque después que reza se come su amante. Pero, también te pareces a un caballito del diablo.

AMELIA: I looked like a devil's pony? What do you mean?

DON FELIPE: Pues un caballito del diablo es un ... dragonfly. ¡Sí, ésa es la palabra ... "dragonfly"! ¡Aunque en español esa mosquita no tiene nada que ver con caballitos ni con el diablo, y en inglés no tiene nada que ver con dragones ni con moscas!

[*He laughs at his wit.*]

AMELIA: Okay. So, why do I look like a radioactive dragonfly?

DON FELIPE: Pues, sí, m'ija, ni más ni menos, con ese vestido verde tan chillante.

AMELIA [*changing the subject*]: So, what are you doing with the binoculars you're taking to my tío Antonio?

DON FELIPE: Los estoy probando. Amelia, ¿crees que le van a gustar a mi hermano?

AMELIA: Sure, Dad. But if he's sick in bed, I don't think he's going to want to run around with binoculars, do you?

DON FELIPE: Déjate de "sick in bed." Yo voy ir y lo voy hacer que se levante. Yo lo digo por experiencia, Amelia. Entre más te quedas en la cama, *más* enfermo te pones. Mírame a mí, fuerte y saludable. Achaques quiere la muerte.

AMELIA [*not wanting to argue with him, changing the subject again*]: Where's the case for the binoculars?

DON FELIPE: Aquí, dentro de la caja, pero me los voy a llevar puestos. Así los puedo probar y puedo ver el paisaje a la misma vez. Y segundo, no los quiero llevar en esta caja por si acaso se pierde la caja en algún trastorno, ya sabes cómo corren los trenes allá en México. Y por último, así puestos no me los estrujan los perros en la aduana. ¿Y el Rudy? ¿Adónde está?

AMELIA: Getting ready. Didn't you see him come in just now? I'll go get him. [*Starting to cross, but then stopping*] Don't tie up the box yet. I have to pack my tío's sweater and my tía Oralia's makeup.

DON FELIPE: Makeup? Tu tía Oralia no usa esas cochinadas. Mi cuñada es una "natural beauty" como María Félix.

AMELIA: María Félix? Yeah, right. She'll like it.

[*She* EXITS.]

DON FELIPE [*calling after her*]: Dile al Rudy que se apure, con mil demonios. ¿Qué cree que'l cabrón camión lo va esperar hasta que termine de peinarse? [*To himself*] Esta juventud de hoy en día no le tiene ni un grano de respeto a la puntualidad. Ni a la autoridad. [*Yelling again*] ¡Amelia! Voy a subir mi maleta al carro; dile al inservible que se apure. [*Crossing with his suitcase, still grumbling*] Pero, si no respetan a sus chingados abuelos, ¿a quién chingados van a respetar?

[DON FELIPE EXITS, *grumbling.* AMELIA *and* RUDY ENTER. RUDY *is eating yogurt, and* AMELIA *is pushing him in front of her.*]

AMELIA: C'mon, Rudy, hurry; you know how impatient your tata gets.

RUDY: We still have plenty of time. I still don't see why we have to be at the Greyhound so early. I could've had a hot lunch.

[*He sits down and keeps eating his yogurt.*]

AMELIA: Buy something at the Greyhound.

[*She* EXITS.]

RUDY: Greyhound? Grody. [*Yelling*] And I don't see why I have to go with him. You go.

[**AMELIA ENTERS** *with* **RUDY**'s *backpack.*]

AMELIA [*kneeling next to the backpack and checking contents*]: I already told you. I can't get off work.

RUDY: Well, why can't he go alone?

AMELIA: Rudy, don't start. It's just for one week. It won't kill you to be without Kimberly for one week, will it?

RUDY: Yeah, it will. And it's more than one week counting the days on the stupid train. Do you know how many days it's gonna take just to reach . . . where are we going?

AMELIA: Oaxaca. Oaxaca. [*Refolding his clothes*] You'd better learn to say it, in case you get lost. Say it: Oaxaca.

RUDY [*with mouth full*]: Wah-ca-ca.

AMELIA: Mírame: Oa-xa-ca.

RUDY: Does it start with a *w*?

AMELIA: No, there's no *w*. [*Spelling*] O-a-x-a-c-a. Oaxaca.

RUDY: *X*? I didn't hear any *x*.

AMELIA: Because the *x* sounds like "ja" in Spanish. You know, like the *h* in English.

RUDY: Well, why don't they just use an *h* then? They just like to make things difficult.

[*He puts the yogurt container on the floor under his feet.*]

AMELIA: I hope you learn Spanish when you're in Mexico, burro. Pocho. You should be ashamed of yourself for not knowing how to speak Spanish.

RUDY: But, Mom, who needs it? I'm an American citizen, and I don't want to speak Spanish. Spanish is for *old* people like Grandpa, who thinks he's still living in Mexico. And anyway, what's speaking Spanish gonna do for me, huh? Get me a quick order of tacos?

AMELIA [*picking up the yogurt container*]: I bet you if Kimberly spoke Spanish, then you'd speak it, too.

[*She* **EXITS.**]

RUDY: Kimberly! [*Calling out to* AMELIA] I promised Kim I'd call her before we left. Thanks for reminding me, Mom.

[**RUDY EXITS,** *and* **DON FELIPE ENTERS.**]

DON FELIPE: Amelia, no se te olvide que ya le pagué al muchacho de la vecina—

[**AMELIA ENTERS.** *She is carrying a red sweater, makeup, and candy bars.*]

AMELIA: Warren, 'Apá. Se llama Warren.

DON FELIPE: Sí, [*pronouncing it with an accent*] el Warren. Pobrecito. ¿Por qué le pusieron ese nombre tan feo? Warren. [*Putting on his shirt*] ¿Qué clase de nombre es ese? De seguro que no es nombre de santo.

[**AMELIA** *is too busy removing price tags from the sweater to answer him. She folds the sweater and places it in the box along with the makeup and candy bars.*]

DON FELIPE: Pues, quiero que me riegue bien mis matitas. Despacito. Y no como un burro meando en la arena seca. Des-pa-cito. Tú dile que le voy a pedir que me devuelva todo mi dinero si vengo y hallo mis matitas secas. O muertas. Tú dile, Amelia.

[**RUDY ENTERS** *quietly and kneels by his backpack. He has changed clothing and is wearing brightly colored floral shorts and shirt, shower thongs or sandals, and wild fluorescent shades.* **DON FELIPE** *checks him out with disapproval and disbelief.*]

¿Y este? ¿Adónde cree que va en esas fachas?

RUDY [*annoyed*]: What's wrong with him now?

DON FELIPE [*mispronouncing "shorts"*]: Tus eshorts. No puedes ir a México en eshorts. ¿Qué va decir la gente? Que eres un animal mal-educado, *eso* van a decir.

RUDY: Why can't I wear shorts?

DON FELIPE: No, no, no. Conmigo no vas a ninguna parte vestido como un turista gringo que apenas se bajó del "Love Boat" en Mazatlán. No, no, no.

RUDY [*standing up, angrily*]: That's it, then. I won't go. Don't tell me the Mexicans there don't wear shorts. What kind of place are we going to, anyway?

DON FELIPE: Pues, no vayas; I don't care. Prefiero ir solo que con un payaso. Llévame al Greyhound, Amelia.

[**DON FELIPE** *picks up the box of presents and crosses to* **EXIT**.]

AMELIA: Wait, Dad. [*To* RUDY] M'ijo, put your jeans over your shorts.

RUDY: It's too hot. I want to wear shorts.

AMELIA: You can take them off once you're on the train when your tata doesn't notice.

[**RUDY EXITS**.]

DON FELIPE: ¿Cómo que no voy a notice? ¡Qué creen que estoy ciego, o que ojos de hacha! [*Checking his watch*] Hazlo que se apure, Amelia.

[*He and* **AMELIA** *are tying the box with string.*]

Ya lo veo en el espejo con el "blow dryer." ¿Lo va a llevar a México?

[**AMELIA** *shrugs.*]

Sácalo del baño, Amelia. [*Moving her hands away from the string*] El Greyhound a Nogales sale a las meras tres. Los americanos aquí no andan con pretextos: que'l Greyhound se tardó, que no funciona el aire, que no hay agua, que los escusados están tapados. No señor, toditito a su merita hora. No quiero perder el camión a Nogales; sácalo del baño ahoritita mismo.

[**AMELIA EXITS** *and* **DON FELIPE** *yells after her.*]

¡Y dile que no lleve el "blow dryer" a México porque no hay electricidad en México!

[*He chuckles.*]

[*Offstage* **MUSIC** *is heard.* **RUDY ENTERS**, *his radio's playing loudly.* **AMELIA ENTERS**.]

AMELIA: Lower the radio, Rudy!

[**RUDY** *lowers the volume and kneels to pack his tapes into his backpack.*]

DON FELIPE: Vale más que lleves muchas baterías para esa mierda porque ya te digo que no hay electricidad en México.

RUDY [*to* AMELIA]: No electricity? [*Throwing his backpack down and standing up*] That's it! I won't go. I'm not going anywhere that doesn't have electricity. He can go alone. I don't care if he's sick or not. I'm not going with him.

DON FELIPE: Sick? ¿Quién está "sick"? Mi hermano está enfermo, pero se va sentir mucho mejor nomás me vea llegar, van a ver.

AMELIA: Never mind, Dad. Let's go.

RUDY: I'm not going. Why should I? He criticizes everything I do. Nothing satisfies him. And so what if he talks to himself? He doesn't need me.

DON FELIPE [*ignoring* RUDY *completely*]: ¿Amelia, no has visto mi sombrerito? Yo no salgo de esta casa sin mi sombrero. ¿Adónde está?

AMELIA: On the kitchen table, Dad. Remember? When you had your coffee?

DON FELIPE [*arguing as he crosses to exit*]: ¿En la mesa? No, no, señor. ¿Pero por qué lo voy a dejar en la mesa? Estás segura que no lo dejé afuera cuando fui con el vecino . . .

[DON FELIPE EXITS.]

AMELIA [*explaining patiently*]: M'ijo, can't you see why your tata can't go alone? He's forgetting too many things. He could get off the train at the wrong place. Anything could happen to him. Please, Rudy, I don't even want him to go in the first place, but he's too stubborn. You have to go with him.

RUDY: But, Mom, they don't even want him there. You told me his brother hasn't even talked to him in over forty years.

AMELIA: But that's exactly why it's so important for your tata now. My tío Antonio had a very serious heart attack, and now my dad's afraid his brother's going to die before they make peace. Please, Rudy. This trip means a lot to him.

RUDY: But he's sick, too. What if he—

[DON FELIPE ENTERS *with his old, beat-up hat in his hands.*]

DON FELILPE: ¿Ya ves, Amelia? ¿No te dije que lo dejé en la mesa cuando tomé mi café?

[RUDY *and* AMELIA *exchange knowing look.*]

AMELIA [*softly*]: Please, Rudy . . . Please, m'ijo.

RUDY [*reluctantly*]: All right, Mom.

AMELIA: Thanks. And don't worry, your tata was just teasing you, Rudy. Of course there's electricity in Mexico. And at the ranch. Do you have the earphones?

[RUDY *nods yes and gets them out of his backpack.*]

[*To* DON FELIPE] ¿Ya ve, Dad? You don't have to listen to his music.

DON FELIPE: ¿Y entonces de qué demonios me va servir si va ir ploguiado con esas mierdas de orejas? Mejor debería viajar con una estatua pendeja. Estorbo inservible, ¿cómo voy a platicar con él?

RUDY: Okay, I missed all that. What's he bitching about now?

AMELIA [*exasperated*]: Nothing. Let's go.

[AMELIA *gets her car keys and purse and* EXITS *with the box.* RUDY *adjusts his earphones and is soon listening to the music, oblivious to* DON FELIPE'*s lecture.*]

DON FELIPE [*putting on his jacket as he talks to* RUDY]: Yo te quiero para compañía en el viaje. Para tener con quien platicar. Un viaje puede ser muy aburrido si va uno solo. Bueno, uno siempre encuentra con quien platicar, pero yo quiero enseñarte todo de México, así como le enseñé a tu mamá. Ella tampoco quería ir conmigo cuando la llevé, después que murió Marta, tu abuela. ¿Pero sabes? Tu mamá fue una compañera de viaje muy buena. En el tren. En el rancho. Bueno, allá fue muy traviesa, pregúntale a cualquiera; ellos te dirán de las tremendas aventuras de Amelia. Y ella era mucho más joven que tú. Pero muy traviesa. [*Sitting down with his hat in his hands, playing with it*] ¿Sabes, Rudy? Yo quiero que conozcas México. Y Oaxaca. [*Yearningly*] Mi Oaxaca. Hace más de veinte años que no veo mi Oaxaca. Cuilapan, Oaxaca, tan hermoso mi pueblito.

[DON FELIPE *is lost in his memories as* RUDY *keeps beat to his music.* DON FELIPE *sighs and turns to* RUDY.]

[*Glaring at* RUDY, *annoyed*] Pero no, vas ir pegado con esas orejas de liebre. [*Hitting* RUDY *with his hat, then putting the hat on and crossing, talking to himself*] Oaxaca. Oaxaca de mis sueños, de todos mis anhelos. [*Starting to sing parts of "Llorona"*] "Ay de mí, llorona, llorona de ayer y hoy. Y aunque la vida me cueste, llorona, no dejaré de quererte . . ."

[*He* EXITS.]

[*Singing offstage*] ". . . Y aunque la vida me cueste, llorona, no dejaré de quererte . . ."

[RUDY *looks up and sees that he's alone. He removes his headphones and puts them into his backpack. He puts on the backpack, picks up his radio, raises the volume, and* EXITS, *singing along with the music on his radio.*]

LIGHTS: DOWN.

END OF SCENE 1

* * *

Scene 2

TIME: *Around 1 p.m.*

PLACE: *Greyhound bus station.*

LIGHTS: UP.

MUSIC: *Mid-1980s teenage favorite.*

[*There is general hubbub, with* PASSENGERS *arriving, talking, moving, etc.* DON FELIPE *and* AMELIA *are sitting on a bench.* RUDY *and other* TEEN-AGERS *are grouped away from* DON FELIPE *and* AMELIA, *near a telephone booth. A* BAG LADY *wanders around unobtrusively, talking to herself.*]

AMELIA [*to* DON FELIPE, *who is searching his shirt pockets*]: ¿Qué busca, Dad? Your tickets?

DON FELIPE: No, no, no. Tengo todo aquí en el sobre de la agencia de viajes. Todo bien preparado. Busco mis dulcecitos para el ácido del estómago. Tengo un poco de acedía. ¿Qué comí que me hizo daño, Amelia?

AMELIA: Nada, 'Apá. You didn't want to eat anything because you were too busy packing.

DON FELIPE: Ah, eso fue entonces, por no haber comido. ¿O sería el café? Vale más que compre los dulcecitos aquí por si no los encuentro allá en México. [*Standing up and yelling out to* RUDY] ¡Cuida las maletas, muchacho inservible!

[*He* EXITS.]

RUDY [*crossing to* AMELIA, *irritated*]: How come he always calls me that: [*pronouncing it very Anglo-sounding*] "inservible"? What does it mean anyway?

[*He sits next to* AMELIA.]

AMELIA: "Inservible" means "useless."

RUDY: Useless!

AMELIA [*quickly*]: But he doesn't mean it, Rudy. That's just the way my dad talks. He's really glad you're going with him.

RUDY: Well, he sure doesn't show it, does he?

AMELIA: Maybe not, but this trip means a lot to him. Pobrecito. So be nice—it won't kill you to give up a week of your life for him.

RUDY: Yeah, it will, and it's more than a week, counting the days on the stupid train . . .

[DON FELIPE ENTERS *and stands, somewhat confused. All conversations become louder, and movements become stylized and slow. The* BAG LADY *wanders around the stage, picking up empty soda cans, talking and singing to herself like changing radio stations.* DON FELIPE *watches her intently.*]

BAG LADY [*repeating everything again until she's back to the place where she started*]: An eye for an eye. If God had wanted people to fly, He would've given them wings. From Washington, the cost of living allowance vote was close. "Don't cry for me, Argentina." Memorial Day Sale at the Heavenly Hills Mall. Every time they test a nuclear bomb on the Bikini Islands, it's a proven fact that people's hair and teeth fall out. The astronauts didn't land on the moon, it was all filmed in a warehouse in the Nevada desert, and when Susan Hayward and Gary Cooper brought the sand back for their driveways in Hollywood, they soon died of cancer. "Don't cry for me, Argentina . . ."

[DON FELIPE *struggles to compose himself. He appears dizzy. He takes deep breaths and crosses unsteadily to* AMELIA *and* RUDY.]

AMELIA: Dad, what's wrong? ¿Qué tiene?

DON FELIPE: Nada, Amelia, nada. Parece que tengo un dolorcito de cabeza nomás. Pero ya se me está yendo. Es el calor. Ya me muero por llegar a Oaxaca. Ése sí que es un clima hermoso, no como el de aquí. Un calor de la chin—

AMELIA: Are you sure you're okay?

DON FELIPE: Te digo que no es nada. [*Changing the subject*] Fíjate que desgraciados, Amelia. [*Showing her antacids*] Estos cuestan treinta y cinco centavos en el Safeway, y aquí—adivina cuánto me costaron. Y no son nada más que azúcar.

RUDY: Mom, can I have a quarter to call Kim?

DON FELIPE: No, no, no. No te me vayas; aquí quédate. Ahorita ya van anunciar el camión para Nogales.

RUDY: Yeah, right. We still have two more hours. C'mon, Mom.

AMELIA [*giving him money and teasing him*]: Ten, m'ijo, but pay attention, the bus might leave without you.

RUDY [*crossing to telephone*]: Not even.

AMELIA [*taking a watch from inside her purse*]: Mire, 'Apá, I bought this watch for my cousin, Toñito, and I almost forgot to give it to you to take it to him. Pay attention 'cause it's a very special watch, and I want you to teach Toñito how to use it.

DON FELIPE: No seas sencilla, Amelia; pues si es un reloj es un cabrón reloj, ¿no? Nomás se usa para dar la hora.

AMELIA: Yes, but look, Dad, this watch also has a calendar. See? And it also gives you the phone numbers you put in it.

DON FELIPE [*impressed, taking the watch from her*]: ¿A poco? ¿Un reloj que da la fecha y los números de teléfono? A ver, a ver si es cierto.

[*He shakes the watch like a thermometer until* AMELIA *takes it away from him quickly before he breaks it.*]

AMELIA: See? You press this . . . or this. It's already set for our time, but if you have to change it to Oaxaca time, it gets a bit complicated. And he has to enter the phone numbers that he wants. Anyway here's the instructions, but they're in English. Maybe Rudy can set it for him over there, okay?

[*She gives him the watch and instructions.*]

DON FELIPE: Pero, mira nomás, es increíble que una cosa tan chiquita pueda hacer tanto.

[*Pause.*]

[*Joking*] Dime, Amelia, ¿también puede este reloj tocar "El torito," como la banda de Sinaloa?

[*He puts the watch to his ear and pretends to listen.*]

AMELIA: Play the what? [*Getting the joke*] Oh, Dad.

DON FELIPE [*continuing to pull her leg*]: En serio, Amelia, dicen que los japoneses ya inventaron un reloj que toca, "Oh, say can you see." Para los juegos de pelota.

AMELIA [*believing him*]: Well, this one doesn't play anything. But tell Toñito that I'll send him one of those the next time you go.

DON FELIPE: Pues el otro año que entra, con el favor de Dios. Quiero ir cada año mientras Dios me preste vida. Mi pobre hermano, enfermo, haciéndose viejo, y yo aquí, disfrutando de la vida americana. Tanto año sin ver a mi hermano. [*Pausing as he reflects*] ¿Cuántos años, Amelia?

AMELIA: A ver, we went in '62 . . . '63? No, it was '62. I remember because I was almost twelve.

DON FELIPE: Sí, dices bien. Era en mil novecientos sesenta y dos.

AMELIA: Over twenty years ago! God, that makes me feel so old.

[*Pause.*]

So, how old is my tío Antonio anyway?

DON FELIPE: Todavía está bien joven mi hermano. Apenas celebró sus sesenta y siete años—me gana con dos años.

AMELIA: He'll be glad to see you, ¿verdad?

DON FELIPE: Pues, a ver, quién sabe. En la última carta que recibí de su hijo Toñito, me dijo que mi hermano está muy enfermo. Que desde que le dio el ataque de corazón, no quiere moverse de la silla de ruedas. No quiere hablar. Nada. No quiere hacer nada.

AMELIA: Well, Dad, I hope you two make up and stop fighting. You're both too old to be fighting like little kids.

DON FELIPE: Pues, no soy yo. No, no, no. *Él* es el mula que no me quiso hablar. ¿Te acuerdas cuando fuimos tú y yo? ¿Para que conocieras a tu abuelita antes que ella muriera? Antonio todavía estaba enojado porque me vine a los Estados Unidos, y él no quiso ni entrar al mismo cuarto en donde estaba yo, ¿te acuerdas?

[*Pause.*]

Pero estoy seguro que me va a hablar esta vez. Es mi hermano, y está muy enfermo. [*Getting agitated*] Pero él siempre ha sido muy terco; *él* es el testarudo, no *yo*. No, no, no, señor.

RUDY [*calling out from the phone booth*]: Mom, c'mere. Kim wants to talk to you. Hurry.

[AMELIA *crosses to* RUDY. DON FELIPE, *confused, keeps talking to* AMELIA.]

DON FELIPE: Yo le dije, Amelia, "¿Con que nuestro padre te dejó a ti el rancho, Antonio? Pues quédate con él. Yo ya me voy."

[*He stands up with his suitcase in his hand.*]

LIGHTS: DOWN.

[FLASHBACK *begins. A* PASSENGER, *wearing cowboy shirt and Levi's, boots, and hat, crosses to center stage and becomes* YOUNG ANTONIO, DON FELIPE'*s brother.*]

YOUNG ANTONIO: No te vayas, Felipe. Quédate.

DON FELIPE: No, Antonio, yo aquí no me quedo ni un día más.

YOUNG ANTONIO: ¿Pero por qué, Felipe?

DON FELIPE: ¿Por qué? Todavía tienes el nervio de preguntarme "¿por qué?" Nuestro padre te dejó el rancho a ti, y eso no es justo.

YOUNG ANTONIO: Nadie te pide que te vayas. El rancho nos pertenece a los dos; no hay ningún motivo para que te vayas a ningún otro lugar. Este rancho nos pertenece a los dos.

DON FELIPE: ¡A mí no me pertenece nada! Nuestro padre te dejó el rancho a ti nomás. ¡No es mío!

YOUNG ANTONIO: Felipe, el rancho solo está a mi nombre por ser yo el mayor. Eres mi hermano; siempre hemos trabajado la tierra juntos . . . Nada ha cambiado.

DON FELIPE: ¡Todo ha cambiado! Nuestro padre te dejó el rancho. Es hora que yo camine por otro sendero, ¿no crees? Solo. Cuando mi padre era el dueño, tú y yo trabajábamos para él. Ahora tú eres el dueño y yo no quiero trabajar para ti. ¿Me entiendes? Como dicen, "En un barco, solo un capitán." ¿Y tú? Quédate tú con el rancho, Antonio.

YOUNG ANTONIO: Entonces, ¿para dónde vas?

DON FELIPE: No sé. Al norte. A los Estados Unidos. Tengo veinte y cuatro años y ya es hora que yo empiece mi familia con Juanita.

YOUNG ANTONIO: Tú y yo sabemos muy bien que Juanita jamás se irá de México.

[DON FELIPE *starts to cross past* YOUNG ANTONIO.]

YOUNG ANTONIO: No te vayas, Felipe. [*Trying to block him*] Cambiaremos los nombres en la hipoteca; eso es lo de menos. Mañana vamos con el notario público—

DON FELIPE [*pushing him away*]: No, no y no. Te digo que no, Antonio.

LIGHTS: UP.

[FLASHBACK *ends.*]

END OF SCENE 2

* * *

Scene 3

[YOUNG ANTONIO *turns away from* DON FELIPE *and becomes a* PASSENGER *again.* DON FELIPE *returns to his old self, confused, suitcase in hand, repeating "no, no, no" until* AMELIA *and* RUDY *rush to him.*]

AMELIA: No, what, Dad? What's wrong? ¿Apá, qué tiene?

DON FELIPE: Nada, Amelia . . . nada.

[*Pause.*]

¿Qué compraste?

AMELIA: I bought a map of Mexico for Rudy. See? [*Showing him the map of Mexico*] That way he can go marking the towns he passes on the train, ¿verdad? [*To* RUDY] That's what I did, Rudy, when I went to Oaxaca with Dad. It makes the trip go much faster.

[RUDY *rolls his eyes, takes the map, sits down, and unfolds it.*]

RUDY: God! Look how far we're going. It's farther than to New York. Twice.

AMELIA: No, it isn't.

RUDY: I bet it's over a thousand miles.

AMELIA [*irritated*]: So what if it is? The more you bitch about it, the longer it'll be.

[*Pause.*]

M'ijo, you're gonna like it once you get there. My cousin Toñito has a son your age, ¿verdad, Dad?

DON FELIPE: Sí, se llama Armando.

AMELIA: Rudy, you'll like all your cousins. At first they're real shy and super polite. They shake your hand when they meet you and ask how you are, offer you water, you know, things like that. And that's how your tata wants you to be.

[**RUDY** *scowls*.]

But once they get to know you, they're really a lot of fun, you'll see.

DON FELIPE: ¿Amelia, no han anunciado el camión para Nogales?

AMELIA: No, Dad. We came too early.

RUDY: See? I told you.

DON FELIPE: Ve, Rudy. Ve y pregúntales cuándo sale el cabrón camión para Nogales.

[**RUDY** *crosses but stops to talk to the* **TEENAGERS** *near the phone booth*.]

AMELIA [*trying to distract* DON FELIPE]: Remember, Dad, how angry my tío Antonio got when Toñito and I went swimming in the reservoir? And he punished Toñito, but it was really my fault. I dared him and his friends to jump in the water with me.

DON FELIPE: Fue un milagro de Dios que no se los comieron vivos los alacranes.

AMELIA: Oh, Dad, there weren't any scorpions! That was just a lie to keep us from swimming there.

DON FELIPE: Amelia, esa cisterna está llenita de alacranes, pero tuvieron suerte ese día. Una vez, mi hermano y yo fuimos a nadar en esa misma cisterna con unos amigos del otro rancho, y vieras visto cuánto alacrán le picó a Manuel Andrés, hijo de Don Fernando. Se le puso toditito el cuerpo negro, y una fiebre que lo hizo delirante. Te digo que casi se moría. Por eso castigó a Toñito. Por el susto que le dieron.

AMELIA: Well, scorpions or not, we still had a lot of fun swimming there. And we did a whole lot of other things my tío never knew about. Lots more.

DON FELIPE: Es lo que tú crees. Él se daba cuenta de todo, pero se hacía el disimulado porque eras visita. Y como no me quería hablar, pues te diste vuelo con muchas travesuras. Pero todos se daban cuenta. [*Pausing as he reflects*] Mi hermano era muy bueno para nadar [*pointedly*] en el *río*, no en la cisterna.

[*Pause.*]

Sabes, Amelia, yo quiero ver a mi hermano antes . . . antes que . . .

AMELIA: Before what, Dad?

DON FELIPE: Antes . . . que él . . . no sé. Pero tengo una corazonada que—

[*The recorded announcement over PA system repeats: "Bus to Nogales, Arizona, with stops at Sahuarita, Green Valley, Tubac, Tumacacori, Rio Rico, now loading and receiving passengers at door number three." There is general commotion as* PASSENGERS *line up.*]

DON FELIPE [*looking around for* RUDY]: ¿Y ahora adónde está el inservible?

RUDY [*knowing he's the one* DON FELIPE *is referring to*]: Right here.

[*He crosses and takes* DON FELIPE's *suitcase. The three get in line.*]

AMELIA [*giving traveling instructions to* BOTH]: Mucho cuidado, Dad. And you take care of your tata, Rudy. Watch for him at all the train stops. In fact, you get off with him when he wants to buy something from the vendors. Don't get lost. Me saluda a todos, 'Apá. Especially Toñito. Tell him to come and visit us.

TEENAGER: Rudy, c'mere.

DON FELIPE: No te vayas. Quédate aquí.

TEENAGER [*flirting*]: Rudy, c'mere. Vanessa wants you to show her where's [*mispronouncing it "Chee-who-a-who-a"*] Chihuahua. Bring your map.

[DON FELIPE *and* AMELIA *try to make conversation as they wait in line, but* DON FELIPE *keeps yelling for* RUDY.]

DON FELIPE [*annoyed*]: ¿No te dije? Estorbo inservible, no sirve para nada. ¡Rudy! ¡Ven aquí, cabrón! [*Changing the subject*] ¿Y tú, Amelia? ¿Qué quieres que te traiga de Oaxaca?

AMELIA: Un ranchero muy rico.

DON FELIPE: No seas simple, Amelia; todos los rancheros allá están bien pobres. En serio, ¿qué quieres que te traiga de Oaxaca? Dime pronto. [*Turning and yelling*] ¡Rudy!

AMELIA [*trying to distract him*]: Bring me anything, Dad.

[*Pause.*]

Oh sí, bring me some Mexican candy. ¿Cómo se llama? I remember that I liked a candy that had lots of seeds, little black seeds. I loved it!

DON FELIPE: ¿Semillas negras? Pues quién sabe qué dulce será.

[*Pause.*]

¡Rudy!

[*Pause.*]

Chia. Así se llaman esas semillitas negras, pero hacen un trago de chia, no dulces. Bueno, siempre te lo buscaré o le preguntaré a tu tía Oralia porque ella sabe de todos los dulces. [*Yelling louder*] ¡Rudy! [*To* AMELIA] El cabrón nomás lo hace para que yo me enoje y no lo lleve conmigo.

AMELIA: No, he doesn't, Dad. Mire, there goes the bus driver. [*Joking*] The bus won't leave without him.

DON FELIPE [*illogically*]: Tú crees que no. [*Yelling again*] ¡Rudy! ¡Ven aquí con mil chingados!

[*A reluctant* RUDY *crosses to them. He leaves the map with the* TEENAGERS.]

RUDY: See, Mom? I'm gonna miss the Twisted Sister concert.

AMELIA: Never mind them. [*Giving* RUDY *more travel orders*] Don't forget to drink the Pepto-Bismol before each meal. And peel all the fruit, just in case. Practice your Spanish, m'ijo. And if you can help it, don't drink the water from the well—

RUDY: Mom, I'm gonna starve and die of dehydration there!

AMELIA [*to* DON FELIPE]: Se lo encargo mucho, Dad, please.

DON FELIPE [*annoyed by all the directions and because the bus line doesn't seem to be moving*]: No, Amelia, allá te lo voy a perder en la primera parada del tren.

[*Pause.*]

Hija, seguro que lo voy a cuidar. Y tú, cuida mis matitas. Y mi cheque de la pensión, el día tres del mes. No se te olvide. Me lo guardas bien.

TEENAGER: Rudy, c'mere. Crystal wants to see where you're going. Didn't you say Wahaka? How come we can't find it on the map?

RUDY [*crossing to them; spelling and showing off*]: 'Cause it starts with an *o*, that's why. [*Pointing to the place on the map*] See?

DON FELIPE [*angry*]: Qué hijo de su tal madre. Que se quede, Amelia, que se quede. Yo me voy solo.

AMELIA: Mire, there goes the driver now. [*Changing the subject; pointing to his hat*] A ver si se compra un sombrero nuevo allá en Oaxaca.

DON FELIPE [*taking off his hat and checking it out*]: ¿Un sombrero nuevo? Pero ¿por qué? Si este está bien serviciable todavía.

AMELIA: Buy yourself a new one, Dad. On me. [*Quickly stuffing a twenty-dollar bill into his shirt pocket*] Rudy! Hurry!

[*The line starts to move, and* PASSENGERS EXIT. RUDY *returns to the line, trying to refold the map.* AMELIA *hugs* BOTH.]

AMELIA: ¡Qué Dios los bendiga! Le encargo a Rudy, Dad—take care of him!

[DON FELIPE EXITS.]

Bye, m'ijo, take care of your tata.

[RUDY *starts to* EXIT.]

TEENAGERS [*ad-libbing, very noisy*]: Bye, Rudy. Don't forget to write to us. Bring me a present! [*etc.*]

[RUDY *almost turns to go to them again, but* DON FELIPE ENTERS *and stands at door sputtering, too angry to speak, so* RUDY *hurriedly* EXITS *with him.* TEENAGERS EXIT.]

[AMELIA *looks at departing bus. The* BAG LADY *crosses the stage, repeating the same lines.*]

BAG LADY: An eye for eye. If God wanted people to fly, he would've given them wings. From Washington, the cost of living allowance vote was close. "Don't cry for me, Argentina." Memorial Day Sale at the Heavenly Hills Mall. Every time they test a nuclear bomb on the Bikini Islands, it's a proven fact that people's hair and teeth fall out. The astronauts didn't land on the moon, it was all filmed in a warehouse in the Nevada desert, and when Susan Hayward and Gary Cooper brought the sand back for their driveways in Hollywood, they soon died of cancer. "Don't cry for me, Argentina . . ."

[*The* BAG LADY *stops and looks at* AMELIA. *Their eyes lock.* AMELIA *stares at the* BAG LADY *until she* EXITS, *then she turns slowly and* EXITS *as well.*]

LIGHTS: DOWN.

END OF SCENE 3

* * *

Scene 4

TIME: *Very late afternoon.*

PLACE: *On the train somewhere in Mexico.*

LIGHTS: UP.

MUSIC: *Polka norteña.*

[*The* SOUND *of a train whistle, trains on the tracks, etc., is heard.* DON FELIPE, RUDY, *and* ALL *the other actors are* PASSENGERS *except* AMELIA *and the* BAG LADY. *The* PASSENGERS *will play other roles and will* ENTER *and* EXIT *as directed.* AMELIA *and the* BAG LADY *will also play other roles after they've changed costumes. The ambience should be one of a crowded train, with friendly conversation, interruptions by* VENDORS, *and sharing of food and reading materials.* DON FELIPE *is conversing animatedly with fellow* PASSENGER DON MANUEL, *who is sitting next to him.* RUDY *is sprawled across two seats behind* DON FELIPE, *listening to his tapes on his earphones, clearly bored.*]

DON MANUEL [*to* DON FELIPE]: Sí, señor, Sonora es un estado muy, muy rico. Dicen que es el segundo estado más grande y más rico en toda la república de México.

DON FELIPE [*impressed*]: ¿De veras? Y, ¿cuál es el primero?

DON MANUEL: No sé. Pero una cosa sí le digo: ningún otro estado le puede ganar a Sonora. La pesca, el ganado, la agricultura. No señor, no le ganan a Sonora. Tenemos las playas más hermosas: Puerto Peñasco, Guaymas, la Bahía de Kino. ¿Y mariscos? Uh, camarón jumbo [*pronouncing it as "yumbow"*] de este tamaño. [*Showing six inches with his fingers*] Mire usted, Don Felipe: Baja California, Sonora y Sinaloa son los tres estados con la más valiosa industria de la pesca en México. ¿Sabía usted?

DON FELILPE: No, no lo sabía. Pero todo lo que me dice es muy interesante, Don Manuel. Y ¿cómo es que sabe tanto? Ha de leer muchos libros.

DON MANUEL: No, no. Nada de libros. Los libros son para los intelectuales, y ¿qué saben ellos? Nada. No, señor. Viajando. Así se aprende, especialmente viajando por tren. Yo siempre—

[CANDY VENDOR ENTERS *selling candies.*]

CANDY VENDOR [*repeating these lines while going down the aisle and* PASSENGERS *are buying candy*]: Dulces, dulces, dulces. Dulces de calabaza, camote, cacahuate y cajeta de leche quemada. Dulces dulces, dulces.

[CANDY VENDOR EXITS.]

DON MANUEL [*continuing his conversation*]: ¿Y a usted, Don Felipe? ¿Le gusta leer?

DON FELIPE: ¿Yo? No, no, no. Yo siempre he estado muy ocupado, trabajando. Y ahora veo las noticias en la televisión. Mi hermano, Antonio, a él si le gustaba leer. Digo, le gusta leer. Desde que era muy joven. Leyendo, siempre leyendo. Cuando yo lo interrumpía, siempre me decía, "Espérate, déjame terminar este capítulo." Pero, ¿sabe algo, Don Manuel? ¡Cuando menos me daba cuenta, ya estaba leyendo *otro* capítulo!

FEMALE PASSENGER [*in front of them, turning*]: No es bueno para los ojos. ¿Sabía usted que le puede dar miopía si lee mucho? ¿Verdad, Don Manuel?

DON MANUEL: Oh sí, miopía y cataratas, señora. [*Slightly annoyed at being upstaged by her; turning back to* DON FELIPE] Mire, Don Felipe, yo tengo una tiendita de artesanías en Guadalajara. Por eso es que viajo tanto—comprando y vendiendo artesanías. [*Handing* DON FELIPE *his business card*] Aquí tiene mi tarjeta de negocio. Pase a verme en su regreso de—¿adónde va?

DON FELIPE: Un pueblito cerca de la Ciudad de Oaxaca. Cuilapan.

DON MANUEL: Dispense, pero no lo conozco. ¿Y qué? ¿Va de vacaciones?

DON FELIPE: Bueno, sí y no. Ya no trabajo desde que me jubilé del ferrocarril. En los Estados Unidos. Pero voy ir a ver a mi hermano. Tuvo un ataque de corazón muy severo—pero se está mejorando. Por eso voy . . . a verlo antes que . . . a darle ánimo y—

FEMALE PASSENGER [*butting into the conversation again*]: Té de azahares, Don Felipe. Las flores del árbol de naranja. Eso dele. Es lo mejor para el corazón, ¿verdad, Don Manuel?

DON MANUEL: ¡Oh sí, pero las mejores azahares son las que están en la corona de velo de una novia! Eso le cura el corazón, ¡así pronto! [*Snapping his fingers and laughing at his wit*] ¡Una nueva esposa es lo que recomienda un médico!

[NEWSPAPER VENDOR ENTERS *with her newspapers, novellas, etc.*]

NEWSPAPER VENDOR [*repeating while going down the aisle, selling, giving change, etc.*]: ¡Novelas, novelas! Revistas, periódicos, *Excelsior*, novelas, novelas. Lea la última novela: *Romance después de las cinco*. Lea y descubra lo que pasa cuando el patrón se va de la oficina. ¡Lea y descubra lo que pasa cuando el patrón *no* se va de la oficina! *Romance después de las cinco*.

[NEWSPAPER VENDOR EXITS. *The* SOUND *of brakes, etc., is heard as train stops. There is general commotion as* PASSENGERS ENTER *or* EXIT. RUDY, DON MANUEL, *and* FEMALE PASSENGER EXIT. *A* LOVER BOY *and* LOVER GIRL ENTER *and stand in aisle, feeding each other food from paper plates. A* YOUNG MAN *sits next to* DON FELIPE. RUDY ENTERS *with two Cokes.*]

RUDY [*giving* DON FELIPE *a Coke in a plastic baggie with a straw*]: Here, Grandpa, I bought you a Coke. Are you thirsty?

DON FELIPE: Sí, tengo sed. Gracias. [*Taking a drink and complaining*] Esto no es nada más que azúcar. Mejor me hubieras comprado un agua mineral.

RUDY [*returning to his seat, grumbling*]: I can never do anything right. Old grouch. I should've stayed home. Let him buy his own damn . . . agua mineral . . . whatever that is.

[RUDY *stretches out and puts on his headphones.*]

[SOUND CUE: *Train starts up. There is again general commotion as* PASSENGERS ENTER *or* EXIT, *get resettled, etc.*]

LOVER BOY [*starting to leave*]: Me escribes, mi reina.

LOVER GIRL: Sí, mi amor.

[LOVER BOY *and* LOVER GIRL *kiss passionately.* PASSENGERS *move as though the train has started to move.*]

LOVER BOY: ¡Ay! Ya se va el tren. [*Running*] ¡Te amo, ciao!

[*He* EXITS.]

LOVER GIRL: ¡Te amaré para siempre!

[*She sits behind* RUDY.]

[SOUND CUE: *Train on tracks. Conversations resume.* RUDY *sits up, removes his headphones, and looks around.*]

RUDY [*to* LOVER GIRL, *offering his tapes*]: Do you want to hear my tapes? I can't get the radio, and I'm tired of hearing the same tapes over and over.

LOVER GIRL [*shrugging*]: No hablo inglés.

RUDY [*to himself*]: Oh, great. I don't speak Spanish. But she's cute, so here goes. [*Pantomiming and gesturing*] Mío tapes—tú can listen, okay?

LOVER GIRL: Ah, comprendo. Me prestas tus "tapes." Gracias.

RUDY [*pleased with himself*]: De nada.

[*Soon the two are conversing as* RUDY *tries to identify the tapes to her. He then sits next to her for the rest of the trip.*]

DON FELIPE [*to* YOUNG MAN, *sounding much like* DON MANUEL, *but changing Sonora's status*]: ¿Sabias tú que el estado de Sonora es el estado más grande y más rico en toda la república de México?

YOUNG MAN [*politely impressed*]: ¿De veras?

[*He keeps trying to reach into his bag for an orange half but keeps getting interrupted by* DON FELIPE.]

DON FELIPE: Oh sí. Y la capital de Sonora es Hermosillo. Un gran centro cultural y artístico. ¿Conoces la Universidad de Sonora en Hermosillo?

YOUNG MAN [*still trying to get his orange half*]: No, no conozco la universidad de Sonora.

DON FELIPE: ¡Qué lástima! Pero me puedes preguntar a mí todo lo que quieras. Así se aprende. Viajando y preguntando. Así es como va a aprender mi nieto, viajando. ¿Sabes cómo fue nombrada la capital de Sonora? ¿Hermosillo?

YOUNG MAN [*finally getting an orange half, covered with red chili powder, out of his bag*]: No.

DON FELIPE: Pues es una ciudad muy hermosa, pero no creas que de allí viene el nombre. La capital de Sonora fue nombrada en honor de José María González Hermosillo. Un gran caudillo en nuestra guerra de independencia. No se te olvide. José María González Hermosillo.

YOUNG MAN [*offering* DON FELIPE *an orange half*]: ¿No gusta una naranja con chile?

DON FELIPE [*taking orange*]: Gracias, muy amable.

YOUNG MAN [*gesturing to* RUDY]: ¿Y su nieto?

DON FELIPE: ¡Rudy! Ven, te ofrecen una naranja.

RUDY [*coming and taking an orange half*]: What's the red stuff?

DON FELIPE: Pues chili colorado, ¿qué más va ser?

RUDY: Chili? Grody. Grody to the max.

YOUNG MAN: ¿Qué dice?

DON FELIPE: Que la naranja con chili está "grody."

YOUNG MAN: Y ¿qué quiere decir eso? ¿"Grody"?

DON FELIPE: Sepa la chingada—perdonando la palabra, muchacho. No sé que quiere decir con ese "grody," pero todo lo que ha visto en México, para él es "grody."

YOUNG MAN [*to* RUDY]: Espérate nomás lleguemos a Tepic; venden unos tamales riquísimos. De camarón.

RUDY: Tamales de what?

DON FELIPE: Camarones, burro.

[*Beat.*]

> [*Mispronouncing "shrimp"*] De eshrimp. Eshrimp. Tamales como los que hace tu mamá, pero con eshrimps.

RUDY [*taking little bites of the orange anyway as he returns to his seat*]: Shrimp tamales? Grody to the max.

[*The bag of orange halves gets passed around until* EVERYONE *is eating one.*]

DON FELIPE [*to* YOUNG MAN]: ¿No te dije? Todo es "grody." Los mangos, los tacos, las carnitas, los pollos—todo, todito es "grody." Déjame decirte esto bien rápido para que no me entienda mi nieto gringo, porque aunque se ve poco menso, sí entiende bastante—cuando le conviene. [*Speaking very rapidly*] ¡Cuando estemos en Oaxaca, le voy a dar—chapulines! Y no va a saber qué son, y no me va a decir que son "grody, grody, grody"!

[BOTH *laugh.* MÚSICO ENTERS *singing and carrying a beat-up guitar or maracas.*]

MÚSICO: "No tengo trono, ni reina, ni nadie que me comprenda, pero sigo siendo el rey."

[*He bows and collects donations after applause.*]

GRINGA TOURIST [*dressed outrageously and carrying a giant piñata; calling to* MÚSICO, *practicing her Spanish*]: Mr. Marrachi. Mr. Marrachi.

[MÚSICO *goes to her, rolling his eyes.*]

¿Sabe ... sabe ... un canción ... romántico?

MÚSICO: Sí, yes, my beautiful lady. [*Singing*] "Se murió mi gallo tuerto, que cantaba en la cocina—"

GRINGA TOURIST: No, no. No querendo gallo tuerto. Querendo something romántico. [*Trying to remember a title*] ¿Cómo se dice ...?

MÚSICO [*bored, moving on*]: Una petición, una petición. [*To* DON FELIPE] ¿Una petición, señor? ¿"Los dorados de Chihuahua"? ¿"Siete leguas"?

[*He moves away.*]

DON FELIPE [*calling* MÚSICO *back*]: ¿Sabes "Canción mixteca?"

MÚSICO: ¿"Canción mixteca"? No, no la sé. ¿Qué tal "La cárcel de Cananea"? [*Starting to sing*] "La cárcel de Cananea, 'stá situada en una mesa—"

DON FELIPE: No, no, no. Déjate de cárceles. "Canción mixteca." ¿Cómo que no la sabes? [*To himself*] Otro inservible.

MÚSICO [*with hurt feelings*]: Pues díspense, pero no la sé.

DON FELIPE [*insistent, starting to hum some notes and then singing*]: "Oh tierra del sol, suspiro por verte, ahora que lejos yo vivo sin luz, sin amor ..."

[*The* MÚSICO *and* ALL PASSENGERS *join in. The* MÚSICO *sings and sways with much energy.*]

"... Y al verme tan solo y triste cual hoja al viento, quisiera llorar, quisiera morir, de sentimiento." [*To* MÚSICO] ¿No la sabes?

MÚSICO [*starting to exit*]: No.

GRINGA TOURIST [*jumping up suddenly from her seat and running to* MÚSICO]: Mr. Marrachi! Wait! I remember now. It's "Wantalameera." [*Mispronouncing "Guantanamera"*] "Wantalameera, asina Wantalameera ..."

[GRINGA TOURIST *and* MÚSICO EXIT *dancing.*]

LIGHTS: DOWN *slowly to indicate nighttime on train.*

[ALL *settle down to sleep on their seats.*]

DON FELIPE [*dozing off, half singing and humming*]: "... Y al verme tan solo y triste, cual hoja al viento ..." [*Talking to himself*] A mi hermano le gustaba leer. Trabajábamos la tierra juntos. La siembra. El ganado. Mi hermano, Antonio, ya estaba casado con Oralia y tenía su familia. En las tardes, yo me iba a ver a mi novia, Juanita.

LIGHTS: DOWN.

[FLASHBACK *begins.* SPOTLIGHT *on* JUANITA, *who is wearing an embroidered huipil over a long skirt, and huaraches on her feet. Her hair is braided and twisted on top of her head with red ribbon. She is carrying a bouquet of red roses.* DON FELIPE *continues talking to himself as she stands there.*]

DON FELIPE: Juanita. Yo quería mucho a Juanita. Yo no sé si ella me quería, pero yo si la quería.

[JUANITA *crosses in front of* DON FELIPE, *and he stands up to stop her.*]

Juanita, espérame. ¿Para 'dónde vas?

JUANITA: Al zócalo. Tengo que vender estas flores.

DON FELIPE: Pero te vine a ver. No te vayas; tenemos que hablar.

JUANITA: No puedo. Tengo que vender estas flores.

DON FELIPE: ¡No tienes que vender nada! ¡Cásate conmigo! Vámonos a los Estados Unidos.

JUANITA: ¿Estados Unidos? ¿Pero qué dices? Tú sabes muy bien que no puedo dejar a mi familia. Mi madre está muy enferma, y yo soy la responsable por mis hermanos menores.

DON FELIPE: ¡Pero ya tenemos más de seis años de novios! ¿Cuándo nos vamos a casar?

JUANITA: Cuando se alivie mi madre. Espera, por favor.

DON FELIPE: ¡Estoy cansado de esperar! Cada año es igual: "cuando se alivie mi madre."

[*He tries to hold her in his arms.*]

JUANITA: Déjame ir, Felipe. Después hablaremos. Tengo que vender estas flores.

DON FELIPE: ¡Deja las flores! [*Angrily shaking her, causing some of the roses to fall to the floor*] Tenemos que hablar. [*Holding her by the shoulders*] ¿Nos vamos a casar o no?

[JUANITA *moves his hands away and kneels to pick up the roses.* DON FELIPE *kneels next to her and hands her some of the flowers. She stands up and caresses his cheek tenderly. Beat.*]

JUANITA: No, Felipe. No puedo dejar a mi familia ni mis obligaciones.

[*She* EXITS *running.*]

LIGHTS: UP *slowly as* FLASHBACK *ends. Back to nighttime on the train.*

DON FELIPE: Juanita, no te vayas. No me dejes. Juanita. Juanita. [*Crying softly*] ¡Juanita!

[ALL PASSENGERS *are startled and murmur amongst themselves.* RUDY *wakes up, sees* DON FELIPE, *and goes to him.*]

RUDY: Grandpa, what's wrong?

[DON FELIPE *doesn't seem to recognize* RUDY. RUDY *tries to speak in Spanish.*]

Tata, ¿qué tiene?

DON FELIPE [*confused, looking around the floor*]: Las flores, muchacho, ¿qué no ves las flores?

RUDY: Flowers? What flowers?

DON FELIPE: Las rosas, muchacho. ¿Qué no hueles las rosas? Por allí anda la muerte. Las rosas traen la muerte. Las rosas traen la muerte. Las rosas—

RUDY: There are no roses; we're on a train.

[RUDY *kneels next to him and tries to help him up, but* DON FELIPE *resists.* RUDY *looks around and sees the* PASSENGERS *simply staring now.*]

DON FELIPE [*mumbling*]: Las rosas. Tanta flor, tanta flor. Alguien va a morir, hijo. Tanta flor. Rosas. Rosas.

RUDY: Grandpa, I don't understand you; I don't know what you're saying. "Morir"? Are you saying someone's gonna die?

[*He looks around helplessly at the other* PASSENGERS, *who are beginning to be annoyed at being wakened.* RUDY *stands up and turns to the* PASSENGERS.]

I don't know what to do; can someone help me? Does anyone here speak English?

[*Beat.*]

PASSENGERS [*complaining loudly in Spanish*]: ¡Qué imprudencia! ¿Por qué no dejan dormir? Así son los gringos siempre; no tienen ni madre de prosapia. ¡Callen a ese viejo! ¡Conductor! Tírenlo del tren. ¡Conductor! ¡Conductor! ¡Queremos dormir! [*etc.*]

[RUDY *just stands there, very confused and somewhat frightened.*]

LIGHTS: DOWN *slowly.*

SOUND CUE: *Train wheels clacking on tracks, faraway train whistle.*

MUSIC: *"Canción mixteca" (Instrumental).*

END OF ACT I

INTERMISSION

ACT II

Scene 1

TIME: *Early morning, around three days later.*

PLACE: *Outdoors, on the patio in Cuilapan, Oaxaca, Mexico. There are many plants and flowers.*

LIGHTS: UP.

MUSIC: *Intoduction to "La danza de la pluma."*

[ANTONIO, *dressed in pajamas and a robe, is sitting in his wheelchair. His wife,* ORALIA, *is wearing a simple housedress and apron. Their son,* TOÑITO, *is wearing cowboy ranch clothes.* ORALIA *and* TOÑITO *are standing behind the wheelchair.* DON FELIPE *is sitting next to* ANTONIO.]

ANTONIO [*a bit shyly*]: Me da mucho gusto que hayas venido a verme, hermano.

DON FELIPE [*patting* ANTONIO's *hand*]: El gusto es mío, Antonio.

ANTONIO: Te estábamos esperando desde ayer, ¿verdad, Oralia?

DON FELIPE: Tuvimos un trastorno de la chingada en Puebla.

ORALIA: ¡Felipe! Por favor no hables así!

DON FELIPE: Pero, Oralia, es cierto. Desde ayer hubiéramos llegado si no fuera sido por el cabrón tren. Horas tardes. ¿Cuántas horas nos quedamos sentados en Puebla, Rudy?

[*He looks around for* RUDY.]

TOÑITO: Anda afuera, Tío. Armando le está enseñando el rancho.

DON FELIPE: Qué bueno; jamás en su vida ha estado en un rancho. ¡Verán cuando vea que sale la leche de una "cow"!

[*He pronounces "kau."* ALL *laugh. Beat.*]

A ver, Toñito, pásame la caja, por favor.

[TOÑITO *gives him the box.*]

Yo les traje algunas cositas de allá. No es nada lujoso pero a ver si les gusta.

[DON FELIPE *hands* ANTONIO *the binoculars.*]

Estos miralejos son para ti, hermano.

ANTONIO: Gracias, hermano.

TOÑITO [*to* ANTONIO, *as he helps him with the binoculars*]: Mire, 'Apá, ahora sí se puede sentar en seguida de la ventana y ver todo lo que está pasando aquí en el rancho.

DON FELIPE: ¿Ventana? No, señor. Con estos miralejos puede montar a caballo y galopear por todas las montañas, buscando sus vacas perdidas.

TOÑITO: Usted dígale, Tío. Todos estos días no se ha querido salir de la cama, ¿verdad, 'Amá?

ORALIA: Es cierto, Felipe. Y nomás vieras que tan malo es para tomarse sus medicinas. Malísimo.

DON FELIPE: Oh, déjate las medicinas y las cabronas píldoras, Antonio. Cuando menos piensen, vas a querer una píldora para dormir, otra pildora para despertar, una pildora para comer, y otra pildora para—

ORALIA [*interrupting him on purpose before he can say "cagar"*]: Le van a servir bien los miralejos, Felipe. Gracias.

DON FELIPE [*taking out the red sweater and handing it to* ANTONIO]: Hermano, este suéter te lo manda mi hija, Amelia. Como puedes ver, es un rojo chillante; Amelia adora los colores chillantes. Vieran visto el vestido verde que traía cuando me vine de Tucson. Parecía un caballito del diablo radioactivo. ¡Ni más, ni menos!

[ALL *laugh.*]

ANTONIO: Gracias, hermano. Dicen que el color rojo es muy bueno para el corazón.

DON FELIPE: Es cierto, Antonio. [*Handing* ORALIA *the makeup*] Este makeup es para ti, Oralia.

ORALIA: Makeup? Pero yo no uso maquillaje.

DON FELIPE: Eso precisamente le dije yo, pero Amelia dice que te va a gustar.

ORALIA: Gracias, Felipe. ¿Qué crees que le gustaría de Oaxaca?

DON FELIPE: ¡Un ranchero muy rico! Pero, en serio. Oralia, me pidió un dulce de por aquí. Yo creo que lo comió cuando anduvo por acá. Me dijo que era un dulce con semillas negras. ¿Serían semillas de chía?

ORALIA: ¡Quién sabe! Pero no te preocupes; yo se lo encuentro antes que regreses.

DON FELIPE: Y aquí les traje dulces americanos para todos. Repártelos tú, Oralia. [*Giving candies to* ORALIA] Ay, ya casi se me olvidaba, Toñito. Amelia te mandó un reloj muy especial. [*Joking*] Este reloj, créanlo o no, no solo te da la fecha y números del teléfono—pero también ¡te da la hora!

[*He gives* TOÑITO *the watch.*]

TOÑITO: ¿Cuál es la fecha? ¿Hoy es martes o miércoles?

ANTONIO: Hoy es martes, hijo. ¿Qué no te acuerdas que ayer, lunes, era cuando tu tío Felipe y Rudy estaban por llegar?

DON FELIPE: Y sí hubiéramos llegado ayer, pero tuvimos muchos trastornos en el tren. Una espera larguísima en Puebla. No sé cuántas horas pasamos nomás sentados. No me explico cómo demonios pudieron ganar la gran batalla del cinco de mayo y ni siquiera pueden correr los cabrones camiones a su tiempo.

ORALIA: Camiones, Felipe. Nomás di "camiones."

DON FELIPE: No, Oralia. Tú también dijeras "cabrones camiones" si te hubieras pasado horas sentada. Y el tren era peor. Chubascos en Sinaloa, huelgas en Guadalajara, y en México, sepa la chingada—y aquí en Oaxaca el chofer iba dormido en la rueda, o borracho. ¡Jamás abrió los ojos!

ORALIA: ¡Ay, Felipe! Cuando no andas con tus maldiciones y disparates, sales con puras exageraciones.

DON FELIPE: No son exageraciones, Oralia. Mira, así venía el desgraciado chofer. Así.

[*He shows everyone how the bus driver drove: sprawled, with his head back, mouth open, eyes closed, and with his foot on the gas.*]

[*Sitting up*] Y llevaba miles de santos y vírgenes colgando de la ventanilla. A eso se atenía, el hijo de—¡pues con decirles que hasta yo me puse a rezar!

ORALIA: Bueno, ya basta. Déjame ir a la cocina a prepararles su desayuno. Han de tener mucha hambre después del viaje.

[ORALIA EXITS, *and* ARMANDO *and* RUDY ENTER.]

TOÑITO [*to* ARMANDO]: Ven, hijo, mira el reloj que me mandó Amelia.

[ARMANDO *goes to him.* TOÑITO *shows* ARMANDO *the instructions.*]

Mira, es un reloj que también da la fecha y números del teléfono, pero no puedo leer las instrucciones. Están en inglés.

ARMANDO: ¿Rudy, puedes ayudarle a mi 'apá?

TOÑITO: ¿A poco entiendes español, Rudy?

RUDY [*slowly*]: Un poquito. No más.

ARMANDO: Pero ya está aprendiendo mucho conmigo ¿verdad, Rudy? Escuche, 'Apá. [*To* RUDY] A la tarde vamos a la plaza a ver las muchachas.

DON FELIPE: ¿Qué te dijo tu primo, Rudy?

[*Beat.* RUDY *doesn't answer.*]

ARMANDO: A ver las muchachas, Rudy, [*making a female shape with his hands*] muchachas.

RUDY: Oh, sí. Las babes.

ARMANDO: Babes. Para cuando regrese mi primo a los Estados Unidos, él va a saber hablar español, y yo voy a saber hablar inglés. [*Repeating*] Babes. [*To* DON FELIPE] ¿Cuántos días se van a quedar en México, Tío?

[ORALIA ENTERS *with platters of food.*]

ORALIA: ¡Armando! No seas mal-educado. Nunca se le debe preguntar a un huésped cuánto se van a quedar de visita. Discúlpenlo, Felipe y Rudy.

DON FELIPE: No hay por qué disculparlo, Oralia. Armando, nos vamos a quedar aquí una semana. Regresaremos de hoy en ocho días.

TOÑITO [*checking his watch with great detail*]: De hoy en ochas días será—

ARMANDO: ¡El día después del juego contra Coyotepec! Qué bueno porque nos falta un jugador. Rudy, ¿sabes jugar béisbol?

RUDY [*a bit hesitant*]: Baseball? Sí. ¿Cómo se dice "short stop"?

ORALIA: Se les está enfriando el desayuno. Todos, vengan a sentarse.

[ALL *come to table and start to eat.* RUDY *just looks down at his plate of eggs.*]

DON FELIPE: ¿Por qué no estás comiendo?

RUDY: I don't want to eat these eggs.

DON FELIPE: ¿Y por qué no? ¿No me vas a decir que están "grody"?

RUDY: Well, they *are* grody. I saw where they came from.

DON FELIPE: Pues, vinieron los huevos de las cabronas chickens, ¿qué no?

ORALIA: ¿Qué pasa? ¿Qué dice de los huevos, Felipe?

DON FELIPE: Fíjate, Oralia. Dice que no se quiere comer estos huevos porque él vio de donde vienen.

ORALIA: Pues vienen de las gallinas. [*Teasing gently*] ¿Qué los huevos de los Estados Unidos no vienen de las gallinas, muchacho?

RUDY [*trying to explain, with great difficulty*]: I eat huevos at home . . . but the huevos come in a box . . . no gallina estando alive where I can see it—

[*A very lively marimba band begins playing* MUSIC, *interrupting* RUDY's *explanation.* ALL *except* RUDY *rise from their chairs, animated.*]

DON FELIPE: ¡Marimba!

TOÑITO: Es una sorpresa para usted, Tío Felipe. Mi 'apá los contrató para que le trajeran serenata anoche porque sabe cuánto le gusta la música de marimba.

ANTONIO: Sí, Felipe. Vinieron a darte serenata anoche pero todavía no llegabas.

DON FELIPE [*starting to tell the story all over again as they all exit toward the music*]: Pues sí, desde ayer hubiéramos llegado, pero tuvimos un trastorno de la chingada en Puebla, ¿cuántas horas nos pasamos nomás sentados, Rudy?

[DON FELIPE EXITS *without waiting for an answer.* RUDY *remains sitting at the table; he looks around and sees that he's alone. Beat.*]

RUDY [*looking down at his plate*]: I don't care what anybody says, I'm not eating any eggs that I saw coming out of a chicken's . . . culo!

[*He pushes his plate away and slouches down with arms folded across his chest.*]

MUSIC: UP. *"Jugo de piña"* or other marimba song.

LIGHTS: DOWN.

END OF SCENE 1

* * *

Scene 2

LIGHTS: UP.

TIME: *Late afternoon, middle of the week.*

PLACE: *On the same patio.*

[ORALIA *is chopping herbs while* RUDY *reads a Spanish dictionary.* DON FELIPE *is just puttering around, getting in the way.*]

DON FELIPE [*picking up an herb leaf and smelling it*]: Ah, ya casi puedo saboriar el mole.

RUDY: ¿Mole? [*Checking his dictionary*] How do you spell it?

DON FELIPE: Déjate de diccionario, Rudy. Tu tía Oralia me está haciendo mi mole favorito para mañana. Y ahorita está cortando las hierbas aromáticas para ponerlas a asar. Verás nomás cuando se estén asando, ¡van a oler sus hierbas por toda la vecindad!

ORALIA: ¿Vas a querer mole verde, rojo, o negro, Felipe?

DON FELIPE: Los tres, Oralia. También quiero el mole manchamanteles, Oralia.

[*They laugh at the joke. Beat.*]

[*To* RUDY] Es broma, Rudy. Un . . . joke. Me preguntó tu tía que clase de mole quería—

RUDY: Yeah, I got the colors. Red, green, or black, right? But I still don't know what's mole.

DON FELIPE: No me interrumpas. [*Sounding like* DON MANUEL *on the train*] Oaxaca, Rudy, es famoso por sus moles. [*Aside to* ORALIA] Sí, sí, ya sabemos bien que el mole lo inventaron en Puebla. [*To* RUDY] Y los poblanos creen que ellos hacen el mejor mole, pero ya viste ¿cómo corren los camiones? En Puebla es donde nos sentamos por horas y horas, ¿te acuerdas? ¿Cómo van a hacer el mejor mole? [*Getting back on track*] El mole, Rudy, es salsa hecha de chili, nueces, semillas, frutas y hierbas, que se asan, y se ponen a hervir a fuego lento por horas y horas. Hay siete clases de mole—

RUDY [*interrupting on purpose to stop the lecture*]: So what kind is the one you want? . . . [*Trying to pronounce*] The mancha . . . what?

ORALIA: Manchamanteles. Explícale tus ocurrencias, Felipe.

DON FELIPE: Te dije que era una broma, Rudy. No es nombre de un mole. Solo quiere decir que ensucias todo el mantel—el table-cloth en inglés—con manchas del mole cuando lo comes. Manchamantel.

[*Beat.*]

[*To* RUDY] Ya deja de leer tanto, Rudy.

RUDY: But I want to learn more Spanish, Tata.

DON FELIPE: Pues, nomás lo escuchas y lo hablas; así se aprende, muchacho.

RUDY: Nah-uh, I tried that, and it didn't work. Yesterday, at baseball prac-tice, this real pretty señorita came up to me and asked me if I was "casado," and I said, "sí, estoy casado."

DON FELIPE: Pero, Rudy, hijo, ¡le dijiste que estabas casado! Married.

RUDY: Yeah, I know that now. It's just that I got mixed up; I thought she was asking me if I was "cansado," you know, from playing baseball, so I said yes 'cause I was tired.

DON FELIPE: Pues es la misma chigadera, hijo, ¡casado o cansado!

[**DON FELIPE EXITS**, *enjoying his joke.*]

ORALIA: ¡Felipe! ¡No le digas eso! [*To* RUDY] No le pongas atención, Rudy. Sigue estudiando tu diccionario, aunque ya veo que tu español cada día va mejorando. Es por las telenovelas que ves con Armando y sus amigos.

RUDY [*trying out his Spanish, somewhat hesitantly*]: Oh sí, me gustan las telenovelas, Tía.

[*Beat.*]

Mi abuelo es muy . . . ¿chistoso?

ORALIA: Sí, pero no te creas; él ha sufrido mucho.

RUDY: ¿Sufrido? What's sufrido, Tía Oralia?

ORALIA: Ay, hijo, ¿cómo me voy a dar entender? Tú y tu abuelo tan bien que se entienden. Uno habla español y el otro le contesta en inglés.

[*Beat.*]

Tu abuelo ha sufrido mucho. Dolor. [*Touching her heart and con-tinuing to explain with many theatrical gestures*] Cuando se enojó con tu tío Antonio. "Yo me voy a los Estados Unidos, Antonio."

"No te vayas a los Estados Unidos, Felipe." Y tantos años sin una carta. Antonio sufrió también. Pero muy tercos los dos. Tercos como las mulas. A tu abuelo le gustaba trabajar la tierra, ¿sabías? El ganado y la siembra. ¿Cómo pudo dejarla e irse a trabajar al ferrocarril? No, aquí es donde pertenecía. Aquí en el rancho, con Juanita.

RUDY: Juanita? Who's Juanita?

ORALIA [*fearing she's said too much*]: Oh, oh, tengo que ir a darle la medicina a tu tío Antonio.

RUDY: Wait, Tía Oralia, you have to tell me the rest of the story. Tell me about Juanita, please. Was she my grandfather's . . . novia?

ORALIA [*reluctantly continues*]: Sí, eran novios por muchos años pero ella no quiso casarse con tu abuelo e irse a los Estados Unidos. Y Felipe se fue. Solo. Y allá se casó con tu abuela, Marta. Cuando Marta murió, Felipe vino a ver a su madre—mi suegra—es cuando trajo a la traviesa de tu mamá. Nosotros creíamos que se casaría con Juanita, pero Felipe sabía que mientras Doña Teresita, la madre de Juanita, viviera, aún siempre enfermiza, que jamás Juanita la dejaría.

[*Beat.*]

Bueno, ya tienes la historia completa.

[*She starts to* EXIT.]

RUDY: Wow! This is better than the telenovelas, Tía Oralia. But that can't be the end of the story. Where's Juanita now?

ORALIA [*dryly*]: Enterrada en Zaachila. Pero antes de morir, dejó muchas tiendas de flores en la Ciudad de Oaxaca, dos en Zaachila, y hasta una aquí en Cuilapan. Dejó muy bien establecidos a todos sus hermanos y sobrinos.

RUDY: Flower shops. So what happened to her sick mother . . . Doña Teresita?

ORALIA: Oh, ella vivió por muchos, muchos años. Apenas hace poco que por fin murió. Ya tenía más de los cien años, imagínate. Parecía momia de Guanajuato. ¡Siempre andaba en las florerías, molestando a sus nietos—bisnietos y tataranietos—y a los clientes!

[*She scoops up the herbs into a basket and starts to* EXIT, *but then stops.*]

Ay, m'ijito, las historias que te podría contar, pero nunca me ha gustado el mitote.

[ORALIA EXITS *grandly*.]

RUDY [*going back to his dictionary*]: Bummer.

[ARMANDO ENTERS. *He is dressed in* RUDY's *"Love Boat" tourist clothes and is carrying baseball equipment*.]

ARMANDO [*practicing his English, with an accent*]: Ready, cousin?

RUDY: In a minute, Armando. I just need to find a word in Spanish.

ARMANDO: Nomás pregúntame a mí; I know every word you need.

RUDY: Remember that pretty señorita who asked me if I was tired and I told her I was married?

ARMANDO: You break her heart, cousin.

RUDY: Yeah, she broke mine, too, when she ran away laughing to tell her friends and never talked to me again. Anyway, now I want to tell her I'm not married, and that I'm just . . . well, the word in English is "embarrassed."

ARMANDO: Embarrassed? Eso es fácil. Mira, nomás ve y dile que estás "embarazado."

RUDY: ¿Embarazado? Okay, thanks, primo.

ARMANDO: You are welcome. C'mon, you have to get your equipment for the game.

[ARMANDO EXITS.]

RUDY [*practicing*]: Señorita, no estoy casado; nomás estoy embarazado.

LIGHTS: DOWN.

MUSIC: *Contemporary Mexican.*

END OF SCENE 2

* * *

Scene 3

PLACE: *Patio.*

TIME: *After dinner, the night of the baseball game.*

[DON FELIPE *and* ANTONIO *are sitting outside on the patio after dinner.* ANTONIO *is wearing his red sweater. There is moonlight and shadows.* ORA-LIA ENTERS *with orange-blossom tea for* ANTONIO.]

ORALIA [*giving the glass of tea to* ANTONIO]: Ten, Antonio. Dice Felipe que el té de azahares es lo mejor para el corazón.

DON FELIPE: Sí, es cierto. Bueno, es lo que recomendó esta vieja sabelotodo en el tren.

ORALIA: ¿Y tú, Felipe? ¿No gustas también un té de azahares? ¿O un agua de piña?

DON FELIPE: Después, al rato, Oralia. No me siento muy bien. ¿Sería el mole?

ANTONIO: ¡Más bien era la cantidad! Vas a regresar a los Estados Unidos bien gordito. Has comido mole y todos tus antojitos cada día que has estado aquí.

DON FELIPE: Siéntate, Oralia.

[ORALIA *sits down.*]

Tus moles son deliciosos. Si quedó mole de la cena, mañana me lo das recalentado para mi desayuno antes que nos vayamos.

ANTONIO: ¿Y en los Estados Unidos, Felipe, también comes mole?

DON FELIPE: Oh sí. Amelia me hace mole cuando ve que me estoy poniendo nostálgico por Oaxaca. Ella compra unas frasquitos de mole en el Kmart, una tienda muy grande que vende todo.

ORALIA AND ANTONIO [*amazed*]: ¡Mole en frascos! [*Tsk-tsking about American barbarism*] ¡Qué barbaridad!

DON FELIPE [*soothing feathers*]: Pero, no se crean, ese mole no se compara al de aquí en Oaxaca.

ANTONIO: No, como dicen, para mole, solo Oaxaca.

DON FELIPE: Es cierto, hermano. Solo en Oaxaca.

[*Beat.*]

¿Pero saben? Yo le doy mucho crédito a mi Amelia. Tiene un trabajo con el gobierno muy bueno. Y le gusta cocinarme mis antojitos. Vieran las tortillas que aprendió hacer. [*Making a big circle with his arms*] Miren, así de grandes.

[ANTONIO *and* ORALIA *laugh, not believing him.*]

ORALIA: Ya vas, Felipe, otra vez con tus exageraciones.

DON FELIPE: No son exageraciones, Oralia. Así las hacen en el estado de Sonora, te digo. Miren, así. [*Demonstrating by flipping "tortillas" from one arm to the other*] ¡Las estiran hasta que llegan a los sobacos! ¡Por eso se llaman tortillas "sobaqueras"! En serio, Oralia.

[ANTONIO *and* ORALIA *laugh; they still do not believe him.* TOÑITO, ARMANDO, RUDY, *and other* TEENAGERS ENTER.]

TOÑITO [*to* ORALIA]: 'Amá, voy a llevar a los muchachos al juego; ¿no se le ofrece algo?

ORALIA [*standing up quickly*]: ¡Dios santo! Pues, ¿qué hora es?

TOÑITO [*quickly looking at his watch*]: Son las seis y cuarenta y . . . ¡siete! O, trece minutos antes de las siete, o siete menos trece, o—

ARMANDO: Hora de irnos, 'Apá. Vamos. [*To* ORALIA] Abuelita, ya dejamos todo preparado en la cocina para la fiesta.

DON FELIPE: ¿Fiesta? ¿Va a haber otra fiesta? ¿Con marimba?

ARMANDO: No, Tío. Es solo una reunión de amigos después del juego.

DON FELIPE: Ah, ¡por si ganan!

TEENAGER: Sí, Don Felipe, y también por si perdemos!

ORALIA: Oh, eso sí. Cada año, han perdido cada juego.

DON FELIPE: ¡Han perdido cada año! ¿Contra quién es el juego, pues?

ANTONIO: Coyotepec, Felipe. ¿Te imaginas? Nunca le han podido ganar a los de Coyotepec.

FELIPE: ¡Coyotepec! Te acuerdas, Antonio, cuando le dábamos en toda la—

TEENAGER: Ay, Don Felipe, es que tienen un gorilón en su equipo, así de grande. [*Walking like a gorilla*] Bien fuerte. La única manera que le pudiéramos ganar es si se quiebra un brazo.

ARMANDO: *Dos* brazos. Vamos, pues. Tal vez este año tengamos suerte. Tío Felipe, ¿sabía que Rudy está en nuestro equipo? Él es nuestro short stop. Y es rete bueno, también.

DON FELIPE: ¿Rudy? ¿De veras? ¿Pero cómo se comunican?

TOÑITO: ¿Qué no sabe, Tío, que el idioma internacional de los jóvenes es el béisbol?

ARMANDO: Sí, Tío, nos comunicamos muy bien. Además, Rudy ya habla bastante español. Rudy, dile algo a tu abuelo en español.

RUDY [speaking slowly in Spanish]: Después del juego, vamos con las muchachas y—

ARMANDO: ¡No! ¡No digas eso!

[ARMANDO pushes RUDY out and ALL except ORALIA, ANTONIO, and DON FELIPE EXIT laughing.]

ORALIA [sighing]: Lo que es ser joven, ¿verdad?

[ORALIA EXITS to the kitchen. DON FELIPE and ANTONIO sit quietly for a few beats.]

ANTONIO: ¿De veras hace Amelia las tortillas tan grandes?

DON FELIPE: Oh sí. [Laughing] Bueno, no tan grandes como las de Sonora. Y nomás cuando le alcanza el tiempo. Tiene un trabajo muy exigente; por eso no pudo venir conmigo. Es muy trabajadora mi Amelia.

ANTONIO: Y muy traviesa. Nunca he visto a ninguna tan traviesa como ella. ¿Te acuerdas cuando se fueron a nadar en la cisterna?

[DON FELIPE nods yes.]

Y ¿supiste de la vez que ella y Toñito se metieron en las colmenas?

DON FELIPE: ¿Colmenas? ¿De quién?

ANTONIO: ¡Pues, de todos! Se metieron en las huertas y tumbaron cuanta colmena pudieron. Yo no sé cómo no les picaron las abejas. Y ese año, después que tú y ella se fueron, no hubo ni una gota de miel. [Laughing] ¡Ni una gota!

DON FELIPE [reflectively]: ¿Te acuerdas la vez que tú y yo hallamos aquella colmena en el tronco del roble viejo? Esa sí que era miel. Dulce, dulce. La miel más dulce que he probado en mi vida. ¿Te acuerdas?

ANTONIO: ¡Cómo no me voy a acordar si fui yo quien la halló!

DON FELIPE: ¿Tú? [Starting to get annoyed] Mentiroso, yo fui quien la halló.

ANTONIO [also getting annoyed]: Yo la encontré. Tú andabas por allá, cortando leña—

DON FELIPE [adamantly]: Y tú andabas por allá . . . [sarcastic] leyendo uno de tus libros, de seguro.

ANTONIO: Te digo que fui *yo* quien encontró esa colmena de miel. *Yo.* Era *yo.* Yo la encontré, no, tú . . . [*Yelling*] ¡*Yo* la encontré!

DON FELIPE [*yelling*]: ¡Yo la encontré!

ANTONIO AND DON FELIPE [*together, still yelling*]: ¡*Yo* la encontré!

[**ORALIA ENTERS.**]

ORALIA [*alarmed*]: ¡Santa madre de Dios! ¿Por qué están gritando así?

[**ANTONIO** *and* **DON FELIPE** *sit back, subdued.*]

Los hermanos no deben enojarse así. ¡Qué deshermanables! [*Handing* DON FELIPE *a glass of bicarbonate*] Ten, esto te ayudará con la indigestión, pero nada te va ayudar si siguen discutiendo tan feo. Parecen chiquitos.

[**DON FELIPE** *drinks bicarbonate. Beat.*]

[*To* ANTONIO] Y tú, Antonio, espera nomás le diga al doctor lo que andas haciendo. Sinvergüenzas, los dos. Pero tú eres el peor, Antonio, porque Felipe es tu hermano y tu huésped y vino de muy lejos nomás a verte . . . hmmph . . . malagradecido.

ANTONIO: Pero, Oralia, yo fui el que encontró la colmena con la miel.

ORALIA: ¿A cuál colmena? ¡Oh no me digas, ni quiero saber!

[**ORALIA** *picks up the empty glass and* **EXITS**, *still grumbling. There is a short uncomfortable silence as each waits for the other to speak first.*]

ANTONIO: ¿De veras nomás viniste a verme a mí?

DON FELIPE: Sí, cuando vine con Amelia, en el '62, ni nos hablamos.

ANTONIO [*somewhat insistent but savoring the words*]: Pero ¿de veras nomás viniste a verme?

DON FELIPE [*admittingly but still just a bit stubbornly*]: Ya te dije que sí. Yo quería venir a verte antes que . . .

ANTONIO: . . . ¿antes de qué?

DON FELIPE: No, nada. No es nada.

ANTONIO: Anda, dilo. No tengas miedo, Felipe.

[*Beat.*]

Veniste a verme antes que muera. Yo no tengo miedo morir. Mi vida está completa.

[*Beat.*]

¿Y sabes? Yo también te quería ver antes que muera. Me dio mucho gusto que vinieras a México antes de mi muerte.

DON FELIPE: No vas a morir, ni hables de la muerte.

ANTONIO: ¿Cómo que no voy a morir? Todos tenemos que morir. Ahora o después. Es la cosa más natural en el mundo. Es como cuando terminas de leer un libro. La última página—y ya.

[*Beat.*]

DON FELIPE [*referring to the past*]: ¿Y yo? ¿Qué era? ¿Un capítulo olvidado en ese "libro"?

ANTONIO: No, hermano, jamás olvidado. Mejor dicho, reservado.

[*Beat.*]

Pero sabes, tú y yo, todos tenemos nuestra manera propia de ver la vida. Muchos, así como yo, miran la vida como un libro, y ya terminando el libro, pues llega la hora de despedirnos, de decir "adios."

DON FELIPE: Me gustan tus palabras, Antonio. [*Standing up and walking slowly*] Pero yo no veo mi vida como un libro; la veo como un camino largo, largo. Al principio tú y yo caminábamos en ese mismo camino, pero tú te quedaste aquí, y yo me fui por otro camino.

ANTONIO: Pero regresaste.

DON FELIPE: Sí, regresé. Pero solo para verte. Allá tengo otra vida, mi familia.

ANTONIO: Pues es lo que te he estado diciendo, Felipe. Te dije que mi vida era un libro, y tú dices que la tuya es un camino largo. Tú te fuiste en tu camino y yo me quedé aquí. ¿Qué hubiera pasado si te hubieras quedado? Eso no se puede saber.

DON FELIPE [*sitting down*]: Dices bien, hermano.

ANTONIO: Sí, yo sé.

[*They sit quietly, enjoying the silence.*]

[*Remembering suddenly and exclaiming*] ¡Ajá! Pero lo que no te dije es la vez que tu Amelia convenció a mi Toñito que cortara y comiera todas las tunas de los nopales—o las pitayas, no sé cuál—y se llenaron los dos de espinas hasta ¡por debajo de la lengua!

[ORALIA ENTERS.]

ORALIA: Ya, ya basta de tanta plática. Es hora que los dos se acuesten.

ANTONIO: Pero, Oralia, déjame decirle a Felipe la vez que Amelia—

ORALIA: No, no. No tienen fin las aventuras de Amelia. Ya es leyenda en nuestro pueblito. A dormir los dos. Ahora mismo.

[*She starts to wheel* ANTONIO *out.*]

DON FELIPE: Vayan ustedes. Yo me quedo aquí y espero a Rudy.

ORALIA: No te preocupes por él; él anda muy bien con Armando. Ellos vendrán en cuanto pierdan el juego, y luego bailarán y comerán toda la noche. Y ya mañana nos contarán todos los detalles de cómo llegaron a perder el juego contra Coyotepec. Ya verás. Ve y acuéstate.

ANTONIO AND ORALIA: Buenas noches.

[*They* EXIT.]

LIGHTS: DOWN, *moonlight.*

[DON FELIPE *sits in subdued shadows.*]

DON FELIPE [*continues speaking softly to* ANTONIO, *though he is now alone*]: Pues sí, Antonio, la vida es un camino muy, muy largo. [*Rubbing his hands together*] O también se puede decir que es un círculo. [*Touching his heart*] Y que caminamos en rueda tras rueda. [*Massaging his heart slowly with circular movements, and then repeating*] Y que caminamos en rueda tras rueda. [*Massaging his left shoulder and arm*] Y luego, regresamos al mismo lugar en donde empezamos, para morir. Tal vez.

[*He rubs his left-hand fingers. Beat.*]

[*Looking straight ahead and calling softly*] Amelia. Amelia, ven. Amelia, hija, ven.

LIGHTS: UP.

[*Please note that this is not technically a* FLASHBACK *or a* FLASHFORWARD, *but rather the scene takes place in* DON FELIPE'S MIND. SPOTLIGHT *on* AMELIA. *She is wearing the same green dress as in act 1. She walks to* DON FELIPE.]

AMELIA: ¿Qué tiene, Dad?

DON FELIPE: ¿Viste a mi hermano? ¿Oíste lo que dijo? Amelia, dice que no tiene miedo morir.

AMELIA: My tío Antonio is very sick.

DON FELIPE: Pero no tiene miedo morir. Y yo sí, Amelia. Yo sí tengo miedo morir.

AMELIA: Stop talking like that. Dad, you're not going to die; don't scare me like that.

DON FELIPE: ¿Sabes qué me da miedo? Que voy a morir sin hacer las cosas que quería hacer, lo que debería haber hecho—

AMELIA: Like what, 'Apá?

DON FELIPE: Que me debería de haber quedado aquí en México, esperando a Juanita, haberle hablado a mi hermano cuando vinimos—tantas cosas.

AMELIA: No one can change their past actions.

DON FELIPE: Eso lo sé, hija, pero ahora mi vida está llena de remordimiento. Toda mi vida . . . cuando he querido a alguien . . . nunca se lo he dicho. Nunca le dije a Juanita que la quería. Ni a mi hermano. A Rudy y a . . . ti.

AMELIA: We know you love us, Dad.

DON FELIPE [getting agitated]: Pero yo quería decírtelo—

AMELIA [going behind him and putting her hands on his shoulders]: Ya, Dad, ya. [Massaging his shoulders softly] Póngase en paz, Dad. Be at peace, rest. Déscanse, 'Apá.

DON FELIPE: Quiero que me cuides bien a Rudy. Es un muchacho muy bueno, vas a ver. Estoy cansado, Amelia. Déjame dormir.

[AMELIA EXITS without taking her eyes off DON FELIPE.]

LIGHTS: LOWER. Return to present.

MUSIC: "Dios nunca muere" (Instrumental).

END OF SCENE 3

* * *

Scene 4

TIME: Morning after the game.

PLACE: Kitchen.

[RUDY, ARMANDO, and TEENAGERS are gathered around kitchen table, *eating and talking enthusiastically about the game they won.* ORALIA ENTERS *with food.*]

ORALIA: Tanta comida que dejaron anoche por andar bailando.

TEENAGER: Pero Doña Oralia, ¿cómo íbamos a pensar en comer cuando por fin le ganamos a Coyotepec?

ORALIA: Pues como siempre; todo el tiempo traen hambre. Bueno, díganme, ¿a qué se debe el gran milagro de por fin haberle ganado a Coyotepec?

ARMANDO: Fue Rudy, Abuelita.

RUDY: No, it wasn't me. It was Armando.

TEENAGER [*leading* ORALIA *to a chair*]: Siéntese, Doña Oralia. Okay, Armando y Rudy, díganle cómo lo hicimos.

ARMANDO: Mire, Abuelita, las bases estaban "loaded," y Fernando era el pitcher—

TEENAGER: No, no. Primero, nos iban ganando con seis rons, y luego se lastimó—¿quién?

ARMANDO: Manuel. Es el mejor bateador que tenemos, Abuela. Corrió a tercera y—¡POW! Se lastimó la rodilla. Uhh, sin Manuel, teníamos perdido el juego de seguro. Pero los alcanzamos. Por tres innings el marcador era doce a doce. En el último inning, íbamos por delante con tres rons, pero siempre creíamos que íbamos a perder—

[DON FELIPE ENTERS. *He is dressed for travel and is carrying his suitcase and his old hat. He is pale and seems tired, and* ALL *watch him intently.*]

DON FELIPE: Buenos días a todos.

ORALIA: Buenos días, Felipe. ¿Cómo amaneciste?

DON FELIPE [*joking*]: ¡Pues acostado y en ayunas!

[ALL *laugh at his wordplay. He puts his suitcase down and places his hat on top of it. Beat.*]

DON FELIPE: Bueno, bueno, ¿por qué tanto ruido y escándalo? ¿Qué viene el Papa a México otra vez?

FEMALE TEENAGER: No lo va a creer, Don Felipe, pero anoche le ganamos a Coyotepec.

ARMANDO: Ganamos, dice la mosca.

FEMALE TEENAGER: Pues, nosotros también ayudamos, ¿no? Con nuestro entusiasmo. Cheerleading.

[*She and* OTHERS *give a quick cheer in Spanish:* "*¡A la bim, a la bum, a la bim, bum, bam, Cuilapan, Cuilapan, ra, ra, ra!*"]

DON FELIPE: ¡Le ganaron a Coyotepec! Ya era hora que le ganaran a esa bola de hijos de la—

ORALIA [*interrupting him before he says a "bad word"*]: Epa, epa. [*Offering him a plate of food*] Ten, come.

DON FELIPE: Gracias, pero no tengo hambre.

ORALIA: Tienes que comer algo; no es bueno viajar en ayunas. Además, no se sabe cuántas horas tendrán que esperar en la central camionera esperando el camión a Puebla.

DON FELIPE: Es cierto. Bueno, pero poquito.

[*He walks to sit down very slowly. Beat.*]

[*Changing the subject; to* OTHERS] A ver pues, terminen de decirme cómo le ganaron por fin a Coyotepec.

[ALL *will demonstrate the moves as they show* DON FELIPE *and* ORALIA. *They will quickly change baseball positions as they pantomime their moves with lots of physical movements, gestures, voice changes, and enthusiasm.*]

ARMANDO: Mire, Tío. Ya casi se terminaba el juego; el marcador era doce a doce, y en el último inning, les íbamos ganando con dos rons. Pero en el último inning de Coyotepec, ya íbamos a perder de seguro. Estaban las bases llenas, sin un out, y luego Manuel—es usted, Abuelita.

[ARMANDO *positions* ORALIA *as the pitcher.*]

ORALIA: Pero no se les olvide que ando manca.

[ORALIA *limps.*]

ARMANDO [*continuing*]: Okay, Manuel tira la pelota, bases loaded, Rudy es short stop, y el bateador de Coyotepec es el gorila—usted, aquí, Tío Felipe—

[ARMANDO *takes* DON FELIPE *and places him as batter.* ORALIA *pitches.*]

—le pega a la pelota—¡ZAZ!—y la pelota se va derechito a Rudy, Rudy coje la pelota, la tira a home, de home a tercera, de tercera a segunda . . .

[DON FELIPE *runs to bases, helped along by others.*]

    ... TRIPLE PLAY! ¡Le ganamos a Coyotepec catorce a doce!

[ALL *cheer and dance around, hugging.*]

DON FELIPE [*very pleased, with his arm around* RUDY's *shoulder*]: ¿De veras, Rudy? ¿Les ayudaste a ganar el juego?

RUDY: Yeah, I helped, but they're good, and the guys from Coyote-something are good, too. But just wait till we get them next year.

DON FELIPE [*to* OTHERS]: ¿Ya vieron? El inservible de mi nieto les ayudó a ganar el juego.

[DON FELIPE *hugs* RUDY. TOÑITO ENTERS, *holding one hand over his eye and moaning. He is pushing* ANTONIO *with his other hand.*]

TOÑITO [*pretending to be in pain*]: Ay, ay, cómo me duele.

ORALIA [*going to him quickly*]: Dios santo, ¿qué te pasó?

TOÑITO [*joking*]: Alguién me dio con una pelota mientras cruzaba el pasillo.

[ALL *laugh and return to table.*]

DON FELIPE [*to* RUDY]: ¿Qué estás comiendo tan sabroso?

RUDY [*pronouncing it slowly*]: Cha-pu-li-nes. They're delicious—want some?

DON FELIPE: ¡Chapulines! ¿Sabías tú que estás comiendo chapulines?

RUDY: Sure, and I bet they're pure protein. If I can figure out how to dry them and grind them into tablets, I'll get rich.

ORALIA: ¿Qué dice, Felipe?

DON FELIPE: Pues, dice el capitalista aquí, que va secar todos los chapulines y los va a moler a pastillas de proteina, y ¡hacerse un millionario!

[ALL *laugh.*]

ANTONIO [*holding up binoculars*]: ¿Ya vieron todos los miralejos que me trajo mi hermano de los Estados Unidos? [*Looking through them and stopping at* ORALIA] Ay, Oralia, ¡jamás te he visto las mejillas tan color de rosa!

ORALIA [*getting slightly flustered*]: Es que me puse tantito blush [*pronouncing it as "bloosh"*] que me mandó Amelia.

[ALL *tease her, ad-libbing:* "Qué moderna," *etc. Beat. She remembers something suddenly, anxious to leave the room.*]

Ay, ¡los dulces para Amelia! Ya casi se me olvidaba darles los dulces de Amelia.

[ORALIA EXITS.]

ANTONIO [to TOÑITO]: Bueno, hijo, ¿hiciste el mandado que te pedí? ¿Adónde está?

TOÑITO [getting a hat box that's nearby; to DON FELIPE]: Mire, Tío. [Taking out a new hat] Ya puede tirar ese sombrero viejo. Un regalo de parte de mi papá. [Putting the new hat on DON FELIPE's head] A ver, a ver.

[ALL admire.]

DON FELIPE [to ANTONIO]: Gracias, hermano. [To TOÑITO] Toñito, dame la caja; no voy a llevármelo puesto. No, señor, este sombrero está muy maravilloso para llevarlo puesto en el tren. Cuando llegue a Tucson, entonces me lo voy a poner. Quiero que me vea Amelia bajarme del Greyhound con mi sombrero nuevecito de México. [To ANTONIO again] Gracias, hermano. [To ALL] Gracias a todos. Muy amables, como siempre. Y no olviden que allá en Tucson tienen su casa. Visítenos. Pero les voy advertir, hace mucho calor. Hace un calor de la ching—

[ORALIA ENTERS.]

ORALIA [stopping him from saying a "bad word"]: Ay, Felipe, ¿cuándo se te va a quitar lo mal-hablado? [Giving him a bag of candies] Ten, los dulces de Amelia.

DON FELIPE: Chihuahua, Oralia, Chihuahua. Yo iba decir que Tucson tiene un calor de la Chihuahua. Tú eres la mal-pensada, Oralia.

[Beat.]

[To RUDY] Bueno, Rudy, ¿ya tenemos todo listo? [To ALL] Tenemos que decirles adiós, pero solo hasta la próxima visita, con el favor de Dios. [To ANTONIO] Y quiero venir a hallarte andando, nada de estar sentado en la silla de ruedas, ¿me oyes?

ANTONIO: Hermano, el año que entra, te voy a esperar cerca del portalón, vas a ver. Y cuando te devise con mis miralejos, voy a correr a saludarte.

[ANTONIO and DON FELIPE hug. RUDY goes to each relative and friend and very formally shakes hands and hugs each one as DON FELIPE beams proudly. Then DON FELIPE shakes hands and hugs everyone. ALL ad-lib good wishes *messages to* AMELIA, *etc.* DON FELIPE *bends to pick up his suitcase, picks it up, and then suddenly drops it.* ALL *rush to him, concerned.*]

DON FELIPE: No, no, no es nada. Fue solo un dolorcito.

[*He sits down.*]

ORALIA: Deberías acostarte un rato, Felipe.

DON FELIPE: No, no. Te digo que solo era un dolorcito. [*Rubbing near his heart*] Ya se me quitó. Nomás era ese cabrón juego de pelota que me hicieron jugar. Eso fue.

RUDY: Tata, do you want to stay and rest? We could leave later in the week.

DON FELIPE: No, no, no. Ya tenemos todo bien planeado. Ya me siento mejor. No señor, uno nunca debe cambiar los planes de viaje. Es mala suerte. [*Explaining*] Es nomás porque la maleta está más pesada que cuando la traje. Llevo muchos regalos. Gracias. [*To* RUDY] Vamos, Rudy.

[*The two start to* EXIT.]

RUDY: Wait, Tata. [*To* ARMANDO, *handing him his radio*] Here, Armando. I want you to have my radio. Take it—it's yours.

ARMANDO: ¿Me das tu radio? Pero no lo puedo aceptar. Es muy valioso y yo no tengo nada para ti.

[*He pushes the radio back to* RUDY.]

RUDY: Armando, if you don't take my radio, I won't return next year to beat the guys from Coyotepec again.

ARMANDO [*understanding, taking the radio and immediately starting to play with the dials*]: Gracias, primo.

[DON FELIPE *comes over to* RUDY *and puts his arm around his shoulders. Then, surprising himself and others, he announces with obvious pride.*]

DON FELIPE: Como quiero a mi nieto. [*To* RUDY] Rudy, in Spanish I say I love you.

RUDY: I know, Tata. I love you, too.

[*Beat. Both turn to* EXIT.]

ORALIA [*giving lunches to* ARMANDO]: Esperen, les preparé algo para el viaje.

ARMANDO: ¿Qué es?

ORALIA: Taquitos de lengua, salsa de nopalitos, gorditas con flor de calabaza, y queso de aquí del rancho.

RUDY [*smacks his lips*]: Mmm, ¡qué rico y delicioso!

DON FELIPE [*surprised*]: Pero, Rudy, ¿sabes que es lo que te preparó tu tía Oralia?

RUDY: Sure, Tata. Tongue tacos, cactus salsa, gorditas with—wait, let me think—pumpkin flowers! And cheese made right here in the ranch, todo bien rico—you'll have to try some.

ARMANDO [*practicing the English he's learned from* RUDY]: Tacos, you make it with cow's tongue! Grody, grody to the max, gag me with a spoon.

[*He turns up the volume on the radio.*]

[*More hugs and all* EXIT.]

MUSIC: "*Las golondrinas.*"

END OF SCENE 4

* * *

Scene 5

PLACE: *At the bus station in Oaxaca City.*

MUSIC: *Mexican radio music, very full of static.*

TIME: *Late afternoon.*

[*General milling around a busy bus station,* VENDORS *and* PASSENGERS *conversing, greeting, etc.* DON FELIPE *is sitting down and seems to be dozing.* RUDY *is talking to a* TOURIST, *sounding very much like* DON FELIPE *or* DON MANUEL, *now a very experienced traveler.*]

RUDY [*showing* TOURIST *a page from dictionary*]: My tata insists that mole was invented in Oaxaca, and you can't argue with him. But really mole was discovered in Puebla. You see, the verb "moler" means "to grind." So anyway, these nuns lived in a very poor convent, and they barely had enough to eat. And one morning the mother superior announces that a very important archbishop is coming to visit the convent; they have to prepare something impressive for him to eat. The cupboards are bare, so they run around and gather herbs and spices and put one of the younger nuns who just arrived from the country, la provincia, to grind—moler. So she's grinding all the herbs and spices on the molcajete—isn't that a great word? Molcajete. Can you say it?

TOURIST [*pronouncing it slowly*]: Mol-ca-je-te. Yes, it's a great word. Like cacahuate, no?

RUDY: Right. So the archbishop strolls by the kitchen, sees her, and asks her what she's doing. And the nun replies, "Aquí nomás, mole, mole." And that's how mole came to be named mole. Got that?

TOURIST [*hesitantly*]: Yes, I think so. That's very interesting.

RUDY [*explaining futher*]: You see, she meant to say "moliendo," but because she was so tired, she said "mole" instead. Get it?

TOURIST: Yes, *now* I get it!

[SOUND CUE: *Recorded announcement: "Pasajeros rumbo a Huatulco, Juchitán, puerta número uno, camión número uno-tres-cuatro-cuatro; Lagunas de Chacahua, Jamiltepec, Guelatao, puerta número tres, camión número uno-siete-ocho-ocho, rumbo a Santa María del Tule, Tehuantepec, Yanhutilán, Tlacolula, Ocotlán . . ."*]

DON FELIPE: ¿Rudy, no han anunciado el camión para Puebla?

RUDY: No, not yet.

[*Beat.*]

Do you feel okay? You look pale, Tata.

DON FELIPE: Ha de ser la altitud. Eso ha de ser. Espera nomás que lleguemos a Tucson, Rudy. ¿Te imaginas? Le hecho menos al cabrón calor que viene directo del infierno. Pero créemelo o no, ya me estaba fastidiando el clima de aquí de Oaxaca. No tiene . . . sabor. No hace calor ni frío; ¿cómo va a saber un cristiano si es verano o invierno? Ahorita parece que hace un poco de frío, pero mírame— estoy sudando.

[*He takes off his hat and wipes his forehead with his handkerchief.*]

RUDY: Tata, if you don't feel well, we could stay a few more days here so you could rest.

DON FELIPE: ¿Descansar? Pero si no he hecho nada. Nada. Puro comer y visitar. Las vacaciones perfectas, ¿no crees?

[JUANITA ENTERS *as* FLOWER VENDOR. *She is carrying bouquets of flowers with trailing ribbons. She moves swiftly among* PASSENGERS *who buy flowers from her.*]

JUANITA [*almost chanting or singsong*]: Flores, flores, flores, rosas, gardenias, jazmines y claveles, flores, flores.

[*She stands in front of* DON FELIPE. *They exchange looks, and then she moves away quickly, repeating her sales chant.*]

DON FELIPE: ¿Viste, Rudy? Se parece tanto a mi Juanita. ¿La viste?

RUDY: Tata, I don't even know what Juanita—

DON FELIPE: Juanita era mi—nevermind.

[*Beat.*]

Rudy, ve a ver cuándo sale el camión.

RUDY: It doesn't leave until ten, Tata; we're early.

[*A* WOMAN *dressed all in black* ENTERS. *Her head is covered with a black shawl, and she carries a prayer book and rosary. She prays as she walks among the* PASSENGERS. *At times she stops, and blesses a* PASSENGER *who then pays her.*]

WOMAN IN BLACK [*praying*]: Bendito sea Dios en su reino y en la tierra. Bendito sean sus ángeles y sus apóstoles. Bendito sean los pasajeros, peregrinos en un largo camino, que el ángel de la guardia guíe sus pasos. Tenlos en tu vista, Dios nuestro, padre de todos los peregrinos que caminan por este mundo.

[*She stands in front of* DON FELIPE *and continues praying softly.*]

RUDY: What's she doing, Tata?

[DON FELIPE *doesn't respond and stares intently at the* WOMAN IN BLACK.]

TOURIST: She's blessing the travelers

[*The* WOMAN IN BLACK *moves away and blesses another* PASSENGER.]

RUDY [*still looking at the* WOMAN IN BLACK]: Blessing?

TOURIST: Yes, watch.

[*They both watch her.*]

She prays for a safe journey and then they pay her.

RUDY: I think I understand. They pay her for praying. And she's praying here at the bus station 'cause everyone's going on a trip; that's neat. Like flight insurance—I like that.

DON FELIPE [*confused*]: Toñito, ve y ayúdale a tu papá; no te tienes que quedarte aquí conmigo.

RUDY: Soy Rudy, Abuelo.

DON FELIPE [*catching his mistake*]: Sí, Rudy. Todo corre tarde aquí, nada a su hora. Quién sabe cuándo nos subamos en el camión a Puebla, y luego el tren a México. Nada corre a su tiempo. Ve, Toñito.

[*He leans back and closes his eyes. Beat.*]

[*Rousing himself, confused*] ¿Amelia, Amelia? Ven, Amelia.

RUDY: Tata, it's me, Rudy. We're still in Mexico. Are you all right?

DON FELIPE [*looking around and getting his bearings*]: Sí, sí. Yo sé. Es que estaba pensando en tu mamá. Ya nos ha de estar esperando. Mira, ¿ves allá? [*Pointing offstage*] Ve y cómprale a tu mamá su dulce. Ella quiere un dulce con semillitas negras. Chía, yo creo que eso es lo que me dijo. Ve y cómprale el dulce a tu mamá.

RUDY: But my tía Oralia already packed her some, remember?

DON FELIPE [*still arguing weakly*]: No, no. Te digo que vayas y se lo compres. Yo no me voy sin el dulce para mi hija. Ella me pidió dulce de Oaxaca. Anda, ve.

[RUDY *starts to cross and meets* JUANITA. *They look at each other intently and then counter cross.* RUDY EXITS.]

JUANITA: Flores, flores, flores, rosas, gardenias, jazmines y claveles.

[*She goes to* DON FELIPE *and stands in front of him. Beat.* DON FELIPE *looks up at her.*]

¿Flores, señor?

DON FELIPE: ¿Juanita? *Ahora* estás aquí. ¿Por qué no te fuiste conmigo aquella noche? Te pedí que te casaras conmigo, pero me dejaste para ir a vender tus flores. Por eso me fui de México. ¿Porqué no te quedaste conmigo?

JUANITA: ¿Flores, señor?

DON FELIPE [*trying to stand up slowly*]: Juanita, llévame contigo.

[*She takes his hand and helps him stand next to her.*]

WOMAN IN BLACK [*coming to* DON FELIPE *and praying*]: Bendito sea Dios en su reino y en la tierra. Bendito sean sus ángeles y sus apóstoles. Bendito sean los pasajeros, peregrinos viajeros . . .

[DON FELIPE *falls to the floor, slowly dying; his hat falls from his head.*]

JUANITA: Flores, flores, flores, rosas, gardenias, jazmines y claveles.

WOMAN IN BLACK [*her voice growing stronger in prayer*]: . . . que el ángel de la guardia guié sus pasos. Bendito sea Dios en su reino y en la tierra . . .

JUANITA [*her voice also growing stronger*]: . . . flores, flores, flores, rosas, gardenias, jazmines y claveles . . .

WOMAN IN BLACK AND JUANITA [*together, continuing to repeat prayer and chant until* MUSIC]: . . . bendito sean sus ángeles y sus apóstoles . . . [*Voices lowering as they continue praying and chanting softly*] . . . flores, flores, flores, rosas, gardenias, jazmines y claveles . . .

MUSIC: RISES. "*Llévame oaxaqueña.*"

LIGHTS: *Varied.* OUT OF BODY EXPERIENCE *begins.*

[DANCE: *The* WOMAN IN BLACK *and* JUANITA *pick up* DON FELIPE. *They entwine arms with him and begin to dance.* ALL OTHER PASSENGERS, *including relatives from ranch,* AMELIA, *and* RUDY *join the dance. The* WOMEN *are carrying the ribboned bouquets. It is a joyful yet courtly dance.* DON FELIPE *beams at* JUANITA. *At the drum section of the song,* ALL *stop dancing and* FREEZE. DON FELIPE *and* JUANITA *embrace tenderly.*]

MUSIC: DOWN *and* OUT.

LIGHTS: DOWN *and* UP. OUT OF BODY EXPERIENCE *ends.*

[JUANITA *and the* WOMAN IN BLACK *lead* DON FELIPE *back to his place on the floor. They kneel next to him and pray softly.*]

[SOUND CUE: *Recorded announcement:* "Pasajeros rumbo a Huatulco, Juchitán, camión número tres-dos-ocho-nueve; Lagunas de Chacahua, Jamiltepec, Guelatao, puerta número cuatro, camión número dos-cuatro-siete-seis, rumbo a Santa María del Tule, Tehuantepec, Yanhutilán, Tlacolula, Ocotlán . . ." *The recording keeps repeating as* ALL *begin to move and* EXIT. RUDY *crosses to* DON FELIPE. *The* WOMAN IN BLACK *and* JUANITA *move away and* EXIT *slowly.* RUDY *picks up* DON FELIPE'*s beat-up hat and goes to* DON FELIPE. *He picks up* DON FELIPE *and cradles him gently in his arms.*]

MUSIC: *Introduction "La danza de la pluma."*

LIGHTS: DOWN *and* OUT.

ABOUT THE PLAYWRIGHT

Silviana Wood is a bilingual actor, director, playwright, and storyteller who received her MFA from the University of Arizona. Her plays have been previously presented in Arizona, Texas, California, Massachusetts, New York, and Mexico. She is presently preparing a collection of short stories entitled *And Where Was Pancho Villa When You Really Needed Him?*, a collection of short plays entitled *Cuentos del diablo*, and a novel entitled *La Quinta Soledad*.

ABOUT THE EDITORS

Norma E. Cantú received her PhD from the University of Nebraska–Lincoln in 1982. She is currently a professor of Latina/o studies at the University of Missouri and a professor emerita at the University of Texas at San Antonio. She is the author or co-author of ten scholarly works, including *Ofrenda: Liliana Wilson's Art of Dissidence and Dreams* (Texas A&M University Press, 2015), *Moctezuma's Table: Rolando Briseño's Mexicano and Chicano Tablescapes* (Texas A&M University Press, 2010), and *Paths to Discovery: Autobiographies from Chicanas with Careers in Science, Mathematics, and Engineering* (UCLA Chicano Studies Research Center Press, 2011).

Rita E. Urquijo-Ruiz earned her PhD in literature from the University of California, San Diego, in 2004. She is currently an associate professor in the Modern Languages and Literatures Department at Trinity University (San Antonio, Texas). She is the author of *Wild Tongues: Transnational Mexican Popular Culture* (University of Texas Press, 2012), and co-editor of *El Mundo Zurdo 2: Selected Works from the Meeting of the Society for the Study of Gloria Anzaldúa, 2010* (with Sonia Saldívar-Hull and Norma Alarcón, Aunt Lute Books, 2012), *Global Mexican Cultural Productions* (with Rosana Blanco-Cano, Palgrave MacMillan, 2011), and *El Mundo Zurdo: Selected Works from the Meetings of the Society of the Study of Gloria Anzaldúa, 2007 and 2009* (with Norma E. Cantú, Christina Gutiérrez, and Norma Alarcón, Aunt Lute Books, 2010).